D1569961

Looking Back at the *Arkansas Gazette*

LOOKING BACK AT THE

Arkansas Gazette

An Oral History

Edited by Roy Reed

THE UNIVERSITY OF ARKANSAS PRESS
FAYETTEVILLE
2009

ISBN-10: 1-55728-899-2
ISBN-13: 978-1-55728-899-8

13 12 11 10 09   1 2 3 4 5

Text design by Ellen Beeler

⊗ The paper used in this publication meets the minimum requirements of the
American National Standard for Permanence of Paper for Printed Library Materials
Z39.48-1984.

Library of Congress Cataloging-in-Publication Data

Looking back at the Arkansas gazette : an oral history / edited by Roy Reed.
    p. cm.
Includes index.
ISBN 978-1-55728-899-8 (cloth : alk. paper)
1. Arkansas gazette (Little Rock, Ark. : 1889) I. Reed, Roy, 1930–
PN4899.L55A74 2009
071.67'73—dc22

                                                                    2008046471

Dedicated to the men and women
who worked for the *Arkansas Gazette*
from November 20, 1819, to October 18, 1991.

Contents

Preface

The *Arkansas Gazette* was John Netherland Heiskell's newspaper for seventy years. He became its editor and one of its principal owners in 1902, at the age of thirty. He relinquished his grip on it in 1972 a few weeks after he turned one hundred, and they buried him in Mount Holly Cemetery. In many ways, it remained his paper for several years afterward during the stewardship of his son-in-law, Hugh B. Patterson Jr., who already had nudged it into the modern age and made it financially stable. Then came the age of the corporate chains, and Mr. Heiskell's paper went the way of many other American newspapers, good and bad. But for most of the twentieth century, the paper was one of the nation's finest. Those golden years are called up in the first part of this book through the memories of people who worked there.

The dismal years are recorded here too. They are not pleasant reading, but serious readers—people who keep abreast of public affairs—need to be reminded just how bad things can get when the messenger becomes part of the problem.

The format of the book is straightforward. Most of it is excerpted and compressed from millions of words of tape-recorded interviews with scores of former *Gazette* employees. The interviews were conducted by about two dozen men and women with large experience in the art of asking questions. The aim of the questions was not to expose shameful or questionable conduct—as it is in many newspaper interviews—but to flesh out history and memory of a time and place that was treasured by those on both sides of the tape recorder. As the editor of the book, I have removed a few memories that I judged hurtful to this or that person. I do not apologize for that.

The book follows a loose chronology for the most part. Mainly, though, the chapters explore specific subjects: what the people were like, the sounds and smells of the newsroom, parties, anecdotes, language, lore, big stories, etc. The italicized passages are my introductions to chapters or my comments interspersed to place the material in context.

The *Gazette* was inextricable from Arkansas's history from 1819 until the paper's death in 1991. It reported in breadth and depth the events that led to statehood, the coming and going of slavery, the divisions of civil war in both the state and the nation, the pains of Reconstruction, the numerous political and economic upheavals, the constant frictions of race, and the creeping pace of progress through it all—the daily history told with patience, intelligence, and wit.

The paper's editorial advocacy ranged widely. Some years it was reactionary; most years it was progressive. It never shrank from firm positions, not even during the bleak years of its terminal illness when a cadre of aging loyalists told the new chain owners what they could do with their unwholesome opinions about public affairs. I have strong feelings about the paper's decline and the reasons for it, and I shall not hesitate to express them. But mainly I will let the people who were there at the end—in the newsroom, the editorial offices, the business office, the back shop—tell about the decline and fall as they saw it unfold.

The memories preserved here tell a story that goes back to the early years of the twentieth century. Several of the people interviewed went to work for the paper soon after World War II. Some were army, navy and air corps veterans. Their memories were colored by the war as well as by the performance of the paper they came to love. One veteran spoke for the first time outside his family of the day when the bomber he was piloting over Germany was accidentally rammed by another American plane. He and his crew bailed out and survived. The other crew did not.

The editors and reporters of that era also remembered *Gazette* people who had worked there before the war. Some of those postwar staffers, storytellers all, brought to life the great characters of the early years of the century: not only sober J. N. Heiskell but also his brother Fred, the bon vivant, and a long string of colorful journalists. There was the managing editor who never shrank from a fistfight, the reporter who never came to work sober on purpose, and the editor who threw a governor down the back stairs, etc., etc. And through it all, the paper came out every morning with its pages showing no hint of the tomfoolery, fits of temper, and drunkenness that went into the making of it. This is the story of a proud institution peopled by proud journalists, men and women who knew precisely who they were, suffering no latter-day crises of identity. They knew that the *Arkansas Gazette* was not only the oldest newspaper west of the Mississippi River but also the best paper for hundreds of miles in every direction, famous right around the country and respected by newspaper people from the Atlantic to the Pacific. In Arkansas, even those who hated it were suspected of being quietly proud of it.

The *Gazette* story does not have a happy ending. We shall put that off as long as possible. The last gasp is a tale of stubbornness, stupidity, arrogance, and willful ignorance in the upper reaches of a large national company.

But I must be patient. First, the golden years.

Roy Reed

May 20, 2008

Hogeye, Arkansas

Acknowledgments

The David and Barbara Pryor Center for Arkansas Oral and Visual History at the University of Arkansas is the repository for the interviews that are the basis of this book. More than that, David H. Pryor was the original inspiration for it. When he retired from the United States Senate, he donated the money to start the center. Then he prodded and cajoled large numbers of his considerable body of friends to get behind the idea of preserving the memories of the state's citizens and its leaders. The first major project under his leadership was the *Arkansas Gazette* oral history. As a longtime friend, it fell to me to line up interviewers. Old *Gazette* colleagues like Ernest Dumas and Jerol Garrison stepped forward at once, and in time about two dozen others joined them to sit down with all the old editors, reporters, copy readers, clerks, and business office people that we could locate. Some were run to ground as far away as California and New York. All sat patiently and submitted to the unaccustomed role of answerer instead of questioner. In all, some 150 interviews were conducted. Transcripts of the full interviews may be read online at the web site for Mullins Library at the university.

The *Gazette* project was launched by a generous contribution from the Patterson family, Hugh B. Patterson Jr. and his sons Carrick and Ralph. Hugh Patterson was married to J. N. Heiskell's daughter Louise. The Pattersons and other Heiskell heirs owned the paper during its last years before it became the property of the Gannett Company. They contributed not only their money but also their enthusiasm.

My thanks to Walter Hussman, who won the newspaper war and took over the rival *Gazette,* for permission to reprint several photographs that belong to WEHCO Media. Thanks to him too for agreeing to a full-length interview. Al Neuharth, who was head of the Gannett Company when it bought the *Gazette,* granted our interviewer ten minutes. Walter Hussman sat for four hours and answered every question.

The Gannett Company is not remembered fondly by many of the old *Gazette* hands. Nevertheless, the company is represented here by a few other men and women who consented to be interviewed. They deserve special thanks. They responded with becoming grace in the face of not-always-friendly questions.

T. Harri Baker, a historian at the University of Arkansas at Little Rock until his death, and Jeannie Whayne, chair of the Department of History at the University of Arkansas in Fayetteville, were particularly persuasive in arguing for the *Gazette* project. Tom Dillard, head of the university's Special Collections, along with James Defibaugh and others on their staff were helpful throughout. My thanks to Special Collections for permission to use the oral histories deposited there.

Among those who laboriously transcribed the tape-recorded interviews, the most active and encouraging was my neighbor and friend, Cheri Pearce. A special thanks to her.

Larry Malley and his staff at the University of Arkansas Press were patient and helpful.

Finally, thanks to my wife, Norma, for her unflagging good humor and encouragement.

The Cast

Following is a brief description of the participants in the *Arkansas Gazette* oral history who are quoted in this book. They make up only a minority of the hundreds who were employed at the paper from World War II until the paper's merger with the *Arkansas Democrat* in 1991. But the group quoted here constitute a strong cross section of the players who occupied the stage for what Polonius might have called the tragical-comical-historical drama of the *Gazette*'s sunset years. Each person listed here is identified by full name the first time he or she is quoted in the book and thereafter by last name only. Their recollections and comments are recorded in their own words but are occasionally compressed and elided to save space. Each interviewee was given the opportunity to edit and correct the interview transcript. Even so, the telling of some stories and events varies in minor ways from one person to another. The editor occasionally decided close calls by relying on his own spasmodically reliable memory. For better understanding you are advised to read through the entire "Cast of Characters" before you begin the book proper.

Charles Allbright became a reporter at the *Gazette* in 1955. He began writing a column in 1956. In 1966, after a period of writing editorials, he left to work for Winthrop Rockefeller in his successful bid for the governorship. He returned to the *Gazette* as the Arkansas Traveler columnist in 1973 and remained until the paper closed in 1991. He then became a columnist at the *Arkansas Democrat-Gazette*.

Nate Allen covered Razorback sports for the *Gazette* for fourteen years. Then he went on covering them for the Donrey Media Group and for his own company, the Nate Allen Sports Service.

Richard Allen was a copy boy and sportswriter at the *Gazette*. He later worked as an editor at the *Arkansas Democrat, Newsday,* the *New York Times,* and the *International Herald Tribune* in Paris.

Richard Allin became the Our Town columnist at the *Gazette* after covering the capitol as a reporter. He continued the column with the *Arkansas-Democrat Gazette* after the *Gazette* closed. He died in 2007.

Harry Ashmore was executive editor of the *Gazette*. He won the Pulitzer Prize in 1958 for his editorials on the 1957 school desegregation crisis in Little Rock. He died in 1998.

Jim Bailey was a sportswriter at the *Gazette* from 1956 until it closed in 1991. He then became a columnist for the *Democrat-Gazette*.

Jim Barden was a reporter at the *Gazette* for one year. He later worked for various newspapers and wire services, then became a copy editor at the *New York Times*.

Eddie Best joined the *Gazette* in 1954 when he was a senior in high school. He worked twelve years as a sportswriter under Orville Henry. He joined the advertising–public relations firm of Faulkner and Associates in 1965, then went to the International Data Group, publisher of *DOS For Dummies*. He retired from Yarnell Ice Cream Company as its advertising director.

Pat Best was a switchboard operator and news department secretary at the *Gazette* for twenty-one years.

Denise Beeber was a copy editor at the *Gazette* for two years. She later worked at the *Atlanta Constitution,* the *Los Angeles Times,* and the *Dallas Morning News.*

Wayne Bolick went to work as a printer at the *Gazette* in 1953 and retired six months before the paper closed. He set type on a Linotype machine, then became night foreman.

Max Brantley was a reporter, city editor, and assistant managing editor at the *Gazette*. After the paper closed, he became editor of the weekly *Arkansas Times.*

John Brummett was a capitol reporter and columnist at the *Gazette*. He later became a columnist for the Donrey Media Group.

Liz Carpenter and her husband **Les** were Washington correspondents for the *Gazette*. She was later press secretary to Lady Bird Johnson in the White House.

T. Patterson (Patt) Clark was a graphic artist at the *Gazette* for six years. He later worked at the *Miami Herald* and the *Washington Post*.

Fred Coger joined the *Gazette* as a copy editor in 1957. He moved to the *Phoenix Gazette* in 1959 and from there to the Philadelphia *Evening Bulletin* in 1963. He was night telegraph editor there when that paper closed.

Harvey Cooper was a *Gazette* copy editor for four years before returning to his native New York, first at *Newsday,* then at the New York *Daily News.* He had earlier worked at the *New York Times* news service. He could not drive a car and during his first week asked directions to the nearest subway station. When he was set straight, he bought a car and took driving lessons.

Jan Cottingham was the last city editor of the *Gazette.*

Pat Crow was a copy editor at the *Gazette* from 1960 to 1962. He then worked as an editor at the *New York Times,* the *New York Herald Tribune,* and the *New Yorker.*

Kenneth Danforth was a *Gazette* copy editor. He was one of several hands known in he newsroom as the "El Dorado Mafia," a network of reporters, editors, and photographers brought together by managing editor A. R. Nelson, a south Arkansas man. Danforth left the paper to become a foreign correspondent for *Time* and a writer and editor for the *National Geographic.* He shepherded a group of writers and produced a *Geographic* book entitled *Journey Into China.*

Tom Davis joined the *Gazette* after working for papers in Oklahoma and Texas. He covered city hall, then became news editor. He later worked as a reporter for the Detroit *Free Press* and as executive editor of the *Delaware County Daily Times* in Chester, Pennsylvania. He spent several years teaching journalism at Arkansas Tech University and Marshall University School of Journalism in Huntington, West Virginia, then retired to Fayetteville.

Jerry Dhonau was the last chief of the editorial pages of the *Gazette.* In 1957 he covered the Central High School crisis from the streets. He also worked at the *Minneapolis Tribune* and the *Daytona Beach News Journal.*

Leroy Donald was the *Gazette* state editor for many years. He became a columnist at the *Democrat-Gazette* after the *Gazette* closed.

Martha Douglas was a general assignment reporter and the radio-television columnist at the *Gazette* for thirty-three years. She married Bob Douglas, a coworker, in 1955.

Robert R. (Bob) Douglas was an enlisted man in the navy during World War II. He saw heavy combat on an aircraft carrier in the Pacific. He joined the *Gazette* in 1948 and was named managing editor in 1972. He left in 1981 to become chairman of the Department of Journalism at the University of Arkansas. He died in 2002.

Gerald Drury learned Chinese in the Air Force. He was a copy editor at the *Gazette* for nineteen years. He retired from the *Arizona Republic.*

Ernest Dumas was a reporter and editorial writer at the *Gazette* from 1960 until the paper's death in 1991. He wrote especially about politics and government. He later became a columnist for the *Arkansas Times.*

Dean Duncan was a cryptographer for the army during World War II. He spent thirteen months in the Azores. He spent six years as a reporter at the *Gazette,* then worked at the Memphis *Commercial Appeal* and the Louisville *Courier-Journal.* He was in the Peace Corps two years. He taught journalism and directed the public information office at the University of Central Arkansas.

Rodney Dungan shot some of the *Gazette's* most memorable photographs during the tenure of Governor Orval Faubus, including the desegregation of Central High School in 1957. He later became a video and political consultant. He died in 2003.

Leland DuVall worked at the *Gazette* for thirty-five years. He wrote analytical columns and editorials, mainly on economics, business, and agriculture. He died in 2006.

Ronald Farrar was a reporter for the *Gazette.* He later taught journalism at Indiana University, Southern Methodist University, the University of Mississippi, the University of Kentucky, and the University of South Carolina.

Anne Farris worked for several news organizations, including the *St. Louis Post-Dispatch,* the *Kansas City Star,* the *Greensboro Daily News,* and the Newhouse News Service before joining the *Gazette* as a reporter in 1985.

George Fisher served with the army in Europe during World War II. He became a commercial artist and began his career as an editorial cartoonist for the *North Little Rock Times* in 1964. He joined the *Gazette* in 1976. After the *Gazette* closed, he drew cartoons for the *Arkansas Times* until he died in 2003.

Gene Foreman joined the *Gazette* in 1957 as a reporter and became assistant city editor late that year. He was made state editor in 1960. After leaving the *Gazette* in 1962, he worked at the *New York Times,* the *Pine Bluff Commercial,* the *Arkansas Democrat, Newsday,* and the *Philadelphia Inquirer.* He was managing editor of three papers, the *Commercial,* the *Democrat,* and the *Inquirer.* He retired from the *Inquirer* in 1998 to teach at Penn State University, from which he retired in 2006. He was president of the Associated Press Managing Editors in 1990. He was a Pulitzer Prize juror three times.

Jerol Garrison covered the federal beat for the *Gazette* during most of his fourteen years on the paper. He later worked in public relations for the University of Arkansas at Little Rock and for the Arkansas Power and Light Company.

Romeo Gatewood was head of maintenance at the *Gazette* from 1967 until the paper closed.

Ed Gray was a copy editor at the *Gazette* for fifteen years. He later became editor of the Perspective and Book Review sections at the *Arkansas Democrat-Gazette.*

Carol Griffee was a reporter for the *Washington Star* and other newspapers before moving to Arkansas. She was a reporter for the *Gazette* for twelve years. She established a freelance reporting agency serving clients in and beyond Arkansas.

Michael Haddigan spent several years in Southeast Asia before joining the *Gazette* state desk.

Tom Hamburger joined the *Gazette* in 1975, left to work for the *Minneapolis Tribune,* then returned to the *Gazette*'s Washington bureau. He later became a well-known investigative reporter for the *Los Angeles Times* in Washington.

John Hanchette worked as a reporter and editor for the *Niagara Falls Gazette,* the *Buffalo Evening News,* and the Gannett News Service. He was a founding editor of *USA Today.* He won a Pulitzer Prize for reporting in 1979 for a story on the misuse of funds in the Catholic Church. He left the Washington bureau of Gannett News Service in 1988 to become managing editor of the *Gazette.* He left in 1990 and returned to Gannett News Service. He later became a professor of journalism at St. Bonaventure University.

Peggy Harris was a reporter at the *Gazette* from 1984 until the paper closed. She then went to work in the Little Rock bureau of the Associated Press.

Sean Harrison, a self-described hotshot photographer (he was not; he lied to the hiring editor), flooded the Little Rock newsroom with photos and stories from Searcy for eighteen months. He moved to the capital to cover the county courthouse just weeks before the paper closed. He then opened a Little Rock bureau for Donrey Media Group. He went on to work in public relations.

C. S. (Chuck) Heinbockel covered the county courthouse and business affairs. One of the "Oberlin Mafia" who had drifted to Arkansas to get into newspapering, he joined the paper as a copy editor in 1977 from the *Pine Bluff Commercial.* On the copy desk, he joined Jack Bradley, a Princeton graduate; Harvey Cooper, an alumnus of the *New York Times* news service; and Jonathan Portis, the youngest of the Portis brothers of Hamburg, Arkansas. Heinbockel left the *Gazette* in 1990 to become a financial planner.

Orville Henry went to work for the *Gazette* in 1942 at age seventeen. He became the sports editor in 1943. He left in 1988 to work for the rival *Arkansas Democrat.* He died in 2001.

Maria Henson worked for the *Arkansas Democrat* before joining the *Gazette* as a reporter in 1984. She went to the paper's Washington bureau in 1987, then became an editorial writer at the *Lexington (KY) Herald Leader* where she won a Pulitzer Prize for a series on domestic abuse. After a Nieman Fellowship, she wrote editorials for the *Charlotte Observer,* the *Austin American,* and the *Sacramento Bee.*

Martin Holmes worked briefly as a reporter at the *Gazette.* He was a sportswriter, general assignment reporter, and news editor at the *Democrat* before moving to the *Modesto (CA) Bee,* where he retired as makeup editor.

Paul Johnson was at the *Gazette* from 1966 until it closed. He was a copy editor, assistant news editor, TV columnist, and running columnist.

Jerry Jones worked at the *Gazette* thirty-five years, most of the time as assistant city editor. He joined the *Arkansas Democrat-Gazette* as a copy editor after the *Gazette* closed and worked there until he died in 2005.

Julia Jones wrote about brides and fashions at the *Gazette*. She was also assistant editor of the paper's magazine. She joined the *Phoenix Gazette* in 1985. Her husband, Gerald Drury, worked for the *Arizona Republic* in Phoenix.

Wayne Jordan was a reporter at the *Gazette* from 1966 until it closed. He then worked for the Arkansas State Police.

Laurie Karnatz joined the *Gazette* in 1990 as editor of the Journals page and stayed until the paper closed. She had worked earlier as a reporter at the *El Dorado News-Times* and the *Springdale News*. She worked as a journalist in Florida after the *Gazette* closed.

Steve Keesee was a military photographer stationed at the Little Rock Air Force Base. He landed a job at the *Democrat*. A. R. Nelson, the *Gazette*'s managing editor, hired him away during a game of pool at a Markham Street hangout. He shot photos for the *Gazette* from 1972 until the paper closed.

Harry King wrote sports for the *Gazette* before joining the Associated Press. He was sports editor for Arkansas for many years. He then became a sports columnist for the Stephens Media Group.

Bill Lewis spent thirty-three years at the *Gazette* as a reporter, music reviewer, and travel writer.

Robin Woods Loucks was head librarian at the *Gazette* during the mid-1960s. She left to sell real estate in Jasper, then moved back to Little Rock. She was a daughter of the paper's food editor, Mildred Woods.

Walker Lundy was the first editor brought in by Gannett after the company bought the *Gazette*. Before coming to Little Rock, he edited papers at Fort Worth, Charlotte, and Tallahassee and had been city editor of the *Detroit Free Press*. He later was editor of the St. Paul *Pioneer Press* and the *Philadelphia Inquirer*.

Deborah Mathis was a columnist and editorial writer and was at the paper when it closed. She worked at the *Arkansas Democrat* and in television before joining the *Gazette*. After the paper died, she moved to Washington with the Gannett News Service. She wrote two books, *Yet A Stranger: Why Black Americans Still Don't Feel At Home* and *Sole Sister: The Joys and Pain of Single Black Women*. She also became a commentator on America's Black Forum.

Jerry McConnell was a sportswriter at the *Gazette* for sixteen years. Afterward, he was managing editor of the *Arkansas Democrat* and executive sports editor of the *Daily Oklahoman* and the *Oklahoma City Times*.

Robert McCord owned the *North Little Rock Times* and was executive editor of the *Arkansas Democrat* before joining the *Gazette* as associate editor in 1981. He created the paper's op-ed page. In 1976 he was elected national president of the Society of Professional Journalists.

Sid McMath was governor of Arkansas from 1949 to 1953. He died in 2003.

Jack Meriwether was city manager of Little Rock before joining the *Gazette*. He spent seven and a half years at the paper as assistant business manager and business manager. He then became a lobbyist for the University of Arkansas.

Joe Mosby worked on the sports desk of the *Gazette* for twenty-two years. He was the outdoors editor eighteen years.

Ray Moseley covered the Central High desegregation story for the *Gazette* in 1957. He later worked for the *Detroit Free Press* and the *Rome Daily American* and for United Press International in Rome, Cairo, Belgrade, London, Moscow, and Brussels. He covered the State Department for the *Philadelphia Bulletin*. He was chief European correspondent for the *Chicago Tribune* until he retired to live in London.

Keith Moyer was the last editor of the *Gazette*. When it closed, he moved to another Gannett paper in Rochester, then joined the McClatchey company. He was editor of the *Fresno Bee,* then publisher of the *Star Tribune* in Minneapolis.

Al Neuharth was CEO and chairman of the Gannett Company when it bought the *Gazette*.

Paul Nielsen was a copy editor at the *Gazette* for six months. He later worked at the *Arkansas Democrat, Newsday,* the *Philadelphia Inquirer,* and the *New York Times.*

Mark Oswald covered city hall and the capitol for the *Gazette* until it closed. He moved to New Mexico and became an editor at the *Albuquerque Journal.*

Patrick J. Owens was a reporter and editorial writer at the *Gazette.* Later, he was executive editor of the *Pine Bluff Commercial,* a labor writer at the *Detroit Free Press,* and a columnist at *Newsday.* Before the *Gazette,* he worked for several newspapers and radio stations in Montana, the Pacific Northwest, and New York. He was court-martialed in the army over a disagreement about the camp newspaper. He attended eight or nine universities. He died in 2002.

Ken Parker was state editor of the *Gazette.* He worked in public relations for Arkansas Valley Industries, Georgia-Pacific, Murphy Oil, and Reynolds Aluminum. He published the *Arkansas Legislative Report* and a workmen's compensation newsletter.

Carrick Patterson is the elder son of Hugh Patterson and a grandson of J. N. Heiskell. He studied music at Stanford University and joined the *Gazette* in 1968. He was executive editor when Gannett bought the paper, after which he said, "I was encouraged by the Gannett people to find other employment." He opened an advertising agency, then became a freelance writer and photographer.

Hugh Patterson spent forty years at the *Gazette.* He started as national advertising manager in 1946. In 1948 he helped engineer the Heiskell family's buyout of the Allsopp family interests, and in that year he became the publisher. He and Louise Heiskell, a daughter of J. N. and Wilhelmina Heiskell, were married in 1943 while Hugh was an officer in the army air corps.

W. L. (Pat) Patterson was a photographer for the *Gazette* until it closed. He then went to work for the Arkansas State Police.

David Petty started at the *Gazette* as a copy boy. He worked his way up to managing editor and, under Gannett, assistant editor before the paper closed. He stayed with Gannett as editor or publisher of three of the company's papers in Jackson and Hattiesburg, Mississippi, and Monroe, Louisiana.

Linda Pine was a librarian at the *Gazette*. She left to become head of the archives and special collections at the University of Arkansas at Little Rock.

Charles Portis was a marine veteran of the Korean War. He joined the *Gazette* in 1959 and worked as a reporter and a columnist. He went to the *New York Herald Tribune* in 1960. He covered civil rights in the South and spent a year as a correspondent in London. He returned to Arkansas to write fiction in 1964. He has written five novels: *Norwood, True Grit, Dog of the South, Masters of Atlantis,* and *Gringos.*

James O. Powell was editor of the editorial page of the *Gazette* from 1960 to 1985. He came to the paper from the *Tampa Tribune.*

Gene Prescott, who served with the marines in World War II, was a photographer at the *Gazette* for thirty-eight years. He retired in 1989.

Wes Pruden was a reporter at the *Gazette*. He left in 1956 for the Memphis *Commercial Appeal.* He moved to Washington to join the *National Observer* and stayed to become the editor of the *Washington Times.*

John Reed was a reporter at the *Gazette*. He left to become the information officer for the Arkansas Senate.

Leon Reed was circulation manager of the *Gazette* for twenty-six years.

Roy Reed was a reporter at the *Gazette*. He was a national and foreign correspondent for the *New York Times,* a professor of journalism at the University of Arkansas, and a biographer of Orval Faubus. (Unless otherwise specified, "Reed" in the interview texts of this book refers to Roy Reed.)

Charles Rixse was a sports and general assignment reporter and assistant city editor at the *Gazette*. He was managing editor of the *North Little Rock Times,* then worked in convention bureaus in Little Rock, Hot Springs, Knoxville, Kansas City, Las Vegas, and Myrtle Beach.

Margaret Smith Ross was the *Gazette* historian for twenty-eight years. The job was created for her by J. N. Heiskell in 1957. She died in 2002.

Jason Rouby was a reporter covering city hall, then a copy editor. He was on the desk the night that Governor Faubus surrounded Central High School with National Guard troops to block the integration of the school the next day.

Bill Shelton was a bomber pilot during World War II. He and his crew had to abandon their plane over the Balkans after another American plane collided with it. They were rescued, and he resumed flying missions over Germany. He went to work as a copy editor at the *Gazette* in 1950 and became city editor in 1952. He died in 2005.

Aubrey Shepherd was an outdoors writer at the *Gazette* from 1988 until it closed. He went to work as a copy editor at the *Morning News of Northwest Arkansas*.

Bill Simmons was a copy boy and sportswriter for the *Gazette*. He was a capitol reporter and bureau chief for the Associated Press until 1996, when he became political editor of the *Arkansas Democrat-Gazette*.

Doug Smith was a reporter and editorial writer at the *Gazette*. He wrote a column on word usage at the *Gazette* and wrote a similar column later for the *Arkansas Times*.

Margie Snider dropped out of Radcliffe to write obituaries for the *Gazette*. She worked for the *Pine Bluff Commercial* and then spent twenty-one years in Washington as an editor and writer for the Service Employees International Union. She took early retirement in 2007 and moved to West Virginia to become a freelancer.

Julie Baldridge Speed worked as a *Gazette* copy editor in the 1970s. She was a press secretary for Bill Clinton when he was attorney general and governor. She later worked for the University of Arkansas raising money to refurbish Old Main. She then ran U.S. Representative Ray Thornton's Little Rock office. After that she became external relations director for the Law School of the University of Arkansas at Little Rock.

Tucker Steinmetz was a reporter at the Crossett *News Observer*, the *Pine Bluff Commercial*, and the *Arkansas Democrat* before joining the *Gazette*. He and **Jimmy Jones** formed a distinguished investigative team. Jones died young. Steinmetz worked briefly at the *Philadelphia Inquirer*, returned to the *Gazette*, then left in 1976 to become a social worker. His father Cecil was the *Gazette*'s stereotype foreman until he retired in 1966.

Donna Lampkin Stephens covered sports for the *Gazette* from 1984 until the paper closed. She then taught journalism at the University of Central Arkansas.

Mort Stern was a reporter at the *Gazette*. He later became managing editor of the *Denver Post*.

Scott Stroud was a reporter at the *Gazette* for two years. He later worked at the Lexington *Herald-Leader* and the *State* in Columbia, South Carolina.

Tish Talbot was a reporter at the *Gazette* for seven years during the 1970s. She later worked in public relations at the University of Arkansas for Medical Sciences and for the Watkins and Associates agency. She became director of communications, public relations, and instructional issues for the Arkansas Education Association.

David Terrell covered the capitol for the *Gazette* then worked for the Memphis *Commercial Appeal*. He became a speech writer for Senator Jim Sasser. He went on to the Bureau of Reclamation and the U.S. Geological Survey.

Mike Trimble worked at the *Gazette* for eighteen years as a reporter and columnist. He later worked at the *Democrat-Gazette* and the *Arkansas Times*. He was city editor of the *Pine Bluff Commercial*. He was city editor then opinion page editor of the *Record Chronicle* in Denton, Texas.

Scott Van Laningham covered city hall, politics, and the capitol for the *Gazette* from 1980 until the paper closed in 1991. He then worked for a consulting firm and became the chief executive officer of the Northwest Arkansas Regional Airport.

George Wells was a reporter at the *Gazette* from 1979 until the paper closed in 1991. He covered the federal beat during most of that period. He also worked for the *Pine Bluff Commercial* and the Louisville *Courier-Journal*.

Ray White was a reporter at the *Gazette* for a year. He later worked at the *Arkansas Democrat* and the *Philadelphia Inquirer*. He became a design director at the *Arkansas Democrat-Gazette*.

Bill Whitworth was a reporter at the *Gazette* from 1960 to 1963. After that, he was a reporter for the *New York Herald Tribune* and a writer and editor at the *New Yorker.* He was editor of the *Atlantic Monthly* for twenty years.

Gaston Williamson was an attorney with the Rose Law Firm from 1948 to 1990. He represented the *Gazette* and the Heiskells in various legal matters and was a member of the paper's board of directors from the 1950s until the 1980s.

Farris Wood lied about his age and got a job as a printer's devil in 1939 or 1940. He was fifteen or sixteen. He served as a radar technician with a bomber squadron in the South Pacific during World War II. He returned to the *Gazette* as a printer and stayed until the late 1960s.

Mildred Woods studied voice in Italy and was on the New York stage before becoming food editor of the *Gazette.* She died in 1968.

Diane Woodruff covered the county courthouse and the federal building for the *Gazette* for eight years.

John Woodruff was a reporter at the *Gazette* for twenty-two years, twenty-one of them covering North Little Rock. He was a marathon runner and ran his last race only a few weeks before his death in 2007.

John Workman was a Methodist minister and the *Gazette's* religion editor for ten years. He wrote a column for another two years until the paper closed, then continued it for a year at the *Arkansas Democrat-Gazette.*

Looking Back at the *Arkansas Gazette*

1

Mr. Woodruff's Newspaper

The *Arkansas Gazette* was born in a log cabin November 20, 1819, on a bank of the Arkansas River. A local establishment donated a barrel of whiskey to celebrate the event. The first issue carried a complaint from a citizen that the town had too many lawyers. When the paper died 167 years later, the problem was not lawyers but corporate executives who had found themselves, to their confusion, in charge of the oldest newspaper west of the Mississippi and not knowing what to do with it.

William E. Woodruff of Brooklyn, New York, was a printer who had made his way west, honing his skills as he went. He acquired a used press at Nashville and floated it down the Cumberland, the Ohio, and the Mississippi rivers to Montgomery's Point. There it was unloaded and placed on a pirogue for its torturous journey up the White River to the "cut-off" into the Arkansas and thence to the seat of the government of the Arkansas Territory, commonly called Arkansas Post because it was next door to a military stockade. The town was then 133 years old. It had been a trading post for the French, the Spanish, the French again, and, since 1803, the Americans.

The aged press was subjected to another river trip in 1821. Woodruff relocated it and his business to Little Rock, where he installed it in still another log cabin. He quickly prospered and became one of the leading businessmen of the territory. He eventually owned a store, an interest in a salt manufactory, a steamboat, a ferry business, thousands of acres of land, and fourteen slaves. His attitude on race was in harmony with that of other white people in Arkansas and, lamentably, of many in his native New York. As editor he advocated removing free blacks from Arkansas, and he asserted that Southern slaves were better off than free blacks in the North. He also editorialized against dueling and drinking.

Woodruff sold the paper to Edward Cole in 1836. Cole sold it the same year to George H. Burnett, who died in 1841, at which time it reverted to Woodruff. He sold it again in 1843 to Benjamin J. Borden, who converted it into a Whig organ to support Henry Clay for president. That annoyed Woodruff, and in 1846 he responded by establishing the *Arkansas Democrat* (no relation to the later publication of that name). Under still another owner, the *Gazette* went downhill and was set to suspend publication when Woodruff bought it once more, folded it into the *Democrat* with the *Gazette* name alone at the top, and coaxed it back to life. He sold it for the last time to Christopher Columbus Danley in 1853 and went on to a lengthy retirement. He died in 1885 at age ninety.

Various men owned the paper during the last half of the nineteenth century. It suspended publication from September 1863 to April 1865 because of the Civil War. It came back as a daily paper in 1865, and William E. Woodruff Jr. bought a share of it in 1866. He became sole proprietor in 1873. When the Gazette Publishing Company was incorporated in 1889, another son of the founder, A. M. Woodruff, was among the stockholders.

The *Gazette* was a Woodruff family paper for most of its first century. It was to be a Heiskell family paper for most of its second. On June 17, 1902, a controlling interest was bought by Fred W. Allsopp and by Judge Carrick W. Heiskell of Memphis, a former Confederate colonel, and his sons John Netherland and Fred. It was J. N. who became editor, Fred managing editor, and Allsopp business manager. Some years later, the Heiskells bought the Allsopp interest, and they and their heirs were the sole owners until they sold it to the Gannett Company in 1986.

J. N. Heiskell, a conservative Democrat, was proud to say that the *Arkansas Gazette* had always supported Democrats except for the Whig aberration and a necessary interlude in the 1960s when Winthrop Rockefeller made Republican reform more desirable than Democratic lassitude. After 1986 the Gannett managers tried to nudge the editorial page into conservatism, but the longtime editorial page writers played dumb and never took the hint. For its last half century the paper had mainly been a solace to liberal Democrats and an irritant to Republicans and conservatives. If the *Gazette* had been buried at Mount Holly Cemetery alongside J. N. Heiskell and William E. Woodruff, its tombstone might have read, "Here Lies The State's Oldest Democrat."

2

The Old Man

We called him old because he was. He was born in 1872 and became editor of the Arkansas Gazette in 1902.

Bob Douglas: We didn't have the same frame of references. We were running a bunch of stories about layoffs once, so he called me in and said, you know, "This isn't news. We have to be concerned about scaring people here, you know, overplaying these things." He had a point, of course, but I didn't think he did. He said—well, he's remembering the Depression when he thought the country talked itself into a depression. "Mr. Heiskell, that is not the way I remember it. I remember that they kind of tried to sweep it under the rug at first, and everybody was giving these rosy forecasts, and then it knocked the hell out of the country." Well, I was talking about 1930, and he was talking about 1898.

Charles Portis: Jerry Neil told me that Mr. Heiskell stopped him once in the hall and said, "Mr. Neil, have you ever stopped to consider just how different things might be if General Lee had had just one scouting airplane at the Battle of Gettysburg?" Jerry said he hadn't.

Jerry McConnell: Carrick Patterson, his grandson, came home on vacation, and he was standing in the newsroom, and Mr. Heiskell came out and was surprised by Carrick being there. He said, "Well, Carrick, what are you doing home?" He said, "Well, I came home for Easter vacation, Grandfather." Mr. Heiskell saw him, and he said, "You know, I don't believe we had Easter vacation when I was in college. Of course, Christ wasn't dead yet."

Rodney Dungan: Mr. Heiskell did not even have a private restroom. He went with the rest of the guys. He was supposedly in the bathroom one day, and

5

some young new copy boy came in. Mr. Heiskell felt like he had to say something. He said, "Good morning, young man. How long have you been with the *Arkansas Gazette?*" The guy said, "Two days." He said, "How long have you been here?" Mr. Heiskell said, "Fifty years." [*Laughter.*]

Roy Reed: This was the oldest newspaper west of the Mississippi.

Douglas: It was founded in 1819. During the Central High segregation crisis, the legislature, as you will remember, was out to punish the *Gazette* and anybody else who thought maybe that the pursuit of law and order was desirable. Well, somebody introduced a bill to prohibit the *Gazette* from using its logo. It's the thing with the eagle in the name plate, which was the same as the Arkansas seal. Mr. Heiskell pointed out that the *Gazette* had it first, and we had no objection to the state continuing to use it.

Ken Parker: In 1948, when Truman and Dewey were running for president, Harry Ashmore told the story about being in Mr. Heiskell's office, and they were commenting on the fact that a number of Southern papers were supporting Dewey, and that morning the Memphis *Commercial Appeal* had endorsed Dewey. Harry said, "Well, Mr. Heiskell, I don't suppose there's any chance that we'll bolt the party, is there?" Mr. Heiskell said, "We'll stay with the party." Harry asked if the *Gazette* had ever bolted the Democratic Party. He said that Mr. Heiskell looked around to make sure no one was listening and said, "Well, I don't like to talk about it, but we did go Whig one time."

Reed: Do you remember when the Old Man quit driving a car?

Douglas: I don't remember what year, but, yes, he was in his nineties. He probably should have quit a little earlier than he did [*laughs*]. He used to—when he lived on Louisiana Street—and he lived there for years and years—he didn't pay any attention to stop signs. He came to work and went back without stopping.

Reed: The story I had heard about his driving was that he came in one day to announce that he had quit driving not because of his age but because he had begun to notice that there were so many damned fools on the road that he felt unsafe to be out among them.

Douglas: He had his taboos, and one of them was running a picture of snakes, which I violated a couple of times, or at least once. And I never heard anything from him. I knew it was something I could justify. A little animal sideshow had broken down in Little Rock, and a lot of the animals escaped. And there was a snake truck that had broken down. And there was a picture of one of the snake trainers trying to corral a snake, a great big snake—I guess a boa—I don't know. She had it about the middle with her hand, and it was biting her on the butt. So I ran that on page one [*laughter*]. He had another one [taboo] about running dead bodies, and I violated that a couple of times because—I never ran a gory picture, but sometimes it was absolutely essential to the picture that the body be visible. If you exercised what you thought was good news judgment, you . . . He was always conscious of the fact that the *Gazette* was a breakfast table newspaper, and he didn't think that people ought to be upset by what they would see in the paper—as far as pictures were concerned—while they were having breakfast.

Margaret Smith Ross: And you know the famous story about when he came in one day and stopped to . . . see what was on the wire, and he pulls this off and takes it over to whoever was in the slot and said, "Be sure this gets in the paper. It's about a fifty-five-year-old woman who had a baby. That will amaze half our readers and scare hell out of the other half."

Jerry Jones: Every now and then, he would come by the city desk, clear his throat, and say, "Mr. Shelton, I think we ought to do so-and-so," and he would make a suggestion for a story. Those were called "JNHs," and we had a file of JNH stories. One time one of his suggestions was, "There are three kinds of rabbits in Arkansas: swamp, cottontail, and jack." That was it. Well, Bill Lewis drew that assignment, and I think he put it off as long as he could, and I don't blame him. But one day, he cranked out this long, long piece about the rabbits in Arkansas—what kind of rabbits we had. It was a dandy. It was a jim-dandy.

Carrick Patterson: The *Gazette* was one of the few papers anywhere to employ an actual historian, and her name was Margaret Smith Ross. She wrote a weekly feature called the Chronicles of Arkansas, which was literally that. It was about Arkansas history and was one of the few really good sources of Arkansas history. It's her work. And she worked very closely with J. N. Heiskell because that was a subject that he dearly loved.

Reed: Tell what [Mr. Heiskell's] desk looked like.

Ross: Stacked pretty high. His desk looked good compared to the table behind his desk where the papers were stacked, and they just went up the wall . . . Charles J. Finger put in print a story that he went there one time to talk to Mr. Heiskell about something or other, and there was a big stack of papers there, and he put a mark on the top one. And then he went back a couple of years later and found that that paper was still there.

Douglas: He wasn't a stick in the mud at all about newspaper tradition of that sort. I mean, he was all for improving the makeup. He originated the In the News column on page one, which became a *Gazette* trademark, and he didn't want that changed.

Kenneth Danforth: Leland told me that one time Mr. Heiskell came into his office and said, "I don't like the way you phrase this, Mr. DuVall." He was always "Mister." Everybody was "Mister" to Mr. Heiskell, a very courtly gentleman in his nineties, upper nineties. And he said, "I want you to change this, or quit doing this." Whatever it was. And Leland told Mr. Heiskell, "Mr. Heiskell, if you tell me to spell *shit* with two *t*'s, I'll do it." And Mr. Heiskell said, "Well, thank you, Mr. DuVall," and walked down, and he came back in about two minutes and poked his head in the door and he said, "By the way, Mr. DuVall, it used to be spelled with two *t*'s." [*Laughter.*]

Parker: He came out to the newsroom one day with a clipping from the *Gazette* in which Fillmore Street was spelled with one *l* and told Sam Harris that street was named for President Fillmore, who spelled his name with two *l*'s. So Sam took it to Tom Davis, who had written the story, and Tom said, "Well, I looked in the phonebook, and it's spelled with one *l* there." So Sam said, "Okay, call the phone company and ask them why they're misspelling Fillmore." And he did, and they said, "That's the way the city engineer's office gave it to us." So he called the city engineer's office, and they said, "The ordinance establishing that street spells it with one *l*." So Tom wrote a little feature story on it, and the next day the editorial page had an editorial saying we need to correct the spelling of Fillmore. The city council met in a couple of nights, and someone introduced a resolution to correct the spelling of Fillmore Street. Alderman Mills objected to the second reading. He said it was a bunch of foolishness, just something the *Gazette* was doing for attention. There was no need wasting time. Fillmore was dead, and he didn't care about how we spelled his name. So for the next two weeks, until the next council meeting, the *Gazette,* in the news columns and on the editorial page, mentioned Alderman Mills at every opportunity and spelled his name "Mils" every time. So the next meeting of the city council Alderman Mills moved that they adopt that resolution.

Ross: His wit was based more on puns than anything else, but it was nearly all very funny. . . . I told you about the world's highest dam, didn't I? . . . He was in the news library one day, reading an out-of-state newspaper, and the telephone rang. Betty Jo answered it; she puts the phone down and said, "Oh, good Lord, some lady wants to know what's the world's highest dam!" And she reached for the almanac, and under his breath, without looking up, he said, "God damn." And . . . you remember Ernest Dodd, that was composing room foreman? . . . He was all-powerful in the composing room, and Mr. Heiskell privately referred to him as Dodd Almighty.

Charles Allbright: I remember he had an operation, a prostate operation, and, around Christmas time, we all got back together, and this was a Christmas open house. And I hadn't seen him, and I said, "Mr. Heiskell, you are looking great," which I thought he was. "Mr. Allbright, the operation was not on my face." He was backed up to the fireplace at that time. There was no way you could ace him.

Reed: On this matter of editorial policy, I think I've mentioned that I've just finished reading John Thompson's manuscript . . . and one of the things that he and Bill Rutherford go into at considerable length is the editorial positions that the Old Man took on a whole range of issues right across the seventy years he had the paper. And, on the one hand, there's a whole litany of what we would refer to as very progressive ideas. He . . . always was trying to reform city government back in the old days. Along with these progressive editorials, Thompson and Rutherford point out a whole series of editorial positions that we, today, would consider . . . reactionary—on race problems, for example, labor radicals and immigration.

Ross: The racial thing is the part that just takes your breath away, because when you go reading along in 1903, '04, '05 in there, and there were a whole bunch of lynchings, . . . and it didn't bother him a bit. He was . . . it was very anti-Negro . . . But evidently, this was something that—he grew up in Memphis.

Reed: He had some fairly approving editorial remarks about the Ku Klux Klan. . . . I should say he did come out against the Klan later on, but . . . On this race question, can you trace when he began to change, or did he actually change, or did he just kind of give up and quit talking about it?

Ross: I'll tell you something that I probably shouldn't say. In my opinion, he got that Pulitzer Prize for losing his daily battle with Hugh and Harry. He agreed to . . . take the position of law and order. This is the law—obey it. He thought Harry went way beyond it. The general public thought Harry went way beyond it.

Hugh Patterson: It was an issue that I don't recall our having ever had occasion really to take up editorially. Now, he had always been taught to be a champion for—well, civil rights doesn't seem to be the appropriate word now —but due process, legality, all that kind of business. Yet it was recognized that his father, having been a colonel in Longstreet's army, you know, had sort of engendered a feeling of racial superiority or whatever: separate but equal and not conceding that it was not equal and never was and never would be under that theory.

Reed: Did you see changes in his attitude on race during your long acquaintance with him?

Patterson: Well, I had to confront him rather directly, and I'll tell you the case in point. By that time, you know, I had gotten involved in educational issues. Forrest Rozzell [executive secretary of the Arkansas Education Association] had recruited me to take an active part in trying to get aid for public education funds. And he and I had strategized, and I had begun as sort of chairman of an ad hoc state group that was called the Governor's Advisory Committee on Education. There were sixty of us who were in what was called the National Council for the Public Schools, or something like that. It was the organization that Dr. Conant [president of Harvard University] had inspired to try to lead to a national policy of lending federal aid to public education. And I had been made the chairman of the southeast U.S. group of that body. We met at Lookout Mountain for a regional meeting, and in the course of that, an AP reporter interviewed me, and in the discussion of the race issues I said, "Well, of course, it's got to be recognized that the Supreme Court decision was the only decision they could have made. We have to recognize that this is a transitional time in terms of public policy, and it will, perhaps, take some time for that to be realized, but there's just no option to this. It's a fundamental matter." And so that managed to get printed, sent out on the wire, and managed to get to the *Arkansas Gazette*. And this was a meeting up there over a weekend. When I got back on a Sunday afternoon or something like that, we were with the Ashmores. Harry said, "Hugh, I don't know whether you have a job!" [*Laughs.*] The Old Man, apparently, had been pretty . . . The following Sunday, the Heiskells came by, as they usually did on a Sunday afternoon, to see the grandchildren, and in the course of the conversation—Louise there, and her mother and me—the subject came up. And I said, "Well, you know, deep down we're talking about your grandchildren's generation. And we feel that we can't misrepresent these issues to them. We can't bring them up feeling that what is inevitable is not true." And Louise supported that position entirely. That was the last time it was ever discussed. And when Ashmore heard about that, for the first time he was able to deal more realistically with the question textually in the editorials.

Reed: Do you remember Mr. Heiskell's reaction, his stated point of view during that conversation?

Patterson: Well, I think it was possibly a degree of reluctant acceptance or inevitability. I think he knew, in a sense, that he had outlived his time.

Harry Ashmore: Mr. Heiskell was an interesting case. The Old Man was a real civil libertarian. He was a real-free speech man. He didn't want them to be shut up, and he certainly didn't want anybody lynched. He didn't want it to become violent. Well, I think Mr. Heiskell was one in his generation who believed that, certainly, that blacks should be treated fairly and be treated decently. This was a part of the gentlemanly tradition.

James O. Powell: In the Central High affair and in the years of dispute that followed, it was he, as the owner, who in the end had to sustain the financial penalties and the personal risk when the *Gazette* lost twenty thousand subscribers. He was never much on integration, as such, but he knew that the *Arkansas Gazette* had to do right and stand for the rule of the law, and he backed up Hugh Patterson and Harry Ashmore in the *Gazette's* heroic stand.

Jerry Dhonau: The *Gazette* editorials became increasingly liberal in the seventies because we didn't have his restraints. Yes, he was fairly conservative. I've never really revealed this before, but they're all gone now. It wasn't too long after I was named editorial page editor. I've forgotten the occasion, but there was a reception of some sort. It may have been a birthday for the publisher, but, anyway, it was up at the Capital Hotel. We were on the mezzanine, and for some reason I fell into a conversation with Louise Patterson [Heiskell's daughter and Patterson's wife]. I'd never really had much of a conversation with her before . . . And she brought all this up about in 1957, how it all came about, of the position they took and stuck with. She told me that they had a family tradition that every Sunday the family would gather at the Heiskell house and have lunch or dinner. I think at the time they had Ashmore there too because this was a big, big topic. When it first came up about what the *Gazette* should do, Mr. Heiskell did not want to take the stand that he subsequently did. He was more conservative. He didn't even want to say, "Let's follow the law. Let's have law and order." He didn't want to get into it. She wasn't explicit about it. Anyway, they had to work on him, she said. Hugh, mainly. Hugh and Harry Ashmore and she talked long and hard to Mr. Heiskell to bring him around on that occasion, and they succeeded. She said that's how it happened. And so, I don't know if she told that to anybody else or not, but I've kept that—she didn't say that was in confidence, but I've kept that in confidence. But it may be good for the historical record.

Reed: I have the impression of a man who came very slowly to the idea that a newspaper page ought to be anything but words.

Ross: He was a word man, all right. But he had a daily, ongoing battle, he told me, with the Allsopp faction—he and his brother—to try to modernize the paper. It took them, I've forgotten how many years he said, to get the ads off the front page below the fold and then, finally, to get them off altogether. And he said they would suggest something like that, and Mr. Allsopp would say, "Well, I'm against it now," implying rather that you can ask me later. They'd bring it up a year later, and he'd "Well, I'm against it now." It was always that. He was against anything that cost money. When they wanted to buy comics, he was against it now. When they wanted to go to color comics, "I'm against it now." You know, he was against everything. And they were going to these newspaper meetings nationally; they knew what was going on nationally, and they wanted the *Gazette,* you know, to be in step with the times. They didn't want to be followers. They wanted to be leaders. Mr. Allsopp didn't, and, I guess, really it came to a head after Fred Heiskell died. He died in 1931, and lots of big changes after that because that's in the middle of the Depression.

Reed: Computers would probably have not . . .

Ross: Oh, forget it. Well, he never even learned to type.

Reed: He wrote his editorials by longhand?

Ross: Yes. Or dictated them. Originally, he wrote them longhand, and I guess they sent them to the back shop that way.

Not every story told about Gazette *people was 100 percent accurate.*

Ross: One story says Joe Wirges, and others say it was a brand new reporter. But some say the cub reporter was sent in there as a gag to ask the Old Man if he had [a spare typewriter] under that stack of newspapers, you know. So he went in and asked for it, and the Old Man said, "No, I don't have a typewriter. Why would I have a typewriter in here? I don't even type." And . . . whoever the reporter was, he persisted, and finally he said, "Well, you can look if you want to, but there's not one there." And he looked, and the kicker was—according to James Street's "South," he's the one that really elaborated on the story—that he found not one typewriter but two and the corpse of a young reporter.

Sam Dickinson had to bring his own desk, and he bought a secondhand card table . . . And you know the story about Mrs. Heiskell when she came in his office one day—she very rarely came to the office. She and Louise both came down there about once a year to the stockholders' meeting, and that was it usually. But one day she came to his office for some reason, they say, and saw the mess it was in and said, "Ned Heiskell, this room is a disgrace. It's bound to be unhealthful." And he said, "Yes, I guess that's the reason I died so young."

Reed: His office was an absolute mess! His secretaries down through the years never were able to do anything with it. His desk—in fact, I ended up with one of his desks. They bought new furniture one time and did away with the old ones. I realized that his desk must have ended up in the library, in the newspaper library. We were invited to take these things, chairs, desks, whatever. I had his desk for years and finally gave it to somebody after transporting it to England and back. It was a huge, old, wooden desk. It had no great distinction. It would be piled, literally, three or four feet high on the back side and on the wings with newspapers. Old copies of the *New York Times,* or whatever newspaper would come across his desk that he wanted. Usually, he hadn't quite gotten around to reading it, but he wouldn't allow it to be thrown away. Then he had tables that were stacked high with old newspapers and clutter.

Ray White: I heard any number of times the story of Heiskell being offered—somebody walked into his office and had a cashier's check for a million dollars and said, "Here's a check for a million dollars if you'll just hand over the . . ." And Heiskell, just taking that very lightly, said, "Well, I don't think I need this." . . . [The prospective buyers wanted] to buy the *Gazette* so that they could change its direction. The *Gazette* was out of sync with the state of Arkansas. It was a liberal paper in a very conservative state.

Reed: He never advertised himself as the owner of the *Arkansas Gazette* . His title was "editor." That carried enormous implications for the kind of paper that it was. He had an executive editor that he trusted to get the paper out day by day and to run the daily operations. That was Harry Ashmore. J. N. Heiskell, himself, was the editor. He was finally responsible for everything that went into the paper: ads, news content, and everything. We all understood that, and everybody in town knew that. Occasionally, somebody would complain bitterly enough about some news coverage or some editorial, and it would end up on the Old Man's desk. He would write a carefully crafted letter explaining, "If you have a problem, it is not up to Mr. Ashmore or somebody else. I am the editor of this paper. I am responsible."

He had a great interest in history. He had a bunch of standing assignments, of stories that he wanted done, at no particular time but as time allowed. All of us reporters had a drawer full of these "JNHs," as they were known. They usually always had to do with history. I remember writing a lengthy story—it took me days and days to finish it—about some North Carolinian who had opposed secession before the Civil War and was pretty much hounded out of the state for it. Mr. Heiskell was deeply interested in this man and his story in the 1950s.

Bill Lewis: I remember once, during the Congo strife in Africa, Mr. Heiskell came out and said, "There's a Congo in Arkansas. Let's go down and see what it's all about." So I had to go down to Congo and make a story, I mean, literally! He was always picking these things up at the Little Rock Club. He came in once and said, "There used to be ferry on Moro Bay." This was in the 1800s. That became a JNH. I had to do something on it, Lord knows what. I can't remember now. And another one was he had seen something on television about the vast number of conduits and pipes and subway things and so forth underground in New York. Well, he wanted a similar story on Little Rock, and you can imagine! And then there was the old town branch. There was a creek that ran under downtown that had long since been covered over. He was fascinated by that, for some reason or other . . . I admired that old man, though. He was just a perfect Southern gentleman.

Reed: Did you spend much time with him?

Lewis: No, and I often wondered if he even knew who I was. I think he must have. I wrote the lead story in his hundredth-birthday supplement. We ran a little tabloid supplement. It was a big surprise, and they said that if he had found out about it then, he'd have put his foot down. He would not have allowed it for financial reasons. And, as I recall, he was quite pleased with that piece. I didn't write his obit, though. I think Margaret Ross probably did that, if I remember.

Reed: Tell me about your Grandmother Heiskell.

Carrick: Wilhelmina Mann Heiskell. Her father was George R. Mann, who was a great architect in Little Rock, and among other things designed the present state capitol and the *Gazette* building . . . They were wealthier than a lot of people. But they also understood that a life of service was called for. If you were called on to do that, if you had the resources to do so. He, for instance, had helped found the Little Rock Public Library. He had library card number one.

Reed: Your, I presume, namesake, Carrick Heiskell, had been in line to be the editor.

Carrick: That's right. That was my uncle. He was killed during World War II, and that's one reason my father came to the paper. There was a gap there, and I don't think there was any question of it going out of the family line somewhere, so it shifted over there to him to keep the management in the family.

Charles Portis: He was in his nineties then, but still fairly active. He would come through the newsroom now and then, usually with a galley proof in his hand and some questions. I remember doing a story about the river. The Corps of Engineers had told me that the Arkansas River would soon run blue through Little Rock, when all these new locks and dams were in place. Mr. Heiskell came by to ask me about that. The muddy, reddish old Arkansas out there flowing blue? Was I quite sure of that? "Blue, Mr. Portis?" I said I was sure the claim had been made. He went away shaking his head over the absurd claim, or my gullibility, or both. But the engineers were right, you know. The river is blue at times.

Fred Coger: One afternoon, when I had not been there long, all of us copy-deskers were called into the office of the editor, J. N. Heiskell, a legend at a very old age, still putting in a full day everyday and reading the paper, every line. He lectured us briefly on some specific things he wanted done in the way of editing. I do not remember all of them now, but one sticks in my mind. He put up on a little board a very short item from that day's paper; it must have been five or six lines only, and he showed us how one extra word in that item made it one line longer than it needed to be. This was important, he said, because if we eliminated that line, we would have just one line more for something important in some other story. He wanted us to be careful to that fine a point. This is how closely the man watched his newspaper, and he did it on so many levels for so many years.

Orville Henry: About a week after I was hired, he kind of came—he had a little loping style. It was very graceful, but [there was] almost a limp too. But he walked down, shoulders turning, walking through. I saw him coming. He walked in, and he kind of grinned at me. He had a newspaper in his hand— you never saw him without a newspaper—and he said, "Mr. Henry, I would like to make a deal with you. This is your first week on the job, and if I don't have to read the sports page, you don't have [to read the] editorial page." And we had the greatest relationship, and maybe five times in all the years I would get a note from him, and I would go in, and I would explain to him why we couldn't do this. And his country club pals would put him on things, and I would tell him why it didn't fit our policy or whatever. And he said, "I'll accept that. Okay." So when he had his hundredth birthday, he sat on a little dais at the country club. When I got to him, I almost had tears in my eyes, and he grinned. And he said, "Well, Mr. Henry, you and I have become a couple of old fogies together, haven't we?"

Dhonau: We met every morning, like nine or nine thirty, in Jim Powell's office. We'd all sit in chairs looped around the room, and Mr. Heiskell would preside. Mr. Heiskell had gone over the paper and made notes to himself about what he wanted to talk about. He would hold forth and sometimes hold forth and hold forth. And somehow something came out of that.

Ernest Dumas: He would've been ninety-one in sixty-five.

Dhonau: Yes, I think so . . . Although he seemed to be somewhat frail physically, he was mentally very sharp. He would have little asides. He would preside over these meetings at which different matters were discussed, some of which were editorial. After that, Jim would get with us and decide who's doing what . . .

We all came in on Saturday morning because [Mr. Heiskell] came in on Saturday morning. And he meticulously edited all our copy. He did some during the week. If Jim wasn't there or something, he'd do it. And he wielded a heavy pencil . . . He slashed. He would take an editorial and cut it by as much as half or more. I mean, he really wielded that strong pencil and scissors. Sometimes he'd scissor them apart and paste them back together. You didn't know what you were going to get back.

Jack Meriwether: As he'd go to lunch, he would drop by the business office in the advertising department, go to the cash register, open it up, get some money, and off he would go to eat lunch. And when they were trying to help him install a business system, this hole in the bucket was there. They finally got up the courage to approach him. After all, it was his paper, and it was his money, and he knew that. I think whoever it was—and it could've been Hugh or it could've been the auditor—whoever, said, "Well, Mr. Heiskell, it's quite all right for you to do this, but would you leave a note in the drawer, because we're having trouble tracking our petty cash. Just leave a note in the drawer, you know, that you've taken . . ." And so he said, "Well, I don't mind doing that at all." And the next day they went down there, and there was indeed a note in the drawer. And it said, "I took it all."

Powell: I remember his hundredth birthday party when he had a big blowout at the country club. Governor Bumpers and Senator Fulbright came, and we all gave him a big accolade. He sat there and received them in a stately fashion. He was never one to deny what was his due. The next morning I went around to see him, and he was feeling better than I. He said, "You know, Mr. Powell, you should start preparing my obituary editorial, in case I should die at an unexpected hour or on the *Democrat's* time." As a matter of fact, I had already started to formulate it, just in the event, although I had no idea that the event was so near. He suddenly got sick and died six weeks later.

Ross: You know, they used to ask him how he got so old, and he thought up several pretty clever answers. Mary Powell [his long-suffering secretary] had the perfect answer: he was serving out the unexpired terms of all the people he had driven to an early grave!

3

Mr. Heiskell's Newspaper

The Arkansas Gazette *was the state's newspaper of record for most of two centuries. During its second century, its standards of language, editing, and reporting compared favorably to those of the nation's best newspapers. Even those readers who disliked its liberal editorial page during its closing generations depended on the* Gazette *for news of the state, the nation, and the world. Its high-quality advertising nudged forward the commerce of the city and state. It also provided the money for J. N. Heiskell and his people to publish the kind of newspaper that their standards demanded.*

The Gazette *had shortcomings that would become clear in the shifting tracings of hindsight. During much of its history, it nurtured a narrow view of the great problem of racial inequity. That was especially true in the nineteenth century when the Southern white establishment and the Democratic Party, stung by the Civil War and Reconstruction, used every device of state-sanctioned segregation to keep the ruling class in power and the black underclass "in its place." The* Gazette *consistently lent its prestige and influence to that cause. The paper expanded its vision during World War II and its aftermath. Even then, while the racial minority was gaining ground elsewhere, the* Gazette *was one of the last major newspapers to hire African Americans in any appreciable numbers. Women did not find a substantial place in the newsroom until the last quarter of the century.*

From the beginning, a thread of hubris coursed through the paper that fired resentment among its competitors and many readers. There was always the sense among Gazette *people that their paper was superior to any other around. It almost always was.*

Leroy Donald: I guess a lot of it was institutional memory because so many people at the *Gazette* had been there and they could remember things . . .

17

The *Gazette* was the paper of record. That it was a chronicle. And that was drummed into your skull from the minute you got there, that this is history. What you write is history . . . It was a state paper. It was our paper. I think, later on, that is where Gannett made its big mistake, forgetting that it was our paper and not Gannett's, not their paper. I mean, whether people liked or didn't like the *Gazette*, it was still our paper. It was Arkansans' paper, and they were proud of it, even though they didn't agree with it many times. It was still the paper that they read. They felt some ownership.

John Thompson: Maybe the *Gazette* was special because it was old.

Donald: Oh, yes. When you walk down that hallway with all those Pulitzer Prize plaques and things stuck up on the wall and the old printing press and all the pictures of the grand old men looking down at you, it was quite impressive.

Wes Pruden: The *Gazette* had a special place in Arkansas. A lot of people said they resented it, but everybody read it, and I think they resented it because it was a newspaper that tried to find out what was going on everywhere and report it. I suppose that there were people on the *Gazette* who were arrogant —most newspapers suffer from that, I think—but it was really a state institution, you know.

Paul Johnson: I never saw and I never knew of Hugh Patterson or J. N. Heiskell ordering a story that had already been written and produced be pulled back or taken out of the paper. We lived in what I now realize was an air of unreality. I don't think there were very many papers that had an absolute fire wall between the business office and the editorial function as it existed at the *Gazette*. I didn't understand how lucky we had been until later in my life when I saw newspapers where that separation didn't exist and where business decisions governed how things were covered or if they were covered or if they were not covered. I think that we all took it for granted that Bob Douglas, A. R. Nelson, Bill Shelton, and those men were pretty much free to cover the news as they saw fit.

Fred Coger: I started reading the *Gazette* when I was in sixth grade. I remember reading about the war, World War II. Even then I was like most everybody else in Arkansas; we relied on the *Gazette* to tell us what was going on throughout the state and in the world. I believe one of the strong things about the *Gazette* throughout those years was how it unified people in Arkansas and helped us think of ourselves as a community. We always in those years had the Arkansas "state news briefs," at least a full page, maybe more, on an inside page. As in *USA Today*, a page of little things from each area. Of course, people in one area would mostly read their items and only be vaguely aware of most of the others, but even if you lived in the little northern town of Hardy, you knew that there was a place in south Arkansas called El Dorado. Even if you did not read all of those stories, you knew that down there were other parts of your culture and your experience as an Arkansan. Over a lot of years, that created a strong community bond, statewide. Nobody else was doing that. That was part of Mr. Heiskell's notion, we are going to edit tight and we are going to make room for this community coverage.

There were others who helped to make the Gazette *a statewide institution. They were mostly invisible.*

Donald: We did a lot of telephoning and used those correspondents, those stringers, around the state. I remember the stringers actually sending in strings to get paid. At the end of the month, the correspondent out there takes all the little copy he wrote that got in the paper, and he puts it down and takes a string and measures the length of copy and cuts the string off. . . . He sends in the string, and then he got paid by the inch.

Laurie Karnatz: The journal page was made up of briefs from all over the state and usually a story or two. It had a 70 percent recognition rate among readers. . . . They would go and pick out just the one area of the state that they wanted to check. . . . When Bob [Douglas] hired me, there were about fifteen or sixteen stringers throughout the state that I would talk to every day. The idea was that I would condense as much as possible into little bitty stories so that you could get the who, what, when, and where in a couple of paragraphs.

In the News, *a column of news briefs on the left side of page one, had been a* Gazette *tradition for years.*

Gene Foreman: I think that [Bob] Douglas invented that. He certainly championed it and brought it to an art form. As I recall, there were three important features. First was the names in boldface, and you start the item with the name. Second was it was all one sentence. And third was that "yesterday" was understood. My favorite—and I think that Douglas would always put it as the first item—was "President Eisenhower played golf at Burning Tree Club in Maryland." That was the lead item just about every day of the week.

The Gazette's *editorial page was considered liberal for its time.*

Doug Smith: The editorial page would be considered more liberal than most papers in the country, big and small. . . . I think we were probably, in the South at least, one of the first papers that went out of our way to try to get black comments and some black representation in the paper, although we didn't, perhaps, do as much as we should have done, even then. . . . I think some of the segs even commented on it, thought that there were too many pictures of black people in the paper. And there was still occasionally a thing that the editorial page was, as I said, was generally liberal. But while Mr. Heiskell was alive, there were some occasional things that they did just because [it was] his special interest.

James O. Powell: From 1957 on for those first few years, I think the *Gazette* said all it could say and survive, which was to argue the case for law and order and decency and the rule of law. We were still saying that in the early years that I was editor.

Ernie Dumas: You had the Civil Rights Act of 1964. In the early stages of that fight, the *Gazette* had some reservations about the public accommodation section.

Powell: I remember there was an evolution, for me, in that period, and I'm afraid that on the public accommodations thing I made the mistake because I had some instincts against the government intervening in some areas. I was totally in error. But that suggests the development or evolution of my own thoughts on that issue because it was in that period that the *Gazette* was moving into the advocacy not only of desegregation and integration as a point of principle and morality and not just as a matter of following the national law. I think it was the editorial on public accommodations that, fairly soon, I became embarrassed about having written it. When we evolved, we went past all that, and we became stout advocates of desegregation and integration and full opportunity under the law.

The sports editor had his own non-ideological problems—a recalitrant back shop, for example.

Henry: Dodd [the back shop foreman] would routinely—of course, sports copy is late because ball games happen at night and so forth, but when you're on deadline, trying to make a second edition and even the city edition— Dodd would routinely shuffle sports to the bottom of the pile and leave anything on news side on top. We protested this endlessly, and finally they put in a stamp where you stamped the time on copy as it made various stages. And one of the happiest days of my life was when we sat down in an emergency meeting of, I guess, the department heads in Williamson's office downstairs, and . . . I said, "Mr. Dodd, isn't your philosophy that since sports happens late, we might as well put the blame on it?" He said, "Yes." He finally admitted that he was doing exactly what you said. He was just rolling our stuff over so it would be last, and we would be standing there with a makeup page and an empty form there, not a thing in it.

Jim Bailey: Oh, I have seen him take his hands and shuffle those papers.

Henry: Yes, yes. And so they could always make us the goat for everything. And, of course, they blamed us for expenses since we had to travel. We were the ones who cost them. The news department didn't do near the travel we did. Nothing took place in Little Rock.

Change sometimes came hard at the Gazette. *When the women's movement gathered steam during the 1970s, Assistant Managing Editor Carrick Patterson, the heir apparent, grandson of J. N. Heiskell, came up with a way to accommodate to the new reality. Or so he thought. He started a new section offering spot news on "soft" subjects.*

Carrick Patterson: Meaning features and entertainment and cooking and that sort of thing. We still had a society section, and it was a society section. It was not just a women's section. It was the society section that went to elaborate lengths to rank, for instance, brides by their social importance. And covered the debutantes and so forth. And the whole process of ranking the brides by their social importance was a big deal in those days. They took up a lot of space with it. Despite the *Gazette's* reputation for being a liberal racial institution, it didn't apply in the society pages. If you were a white Little Rock person who was engaged, your picture was in the paper, and then, when you were married, your picture was in the paper. It was almost like the right to an obit. [*Laughs.*] But you made the front page if you were socially prominent. And you made the upper-left-hand side of the front page if you were really socially prominent enough. Well, being a young, liberal person, I thought that perhaps the day for that was passing. And I persuaded the powers-that-be at the *Gazette* to let me start up a general features section using the resources that, among other things, had been put into that elaborate bride business. And we called that the "Omnibus" section, the daily features section. And it was to be modeled in my mind—even though I hadn't heard of this—I somehow wasn't aware of it—but it was the same idea as the

Washington Post Style section—that it would be a spot section. It would cover not only human-interest-type stories, but art, culture. It would have spot performance reviews. It would cover, you know, somebody interesting visiting from India as well as the ballet and the opera and the arts center and—what else happened?—but it would be very much a timely spot-type section. Well, I had really miscalculated what people in the newsroom would think about that. There was a lot of resentment in the old, traditional newsroom about it.

Reed: Why?

Patterson: I don't know, but Bill Shelton and Bob Douglas and people like that thought it was frivolous to be doing and didn't want their spot material used in it. And because of press considerations, it was decided to make it an advance section. So I never had the power, if you will, to get it made a spot section. It was always a twenty-four-hours-later section. But, gosh, before we made those changes, we still literally had a column called Among Ourselves. . . . And it was just—it was the 1970s, you know. We were very much conscious, or at least I was at that time, of how things needed to change a little bit. I thought so anyway. But the Omnibus section, I was proud of that, and I think everybody who worked for it was. We still covered—we were the newspaper of record for all the governmental, politics, and everything else, but it just added that element that, I think, rounded out the paper a little bit more. But finally the pressure from the people who resented it and also the notion that it should become more aimed toward attracting advertising took over, and it stopped being that same kind of section. They brought in a new editor, a guy named Bill McIlwain, to try to shake loose the obstreperous young man who insisted on doing all this stuff.

Among the unsung heroes of a newspaper are the men and women who deliver it, usually before daylight, to the readers' houses.

Leon Reed: When I got to the *Gazette*, transportation for the *Arkansas Gazette* was done by the Film Transit Company out of Memphis. The way they were doing it, we were really late getting into places like Texarkana because trucks hauling our paper stopped all the way along the line to drop off film. I followed them one night. I wanted to find out why the hell it was taking so long. I followed this truck. Every driver was stopping, dropping film and picking up film. They're getting to Texarkana late in the morning. They should be there at two. I told Hugh, "We can beat this. We'll start a contract hauling deal." . . . The guy owns a truck, gets a contract, and he has to drive seven days a week. He is in business for himself. Give him a contract for a given amount of money to drive from Little Rock to dealerships every night. If he's sick, if he has a problem, he gets a truck and driver. You've got to have a standby. . . .

See, we had three editions. The first edition, as you know, was in the outside fifty counties. Then the trade zone, the inside twenty-four counties, and the city edition, that was Pulaski County. . . . We got it all together. We were having all these papers getting there on time. It worked out really well. We never had any problem because they all had backups. Then we had a deal with Hertz. Any time a guy couldn't run his truck because something was wrong with it, Hertz had a deal for him. They would furnish the truck for him. Yes, he was expected to pay, but at a very cheap price, so Hertz was willing. That trucking system worked really well, but one of the funny deals about that, Roy, is during an ice storm—I don't know which year it was, but something like we just had the other night—the driver—I don't know who it was—was going to Eureka Springs, Harrison, taking a run up that way. He got to the fork at Clinton to the Harrison road, and the state police had the road blocked off. They wouldn't let him through. He called back to the office, and they called me. At that time, our state police director was Herman Lindsey [Governor Faubus's state police director]. I called him and he explained to me, "Mr. Reed, that road is a mess. The only things we're allowing through are perishables." I said, "Well, sir, can you think of anything more perishable than today's newspaper?" [*Laughs.*] "No," he said, "I guess you're right. Well, I'll call him and lift it. You know your trucks are at their own risk." I said, "When aren't they?" They let us through. The next couple of nights later he comes through, and they stop him. The cops were still there closing that road off. The driver got out, and he said, "We made arrangements with the state police to go through." "Oh, we know that. We just got a couple of squad cars going to Harrison that would like to follow you," they said. "This guy knows that road like the inside of the palm of his hand." . . .

We had a big problem up in Fayetteville with the first edition paper there. Fayetteville High School had that big game last night, they won, and they're not even in the paper. Orville [Henry] told me, "Man, we get a lot of guff on that." I went and talked to Central Flying Service to find out, on a Friday night, what it would cost us . . . We made a deal where, on Friday nights during the football season, we'd take these papers out to Central Flying Service, and they'd put them on. At that time, they had the Beechcrafts, the old twin engine. . . . But you could only get so many on that thing and get off the ground. We'd fly the papers into Fayetteville, into Jonesboro, and we'd fly papers into El Dorado. Three flights every Friday night. They'd fan out from there, but they had the football scores. I think that really picked up the circulation for us in outer limits of the state. Orville Henry was wild about the idea. We'd only do it on one night, but it gave the people the idea that we were doing it every night. When we started flying those papers up there, we had a tremendous increase. I think, at one time, we had close to four hundred carriers, boys. At that time, all the routes in town were handled by boys. There was no such thing as the motor routes in town. Out in the county, we had motor routes. Out in the trade zone, we had routes.

The biggest discussion, of course, was time, press time. I can remember when there would be a certain story, sudden breaking news, [the managing editor would] want to hold up the paper for it. I didn't want to hold the paper up because [if] you holdup the first edition, then your third edition is late, the city is late. We had a couple of pretty good discussions about that . . . I had a little trouble in the newsroom making these guys realize how important that break was. Guys are sitting down there, and pretty soon you have a traffic jam because the second edition trucks are coming in and the first edition trucks haven't left yet. You got presses rolling, you got to speed up the press and chance [paper] breaks. It doesn't sound like much, but ten or fifteen minutes is a lot of time if it's ten or fifteen minutes late. Then, you got a lot of boys out on the street, waiting on the their papers, and they're not there. Pretty soon parents get involved. He's late for school . . . Nobody knows more than I do how important that breaking news story is to the paper, but if it doesn't get there, the story doesn't mean a thing!

J. N. Heiskell was often described as the owner of the Gazette. *That was only partially true. First, there were the Allsopps . . .*

Hugh Patterson: At the time, Roy, I had assumed that Mr. Heiskell had absolute control of the 75 percent that the family didn't have, the Allsopps. The Allsopps were there when the Heiskell family bought the majority interest. Later on, I learned that Mr. Heiskell had really maybe just about 25 percent, and his late brother's estate had a lesser amount, and the rest of it was divided among his two maiden sisters and his two widowed sisters because his father, who had been the major owner, had left equal amounts to the six children. And that's the way it worked out. So the J. N. Heiskell family did not even have a majority. When I learned that, boy, it sent a chill up my spine. But we rocked along there, and Will [Allsopp] just wouldn't give me any kind of consideration for anything progressive that I wanted to do in my role as national advertising manager. I've forgotten how long it took, but about September of 1948 he had a lawyer approach us with the proposition that he would sell the Allsopps' stock to us for a million dollars. Well, a million dollars was a lot of money back then, but I found, by then, that he had been presiding over an accumulation of earnings that amounted to about a half-million dollars, which he had not in any kind of interest-bearing investment but just purely in a checking account. And they had him on the board of directors at the bank, you know. That was characteristic of the way things were done ... We were able to work out a loan, but at that time I don't remember just how much money we were to borrow. It was a significant part of the million, perhaps four or five hundred thousand, something like that. And so not too long after that we settled the proposition: I was made vice president, secretary, and treasurer, with the title of publisher. [That was] in November of 1948.

Patterson soon installed a modern system of accounting that kept closer track of how much each part of the operation cost: circulation, printing, etc. His ideas eventually were adopted by other newspapers across the country. He modernized the Gazette's outdated equipment. Then he dealt with another threat to J. N. Heiskell's control of the paper. W. R. (Witt) Stephens, the hard-knuckled financier and political kingmaker, managed to buy a substantial block of Gazette shares from an heir, apparently with the intention of acquiring a voting majority. Patterson quietly arranged to place the remaining shares in an inter vivos trust with J. N. Heiskell controlling it. He related what happened when Stephens came to his first board meeting.

Patterson: I said, "Witt, I don't know why you bought this because it's not going to make any money for you. I don't know what asset you saw in it to justify your doing that." And he said, "Well, Hugh, I saw that you had a considerable inventory of newsprint, and I know that newsprint is demanding a good black market now." And I said, "Well, that's fine, Witt, but that's what we use to print the newspaper, you know, so that's not for sale for a quick profit." And then he said, "You've got more building than you need, and you've got real estate and what not." And I said, "That's right, and that's all in the plan for expansion as we need it. So I'll be happy to have your suggestion on financial matters and things of that sort; you just won't be involved in any policy decision-making and that kind of thing." Well, we rocked along there. So the time passed, and he kept making veiled threats that he could sell the stock one share at a time to other people who would like to buy stock in the *Gazette* and all kinds of silly stuff. And I said, "Now, Witt, don't go around waving an empty gun at us!"

After a year, Stephens threw in the towel and sold his shares to the Heiskell family, giving the patriarch J. N. Heiskell undisputed control.

Reed: You know, it's not like Witt to have overlooked the possibility that you all had sewn up the . . .

Patterson: He thought I was a yokel! [*Laughs.*] I suppose that was the best poker hand I ever played.

Reed: I heard somewhere that he once said in your presence that you were the only man who had ever bested him in a financial deal.

The American Newspaper Guild tried unsuccessfully to organize a local chapter at the Gazette during the late 1940s. A large number of reporters and editors went on strike. Farris Wood, a printer, watched the guild's effort fail. He had already seen a decline in his own union.

Wood: We had a groundswell of union growth in this country, and we had a different political climate then. They discovered that they could get one man, one representative in the legislature, and do more good for their cause at that time than they ever could by honest negotiations. In my opinion, that is when the union started its decline. There's a long, gentle decline down the toilet into the sewer. . . . The [guild] strikers made two serious mistakes: one, they just knew that printers would not cross the picket line. They just made that assumption.

Dumas: That decision would have been made in Colorado at national head-quarters?

Farris Wood: Yes. They got Colorado's attention too late, and they were out on the picket line, and they [Colorado headquarters] told us, "This is not your quarrel regardless of how you feel about it. You are under contract with the *Gazette*. Go back in there and go to work." That was the first mistake they made. The second mistake they made was about six months later. Now, this was the American Newspaper Guild. About six months later, they embraced the circulation workers and the Teamsters Union. One night they got every edition of the *Gazette* that they could possibly get on two or three trucks. They took them over to the middle of the Broadway Bridge, and they threw them in the river. Well, I know where the next edict came from, and it wasn't Hugh Patterson. It was Hugh Patterson's father-in-law! He said, "That did it. That union is not going back to work for this company. I don't give a damn if it costs every nickel I've got. Give anybody out there twenty-four hours to go back to work. Otherwise they're cooked. And to hell with those people who destroyed our property!" And, really, in all honesty, I don't see how anybody could blame him for doing it. Nobody has ever said so, but I'm certain it came from Heiskell because if you backed him into corner, he could make a decision! [*Laughs.*]

Robert Douglas: The strike was in December '49. We formed a chapter of the American Newspaper Guild in early fall of '49. We won an election. And the way that happened is that—I wasn't in on this—they'd had some kind of jackleg union. They were affiliated with the Teamsters. I don't know how it worked. It didn't work very well because they didn't get anything. The word was that Mr. Heiskell had promised that the newsroom would get a raise any time the printers got a raise, and they got raises fairly regularly because they were a union, a strong one. They made more money than we did. But Hugh Patterson had come and, I guess, he became publisher about the time Harry [Ashmore] became executive editor, September '48. And Hugh, in the service, in the army, had been a personnel officer, so he had some ideas about structure. Well, instead of a raise, we got a system. Everybody was in a certain notch. You know, if, say, you're a copy reader, well, you would be a junior copy reader, then a maybe a middleweight copy reader, then a senior copy reader until you got to the end of your graph. That was the most you could make at that level, and then you moved up. The problem with that, in the first place, nobody was very excited about it. But the real problem was that nobody got a nickel. Everybody, just coincidentally I'm sure, wound up right where they were. [*Laughter.*] . . . So we started talking about guild and got a union representative and held an election, which we won, won overwhelmingly. Well, I learned later, and somewhat suspected at the time, we weren't going to have a guild. We were going to be forced into a strike. Of course, we were forced a whole lot earlier than we should have been. It was a dumb mistake. We asked for a model contract. You had to do that. It was somewhat ridiculous. We weren't going to get that, and we should have known it. Well, the *Gazette* seized on one or two requests—not requests, demands, guild demands for a contract—and we asked for a voice in hiring and firing. The whole thing was for higher wages. So we went out in December, near Christmas '49. It snowed immediately, of course. We walked the picket line in ice and snow.

Reed: How many of you went out?

Douglas: About twenty-six, twenty-seven including Joe Wirges [long-time police reporter]. Spider Rowland [a popular columnist] joined us for a couple of weeks. Spider's complaint was Ashmore changed some of his copy. [*Laughter.*]

Reed: I've never heard of a better reason to go on strike.

Douglas: Our weapon was supposed to have been the circulation department . . . They got the circulation people to join us, and we blocked the newspaper for a few days. There were some deliveries, but a lot were late, and a lot of them never got there. We'd picket all these carrier folks, which was a rotten thing to do. It was not a good time. I sometimes felt it was silly . . . It lasted until summer. Well, officially, it lasted about two years. [It was] about a year and a half, though, before the picket line was dissolved. People started scattering, and I did too, although I think I was about the last to leave the picket line. Because I was president, I didn't feel I could go. I got a job with a radio station, KARK, and was striking also at the same time. But I got an offer from the Asheville [North Carolina] *Citizen.* Walt Damtoft was working there. They had a gambler, a racketeer, who had been picked up in Little Rock, and there was a series of extradition hearings to get him back to North Carolina, and they asked me to cover that. So I covered that for them, and then they offered me a job. So I went up there. The *Gazette* offered me a job back. I should have taken it back, but I figured it wasn't quite seemly as president of the guild. The strike wasn't officially over. So I went to North Carolina for nearly a year and a half. Went there in the spring of '50 or '51. I came back in '52, October of 1952, because I wanted to.

Reed: Were there any hard feelings when you came back?

Douglas: No, not as far as I know. I'd stayed pretty friendly. Carroll McGaughey [J. N. Heiskell's nephew] was a very good friend of mine. During the strike he got married in Virginia, and I went up as the best man for the wedding. [*Laughs.*] I stood with Mr. Heiskell and Hugh Patterson, and we all partied together. It was a heck of a party too. A Virginia party is a nice thing to attend.

The Gazette saw a second attempt to organize a newspaper guild during the early 1970s. It was as ill-fated as the first.

Douglas: There was, again, another terrible period. We had strike number two, although it wasn't a strike: guild movement number two, which I fought tooth and nail and won that one. That would have been about 1973. I had just been named managing editor. Kind of got hit with that. They were justified in asking for more money, God knows, but we were under [federal anti-inflation] guidelines. Nobody was supposed to get any raises nationwide.

We had four days of representation hearing and then had an unfair labor practices charge. We won every point. I knew something about unions. I had been president of a guild chapter.

Dumas: That episode was unusual in that the *Gazette* was, as I recall, a place where we were relatively happy, were we not? At least, compared to across town. At the *Democrat* across town, people were miserable, pay was much less, hours worse, fringe benefits poor, yet the *Gazette* is where we had a union drive. What do you think the genesis of it was?

Max Brantley: You know, I don't know. To this day, I don't really know . . . In a way, it was a lark for me. The notion of a union, of solidarity, of group negotiation, of being able to press complaints, not just about pay but about other things, as a solid front, was an appealing thing to me. Philosophically, that was most of its appeal to me, but it's true that we were sort of a plantation. I guess the tradeoff, in a way, was being a plantation. I think people, some underperformers, were tolerated probably and some quirks were endured and some problems were endured because that was just the way the *Gazette* was. It's kind of like Harvard. They say if you get in, you'll graduate. If you got on at the *Gazette,* you would stay unless you did something just extraordinarily awful. I think maybe that was the tradeoff for less pay. And I know today, twenty-seven years after the fact of hiring, that the pension plan that existed then just almost couldn't have been worse. Except none at all. That would have been worse. In terms of pension and health benefits, the best thing that ever happened to a *Gazette* employee was Gannett's purchase of the newspaper. That's another story.

The Gazette *had always prided itself on being the "Old Gray Lady."*

Gene Foreman: We weren't too much on modern information graphics in those days. As a matter of fact, Shelton would sketch out little maps of his own if he thought we needed one. Bill had a lot of qualities as a journalist, but art was not one of them. I can remember when the decision was announced by the Defense Department that they would build Titan II missile silos in central Arkansas. Bill looked up what the range of these missiles were, and he drew a flat map that concluded that these missiles could not reach Russia. This is really confusing that we're building all these missiles and they cannot reach Russia. Later that day they told him that he used the wrong direction for the missiles. He's a stand-up guy, so the next day he ran the map again and said, "Wrong, all wrong." That was the heading. You can look it up. It explained that if you went over the North Pole, you could hit Russia.

Patt Clark: I think it was around 1985. The *Gazette* was buying new presses, and Mary Jo [Meade, the new graphics editor] was there to shepherd the color just as it started showing up more often in the paper. She had a color sensitivity that was very sophisticated. Often, when papers get color, they splash whopping 100 percent yellow globs of yuck onto their pages, really strong saturated colors. It makes the paper look garish and unrespectable, like a beach ball. The *Arkansas Democrat* was guilty of that. Gaudy color. Mary Jo's approach was more subtle. She used light touches of color, muted color that complemented all that endearingly gray type. Newsprint is already pretty gray, so if you use gray colors with them, it looks more sophisticated. It looks more serious. And it helped the Old Gray Lady stay the Old Gray Lady . . . Just a little makeup on the Old Gray Lady. A little blush.

George Fisher, the political cartoonist, became famous for his caricatures and biting portrayals of the state's political leaders. He took on friends as well as enemies. Sometimes, he and the editors decided against publishing them for fear of offending readers' tastes, like the one he drew of the capitol dome as a woman's breast after a series of Washington sex scandals.

Dumas: There's another one of David Pryor, when he was governor of Arkansas and came up with the "Arkansas Plan" to shift state taxes and expenditures to the local level. The legislature just cut it to pieces. And you drew a cartoon of Pryor, lying on the gurney as a surgical specimen, I guess.

George Fisher: That's Rembrandt's "Anatomy Lesson."

Dumas: You have all these physicians gathered around the prone body of David Pryor, and they're looking over his abdomen. The surgeons are members of the legislature.

Fisher: The lead surgeon happens to be Ben Allen, who later became fast friends of David Pryor, you remember? Ben has his scalpel, pulling tendons out of his arms in demonstration. You don't do that in the newspaper.

Dumas: People are squeamish about it.

Fisher: Photographs of accidents showing somebody's body parts, part of a hand showing, blood and all that. Readers don't accept that. It's too gruesome.

Dumas: Another one was of Orval Faubus as a monkey. And he says, "I'm not yet ready to accept evolution." And the cartoon of Nixon in the manger. He's the baby Jesus.

Fisher: He's a little large for the manger, but he's saying . . .

Dumas: "You say there'll be gifts?"

Fisher: I got more criticism for using religious metaphors than any other subject, and it got me in trouble. I mean real trouble. I remember the donkey after Jimmy Carter won the Democratic nomination. I drew a donkey coming up out of the water. The caption was "Born Again." That got me in trouble. A lot of people wrote letters to the editor, complaining about that cartoon.

Dumas: Did you ever get much personal abuse as a result of your cartoons? People calling and harassing you?

Fisher: Oh, yes. I never minded so much when they called me directly, but when they called my wife and told her to "tell your husband to watch it," she'd say, "Watch what?" "Well, just watch it, that's all." They won't go into details. She used to get a lot of those calls. When they called me, I'd talk to them about the cartoon. That's okay if people do disagree. And I was always kind to people. I always treated them with dignity. That way they're not so scornful.

Dumas: Were these usually about race? Was that one factor that would get people riled?

Fisher: Race was one of them, yes. Race, of course, and religion. But that's okay. That means somebody read it, and that they were readers, so I never objected to that.

On the huge question of race, the Gazette *was slow to change.*

Reed: How did the *Gazette* cover black athletics?

Jerry McConnell: Not very much when I first started. Generally, we would call, they would call. But we hardly ever staffed a, at that time, a black-on-black ball game or anything like that. I am sure, you know, at some point in time that began to change . . . Before I left, we had hired Wadie Moore [a black reporter]. When I first started, the newspapers in Little Rock ran white and black obituaries, but they had a separate section for black obituaries. And my hazy recollection is that they did not ever call blacks "Mr." or "Mrs."

Reed: What was the policy on the handling of news about black men?

Bob Douglas: Well, mostly we just ran police stories. There were never any positive stories about blacks. They were not called "Mr." and "Mrs." That changed. Ashmore effected one change. He talked Mr. Heiskell into using the honorific "Mrs." But we still couldn't call black males "Mr." I did it, and Mr. Heiskell got on me once. I think I used "Mr. and Mrs. Martin White," and Mr. Heiskell reminded me it's "Martin and Mrs. White."

Bob Douglas, one of the paper's best managing editors in its long history, found himself in an untenable position when Carrick Patterson, the older son of Hugh and Louise Heiskell Patterson, rose through the editing ranks and started training to become managing editor. Douglas moved to Fayetteville and became the chairman of the University of Arkansas's Department of Journalism. His leaving coincided with other changes at the Gazette.

Dumas: There was a point when Douglas was effectively fired as managing editor of the *Gazette.* Carrick was promoted and Bill McIlwain was named the editor. He had been editor of the *Washington Star.*

Brantley: He was to groom Carrick to assume the role of leadership of the paper. . . . McIlwain was the first of many outsiders who came in and had an awful lot of harsh things to say about the way we were doing things . . . It was under McIlwain's reign that we really beefed up and improved the feature section, which was a good thing. A new design team came in and changed the look of the newspaper. In a lot of ways that truly, I thought, were an improvement. It may have been in that period that we switched from eight-column to six-column format . . . But one of the things he was not happy about, and it would be a theme that would echo and reecho as subsequent new leadership came in, was that we were too boring, too stodgy, too concerned with matters of record and not enterprising enough and not colorful enough and not in tune with everyday concerns enough, and we needed to have a whole lot more of that kind of writing in the newspaper.

Dumas: Did you agree with that assessment of the *Gazette?* Was it behind the times?

Brantley: You know, probably yes, but I had been schooled in it, and it seemed fine to me . . . There is a great deal of reassurance in approaching things in a formulaic way. I mean, you're never bad wrong. If your lead is a classic "who, what, when, where, why" lead every time, it may be boring, but it won't be wrong. You don't take near the risk on skewing context that you do when you reach for an anecdotal lead or reach for an interpretive lead.

The back shop, the domain of the printers, was a different world. Farris Wood, a longtime member of the International Typographical Union, saw many changes during his time.

Wood: We had a battery of twenty-three Linotype machines, plus strip-casting machines, plus displaying machines. All of them were hot metal. . . . They would dump pied type [discarded type] into the top pot, melt it down, and it would feed the next pot. Those pots, they ran from 500 to 515 degrees each, and that—twenty-three times two times the strip casters and the display—in one room, it gets pretty hot! Temperatures would run 110 or 112 degrees at midnight, and it was beginning to cool off a little bit then.

Dumas: You had mentioned earlier about the large number of hearing-impaired people who worked at the *Gazette.*

Wood: It's an excellent trade for the hearing impaired because, for one thing, they're not bothered by the noise. Their concentration is better. Now, they're a little bit harder to train because you're speaking another language. I was always going to learn to sign, and I never did quite get around to it, which meant if we were going to get technical about any problem, I had to have an interpreter. Either that, or I had to write it down. . . . We had a deaf man with a PhD back there. . . . The deaf people would call me over and take my hand and put it on the machine. And I thought, "What the hell do you want from me?" Well, he felt something in the rhythm of that machine that wasn't right. I can't figure it. I don't know what you call it. Then he'd write me a note, "It's going to break within the next ten minutes." [*Laughs.*]

Talking about disabilities, part of the territory in the newspaper business —I don't know how it is now, but I suspect it's the same—whether you're a printer, a pressman, a news reporter, or an editor, is alcoholism. As a matter of fact, I'm an alcoholic. But that just goes with the trade. I had a feeling about this. I've never seen a study on it or anything, but you've got a high-tension job. You're meeting, if you're a printer, sometimes dozens of deadlines a day. You go home at the end of the day, and you're really tied in knots. Basically, reporters are the same way.

A long day's work—reporting, writing, and editing the stories; setting them in type; arranging the type in page forms—all this was prelude to a miracle of timing and skill that was repeated in the back shop every night of the year in the last ten minutes before the paper hit the streets. Wayne Bolick, another printer, witnessed the miracle every day.

Wayne Bolick: We really had it streamlined . . . We'd get the last piece of type across the dump to makeup and put in the page and lock it up. From that point to the street, with a curved, metal, lead plate, was about ten minutes. Pretty damn good. In other words, you could almost set your clock by it. They have an assembly line back there in the plate-making department. They'd roll that plate back there, and roll the mat, put it in the dryer, then they'd put it in a thing and pour the hot lead on it, then shoot it up. One guy would shave this, one guy would shave that, slap it on a press, turn that press on, and they were gone. It was pretty quick starting up the old metal plates.

That was in the old days. Then came a new form of printing.

Bolick: When it got to offset printing, the start-up was a little more complicated. You have to get your ink and water regulated. The paper starts out black. It takes about four or five hundred papers to get started. You have a lot of waste in there. . . . We didn't change over to offset until we got in that new building [in the east end of Little Rock] . . . That must have been '87, or '88, somewhere around there . . . You couldn't convert a letterpress to offset without major expense and major downtime—I'd say six months . . . We went through some gradual changes to kind of prepare for doing cold type . . . Then, when the offset press started running full time, that was a drastic learning experience for all the pressmen because they were letterpress printers and they had to learn to run an offset press. I'm sure it was just as drastic for them as it was for the composing-room people, but they got along very well.

. . . When I went to work there, in '53, everybody in the composing room was in the printers' union [International Typographical Union]. Next, plate-making department in the stereotypers' union. The next department was the pressmen's union. And the next department was the mailers' union. They all just flowed one right after the other. Each one had its own contract and jurisdiction, and so forth. In the composing room, you couldn't touch any type. Editors used to use a pencil to point to type. The minute an editor touched any type back there, some of the old stalwarts would say, "You can't do that!" Boy, they'd complain. The boss would tell the editor, "Don't do that. You'll disrupt things." . . . As the technology changed, the printers' union began to lose strength because of the newer ways. The electronic stuff was more complicated to begin with, but when it worked, it was so fast and good that it saved a lot of labor. I can remember when we changed over to cold type, one of the things that they were very proud of at the *Gazette* was that they didn't put anybody out of work. Just through attrition and retraining, we changed that whole mess over. And over a period of years we had a lot less paperwork in there because we just didn't need that many people. The main thing involved the typesetting. The copy came in already set. The editors would call the AP copy up on a computer screen electronically, edit it, send it to the composing room in the *Gazette* style, and we'd put it right in the paper . . . The reporters did the same thing. . . . They'd input it, it would go over to the rims, the editors would put the style in it, pass it over to the news editors, the editor would look it over, okay it, and send it to composing.

Reporters' salaries everywhere were pitiable in those days. There was a feeling in management that reporters should be willing to work for the glory of the thing. We groused about the low pay, but many of us would have paid the paper for letting us work there. Wayne Jordan's salary negotiation was typical. He was a reporter from 1966 until the paper closed.

Wayne Jordan: And we talked about that for a little bit. Then he [the managing editor] said, "How much money would you want?" I said, "How about $125 a week?" He said, "$125 a week!" He kind of laughed. He said, "No, I don't think so." He said, "I'll tell you what we'll do. How about starting out at $85?" And I thought about that, and I said, "Mr. Nelson, I'll tell you what: I will do that if you promise me one thing. If I do well and if I come up with some good news stories, you will pay me what I'm worth." And he got up and put his hand out, and he said, "Sounds like a good deal to me." [*Laughter.*] So that's how I was hired.

Dumas: I started off at $80 there several years before, but they acted like they were paying me more than they'd ever paid anybody.

Jordan: Yes, they acted like it was coming out of the national treasury and that if we got too much money out of that treasury, it would bankrupt the country. And whenever Douglas got us that huge raise that year, I'll never forget that. I could not believe it. Whew, boy!

The Gazette *could be tightfisted on more than reporters' salaries.*

Bailey: I have heard like in the 1940s, the wartime years, you couldn't even make a long-distance call unless the managing editor gave prior approval.

Henry: That's right. To make long-distance calls, for four or five years, you had to tell him what it was for and why. . . . The *Arkansas Gazette* never had a lot of money. . . . There was nothing in the budget for a three-, four-, five-, six-, seven-man sports department. But what they did let me do is every once in a while I could add a part-time employee. If he was any good, then we would keep him. And I really—it was a problem for me. I was so damn young, and I didn't know how to be a sports editor. I didn't know how to write sports. . . . They did not really want a sports department at the *Arkansas Gazette.* They spent all their money on the editorial page—three columns. There would be six men, eventually, and some of them making big money, writing editorials or doing nothing all day. So here's what I had to—if I asked for anything, I was not apt to get it except on the basis of compromise. I got part of my help [from] people like Chuck Miller and Bill Bentley, people that they had hired as reporters who did not fit the niche that they were hired for. They were not really doing well. So they said, "We can give them to sports." . . . And the other thing was, I had the Friday-night extras. On Friday night we would have up to six, eight, ten high school kids who would take football games over the phone. Wally Hall [later sports editor of the *Democrat*] was one of them once—and so that is where I found the jewels.

Bailey: Well, you hired at least three guys, Dygard, Robert Shaw, and Bill Simmons, who became AP [Associated Press] bureau chiefs.

Henry: How about Tom Dygard, who became the number-two man in the Associated Press in this country? How about Gene Foreman [managing] editor of the *Philadelphia Inquirer?* How about Wes Pruden, editor of the *Washington Times?*

Newspaper rules about freebies were fairly relaxed until the closing decades of the century. At the Gazette, *we all looked forward to the Christmas parties given by the utility companies and others and to the cases of booze that lined the newsroom wall during the same season. We were not entirely without scruple; no one took more than one bottle from each company. Then there were the free trips. We all envied Bill Lewis, a former United Press reporter and a stalwart in the newsroom, who traveled the world at no expense to himself.*

Bill Lewis: I got more response from the travel stuff than almost anything else. I guess they may have been able to see that this might be a nice addition, so they began letting me—I started working on developing the trips. Of course, I never paid for anything, and they were all free. It was freebie city as far as I was concerned, and most of them were all first class—airfare, hotels, restaurants, totally guided. Typically, the German government tourist agency, Pan-Am, all the other airlines. . . . I wound up going to fifty countries, give or take one or two, including some of the little Caribbean island countries that are independent. . . . Then, when Gannett came in, accepting free trips was one of the no-nos. They did not allow anybody to accept anything free. I remember once going to cover some kind of meeting which started with a cocktail party. I shunned everything in accordance with Gannett's policy. I came back and told [Managing Editor] David Petty, "That was the last time I'm doing that. I'm going to go and have a drink, eat whatever, and to hell with it!" [*Laughs.*] It was really, really awkward to do things like that. . . . So

I cannot tell you more emphatically that I cannot remember ever being influenced positively or negatively by the fact that I took the free stuff. It just didn't occur to me, and if there was anything negative about it, I always wrote it. I think I was as fair about that as I tried to be with everything else.

Reed: Did you get any backlash from the sponsors when you'd write negatively about anything?

Lewis: I never did. Now, one or two times, I had heard from others that if an airline, say, flew you to Europe, they would like at least a mention in your column. I always did, anyway. I thought that was only fair, but it wasn't "What a marvelous flight this was."

The Gazette had a traditional society section, later known as the "women's section." Julia Jones wrote about brides and fashions and was assistant editor of the paper's magazine.

Julia Jones: We were in the bride business. That's what drives a woman's section. During Betty's time [Betty Fulkerson, woman's editor]—she was a widow at this point—but when she was a young woman, a woman would only have her name in the paper three times: when she was born, when she was married, and when she died. So we were sort of still operating under that attitude. . . . On Monday and Tuesday, we would all cram into Betty Fulkerson's office, and we would go through these brides to rank them, to see if they had a known family name, what kind of dress they were wearing, who designed it, and where the wedding was going to be and where the honeymoon was going to be, look at all the attendants to see if they were "anyone." We looked at the jewelry she wore. We even looked at the photographer. All these things would give the bride points, and if you got enough points, then you got to be on page one. You got the most points if the bride's father brought the picture in. We even had a special, flowery way of writing for the page-one brides. It was really depraved. It was an amazing amount of time and effort. Then the pages were made up on Thursday for Sunday.

Somebody had to go out in the composing room and kind of hang around while they were making up the pages in case there was a trim of a few words or whatever. Betty usually did that herself because she didn't like for us to go out in the composing room. She didn't like that because, of course, they were all men. She apparently felt that they were almost animals. And it was okay if one of us "older" women went out in the newsroom to get the mail, but if it was a summer intern, then they had to go in pairs, like a chaperone. She was really concerned about protecting her interns. She would tell them to be sure and kneel down to get the mail in the newsroom. Our box was right down on the floor, the bottom shelf. In those days we were all wearing skirts several inches above our knees, and she did not want you to bend from the hip and get that mail out of that box because it would show way too much leg to those animals in the newsroom.

As more women were hired as reporters and editors, they learned to negotiate obstacles that had never been there for men.

Denise Beeber: Were they protective of you? Did they warn you about things they thought you needed to know?

Maria Henson: Yes. They were good about that. And frankly, the legislature was just such a gauntlet for a young woman to be running through. There was just, time and again, weird stuff that would happen over there. Like, you'd have one legislator who was in AA [Alcoholics Anonymous], bringing his biggest squashes and produce into a committee meeting and then plop down with a big kiss right on my cheek. I'm trying to cover the thing, thinking, "Oh, boy, is this part of the job?" Because I was so young, I didn't understand. I didn't put these folks in the paper when I should have. They were just out of line so many times. But I thought, "Oh, well, that's what you have to put up with. It's such a guy's world over here." And there really weren't that many women. Deborah Mathis was from TV. There were a few TV reporters around. But there really were not that many women covering the legislature, and it was just outrageous, some of the stuff they said and did. I remember Senator Knox Nelson blocking my way to get into the Senate. He wouldn't let me through. He said, "You're going to have to give me a kiss and come sit beside me," which I didn't do. But it was that kind of thing all the time. And in my case, I would laugh and move on.

Anne Farris: Peggy Harris and I were really two of a few number of women reporters. And we sat right next to each other, and because of our names, Anne Farris and Peggy Harris, people were always confusing us. The guys in the newsroom just gave us grief to no end about one thing or another, but it was always good hearted. No one was ever patronizing to us. They were always respectful of us. They treated us as equals, except when they would jab us about certain things that were just male-female differences sometimes. So we were really accepted into a very male-dominated climate there. . . .

There was one reporter that Gannett sent down when Bill Clinton was running in 1990 for reelection for governor. Let me just clarify it was not John Hanchette. Anyway, the guy they sent was a real lech. [*Laughs.*] He was always making sexual comments about the length of your skirt or nice legs. He was just a real sleaze.

Don Troop: And he was the big city reporter? [*Laughs.*]

Farris: Yes, yes. I guess he thought, "Well, I can just sashay in and take advantage of these little country bumpkins down here." [*Laughs.*] I had to read him the riot act a couple of times. He was really obnoxious. When you work in a male-dominated work environment, you get used to that, and you just blow it off. But, you know, it does get a little aggravating. [*Laughs.*]

Hugh Patterson, the publisher, and Bob Douglas, the managing editor, tapped two of the paper's best reporters, Tucker Steinmetz and Jimmy Jones, and cut them loose to do investigative reporting. The pair turned up numerous stories of corruption and malfeasance.

Tucker Steinmetz: When Bob Douglas and Hugh Patterson made a commitment to this project, they said, "We will never interfere with what you find. We are not going to tell you what to find. You tell us. You take as long as you need to finish a story." And we were kind of slow at times and never were rushed. One time, we really got dragging along and weren't making much progress, and Douglas called us in one night and said, "Guys, let's get this wrapped up." And we said, "Bob, we're right on the brink of it, but we are not there yet." And he was kind of irritated with us. And the next day we came in, and he came up to our office and apologized. "You guys tell me when you are ready." They never backed up on their commitment, and they never interfered. . . . When we wrote about the poverty programs, the *Gazette* had been extremely supportive of those programs, but we had reports of general corruption in those things, so we went out and wrote about it. And both of us, it bothered us because we were both inclined to be supportive of those efforts.

Language was important at the Gazette. There was an insistence on proper grammar and usage. There was also a strong element of quirkiness.

Ray White: There were things I couldn't get about the language, like the *who/whom* thing. I never got that. "Sequence of tenses" was a mystery to me until I got to Philadelphia [*Inquirer*] and had to be a copy editor . . . I never heard of [H. W.] Fowler until Gene Foreman threw it at me one day. That big book on usage. And Ed Newman. I hate Ed Newman. They want to put language in a box. So does Fowler. But they do have something to say. If you're trying to be literate, that is part of the deal. You've got to understand those rules before you break them. But we were just going out there and breaking them. We didn't know anything, and we just went ahead.

Donald: I remember one time they got in a big fight over whether a weapon used in a holdup of a gambling hall down at Crossett was a Thompson sub-machine gun or some other kind. It was late at night, and we were trying to beat a deadline. We didn't have time to go back and determine the exact caliber of the weapon . . . You had the people in there, like Shelton, Jim Clark, and Mr. J. N. and A.R. Nelson, who were real wordsmiths and knew the English language and grammar backwards and forwards. And you rarely, rarely ever saw a punctuation mistake or a grammatical mistake in the *Gazette*. I am talking about no split infinitives. Prepositions were used properly. It wasn't necessarily the *AP Style Book,* but every rule of grammar and punctuation and spelling was closely adhered to.

Carrick: We didn't have an official style book at that time. We had a collection of loose-leaf folders, which was mainly full of things like memos from J. N. Heiskell, that had established the style. And some memos from the other people like Bill Shelton, the city editor, and A. R. Nelson, the managing editor. But the JNH legacy was the major part of our style book. He had some really interesting rules, for instance the possessive of the word *Arkansas* was always to be spelled *-s's.* And his reasoning on that was that, . . . in the word *Arkansas* itself, the final *s,* though written, was not pronounced in the French form. But when you added the possessive, it was . . . [Editor's note: He was right, by God.] He had a number of other spelling styles. For instance, the word that is now almost always spelled D-R-O-U-G-H-T, meaning a dry period, at that time was pronounced "drouth" in the South. And so, in the *Gazette* the word was spelled D-R-O-U-T-H.

Henson: Bill Shelton, the city editor, the first day or two I was there, said, "The first thing you have to know is the *Gazette* style." So they put me in a corner, near the windows behind Bill Shelton's desk, and I had this little spot where I was sitting, thinking I might read a style book. I think I'd heard from other people that journalism had that. He brought this big manila folder with little pieces of paper sticking out in every direction, and my memory is that it was a foot and a half high. And I was supposed to read what was referred to as the "style pile." And so I did. I just kept reading these little scraps of paper, and I just remember thinking, "Oh my gosh, this little piece of paper is dated 1910!" And it was J. N. Heiskell. And there are things I still remember to this day—never use the word *nation* unless you are referring to "Indian nation." *Drouth. Employe* with one *e.* Why is that? All these things,

and they were all little tiny yellowed—and I mean really yellowed—pieces of scrap paper, and you were supposed to memorize it. But obviously I didn't. I did think, "Oh my gosh, how could anyone remember all these things?"
Ken Parker: Mr. Heiskell made sure we all knew such things as there are no "tugboats" on the Arkansas River, only towboats. That's not a "twenty-one-gun salute" they fire at a funeral for some retired military man; it's three volleys. A twenty-one-gun salute is fired only for the president of the United States.
Donald: The *Gazette* used a lot of commas, where others didn't. And if you did something, you would get a note from Mr. Heiskell. It was always these fine, fine, very intelligent notes written down. "I noticed that a comma was placed here instead of there."
Gerald Drury: If it wasn't Gibraltar, it wasn't a "rock." A "kid" is a baby goat.

The Gazette *was a kind of graduate school. Scores of cheeky kids—Sorry, Ned—with nothing to recommend them beyond raw desire were turned into functioning newspaper people.*

Henry: One day Clyde Dew [managing editor] came in with a long piece of copy I had written for a column, and he had cut it up and pasted it up and written down . . . He used a number-three [pencil]—little bitty, you know—and he said, "What the bleep does this mean?" And I said, "It means this." "Why in the hell didn't you say so in the first place?" That very moment, I decided, "I'm never going to create a word or a slang or something. I am going to say exactly what it is. I will repeat it over and over." You would have to use five different words for a baseball in a column. You'd call it the pellet, the bean [*laughs*], and that was flowery writing. And I got that out of my system.
Bill Whitworth: That was my professional education. For the *Gazette* to turn me into an at-least competent reporter in four years, I think, was an achievement. [*Laughs.*] I came in there with no real ability to report, and when I left, I could have easily walked into the *New York Times* and covered virtually any story that they would want me to cover. And it was all just the experience at the *Gazette*, observing how they did things and being given the chance to do them myself.

For all its quirks, the Gazette *was the place to be for an ambitious young journalist.*

Mike Trimble: People bitched a lot about the paper among themselves but were furiously loyal to it and defended it against all outsider criticism . . .

Every newspaper person in Arkansas who was any good, their ambition was to work for the *Arkansas Gazette*. And it seemed to me that once they got there, they were content to stay there . . .

Paul Nielsen: Mostly I remember a *Gazette* that was very, very sober. It didn't take itself anywhere nearly so seriously as the *New York Times* did, and does, but it was very serious about what it did . . . It was a conservative paper in the way it looked. It looked in 1968 the way it had looked in 1958 . . . It was the best paper for states and states around . . . You'd have to go to one of the two oceans, I guess, to get a paper that was comparable to the *Gazette* . . . What it had achieved in 1957 and 1958 in the Central High School integration crisis was then, and is now, a benchmark and a standard in this profession for what public service is and shall be and should be. Two events have shaped and defined my professional convictions: the *Gazette*'s performance and Edward R. Murrow's show on Joe McCarthy. They set the model and the standard for the deliberate and appropriate response to the people who seek to bully the news business and interfere with the proper gathering and reporting of information. I am very proud to say I was at the *Gazette*.

Dumas: I think that the *Gazette* kind of looked at itself as a guardian of the state's morals or ethics. And that's the kind of story that Bill Shelton and the others wanted to do, to get out the corruption, the favoritism in the government. It was just kind of a moral mission that the newspaper had . . . I think to most of us it wasn't like a job where you make a living because you didn't make much of a living there. Salaries were better any other place than in the newspaper business in Arkansas, but it was kind of a mission that we were on. And you couldn't see yourself working at any other place or any other line of work.

Reed: I guess we thought that we were better than everybody else.

Dumas: I think so. And I guess we kind of exuded that . . . And there was this kind of resentment that *Gazette* people thought of themselves as superior, and they resented the hell out of it that the people at the *Gazette* thought they were better, on a higher plane of journalism, than the rest of them, and they resented it.

4

Gazette People

At Work and Play

In newspaper language, color is material off to one side of the main story. It is
information that a reporter uses to add savory to a story, like black pepper on
eggs. The occupants of the Arkansas Gazette newsroom were color, a little offbeat
and off to one side of the main flow of the town's citizens. Not one of the editors,
reporters, sportswriters, photographers, or copy boys considered himself or herself
to be unusual. But taken in the totality, the Gazette's newsroom contained the
largest display of eccentricity in Little Rock outside of the state hospital for the
insane, a mile to the west.

   Colorful as they were, the editors and reporters at the Gazette were among the
most serious newspaper people in the United States. The paper they produced
was widely considered one of the nation's best, well written and well edited, sober
as the New York Times. It came as no surprise in newspaper circles that the
Gazette won the Pulitzer Prize for its thorough coverage of the Central High School
crisis in 1957. The paper's work under more-than-ordinary deadline pressure was
simply an extension of the work coming out of that newsroom all the time, year
after year. During their long tenure, the Heiskell and Patterson families had used
their profits not to amass personal fortunes but to build a staff of superb journalists
for the paper they considered a public trust. The years after World War II were
especially golden. The high quality during those years started at the top with
Executive Editor Harry S. Ashmore, Managing Editor A. R. Nelson, and City Editor
Bill Shelton.

   A number of people who worked with and for Bill Shelton considered him to be
the best city editor they had ever met, maybe the best in the United States on a

newspaper of the Gazette's size. He was intimidating and was, to young reporters, thoroughly frightening. His face on most days had just one expression: stern. We called him the "Great Stone Face."

He was unflappable under the daily pressures of putting out a newspaper. Some thought that was because of the war. He was a bomber pilot during World War II. One day, returning from a bombing run over Germany, another American plane collided with his. The crew of the other plane were all lost. Shelton and all of his men bailed out safely over Yugoslavia. He was the last to leave the doomed aircraft, keeping a steady hand on the controls until all the others were out. That same steady hand was evident as he presided over the Gazette's news coverage for many years. Shelton demanded and got the best from his reporters.

Mike Trimble: You would do a story over four, five times before [Shelton] would accept it. Occasionally, he would communicate in writing, but it would be this little telegraphic note. One I remember I kept for years, and I lost it in a move. This was back in the days when they still used typewriters and paper and carbon paper. It was in that telegraphic language he used. He said, "If you cannot learn to spell, could you at least please learn to type? Your failure to do either is driving me crazy." [*Laughter.*] . . . Shelton instilled fear into me, the fear of not being excellent and of not meeting his standards. I don't know if I ever did. I don't know if anyone ever did, but I worked real hard to do it, and I think today the way he went about making me a better reporter probably is frowned on by human resources people, but it worked for me . . . I was a general assignment reporter and then did a stint on the police beat for about six months, at which time Shelton jerked me off and said I was the worst police reporter who had ever been at the *Arkansas Gazette* [*laughs*] and that I was, furthermore, the laziest reporter who had ever worked for the *Arkansas Gazette* . . .

Max Brantley: It was particularly terrible to get beat by [the *Democrat*], since they came out after we did. If we had missed something entirely on our cycle, there was hell to pay with Shelton . . . You would get a note, and there would be some big black circle around it with one of those old number fifteen pencils, you know. The lead is about as big around as my thumb, and he would say, "Why we not have?" And you talk about striking fear in your heart! Just an awful thing to have happen.

David Terrell: I had made a factual error in a story, something I did too often. He came over to my chair, and he was holding a piece of hard copy by the corner as if it were a dying snake, and he pointed at this particular paragraph.

As soon as he did, I realized my error. I knew what he was talking about. I recognized it as the flush rose in my face. With terrible contempt, he said, "Where did you get this? Just from your general knowledge?" And he turned and walked back to the city desk, and I thought I could die. The last thing I wanted to do was disappoint Shelton or embarrass the *Gazette*. And he was accusing me of embarrassing the *Gazette*.

Tish Talbot: He was a difficult task master. He was also the best editor I've ever seen in my entire life. He could cut my copy in half, and I couldn't find where he had cut it . . . There are words that twenty-five years later I still have never used in my life because I got a nasty note from him about it. I will never in my life use the word "utilize." . . . He was not terribly communicative, even when I was his assistant. Sometimes he'd go for three or four days without speaking, and sometimes while we sat across the desk from each other, he would get up and walk across the room [*laughs*] to put a note in my mailbox, and then I would [*laughs*] get up and walk across the room and go get it and read it . . . I got married while I was at the *Gazette*. I told Shelton I was getting married that night, and he told me to wear my beeper during the wedding. [*Laughs.*] I didn't do it.

Tucker Steinmetz: As the *Gazette* newsroom was moving into the era of word processing, Shelton had to live with the early glitches and the frequent crashes, some of which caused immense consternation in the newsroom. One day I heard him yell, "Goddamnit!" I looked up as he grabbed a big bottle of that old glue we used to paste sheets of a story together (a vanishing commodity at that time) and hurled it across the newsroom, striking the west wall and slinging the gooey mess in every direction. We all had those urges in the early days of writing on computers that frequently swallowed and destroyed our copy.

Doug Smith: Shelton was just pretty much aloof, and he communicated a lot by notes, more so than direct conversation with you. And I, for a long time before I worked for him, didn't know what to call him, and so I would, finally, when I had to talk to him, I would just kind of go up and stand there until he looked up, and then I would start talking about whatever it is I wanted to talk about because I didn't feel like—"Bill" didn't sound right, and "Mr. Shelton" after a while—I guess, at the first, I called him, "Mr. Shelton," but then after I had been there, worked for him for quite a while, that seemed too, too formal. And some people just called him Shelton, and I guess, maybe, toward the end, I started calling him that, but, yes, he was a fairly intimidating figure. And, of course, he looked like what a tough city editor should look like too.

Brantley: Toward the end of Shelton's . . . career, it may have been the year that he had announced he was going to retire, they went out and had some drinks one night with several reporters, and they said, let's go drop in on Shelton. Wish him a Merry Christmas. It was kind of an unbelievable thought that somebody would do this. And so they went to his house in Hillcrest and knocked on the door, and he said, "Well, sure, come on in," and poured them all drinks. As many people said, you just had to see Shelton outside of work. Totally different person. Very gracious, very amiable, fun to be with. And finally, Bill Green got around to the issue about everybody calling him Mr. Shelton and . . . wondered what they should have called him. And he said, "Well, Mr. Shelton would be fine."

George Wells: He had some peculiarities, and, in his case, one that sticks out is the word *contact*. We obviously could not use that as a verb, except if we were quoting somebody else . . . He said the only sense I could use it in was an electrical contact. I thought that was excessively narrow, but, then, he was the boss. He was a hard worker too. I remember one time, when I was still on general assignment, I was working the late shift, and there wasn't somebody coming in to fill in for him, for some reason. So he asked me if I would finish it up. He wrote down a number on a piece of paper, and he said, "Now, this is where I can be reached, and don't wait too long because I'm going home to open a bottle of gin."

Charles Portis: I used the word *afterwards* in a story once, and he lopped off the *s*, saying it was unnecessary. I still prefer the *s*, but he was usually right. I don't remember any . . . program of instruction. It was assumed that you knew your job, more or less.

Roy Reed: I didn't realize till twenty or thirty years later, but it was Bill Shelton who taught me sequence of tenses. . . . He was very strict on sequence of verb tenses.

Charles Portis: "To care for him who shall have borne the battle . . ." Lincoln's nice use of the future perfect tense.

Henson: On the night of his retirement . . . several showed up at his house with Bombay gin, which we heard was his favorite. And that was the most time I'd spent with Bill Shelton. It was almost scary to go to his house, but he seemed to really appreciate it. Here he'd been through the wars there. And there was no big party. Apparently he didn't want one. No big goodbye. But he loved gin and tonics, and he could make perfect ones, so we brought him some Bombay gin, and he was very touched.

Reed: [Shelton would] take time to help young reporters, and at the end of the day he would come around and say, "I just wanted to make a suggestion or two about your writing. A little bit more to this angle of the story." He was very helpful . . . I remember Shelton when we came to a parting of the ways. I'd come back from Harvard being a Nieman Fellow, pretty full of myself. And he knew it, and he was going to bring me down to earth a little bit. He sent me off to Blytheville or somewhere up in Mississippi County. He wanted me to do a story about, I don't know, the Farm Bureau convention, some kind of routine story. I ended up spending two or three days up there doing not just that but the story I wanted to do, about the politics of Mississippi County. I came back and dusted off his assignment in about six grafs and wrote my story at a length of about two thousand words. [*Laughs.*] And he ran them both, just as I had written them. We had this custom of going out to coffee at Miller's about the same time every afternoon. The day those stories ran, or the day after, [while we were at Miller's] he said, "I just wanted to tell you what I think about that," and he did. [*Laughter.*] God, I felt about six inches high. Of course, he was exactly right. You don't treat your editor that way . . . This discussion went on for the better part of an hour, very tense. We were both mad and hurt—or I was—but he never raised his voice.

Bill Shelton: I didn't have any experience handling a newsroom crew. None. I'd never done this, and I didn't know them either. They weren't guys that I'd hired . . . That was scary, but I was afraid to turn it down. I might not ever get another chance. So I took it. It took me five years to get control of that job. I just had no training for that, and, man, I worked day and night. And it took five years before I could walk in and feel like I knew how to do this . . . In rebuilding the staff, they had hired whoever they could hire. Nearly all of them, half of them were drunks. I mean, alcoholics. You know, you're not only trying to handle the reporter who's a stranger to you, but he's a drunk.

Bob Douglas was another veteran of World War II. He was a sailor on an aircraft carrier in the Pacific. An enemy shell exploded a few yards from him one day and hurled him across the deck. He got up and went back to his position. At the Gazette, he worked as a reporter, copy editor, news editor, and managing editor. His was another steady hand, but he was also known for his wit. Charles Portis once called him the funniest man in Arkansas.

Portis: That was from a story he told me once about a funeral in a country church, up around Kensett. It was an ordinary church with the two aisles— pews on the left and right and in the middle. The service had already started. The coffin was on a platform, a bier, beneath the pulpit. An old man came in late, making his way down the left aisle, when he caught his foot on a sprung board or something. He went into a stumbling trot, trying to regain his balance, and appeared to be making for the coffin—making a headlong assault on the coffin. Everyone froze. But at the last moment he managed to veer off to the right, short of the coffin, and continue his run down the right-hand aisle. I can't remember now whether his momentum carried him on out the door, or whether he just plumped down into a pew at the rear.

Reed: Once a guy came to town who advertised himself as the "King of the World." Bishop Tomlinson from New York. He'd go from one state capital to another and crown himself "King of the World" and collect his clippings from that day's newspaper and go on. And when he came to Little Rock, [Pat] Owens did the story. A terrific story as I remember. I think I saw the raw copy. Owens could grasp the essence of a piece of an absurdity like this and tell the story very well. And when he got up the next day, the story had been cut to three or four paragraphs. You can imagine how Owens—Owens did not go to Shelton. None of us really had the nerve [*laughter*] to go to Shelton about something like that, but he complained to Douglas about what Shelton had done to his story. And Douglas said, "Well, you know why he did it, don't you? I mean, why he cut the story." And Pat said, "No." And Douglas said, "Well, Shelton's on to this guy. He knows he's not the king of the world."

Robert R. Douglas: I got lucky. I kind of caught [Ashmore's] eye, I guess. They changed the byline rule that summer. You could get a byline if you wrote a story in the city. And something I wrote he liked. I think I was about to get fired. [*Laughter.*] I'd been called in to cover North Little Rock on a substitute basis, and I didn't notice there was a council meeting that night. [*Laughs.*] Well, I came in—I guess it was the following Monday—and there were two notes in my box. One of them was Sam Harris reminding me I'd failed to cover the North Little Rock city council, and the other was Ashmore's complimenting me on a story: "We need more of this sort of thing." So I think he saved my job. [*Laughs.*] I started at forty dollars a week.

Tom Hamburger: There was a party at Brenda Spillman's house in the Heights—her new apartment. Well, she had baked cookies, and we were all drinking beer. Douglas came in, and . . . there was some discussion about the raises that had just been given out. And Gerald Drury, the news editor, did some grousing about the raise and called how much more they would have gotten if there had been a union. And Douglas quieted everybody in the room, and he had his big-stomached editors around him. I remember sitting down like it was a class, and Douglas was up at the front of the room, still with his coat on, saying, "Who else believes that they didn't do enough with this raise?" And he called for a show of hands. And Drury started cat-calling him from where he was seated near me. Douglas said, "Let's have it out right here!" Drury got to his feet and was trying to slug Douglas. Douglas was ready to fight back, and Jimmy Jones and someone else, maybe Tucker Steinmetz, escorted Douglas to the door—kind of whisked him out of the apartment, holding him back. We heard some scuffling out in the hallway, and then the door kicks open, and Douglas's voice shouting at Drury: "I'm still here, Pard!" And some of us from the freshman class at the *Gazette* still use that "I'm still here, Pard!"

A. R. Nelson was managing editor during some of the paper's most trying times during the 1950s and 1960s. He carried his authority with quiet gravity. He could scold a reporter or an editor without leaving a scar.

Ronald Farrar: [The society editor] was a very prominent woman in the community, who had just been widowed and apparently had very little journalistic training, but he made her women's editor. And she was, initially, just a complete disaster . . . One Saturday night, along about midnight, the first edition of Sunday's paper had just come out, and the women's section was just completely wrong, wrong cut lines under pictures and all kinds of things out of whack. So Nelson trudged up the stairs to the third floor, and there was the women's editor—her name was Betty Fulkerson—at her desk crying. And she looked up, and she said, "Are you going to fire me, Mr. Nelson? Are you going to fire me?" And Nelson, a very soft spoken and very deliberate man, said, "No, Mrs. Fulkerson, I'm not going to fire you, not tonight. I'm going to wait for some cold, snowy Christmas Eve." Well, she, of course, rallied, and she became quite good. She was with the paper until she retired.

Julia Jones: Nell Cotnam had been there before Betty [Fulkerson] came, and Nell had been a bridesmaid in Mr. Heiskell's wedding. So, she got to call him Ned. She was the only one on the second floor who did that. Anyway, she wrote a social notes column, Among Ourselves. She was an old lady, but she was fun. I remember one day Mr. Nelson came down the hall, and we knew it was him because he had those half-moon taps on the heels of his shoes, and you could tell it was him. He was always looking for someone to go to lunch with him, and he had stopped to talk with Harriett Aldridge, and then he came on in to our office to see who else wanted to go. Nell started kidding him about how people were going to say that he had a harem if all of us went to lunch with him. She got tickled in the middle of trying to say, "You're going to get a reputation," and it came out, "You're going to get an erection."

So we were all falling around laughing about that. But Nell took off her green eyeshade and stood up and went over and got her hat and put it on and left with never cracking a grin and never said anything.

Leroy Donald: What Nelson told me was, "The only reason I am hiring you is because you got a Southern accent." . . . The paper had gone through all that Central High mess, and people were burning the papers out on the routes. And there was a lot of animosity out there in the populace, and, apparently, a lot of the reporters at the time either had Yankee accents or were looked upon as Yankees or something. So anyway, Nelson said, "We need somebody who can answer telephones and has a Southern accent."

Richard Allen: I had a lot of respect for A. R. Nelson. He hired me. Well, he hired me as a copy boy. He almost fired me as a copy boy because—one of the things you did as a copy boy was you handled the switchboard, right? When the switchboard operator went out, you handled the switchboard that had the wires and poking things in there, and the lights would come on. When I was talking to my girlfriend, I cut off A. R. Nelson, right? Wouldn't you imagine, I was talking to my girlfriend? He calls back and he says, "Were you talking to your girlfriend?" So I was called into his office the next day. I just thought he was going to bawl me out. But he said, "Normally, I would just fire you, but you've got some friends here. Some people came to me and told me that you work really hard, so I'm going to give you one more chance." [*Laughs.*] But I never talked to my girlfriend again after that!

Douglas: Nelson was the most skillful copy editor I ever knew. He could really edit copy. He was probably the best news editor, in many respects, that we ever had . . . His news judgment and his feel for copy were . . . he could cut through the chaff. He could do that better than anybody I ever knew. He taught me a whole lot when I worked under him.

Donald: One of the great things about Nelson was . . . He says, "You think that writing an obit is easy . . . But I will teach you that for every ten words you write, I can edit one word out of it."

Carrick Patterson studied opera at Stanford University and gave up a promising musical career to come home to the family newspaper. As the elder son of the publisher, Hugh Patterson, and grandson of the principal owner and editor, J. N. Heiskell, he was expected to take over the management in due time. He did. He ran the paper until the family decided—reportedly over Carrick's objection—to sell it to the Gannett Company. His uncle Carrick Heiskell had been the family's earlier choice to lead the paper, but he was killed in action during World War II.

Carrick Patterson: When I went away to prep school there in Washington, at St. Albans School, there was not a band there, but there was a glee club, a vocal group. So I went and started singing with them. . . . So, when I went out to college [Stanford University], I was interested in continuing to do some choral music and so forth. To my surprise, I was asked to be the baritone soloist for that choir just on the basis of my audition.

. . . They started a student opera group. I was in that and got some pretty big roles in the opera. I started doing some studying up in San Francisco with opera coaches and singers, and what not, and I really thought about making a little bit of a go of that as a career at one point. I was asked to sing at a summer Bach festival after graduation and really thought about doing it. And I went up to New York and auditioned for some teachers. They were, you know, pretty excited, and I auditioned for the guy who taught Robert Merrill, who was a great Metropolitan Opera baritone. He said, "Yeah, I think you can have a career," you know, "but you've got to learn some." And, just one morning there in that New York thing, I was up there about three days doing auditions, just walking down the street in New York City, and I thought, "I want to go back to the newspaper. That's what I want to do." And so, I did. . . . After I came back here, I sang in the church choir for a while. They started up a local opera company, and I sang with that a little while.

Clyde Dew was managing editor before World War II. They called him "Count Dew."

Farris Wood: Clyde had a habit. When he was into a unit count, writing headlines. He'd count on his fingers. You know, a fourteen-point head had so many units. A twenty-four point had so many units. So he had that part memorized, but he would count on his fingers. . . . But here he goes, you know, with that damned corncob pipe, which he smoked Bull Durham in, and he'd count on his fingers. Well, naturally, he became "Count Dew." Or, they referred to him as "The Count." . . . This took place during the war. He would be concentrating on some copy, and he'd think that corncob pipe was out of fire—he really did smoke Bull Durham in it. He'd shake it over here in a wastebasket and start a fire every night. And the women really didn't want to hurt the old man's feelings. One of them would come over and ask him something while the other would take the wastebasket over to put the fire out! [*Laughs.*] That happened almost every night.

Douglas: Count Clyde Dew, an old Michigander. I don't know how long Clyde had been there, but he was—as far as the newsroom was concerned, he was pretty much the *Gazette*. Arbitrary old son of a gun. He had a way of doing things. He'd been there since the 1920s, anyhow. He read all the copy himself. Didn't matter if it had been read before. . . . Count Dew used to have fights, they said, before I was there. The Count would fight anybody. He never won, but he would fight. He'd had a big argument with a printer and been through a galley, and he went home about midnight or after—walked, I think, about sixteen blocks to the house. He'd gone back to put on his regular clothes, which were nothing to brag about, but they were a little bit nicer than the rags he wore for working clothes. This printer came in and said, "Wait a minute, Mr. Dew. We have to settle this argument." Count Dew said, "Well, will you let me put my work clothes back on?" And he did, and they squared off. They moved the desk back, and they fought, and Count Dew lost.

Orville Henry: In 1947, Carolyn and I were about to be married, and I went to see Mr. Dew. It was early September, and, of course, her mother had set the date—you don't have any choice in that—but I said, "Mr. Dew, I'm getting ready to get married." And he said, "Goddamn it. Another son of a bitch doesn't know when he is well off." He said, "Go ahead, you have a week."

The Gazette *hired and trained good reporters throughout the twentieth century. Many of them stayed at the paper until retirement. Others moved on to larger venues. Morgan Beatty was a* Gazette *reporter before becoming one of the best-known names at the National Broadcasting Company. Some reporters, like Charles Allbright and Charles Portis, were known for their writing skill. Others were valued for their ability to root out the news, even in trying circumstances.*

Reed: Ernie [Dumas] is one of the treasures of the state of Arkansas . . . Here is a young guy who was obviously cut out to be a newspaper guy. He had all the right instincts. He knew how to get the news. He knew how to dig out the facts. He knew how to write it. He wasn't as fast as Bill Lewis. Hell, nobody was. He became one of the walking encyclopedias about Arkansas state government and politics. Years after I left the paper, I would come back to Arkansas with the *New York Times* on this or that story having to do with Arkansas government, and, generally, the first person that I would call would be Ernie Dumas. He always carried the necessary set of facts in his head. Any reporter can give you background information if he has time to go to the clips in the library, the morgue. Ernie carried it all in his head.

Margie Snider: Everybody loved Ernie. I remember when I worked with him at the capitol. I was always just amazed because he didn't seem to take very many notes because it was all in his head. And he knew what was important, and if something was important, he would start writing it down. . . . So I would just always think, "God, Ernie never takes any notes." He would be like the waiter that comes out and everybody rattles off what they want and then you realize this guy didn't even write it down. And then he would come back with everything.

Mike Trimble: Almost everything that was making news somehow ended up in federal court, it seemed to me. Jerol [Garrison] had been there, gosh, eight or nine years and was a fixture over here, and everybody at the federal courthouse and federal building loved Jerol, with good reason. [Judge] Smith Henley called him "Jerol the Thorough" because he never got anything wrong. He always played it right down the middle. He was a serious reporter, not frivolous, and his stories gave the court the dignity that the federal judge thinks he deserves, which is a hell of a lot of dignity. And following him was a really tough act. I mean, I had secretaries say, "Well, I'll just tell Jerol." And I'd say, "Ma'am, Jerol is not going to be back. Jerol doesn't even work at the newspaper anymore."

Henson: Carol Griffee . . . was one of the most intense reporters I've ever seen. She lived it. It seemed to me she had two dogs—and they were bulldogs—and if I'm remembering correctly, this would be her attitude toward every story. She was going to bulldog the story until she got that story. And she was so on the Environmental Protection Agency, the pollution control agency. That woman had a system where she would tell you how many trade magazines you should be reading and how many newsletters, and she actually did all those things she told other journalists to do. And you didn't want to make her mad, either. You listened to her.

Charles Allbright began as a reporter, then became a columnist and later an editorial writer. Before making the last move, he told his readers that it reminded him of a woman he knew who always had to put her car in reverse and go backward several feet before going forward, no matter where she was parked.

Charles Allbright: I remember that Mr. Heiskell, J. N. Heiskell, who was the heart and soul and owner of the *Gazette,* told Jim Powell, who replaced Harry Ashmore, that an editorial I had written—he didn't know who wrote it—was the best that had ever appeared in the *Gazette.* And it had to do with water. Wood and water. Trees and water. It was a stunning thing for me to hear from Jim Powell. I don't know how you can spin and weave about wood and water. But I didn't like writing editorials because I wasn't comfortable with it, and I wasn't qualified to do it. Mr. Heiskell thought, on the basis of what he read in the paper that I had done, "Here's a guy with some sort of depth." It wasn't the case. It has to do with, I guess, the English language. If you don't kick that around and you don't abuse it, you can be mistaken for a thinking individual. My mama and daddy both had been English teachers, and that is all I heard growing up, was decent stuff in the house. So I think that he thought—he kept reading things that I had written, and he thought that I should come back and do editorials. In fact, when Harry told me about this, Harry Ashmore, he said, "I have an indecent proposal to make to you. Will you come back and write editorials?" And so I said yes, but it was a long two years for me. I am not persuaded that I improved the human condition in one way or another. Wood and water, yes. I improved that. . . .

I was not a good reporter. I would cover, say, North Little Rock city council on a Monday night, and while the invocation was being given, I would peep. I would look around, and here were these aldermen, conniving somehow. I couldn't get down and get reverent, Michael, over covering things. . . . I am not trying to sell anything. I am trying not to be bad. That doesn't sound like much of a goal, but there are so many ways I can be bad. I mean, poor—I don't have any sense of mission, other than not embarrassing my dead parents, or not embarrassing my family now or the people of Arkansas.

Three Portis brothers, Charles, Richard and Jonathan, worked at the Gazette *at various times. The oldest, Charles, succeeded Charles Allbright as the Our Town columnist. Richard worked as a copy editor and later became a physician.*

Richard Portis: Buddy [Charles] went to the *Herald Tribune* in like 1959 or 1960. I remember Daddy was really upset with him when he took that New York job and quit as the writer for Our Town. Thought that was his pinnacle, which may very well could have been.

Reed: I always thought Buddy quit the best newspaper job in the world when he left the London bureau of the *New York Herald Tribune*. Remember what Tom Wolfe said about that? He and Wolfe worked together at the *Trib* in New York, and Wolfe later put together this anthology of New Journalism, and in the preface he said, "Back then all of us hotshot feature writers wanted to be novelists," and he said, "Now and then somebody would cut loose and do it." And then he said, "Charles Portis, for example, left this great job as the London bureau chief of the *Herald Tribune* and went home to the hills of

Arkansas, for God's sake, and lived in a fishing shack and wrote this great novel." Actually did it. Lived out the newspaperman's dream. But at the time I couldn't imagine anybody. Of course, I didn't want to write novels, so all I could see was, here he was, he had this terrific job, and threw it over.

Charles Portis: There were four of us in a little furnished house—Jack Meriwether, me, Ronnie Farrar, and a guy named Hawkins, I think it was. The house of abandoned neckties. Jack was an assistant city manager, and Ronnie was a reporter for the *Democrat*. I don't know what Hawkins did. I'm not sure we even knew who Hawkins was, but he slept there and paid his share of the rent. . . . Some previous tenant of that house had left a lot of very wide and garish neckties hanging in a closet. I like to think he had turned his back forever on Twenty-First Street and his old life of wide ties. I wore one to work one day—a big orange tie with a horse's head on it, with rhinestone eyes. Mr. Nelson came over and said, "I don't know, Buddy, that tie—don't you think—I mean, meeting the public. A tie like that . . ."

Jack Meriwether had been city manager of Little Rock before joining the business office of the Gazette *and ending as head of it. His sense of humor came in handy when he had to associate with newsroom people.*

Jack Meriwether: We used to go eat supper out at Lido's at the end of Main Street. . . . You'd get the soup and the salad, a fine supper, for about three dollars. And then coming in the summer, you'd come back down Main Street, and there was generally a tent meeting going on at Twelfth and Main in a vacant lot not too far from Granoff's. And [Charles] Portis was the one who always had to stop, and he would make signs from the back of the crowd that indicated that he thought the preaching was heretical and often draw attention to himself and then quietly slip away and let the preacher vent about—well, he was a different sort of fellow to live with.

Dumas: The queen of England would periodically invite the foreign reporters for audiences. So [Charles Portis] was invited to one, and there were going to be several of the reporters there, so the night before, they were all sitting around at Buddy's apartment, or somebody's apartment in London, and having a few beers, smoking, and playing cards. And somebody could do this trick where they could put a lit cigarette on the end of their tongue, and it would burn down, and they would fold their tongue back in so that the cigarette went into the back of their mouth, and they could close their mouth and open it back up, and the cigarette would be stuck to their tongue, and they would avoid burning the roof of their mouth. Well, Buddy was the kind of guy who always had to take every dare, so he decided that he could do that. So he put this cigarette on the end of his tongue and laid his head back, and the cigarette fell off his tongue, and the lit end of it landed on the end of his nose and kind of stuck there to the flesh and burned the end of his nose. Of course, the next day, he had to go to the palace for an audience with the queen, and he had to go because it was a once in a lifetime thing, and the end of his nose was like a great big red rubber ball. And he could hardly see past this big red nose. It had gotten infected, so he was self-conscious about his nose. Through this whole thing he was trying to use his napkin to try to keep the queen from seeing his nose.

Gazette reporters who had to substitute for Joe Wirges on the police beat were intimidated. As for the Democrat reporters who had to compete with him, theirs was an uphill job.

Douglas: Joe [Wirges] was the police reporter for forty-nine years, and there was never a greater police reporter anywhere. There never had been any police reporter who got the stories Joe did. In fact, he practically ran the police department, the state police. One of my early assignments, about September of 1948, was to fly up with Joe to Yellville and join a manhunt. There wasn't much for me to do. I think I flew back and brought the pictures was all. [But] Joe just took over. He just took charge. "All right, boys, there is no point in looking or doing anything else tonight. Too dark." . . . Joe Wirges worked for practically nothing. You know the *Gazette* never paid anybody. Joe might have got up to sixty bucks a week before the strike after thirty, thirty-three years then. Making sixty a week. There was a radio show called "The Big Story." [It] was about police stories, reporters covering police stories. . . . In Joe's case, he broke a murder case, so they had him on the radio—not Joe, but somebody acting his part.

. . . Some woman had committed a murder, and she was sent to the penitentiary. Joe went in his car. He was going to cover her walking in through the prison gates. It was a men's penitentiary. They got there, and the warden or whoever said, "I can't take her. We can't take her here. Nobody told me anything about this." And the deputy sheriff who brought her said, "I've done my part," and got in his car and went back to Little Rock. So Joe gave her a ride back. [*Laughter.*] And on Saturday night—the one night that we competed with the *Democrat* then—the *Democrat* being an afternoon paper, we competed for the Sunday paper. So Joe drove her around and talked to her until past the *Democrat's* deadline and then put her on a train. She got on a train and never served a day . . . He knew all the crooks, all the criminals. He would go down to death row and eat the last meal with the condemned man. Join him. Well, he got a good meal out of it . . . And he'd talk them out of their corneas. Joe always had bad eyes, and he collected corneas for the eye bank. Would talk them out of their corneas.

Farrar: Joe brought in these pictures, threw them down on the desk, said, "What do you think about that?" And this man had caught another man with his wife, and so he had—the guy was asleep—taken an ax and chopped the man's head off. So the police came. The guy's head was sitting up in a chair. The rest of him, the body with all the stuff sticking out of it, was on the floor. It was the most grotesque thing, and he said, "What do you think about that?" And I said, "Joe, I don't know," and so . . . I carried the pictures back to [Tom Swint, the news editor]. And I said, "What about these pictures?" And he put his arm around me, and he said, "Son, the *Gazette* is a morning newspaper. . . . People read this paper with cereal and eggs. I don't think they want to run into this." And I had to tell Joe, and Joe made some comment about college boys and all that.

Ernest Dumas: Joe got some wonderful stories because he had such a good relationship with the police and the criminals and with people at the state prison. You know, he would take his vacation at the Cummins Unit of the state prison because his best friend was Lee Henslee, the superintendent of the state penitentiary. Joe would go down and stay at the prison. He would sleep in one of the cells, and the story that was told to me was that he would sleep in there, and then he and Lee would go fishing in the Arkansas River, which ran behind the prison. Joe had the run of the prison. He knew most of the inmates, particularly the murderers. The serious criminals were all his buddies, and he'd maybe sleep on death row and pal around with the cons. I remember one great story that he got once while he was down there. He called from down there and dictated it to me, as I recall. He called up and said [in deep gravelly voice], "Hey Ernie, I've got a great story here. You ready?" Joe would call up and just say, "You ready?" And you would have to roll some paper into the typewriter, and he'd start dictating. He just butchered it, of course. It was awful. He always had the facts, but he wasn't a very good writer. This story was about a man named David Reginald Van Rippy. And David Reginald Van Rippy was in the penitentiary on several crimes, one of which was bigamy. His wife had turned him in, and he had a couple of wives, so that was one of the reasons he was down there. According to the story that Joe dictated to me, Van Rippy had refused to have a physical. It took them days to get David Reginald Van Rippy in for a physical. That apparently was a requirement for all of the inmates. When they first came through the diagnostic unit, they had a complete physical, and they couldn't strip David Reginald Van Rippy down to get a good physical. But they finally did and discovered that David Reginald Van Rippy was a woman.

. . . So Joe dictated the story. He had called David Reginald Van Rippy's wife in Oklahoma, the wife who had turned him in and told her that the guards down here had stripped him down in the shower and that he was a woman. She said, "There was always something strange about him." . . . That would have been in the early 1960s. That story ran on the front page.

One of the best-known voices of the Gazette *at midcentury was a columnist named Spider Rowland.*

Bob Douglas: Spider wrote after the fashion of Damon Runyan. He had his own language. Women were quail, and young women were San Quentin quail, and the legislature was made up of county congressmen, and on and on and on. Spider lived on the edge of the criminal community. In fact, he'd been physically shot with a gun several times. When World War II came along, he tried his best to join all three services, and they wouldn't take him for physical reasons. So Spider joined the maritime service [Merchant Marines] and requested tanker duty. He went all over this damned world. As I understand it, he had one or two tankers shot out from under him. He went back, put dry clothes on, and got on another tanker. Well, a couple of times a week he would write columns. When he'd come into the port city, he'd mail them all, put them all in a bundle and mail them back to the *Gazette.* So the *Gazette,* pretty much during the war years, had Spider Rowland's column going for them.

Mort Stern: Spider was a hell of a colorful character. Somehow or other, I met him. I guess Spider had left the *Gazette* before I went to work there. But I covered a speech he made. Somebody said that when Spider gets to drinking, he is kind of interesting. I am trying to remember. As he was talking, he became more interesting. He didn't seem to be touching a bottle. He had access to something in his hand. It looked like it could have been an inhaler. He seemed to get tipsier and tipsier as the talk was going on. When it was over, I came up and asked, "How did you manage this?" He opened his coat and he had a little tank in his pocket with a tube that went up his sleeve, crossed the back of his jacket, and down here hooked to whatever it was he was sniffing. He was consuming liquor on the spot through a tube.

Sid McMath: Spider Rowland . . . was an avid cigar smoker, or cigar chewer. And he had a hat that he wore on the back of his head. He had been shot and was kind of crippled a little bit. He had to lean over, and so forth. Somebody had shot him three or four times. There was a friend of his [Bob Faust]—they'd meet together and talk politics down at the Marion Hotel. He went out to see Spider at the hospital. He said, "Spider, I want you to tell me something. Are you going to make it or not? I want to know because I'm putting some money on it!" [*Laughter.*] Spider said, "Yes, I'm going to make it." . . . So Bob Faust went in the back and cleaned up that Spider was going to survive. He was shot three times. [*Laughter.*] Anyway, he was very much interested in this [election] in Hot Springs. He didn't think that [Mayor Leo] McLaughlin could be beaten because he controlled the machinery and everything, you see. Well, not many other people thought he could be beaten, either. Anyway, he came out to my house, and he liked to have a drink. We'd have some drinks and visit and so forth. He wrote some favorable articles in my behalf during the campaign. He had a keen sense of politics and a wonderful sense of humor, but he always had something germane in his articles that made it worth reading, more than entertaining. He was a good friend. I had a long session—I don't want to get into this, but I had a long session with Spider Rowland when I was trying to make up my mind whether or not to run for governor. See, I was the prosecuting attorney, so I had to make up my mind whether or not I was going to run. I had taken my wife and boys down to Biloxi, Mississippi. We spent time in the sun and fishing, and so forth, and I came back and stopped at the Peabody Hotel in Memphis. Spider Rowland came over there to see me, and he wanted to know what I was going to do. So I discussed it back and forth. He got ready to leave, had put his hat on the back of his head, and had a cigar in his mouth. He said, "Well, I'm going to give you some advice. All it's going to cost you is that cup of coffee we just finished drinking. Never call retreat." That's all he said. "Never call retreat." Pretty good advice.

Reed: Didn't he call you "The Champ?" Where did that come from?

McMath: Well, I was a fighter, you know, when I was in high school. I started boxing in Hot Springs.

A lot of other eccentrics drifted in and out of the Gazette *newsroom over the years. The paper became a magnet for ambitious young people, Ivy League graduates, reporters with good eyes and ears, and restless drunks—almost all of them with a gift for language.*

Carrick Patterson: Deacon Parker ["Deacon" because he had once been the religion editor of a newspaper somewhere] was one of those very typical old copy desk guys. He drank too much. Nelson, the managing editor, would occasionally go rescue him from his rooming house. He lived in a cheap hotel or rooming house just a few blocks from the paper, and he would take his lunch breaks—or dinner breaks I guess they were—and go drink a pint of bourbon and come back. He was very funny, very witty, and I think, to some degree, in constant pain because he had broken his neck at some point and moved rather stiffly, kind of in Frankenstein fashion, and couldn't turn his head all the way. He had to turn his whole body like this when he'd talk to you. But Nelson rescued him from somewhere. I think he was in Pittsburgh at one point. He sent Nelson a telegram saying "I need to come home," and Nelson wired him the money to get him a bus ticket. He was still there when I left.

George Wells: [Ray Kornegay] spent a lot of time picking horses.

Dumas: That's right. He was interested in the horses and Barry Goldwater. He hated Barry Goldwater.

Gerald Drury: In 1974 [Ray Kornegay] got a call from the general manager from Churchill Downs, who had apparently known him since the 1930s . . . [Ray] had spent a lot of time working on campaigns to get horse racing in Texas. He had spent many years in Houston. I think he had his own PR firm at one time. . . . In 1974, the general manager called from Churchill Downs and said, "This is the hundredth Kentucky Derby, and I want you to come." Ray and I were talking, and I said that was a great idea. I would take a week off and I would drive my Volkswagen camper up there, and I would go to the races every day for a week. And you can get me in free for a couple of days, on the really hard days to get into the track. He said okay, so the general manager got him a hotel room and parking passes so we could drive right through the gate even on Derby day. It was a great trip for me. I loved every minute of it. They knew Ray, and they treated him almost like royalty. It was like I knew you since 1935.

Jones: Do you think anybody at the *Gazette* knew anything about his background, or did they just think he was a grouchy old man?

Drury: Mostly they thought he was a grouchy old man. He was a good copy editor . . . and would not work a piece of copy fast. He just had one speed, and that is what he worked at.

Dumas: Kornegay was an old left-winger. Ray was probably sixty-five when we hired him. I don't know where we got him. He was opinionated and argumentative and would come back to me to talk politics. He'd take a little break from the copy desk, and he'd come back and start talking and would just finally wind up screaming and preaching back there, "Goddamn Republicans and Nixon" and whoever. He would just be raging.

Chris Kazan was a Harvard student who went south after graduation. He tried to find work first at the Delta-Democrat Times *in Greenville, Mississippi, because his father, Elia Kazan, the film director, was acquainted with the Carter family who owned it. They sent him to the* Gazette, *where he worked as a reporter from 1961 to about 1970. He returned to his father's estate in Connecticut, taught at Columbia University, and became a novelist and screenwriter. He died in 1991 at age fifty-two.*

Pat Crow: So Chris showed up, and he was hired as—he was doing rewrites, obituaries, and sometimes working on the copy desk. He stayed there probably until about 1970, and then he moved up to his father's place in Sandy Hook, Connecticut. He died maybe—I don't think it's been ten years, but maybe it has. He smoked a pipe a lot, and he had cancer of the jaw. He was a good addition to the staff. In small town newspapers, you don't get a lot of Harvard boys just dropping in. Usually they want to work for the *Times* or the *L.A. Times* or one of the news weeklies or something like that, but Chris was there.

Dumas: Chris was the son of Elia Kazan, and he'd graduated from Harvard. Well, he never really graduated; he went to Harvard, then didn't attend commencement and never got his diploma. For years afterward, Harvard would send a letter down to the *Gazette* to find out where he was. It said, "You need to send fifteen dollars, and you can get your diploma from Harvard." He didn't follow up on it, so it was long after—years later they kept putting Chris Kazan's mail in my box, so I finally sent him—I think he was in Washington at that time. I said, "Chris, goddamn it, you got a degree from Harvard. Get your goddamn degree." So he sent in his fifteen dollars and got the degree and erased his name and found somebody with a nice cursive hand and wrote my name in on his degree, leather bound, and sent it to me. So I had a degree from Harvard. But Chris, after finishing with Harvard, decided he wanted to be a newspaper person and went to Greenville, Mississippi, to the *Delta Democrat-Times,* and saw Hodding Carter.

Hodding said he didn't have a job for him, didn't have any openings there, but he picked up the phone and called Hugh Patterson. Hugh said to send him on up. So Chris showed up at the *Gazette,* and we hired him as an obituary writer. That would have been in 1961, not too long after I went to work there. . . . Nelson told him that he needed to wear a tie. They had an unwritten rule that everybody ought to wear a tie at the *Gazette,* and he didn't have a tie. He wore cheap shirts that he would get at the Salvation Army, but I had an old awful green tie that I had gotten someplace. It was the most hideous, tasteless green and black tie, and I gave it to Chris, and he wore that tie every day for four, five, or six months. No matter if he was wearing a red shirt, orange shirt, whatever, he would have on that old green tie. He got to be a reporter on the city desk. He was a general assignment reporter for a while, and then he went on to the copy desk. He eventually went to the *Washington Post,* as I recall, as a copy editor and was up there for a while. He married while he was in Little Rock. He married Jeannine Donald, who was Leroy Donald's first wife. . . . He was unhappy up there for some reason and came back to the *Gazette* and then decided that he was going to be a doctor and went to medical school here. He enrolled in medical school, and after the first semester he came down with mononucleosis and was out of school for a couple of months, gave up that career as a doctor, and went to Connecticut and lived in a little house on his father's estate in Sandy Hook, Connecticut and wrote screenplays and a couple of novels that did not get good reviews. One was called *Mouthful of Sugar,* which was a kind of a political novel that was a bunch of strung-together old stories that I had told him from Arkansas's political campaigns. I was in the book as a proctologist. I was "Dr. Dumas." I was a proctologist who commits suicide at the end of the book. I jump out and fry myself on a heating unit or something. The book was kind of based on Dr. Dale Alford, a segregationist who was elected to Congress in 1958. It's kind of a mixture of Dr. Dale Alford and me. . . . It was a terrible book. He wrote one or two other books that were published, and then he did screenplays with his father, one of which made a movie. It was a Vietnam movie. It got some good reviews and some bad reviews, but after that Chris wound up teaching film at Columbia University. When my son Chris went there as a graduate student in the master's program, Chris had died of cancer a couple of months earlier. My son Chris said that Kazan was a legend there. Everyone said that he was the best teacher by far that they had ever had. The students were still grieving Chris Kazan's loss. He was a great, great teacher. . . . Chris used to make beer and wine. We had a house on Fourteenth Street, and he would make great vats of beer and bottle it. It was awful stuff, so dark you couldn't see through it. Chris would drink that stuff and just become cross-eyed.

Reed: He used to talk very interestingly about his father's growing up in Turkey. He was Greek, but he'd lived in Turkey. That was the first that I'd heard of the centuries-old trouble between the Greeks and the Turks.

Dumas: He had a son named Nick who was born here at Little Rock when they lived on Alpine Court a block from us. When Nick had graduated from high school, he was killed in a car wreck in Connecticut. That was his and Jeannine's only child. Jeannine had two children by Leroy.

Not all the newcomers were from the elite East. There was one from Montana.

Reed: Patrick J. Owens was a terrific reporter. Pat weighed about 250 pounds. He had hair that was never combed, never. He wore glasses that were never clean. I don't know how he ever saw out of them. It was like a windshield that had been hitting bugs . . . He came to the *Gazette* with a rich background. He never finished college but was probably the best-read person on the staff. He was left wing in his politics but showed no hint of bias in his reporting. He was one of the few people at the *Gazette* who could differentiate between Leninists, Stalinists, and Trotskyites and back it up with historical perspective. He was probably the only member of the staff who much cared about the subject. He had had practically no experience of racism against African Americans before he came to Arkansas, but he had studied the problem more acutely than almost all of us. His only personal brush with racism had to do with the local tribes of Native Americans in his home state of Montana. He argued, with a touch of embarrassment, that the Indians were different and that those of us who did not live among them could not really understand the problem.

Owens was quarrelsome with strangers, especially when drunk, and his friends habitually had to extricate him. The last time I saw him, we were having dinner at a restaurant in Missoula, Montana. He had taken several drinks before dinner and was in the mood for a quarrel. He abruptly started one with a woman behind him at a nearby table. The woman was with her husband and had somehow offended Owens by her looks or her speech or something he had overheard her say. He carried on a lengthy cuss fight with the woman without ever turning to look at her. Neither addressed the other directly; the affair was conducted entirely in the third person. Owens addressed his remarks to me, and the woman spoke her rebuttals to her husband. The husband and I were embarrassed and got our charges out of the place as soon as we could.

Patrick J. Owens: I went in the army. And I went to Panama [the canal zone]. I was editor of the *Caribbean Army News*. It was a mess because I was a corporal and I had this big job and I'd get in a fight every once in a while. I ran with some readers who disagreed with the army. And then I got out of that for some—well, I got out of the job because of my colonel, and he had at one point ordered me up for court-martial. And I got a criminal discharge, and Senator Mansfield intervened on my behalf.

Reed: Were you at my house at a party one night when Pat Owens got drunk and called Amis Guthridge [a segregationist lawyer] on the phone?

Charles Portis: Probably. Pat was a great one for that. At some point in the evening he would go for the telephone. You know, put-ons, pretending to be some earnest but slightly insane person with some questions to ask. Spinning it out. Pretending not to understand the meaning of simple words. The game being not to laugh and to keep the other party on the line as long as possible . . . We turned the tables on him once. Do you remember a guy on the copy desk named Don? Out of California, I think. A heavy drinker. He slept on Pat's couch a lot when he couldn't remember where he lived. Anyway, he left—went back to California or Oregon. Then Jim Bailey and I wrote a letter to Pat, purporting to come from Don, saying he had married a woman with three or four kids, and they were making their way back across the country, in an old car, staying with friends along the way. That they were now in Beaumont, Texas, getting the car repaired and were looking forward to a good long stay in Little Rock, at Pat's house. We arranged to have the letter mailed in Beaumont. I think Paul Johnson knew someone there. We let Pat sweat it out for a week or so after he got the letter, waiting for Don.

James O. Powell: Patrick J. Owens didn't get along too well with Mr. Heiskell, as you can rather imagine, and Pat didn't stay that long either. Once I had taken a vacation, and I was in Florida with a week or two off, and I called Pat to see what was going on. "Oh yes," he said, "I've quit." Pat was a great character and a great writer. I think it was always the case with him, that probably any sort of constraint was too much, I suspect.

Dumas: Owens was one of the great characters there. He was a reporter when I went to work there. Great writer and a great wit and just physically a character. He had all of this baby fat on him. He was just kind of a glob. He always wore a white shirt, but it was always dirty. He always wrote with an old number-two pencil—the really big, thick dark pencils that we used to have in those days . . . Most of us would write with a pen; it was much neater to write with a pen, but Pat always used one of those old black pencils. And he'd have three or four of them in his pocket up here in his white shirt. When he got through writing, he would take the pencil with the point down and stick it down into his pocket. He'd guide it in there apparently by starting the pencil about two inches above the pocket, and then he'd guide it into his shirt, so that by the end of the day you'd have above his left front pocket about twenty-five black stripes going down into the pocket.

. . . About a month or two after I went to work there I went to Memphis with you and Patrick J. Owens when Richard Nixon was running against John F. Kennedy and made an appearance at Memphis, actually across the river to West Memphis, so he could say he had been in Arkansas. You went over to cover it. I guess you were probably writing about it, and Patrick J. was going to go over to see Nixon, and you asked me to go with you. You probably needed someone to drive on the way back because you both probably were going to do a little drinking. So we went over there and, of course, saw Nixon on the riverfront, and you filed a story, and we went to some bar. And Patrick J. Owens almost got into a fight with some Mississippian who was there with a name sounding like J. Archibald Phillips, or something like that. He was a dandified kind of a guy at the bar. So Owens gets up and introduces himself: his name is L. Patrick Owens, and this is J. Roy Reed, and this is L. Ernest Dumas. This guy had a fancy cane. I have forgotten what happened, but eventually they got up and started shoving each other, and it looked like it was going to come to blows. You interceded and got Owens out of the picture. He was always going to fight people and beat them up, and he probably could never have whipped anybody. . . . Remember when he got into the fight with a camera man from Channel 11 at the Electric Cooperatives Christmas party in about 1961 or '62? All of the utilities used to throw these bashes for the press. Everyone would go up there—nobody had ethics in those days. And they'd lay on a big feast of shrimp and cheese and spreads. We'd all go up there and drink and eat at the expense of the ratepayers, and everybody got drunk. And Owens got into a fight with, insulted, a camera man, a big blocky muscular guy. He was like a linebacker, but the guy was drunker than Owens and neither of them could stand up. Both threw a couple of blows and missed, and both of them fell down. We had to get them out.

Reed: While he was covering the labor beat [at the *Detroit Free Press*] they had a newspaper strike . . . It was the longest newspaper strike in history as I recall. It went on for months. They had a little strike paper that the *Free Press* boys put out, and it paid a few dollars, and Pat got bored. He had been divorced from his wife that he had down here and had taken up with a lady by the name of Myra whom he eventually married. But Myra and her two children went off on a trip to Europe, and Pat decided that since he was on strike, he might as well join his girlfriend in Europe and did and stayed over there for the remainder of the strike. One day it was settled, and Pat needed to get home and didn't have enough money to buy his return ticket. I got a telegram from Owens saying, "Please wire twenty dollars to American Express

Paris to help me get home." In a few days he showed up. We were living in Washington at the time. He told me the whole story. He had sent fifteen or twenty of those telegrams to friends around the United States to raise money to get back to the North American continent. It was not a loan; it was kind of a grant, you might say, to get Owens home. That was the first time we had ever had Pat as a houseguest. Norma had dreaded it terribly because she knew his reputation for hell raising, and she remembers to this day that he was the perfect houseguest. He was considerate, cleaned up his room, and all of that. Did everything so unlike Patrick J. Owens. All our son John remembers about him is that he taught him to shoot pool while he was staying. He stayed for weeks before they finally got the new contract fully signed and ready for them to go back to work.

Dumas: He later stayed with us many years later. He stayed with us a few times when he was back in Little Rock visiting, mainly after he went to *Newsday.* I remember when our son was very small. Pat was a gracious guest, thoughtful, except he would drink too much, and then we couldn't get him to bed. We had a two-story house, and he drank and then fell asleep on the couch or in a chair, and you couldn't get him up to go to bed or he'd swing at you. He'd be in some terribly contorted positions making terrible noises, and if you tried to get him up, he would swing. So we finally just said to hell with it and left him down there and went on up to bed. Sometime in the night I woke up, and Chris, our son—he must have been five or six then—came into our bedroom just terrified and got into bed with us because of this terrible racket. Sure enough, Pat was downstairs sleeping, and he was snoring loudly and also yelling. He was having nightmares or something, and he was bellowing things. It was an unbelievable racket down the stairs. We closed the door to our bedroom trying to shut it out. But the next morning he'd be gone. We'd go down the stairs the next morning, and Pat would be gone on his rounds, or he'd be working on a story or whatever.

I remember once when I was in the army in 1962 or 1963 and I was stationed in a little army post out in Long Island Sound from New Rochelle. . . . I would go in on the weekend and stay with Pat Crow, who had been an *Arkansas Gazette* copy editor who went to New York in the fall of 1962 as a copy editor for the *New York Times.* . . . For some reason, Owens was there, and I don't remember now why Owens was there in early 1963. He was there and Buddy Portis was there. Buddy was with the *New York Herald Tribune.* We were all at Crow's apartment, and in the wee hours of the night Owens began to make telephone calls. He called Ross Barnett at the governor's mansion in Mississippi. My recollection is that he succeeded in getting Ross

Barnett on the phone. . . . I think he somehow talked to the security person or someone and told them it was urgent. He concocted some wild story and actually got Ross Barnett or his wife on the phone. And then insulted them with some wild story or something. Then he called James D. Bales, who was the anticommunist professor at Harding College. Bales wrote these long tracts about communism in letters to the editor. He got James D. Bales on the phone at three in the morning and read to him a long sentence out of *Das Kapital*. It was about six hundred words long. This one sentence was about "intellectual capital," but anyway it goes on and on. . . . Owens had a copy of *Das Kapital* that he picked up from down on Union Square from some Communist who was handing them out. So Owens found some sentence, and it was an interminable sentence. Owens read it to James D. Bales and said, "I am working on this book. I've got to have it in the hands of the publisher tomorrow, and I'm hung up on this sentence. Goddamn it, what does this sentence mean? I've got to have it tonight." And Bales said, "Can't you wait until tomorrow?" Owens said, "No, I've got to have it tonight. You don't understand, this publisher is breathing down my neck, and I've got to have it to him in the morning." And he said, "Now, read it to me again." So Owens read it to him again, and he went on and on. Bales was still befuddled by it, and Owens wound up reading it to him for three or four times. Finally, he called Margaret Mead, the great anthropologist, and got her sometime way to hell in the middle of the night. He told her some story about sexual impotency and wanted her counsel about it, and she hung up on him. She said, "Do you know what time it is? It's three in the morning." So she hung up on him. Buddy Portis was offended and left. Calling Ross Barnett and James D. Bales is one thing, but calling this old woman, Margaret Mead, at three in the morning? I mean, that was no longer funny. So Portis got up and left. . . . He was sitting around thinking about people that he could call up. He was fond of doing that. I think he did that one night at your house. . . . I think he called Amis Guthridge, the lawyer who headed the White Citizens' Council, but he also called Jim Johnson and told him that Amis Guthridge had been caught diddling a black boy in the men's room at the bus station, and we had to get him out. Jim had to come down and get him out because it was going to be in the papers, and it was going to ruin the whole Citizens' Council and everything. Jim wasn't about to come down. Amis was going to have to settle that matter himself, Jim said. But Owens was fond of making those calls.

Photographers occupied a special niche. They were expected to be colorful and most were.

Carrick Patterson: [Larry Obsitnik's] title was Chief Photographer. Everybody called him "Chief." He used to have run-ins with the people he took photographs of. He was not a bit above ordering people around to make a better photograph. From the governor on down to anybody, he would say, "Now, stop. Move over here," or "Move to your right," "Move to your left," "Smile," "Hold this up," "No, do it again—you didn't do it right." He would boss them around. A famous story about Obsitnik is—one time the head of the Ford Motor Company came to Little Rock to speak at some event or other. The service club luncheons were a big thing that was always covered in those days, both by reporters and photographers. And, of course, if somebody, Mr. Ford—I forget. It may have been Edsel Ford. I don't know which Ford it was, I must say—came and spoke, and there was a session where the photographers afterwards took a picture of him. Larry Obsitnik, the Chief, took Mr. Ford's picture and said, "Now, Mr. Ford, my . . ."—I've forgotten what model, the cheapest one, the cheapest model of Ford he had—and Mr. Ford said, "We don't like to hear that. Take it into the shop, and tell them I said to fix it." Well, it developed that Larry ended up with a free, new engine out of it, by confronting the head of Ford Motor Company.

Martha Douglas: Larry Obsitnik . . . loved Christmas more than anybody I ever knew. He would put his kids' toys on layaway. He's the only person that I ever knew who put his Christmas whiskey on layaway.

Trimble: [Larry Obsitnik] was one of the bunch that would go up to the downtown Officers Club, where a lot of *Gazette* people drank. He loved to philosophize, and he was talking about original sin at one point, speaking to Lodema Fortenberry, the barmaid, . . . and Larry was talking about original sin . . ." If he hadn't eaten that apple, I'd be sitting here and Jerry Neil would be sitting down there, just like he is now, and you would be behind the bar, and everything would be the same except we would all be naked."

Dumas: And then Chief tried to get a picture of [President] Truman shaving, wanted to get a picture of Truman shaving in the car. [*Laughter.*] And I think Truman apparently just slipped and said, "Goddamn it, get this son of a bitch out of here."

Gene Prescott: Have you ever heard about Larry stopping the Razorback football game? Well, he got into a fight with somebody. Not a fistfight. He stepped across the line, or he was out of place or something. There were only three thousand people there. That's all that ever attended a Razorback game in those days. And it stopped the whole game. And [*laughs*] the argument was with an umpire. Finally, the coach came up and asked them to stop so they could finish the game.

Bob Douglas: Larry was certainly a fun lover and a terrific photographer. He was the father of modern newspaper photography in Arkansas. . . . He could bring in a picture. Whatever the story was, he brought in *the* picture that best illustrated it. He and Gene Prescott both did that . . . And they probably wouldn't bother to tell you what the story [was], if they even really knew what the story was about. [They] just knew enough to know what best illustrated it and get that picture. . . . He loved pictures of pretty girls, of course. I was with him one day—I think he was giving me a ride to work—we had a lot of snow and ice. This girl in a miniskirt was wiping the snow off her windshield, bending over. Well, we got a view when we went past her, and, woo, I mean he hit those breaks, we spun around three or four times, and stopped to get that picture. [*Laughs.*] Of course, Larry would have her lean further and further over. "Now, don't . . . this is not quite it." [*Laughter.*] I mean I walked by a studio by the *Gazette* building once, and he was taking pictures. I think the dance craze was the twist. You remember the twist? And he had a professional dancer in there, a Little Rock dancer. She was doing the twist, and he was taking a series of pictures of the movements. He said, "Bob, would you come here a minute? I need some help." He said, "Don't you think this would be better without the slip?" [*Laughter.*] I had to agree. [*Laughter.*] Serious thought, you know. Wrinkled his forehead.

Michael Haddigan: Now that you mentioned it, let me digress just a little bit and ask you about when Larry Obsitnik was chief and when he died. I understand that the photographers of both papers had a little send-off for him.

Steve Keesee: Yes. I kind of organized it. I did not realize how big it was going to be. I thought a couple of us could go out there—like I said earlier, Larry enjoyed whiskey. We took a pint of whiskey to the cemetery about eleven at night. A bunch of us had to jump over the fence. We all went around there and did a toast and left. About that time, after we had left, the cops were alerted that prowlers were in the cemetery. Nobody was arrested or even caught. It was kind of fun and thought it would be a great tribute to one of us that had gone on. . . . We have a photograph. I am guessing, probably, about twenty to thirty people were out there. Most were photographers and reporters.

Haddigan: Gene Prescott . . . was in World War II and Pearl Harbor. He was in the Marine Corps all the way through the war.

Trimble: Always just a delightful guy. The world to him was wonderful. It was a new day every day. And Gene loved to go on trips, assignments, and every place we would stop to eat had the best cheeseburger, you know. . . . I remember Gene and I went to Fort Smith when [Vice President] Spiro Agnew was going to make an appearance. And I don't remember if he was a candidate or if he was already vice president. But we drove up there, and Agnew came in on the railroad, railroad station. And Gene never much talked about the assignments on the way up. He'd talk about Ruby, his beloved wife, or his house on the lake and stuff. But we got there, and it was a big crush of advance men and secret service guys, and Gene got his shot and, of course, it turned out to be excellent. When he was all done and walked away, Gene said, "Who was that son of a bitch anyway?" [*Laughs.*]

Some employees had private lives that few knew about.

Henry: Nobody knew it—I didn't know it until later—but James Warren was the closest man to Elijah Muhammad. James Warren, who shined shoes and ran errands and was just a handyman at the paper, sent all his children through excellent colleges. And when Elijah Muhammad or any prominent black man came to town, they stayed with James Warren. James Warren was a "Yes, sir, massa" man. He played his role, but he and I had gotten to be good friends because I talked to him. He and I talked like two friends and human beings. . . . He played the role of the old darkie, but he was very shrewd, very smart, and a wonderful person and never recognized in Little Rock for the part he played on Ninth Street.

Jim Bailey: He told me, of course, years after that. He was talking about his son-in-law. His daughter, apparently, had gone to some northern city and married this guy who was a big shot Muslim. And he was talking about how they would come visit, and he would say, "You know who they had with them the last trip?" "No, no, James." "Malcolm X."

Orville Henry: Yes. James Warren, like I say, never recognized in Little Rock, was a very handy man in the black movement before it ever—while it was still underground.

The Heiskell family owned the paper for most of the twentieth century. John Netherland Heiskell was the editor seventy years, until his death in 1972. He outlived a host of family and fellows of the trade, including his younger brother Fred, who worked under him as managing editor from the teens and the Roaring Twenties through the Depression and prohibition. J. N. was sober and circumspect. Fred was not.

Reed: Is it true that Fred Heiskell won James Warren in a poker game?

Margaret Smith Ross: The story went a crap game, but James said it wasn't. . . . Well, James was working for Fred Hotze, who owned the building. . . . And he worked for Mr. Hotze, but Fred Heiskell kept him busy all the time driving him places. He was his driver . . . at night mostly, and James knew a lot he wasn't telling. But one of the stories was that he won him in a crap game. So, I asked James if this was true. And he said, "Oh, no, ma'am. It wasn't exactly like that." He said . . . by putting together what James told me and what Hugh told me because I can't remember whether James knew the whole story or not. He may not have. But the Heiskells didn't like the idea of hiring anybody away from somebody else, particularly a friend. And, of course, they were only renting the building at the time. . . . They didn't own it until later. And it was built for their occupancy, but it was understood that they were tenants from the beginning. And he . . . approached Mr. Hotze on the subject and offered him a certain sum of money. I don't know what, whatever it was. And Mr. Hotze said, "The son of a bitch ain't worth it." [*Laughs.*] And it was "I'll flip you for him" or something. It was not a crap game or a poker game, either one, but it was something similar. I don't remember what.

Mr. Fred had the most delightful sense of humor. I never laid eyes on that man. He died on the day before April Fools'—it's easy to remember—in 1931. And I never saw him, but after . . . our Mr. Heiskell [J. N.] died, I got all the stuff that he kept at home, his papers and things, and he had brought home from Memphis his father's and his sister's papers. And they had all the letters that Fred Heiskell had written home when he was in the Philippines, . . . had written home when he was . . . secretary to Governor Luke Wright in the Philippines . . . He wrote long letters home, and they were wonderful. He was the natural-born writer. He just went with the flow, and he wrote like he talked, and he talked real pretty. And Mr. Ned polished everything he wrote, and . . . he would call Fred at home and read him an editorial he'd written, and he'd call him back several times during the night to read the changes he'd made in it, and Miss Georgia [Fred's wife] told me one time that Mr. Fred said, "Ned polishes all the guts out of an editorial." [*Laughs.*] Which he did.

Reed: I'm a little surprised that Fred commanded the same kind of dignified—from what I'd heard about him, he was kind of a good-time fellow.

Ross: Everybody loved him. Except, now, Nell Cotnam. I heard—someone told me that she used to date Fred Heiskell, and I asked her about that, and she was indignant. She had me know she didn't date people like him. She said one of her beaus wanted to bring him over and introduce him to her one time—one of her best beaus, she said. And I imagine Nellie had quite a few because she was right attractive as a young woman. And she told him that that man was not welcome in her home, and if he brought him over, he couldn't come back anymore!

Reed: What'd she have against him?

Ross: His reputation. It was terrible.

The Gazette *was slow to hire black reporters and editors, but it came to its senses when Deborah Mathis, a local television reporter, knocked on the door.*

Deborah Mathis: I had . . . this wild idea that somebody other than middle- to older-aged white men could actually write opinion for the venerable *Arkansas Gazette.* I thought they were going to laugh me out of the room when I proposed that, especially because I was colored, a TV babe, and that kind of thing—you know, younger, thirty-five years old or something, black, female, and talking about writing opinion for the famous *Arkansas Gazette!* "Are you out of your mind?" To his everlasting credit, Bob McCord [editor of the Voices page] said, "Well, you know, we've got to make some changes around here. Life is changing, the world is changing." . . . I worked in the newsroom for about a year, I guess, before there was a retirement on the editorial board, and I was up for that. There was a little tension there about some other people possibly getting it, but I got it and was the first black woman associate editor of the *Arkansas Gazette.* The *Gazette* meant a lot to me personally in that way, and that was in 1989 when I went on staff . . . I got tons of hate and threatening, very threatening, mail, and somebody showed up at the *Gazette* with a gun and asked, "Where's Deborah Mathis?"

George Fisher's cartoons on the editorial page were known not only for their biting political comment but also for a daily gag. He hid his wife's nickname in practically every drawing.

George Fisher: So they made arrangements for an art college in Bournemouth, [England]. . . . My drawing board faced Rosemary. She was a student there and a sophomore. Her name was Rosemary Beryl Snook. . . . [After the war], I went down to Bournemouth, and there we got married. . . . That was early 1946, in March of 1946. Then we came back to the States. . . . She came over in a merchant ship they used for that purpose, for war brides. They used them to haul troops in and for brides. She got off the ship in New York and got on the train on orders. She was sent by freight. She got off the train in Beebe. . . . Technically, that was the only way they could ship them was by freight. [*Laughs*.] And so she [*laughs*] had a tag around her neck, "First Class Freight."

Dumas: You always hid the word "Snooky," the nickname for your wife, somewhere in the cartoon. When did you start doing that?

Fisher: Almost immediately when I came full time with the *Gazette*. About 1976. Her name when I married her after the war was Snook, a good old English name. All the students from the college over there in England called her "Snooky," and I still do. And so I hid *Snooky* in the paper every day in the cartoon . . . Just kind of a frivolous little thing between myself and her. And I didn't know that anybody would ever see it because it was hidden sometimes so that you had to be looking for it to find it, but it soon caught on after a while, and just everybody knew it was in there. It became a game with people. Dorothy Harwell was my secretary, and she always knew where I hid it. She also knew when I would inadvertently leave it out. People would call up when I'd forget to put it in, and she'd tell them, "He forgot it that day." Somebody called from Pine Bluff and said, "I've been looking for *Snooky* in a certain cartoon for nine months." He said, "Every morning when I come to work, I pull the drawer out, and I get that cartoon out, and I look at it again. For nine months," he said, "I've been doing that. Now, where in the hell is it?" After he gave her the date of publication, she said, "He forgot to put it in that day." He said, "I'm going to kill that man."

Harry Ashmore, the executive editor, was credited and blamed for the paper's elegantly written editorials. What the public did not know was that many of those were written by his associate Jerry Neil. It was Neil, not Ashmore, who wrote the obituary editorial when Senator Joseph P. McCarthy died. It was unlike any of the many that appeared around the country, the speak-no-ill-of-the-dead sort. Neil's editorial consisted of a patient listing of all the harm McCarthy had caused with his sensational Red-hunting campaign and ended with this: "Joe was a bad guy, and the evil that he did will live after him."

Powell: Jerry Neil, of course, was not amenable to much restraint either. Jerry and Mr. Heiskell were often in disagreement. Jerry was, incidentally, a great editorial writer, especially up until the seventies . . . Suddenly, one morning, he just went out of it with what seemed like a stroke. It lasted a few days, and he died, as you recall [in 1978]. But Jerry was a great editorial writer, had his own style, which was different from anybody else's. Long, flowing, Ciceronian sentences, and when they were good, nobody could do it better.

When he was good, nobody could match him.

Jerry Dhonau: Jerry [Neil] was a great guy. Very good writer. He lacked a little discipline. I always thought if he had gone through a rigorous PhD program, he probably would've taught literature at Yale or something. At the time I was there, he—well, let's be honest about it—he started drinking. Maybe he had before—I don't know—but, in any case, his pattern was to come to work early, oh, something like seven thirty in the morning. His wife would always drive him. Jerry would never drive a car. I think that may have gone back to a youthful accident; I never did find out exactly what it was. . . . There was some allusion to something that may have happened in his wild youth. Anyway, Jackie, his wife, would bring him down about seven thirty every day, and he would try to get his writing done by noon. Sometimes he would write some in the afternoon. But as the years went by, he would start taking longer lunches. He'd have it done—I mean, great editorials—have it done before he started the martini lunches. . . . I know that he had offers to go elsewhere. He told me a little bit about this, and I found out, independently, later that they wanted him to come to the *New York Herald Tribune.*

Dumas: In '57, particularly, he wrote some of the great editorials. . . . They were unsigned [and] Ashmore always got credit because he was the editor of the page.

If a reporter was pressed for time, he went to Leland DuVall to get information instead of rifling through the clippings in the morgue. DuVall was at various times the paper's farm and business columnist and an editorial writer. But he was much more.

Dhonau: [Leland DuVall] was the most productive editorial writer I've seen, including myself. . . .Very little formal education, but widely read, very intelligent guy, a hard worker, never complained about anything.

Dumas: He was always right about things. He was the first, maybe the only person in America early on, to write about the impending doom of the savings and loan associations when they got cut loose during the Reagan administration.

Dhonau: Exactly. As a result of some of those editorials, I remember, some of the federal officials from Dallas said they wanted to come in and talk to him and me, which they did, and Leland just laid them flat.

Dumas: The S&L regulators were promoting . . . telling the S&Ls that they needed to get out there and diversify their investments, get out of this strict home mortgage lending, get out there and make some risky investments.

They came in to try to talk Leland out of it?

Dhonau: Yes, and say it's really not that way. It's blah-blah-blah-blah—whatever the particulars, I don't recall. We would politely listen, and then Leland would just tell them the way it was, you know, low-key. It didn't faze Leland at all.

Dumas: He was a great biblical scholar, and so many of his editorials would begin with some parable. He always had this way of starting the editorial that would pull you into it. He'd start it off with some obscure biblical story. At the end of the editorial, he'd tie it all back together. It was as if this was the word of God . . .

Many critics accused the Gazette *of being a hotbed of Communists. DuVall's biography would have given them evidence if they had known.*

Leland DuVall: I went out to [Arkansas] Tech and enrolled in the midterm [after World War II]. So they paid my tuition and got me started. I went to school out there for a year. . . . The [Russellville] *Courier* was a locally owned paper. . . . His news editor was named Seaton Ross. . . . Seaton Ross had been there for years. Nobody knew where he came from, and nobody knew where he'd been. You know, he just got a job from old man Livingston back during the war, and nobody knew anything about him and didn't question anything about him. And Seaton sort of gave me a one-day lesson in journalism, and he showed me what you had to do to put out a paper, you know, things that you'd have to do. And I sat up there and watched him all day long. And he talked all the time about what he was doing. Then he was gone the next day, and I had to put out the paper. [*Laughs.*] And I didn't know until years later when Joe McCarthy got to stirring around, you know, in the fifties, who Seaton was. They were having hearings here and there and one place and another. And I picked up the *Gazette* one morning, and there's Seaton's picture. A big spread there, you know? And he'd just testified before the Senate committee on whatever it was McCarthy was investigating. He'd been the editor of the *Daily Worker* back in the old days. [*Laughter.*] So I was always, after that, able to tell everybody I'd had a one-day course in journalism from the editor of the *Daily Worker*. And that's as much journalism as I had. . . . He had a dining table, one of those old, old dining tables for a desk. . . . . Sort of had too much on the desk. He got up on that table with his feet and kicked all that stuff off in the floor. All of it. And went and got the broom from the back and swept the desk off, and he said, "Now, it's yours."

One of the Gazette's *strengths was its sports coverage.*

Jerry McConnell: Orville Henry was one of the first sports editors (the first I knew about) that recognized that sports writing would be changed by the impact of live television. Since the newspaper could no longer be first to bring the news about Razorback games to the readers, he theorized, the papers should start doing things that the TV did not, such as reporting the reactions of the coaches and players. Thus, he stepped up dressing room interviews and game sidebars. He also recognized that TV was creating increased interest in the Razorbacks and other teams and games, and he was one of the first to delve heavily into the personalities and interests of players and coaches. When a game was televised live, a lot of people thought there would be less interest in reading about it. It turned out that there was more, and Orville was one of the first to figure that out. It was said that Orville would tell you everything there was to know about the Razorbacks, including what kind of toilet paper they used.

The sports department, as I mentioned, received a lot of credit for helping keep the *Gazette* going through the integration crisis, and after that it seemed that Orville could get anything he wanted. He wasn't always in good health, and I remember the paper bought him a reclining chair and put it in the sports department, so he could take a rest during some of his long days. At his behest, they also bought us a color television set, so the people handling the Razorback copy and pictures could watch the game on television. It helped in identifying pictures.

Orville became regarded as *the* authority not only on Razorback football but on SWC football in general. I can remember writers from other papers asking Orville in the press box to explain the theory behind some unusual formation or whatever. That included Dan Jenkins, a great writer who later became a best-selling novelist. Jenkins first worked for a paper in Fort Worth and then one in Dallas, I think.

[Jim Bailey] knew sports backwards and forwards, and he had a great memory. He had, I would guess, almost a photographic memory. He could quote Stan Musial's batting average for every year he was in the major leagues in order. He would start out each year and tell you what he hit that year and probably how many home runs he hit. He could do the same thing for Joe Dimaggio. He was the same way about boxing. He knew boxing backwards and forwards. . . . You used to always get a million calls in the sports department, people calling you up and wanting to settle arguments and bets and stuff like that. So I would take the ones on football and track, and Bailey would take the ones on baseball and boxing and maybe a few other things. But I remember somebody calling up one time, and I answered the phone, and he said, "How old is Floyd Patterson?" I didn't even bother to look. I said, "Hey, Jim, how old is Floyd Patterson?" He said something to the effect, "*I* don't know. He was born February the twenty-eighth of 1927. Figure it out for yourself."

The Gazette, *like many state capital papers, kept a Washington presence. For years, Les and Liz Carpenter, Texans who had moved to Washington when Lyndon B. Johnson first served in Congress, worked part-time for the* Gazette *and part-time for several other regional papers.*

Liz Carpenter: I ended up being the editor of the paper there [Austin High School], and Les [her husband] ended up being the business manager. That's where we first met. So it was a semi–high school romance but more of a college romance when we both went to work on the [University of Texas] *Daily Texan.* Your pathway was then straight out of school.

I graduated in June of 1942, and my graduation present was a ticket to Washington, DC. The war had just taken place, and my oldest brother was there working in one of the departments, and so I could stay with him. I took my scrapbook from—I'd worked on the *Austin American-Statesman* as well as the *Daily Texan,* and I took my journalism degree, as I say in speeches, with my journalism degree and my virtue intact [laughter]. I went to Washington, DC. I still have the journalism degree. Well, anyway, I knocked on the doors. I was not married at this point. Les was in the navy after graduation, and I was in Washington, knocking on doors in the National Press Building, looking for a job with the scrapbook. I got a job. It wasn't hard for a woman to get a job then [because] the men were going to war in 1942. Also, if you were a nice girl, you went to Washington and you called on your two senators and your congressman. My congressman was in room 504, House Office Building, Congressman Lyndon Johnson from Texas, Tenth District. He wasn't there. He was in the South Pacific because, like a handful of congressmen, they had voted for the draft, voted for the declaration of war, and they went and signed up. Roosevelt called them back later. Lady Bird was running his office, so she gave me lots of good advice on what to go see. I was still wide eyed and eager . . .

Henson: Did you take notes by shorthand?

Carpenter: No, I just scribbled fast. You learned how to read somebody's desk with the letters upside down. That still stays with me. I can do that, but the talents were so different then, and few people had recording machines. I mean, you saw a few at White House press conferences under FDR. I went to some of his and Mrs. Roosevelt's press conferences. I treasure those because I was about twenty-two and twenty-three at the time, but what a wonderful, long corridor of history you're looking back over.

Mrs. Carpenter was a pioneer in breaking down prejudice against women reporters.

Henson: Did you encounter any kinds of prejudice against you when you were working the job for the *Gazette?* Would people say, "No, I don't want to talk to you. I want to speak to Les on this topic"?

Carpenter: No, I didn't. The only one I encountered was from the *Tulsa Tribune,* and they labeled in our early bylines, "Les Carpenter, Chief, Washington Bureau," and there were only two of us. I thought, "Well, what am I, the squaw?" And I made so much fun of it that they dropped that term. . . . But I think Mrs. Roosevelt helped move that along just by being news and by it confining her—she wiped up discrimination by discriminating. She wouldn't allow—she only had it open to women. The AP [Associated Press] had to put on a woman who handled news out of the White House. The UPI [United Press International], the INS. They were really days of change, and we didn't realize how much they were changed.

Down the hall from the newsroom were the women's and features departments.

Martha Douglas: I remember Miss Nell Cotnam and Millie Woods. At one point, they had a desk down the hall from each other, and they would call each other on the phone. They both spoke with loud, loud voices, and they could very well have used the same tone and talked down the hall! . . . They took me to lunch one day when I first came there, some of the ladies, and they were telling the story about Miss Nell flying in an airplane under the Arkansas River bridge. . . . And I don't remember who the pilot was, you know, but she was famous for this exploit. And, you know, looking at her, you'd think, "How can this old lady ever have done that!" A real white-gloves-type lady. Millie, you can't describe in a word. She . . . was very intelligent and a good writer, had no newspaper training but managed to write a very interesting food column every week that often included a lot of politics. She talked about her two daughters a lot. But she had grown up, I think, in Pine Bluff and was, I think, was a sort of upper-crust type. I don't know. She was an interesting person and a very opinionated person but someone I liked very much.

Millie's daughter Robin, who worked in the Gazette *library, remembered how her mother turned food columns into political commentaries.*

Robin Woods Loucks: She said, "If I have to write about food, that would bore me to tears." She was an excellent cook, but what she tried to do was introduce social issues and historical issues—any issue that happened to come to her mind or happened to be growing in the community, she would write about it . . . the integration crisis, although the newspaper wouldn't let her do that, but she wrote a very fine food column on separation of church and state.

Reed: I remember a very strong personality. Do you remember how she died?

Martha Douglas: She killed herself. She'd always said—nobody believed her, I guess—that she was never going to linger with any illness, and I think she might have had emphysema. She had been a heavy smoker. She killed herself at her daughter's house while everyone was gone. This was after she'd retired.

Reed: I've heard it said that Ashmore hired Betty Fulkerson because she was a young widow from a good family who needed a job. Her husband had been a prominent young lawyer. . . . Wasn't he at Nuremberg?

Martha Douglas: Yes, he took part in the Nuremberg trials. And died young.

A particularly fearsome man helped the Gazette *break the color barrier.*

Brantley: James Meriwether was not the first black reporter for the *Arkansas Gazette*—I think Ron Coleman may have been—but he was one of the earliest black employees on the news side. He was kind of a fearsome figure, wore muscle shirts to work. He'd been a wide receiver for UCA briefly. He was a football star in high school and well muscled and had a modified Afro hairdo, a bushy black moustache, and a pretty tough physique and was a strong, silent type. Turned out, he was a funny, engaging, wonderful guy, but was a little scary to a guy who went to General Lee's college up in Virginia.

The Gazette *had the customary old-fashioned telephone switchboard. The person in charge was vital to the paper's operation.*

Martha Douglas: Miss Mary Grace . . . She was a dear lady, and she had a pretty sharp tongue, or could have. She was well known for covering for the guys, you know. When the wives would call and she would call out their name, and they would signal whether or not they were there. So she used to cover for them if they'd been out, if they'd gone out for beers. She was very nice about that.

Ken Parker: Mary was without equal when it came to finding people who didn't necessarily want to be found. When I was state editor, there was an embezzlement at the Bank of Dierks. The person with the information was a bank examiner who had faded from sight. I called Mary and told her I wanted to talk with this guy, and he was a bank examiner, and he would be in a motel in the Nashville area. In a few minutes, she called and said, "Parker, is he driving a black Chevrolet?" I replied, "Mary, I don't know if he has a car." She said, "He is coming to the phone." The man answered, and Mary said, "Mr. So-and-So?" He said, "Yes." She said, "You didn't think we could find you, did you?" Then, she left the line and left me to talk with this astonished bank examiner. . . . Mary was great about covering up for employees. If a wife called, she would lie if necessary. But if she found out that the employee was cheating on his wife and was probably out at the moment with his significant other, she would not lie.

Almost everyone held J. N. Heiskell in awe. But not all.

Parker: Elmer Upchurch ("Ma") Grant [a printer] was the senior man on the seniority board of the *Gazette* Chapel of the ITU [International Typographical Union], and as I recall, there was about a thirty-year gap between him and the next person. When he finally retired, he had more than sixty years at the *Gazette*. Ma's other claim to fame was that he was the only person in the *Gazette* building who addressed J. N. Heiskell as Ned. He was at the *Gazette* when Mr. J. N. and Mr. Fred came there, and he called them by their first names. Mr. Heiskell addressed him as Mr. Grant. In the 1950s, Ma Grant worked the day shift, primarily setting editorial page copy. He would occasionally insert his own editorial comments concerning the editorials, such things as "HELL, NED, YOU DON'T BELIEVE THIS CRAP ANY MORE THAN I DO!" He always put his editorial comments in capital letters so the proofreaders would be sure to take them out before they went into the paper. Ma drank on the job. Every afternoon when Ma left, the porter would remove an empty liquor bottle from the cabinet next to Ma's Linotype machine. I never saw him drunk, although there were occasions when he had a bit of trouble hitting the door as he left.

When Ken Parker joined the Gazette *in the late 1940s, the newsroom held memories that predated World War II.*

Parker: Henry W. Loesch was nicknamed Heinie. He started as a sportswriter and eventually moved to the copy desk. When I arrived at the *Gazette,* Heinie was the slot man—and a very good one. Heinie wore a green eyeshade, as did Nell Cotnam and Bill Bentley. As his health deteriorated, Heinie became the day slot man. Nelson would talk him into working on election night but only after he guaranteed there would be a cooler full of beer in the managing editor's office. Heinie had a couple of strokes. He always said his first stroke was caused by Charlotte McWhorter walking through the newsroom in a tight sweater.

James Street, after a short-lived career as "the Boy Evangelist of Mississippi" [he eventually became a well-known writer], wound up some way at the *Gazette,* where he became state editor. This was in the 1920s. At about the time of the 1927 floods, Street heard for the first time of buffalo gnats, and the name struck him as funny, a buffalo being a large creature and a gnat a tiny one. He learned that buffalo gnats were particularly numerous after heavy rains and that they pestered cattle. He decided it was probable that the state prison farm, being in the area that flooded, was infested with buffalo gnats, and he wrote an article about the problem. The next day, the superintendent of the prison called to say he had not seen a buffalo gnat in years. Street was on the verge of being fired when he was hired by the Associated Press and sent to the Atlanta bureau.

Joseph B. Wirges started as a copy boy when he was about sixteen years old and then became the police reporter, a job he held until he retired. Joe was a rather rough-looking character with a crew cut. He had a deep voice. When I first knew Joe, he had been the *Gazette* police reporter for so long that he had "seniority" over every cop in the state. Most of them addressed him as "Mr. Joe." . . .

John Fletcher was the only staff member I know of who put his own byline on his stories. He was good for one story a day, and it was always bylined. When he completed that story, there was nothing the copy editor could do to it. If you took out one word, the whole article would crumble. John . . . had a lot of good news sources, and they trusted him. He wrote articles exposing gambling at Hot Springs, but he was a close friend of Jack McJunkin of the Southern Club [an illegal casino]. McJunkin sent John a set of china when he married the last time. If John was in Hot Springs for fun or rest, he would call McJunkin and tell him. If he was there on business, Jack knew he'd better watch out. John liked to tell about one day when he was walking along Central Avenue and met Owney Madden [mobster and gambling kingpin] hurrying in the opposite direction. John tried to stop him, but Madden said, "I'll be right back." He went about half a block, put a coin in a parking meter, and came strolling back. He explained to John, "With my record, you can't be too careful."

Morgan Beatty was gone from the *Gazette* before I arrived. In fact, when I was in school, I heard him on NBC Radio, where he was one of the top newsmen. Beatty was from Benton, if my memory is correct. He was a reporter for the *Gazette* before going to NBC. When he left, he owed the *Gazette* for quite a few long-distance telephone calls he had made to his girl-friend. Since he did not have the cash to pay for the calls, he gave the *Gazette* his camera. It was the first camera the *Gazette* owned, and it was assigned to Joe Wirges.

[Matilda] Tuohey was an excellent reporter and a good friend. At her funeral, the rector of St. Andrew's Cathedral told of meeting Tuohey soon after his assignment there. A couple of weeks later, he said, as he went up the aisle during the recessional, a clenched fist came out of a pew and in front of him. It was Tuohey's. He held out his hand, and a twenty-dollar bill dropped into it. "What's this for?" he asked. Tuohey replied, "A bottle of scotch. You look like you could use it."

Tom Hamburger: Matilda's nickname was "Tiger." She had a very gruff exterior. . . . She came in, and she didn't speak to me. And Jimmy Jones, who had taken over as state editor just that year shortly before I arrived or about the time I arrived—Jimmy said, "Oh, it takes Tiger at least a year before she will talk to anyone." [*Laughs.*] She didn't bother learning names either, and particularly Yankees'. But we became fast friends.

Farris: How did she fare in that newsroom at that time as a woman? Was she accepted?

Hamburger: It was hard . . . You really had to assume a lot of the affect of the male reporters—and not only do what they did but do it better, which meant drink hard, curse, you know, affect a cynical pose and take on the tough stories. And she did all of it. She cursed like a sailor. She was very funny, very well read, never married. She used to travel the globe, loved going to third-world countries. And she would send us different photographs. . . . She was a voracious reader. She'd bring in books. She loved anyone who read books also, and she always keep a stack of them by her desk. . . . And she read murder mysteries, and she read political nonfiction. She loved, devoured, campaign books each year. She was a real news person, just fabulous. Interested in everything . . . Loved to drink. Loved to cook. . . . As a reporter she had some very tough assignments, and then when she sort of moved up to editor, I think she edited all the time at the state desk . . . [Roy] Bode used to like to call in his stories [from Washington]. This was in the days of telefaxing and so forth, but often he would go to a bar. He was close friends with the Carter administration, . . . and frequently he wanted to call in stories from his favorite watering hole. And Tiger would get right out. "Bode, Bode, I can't hear you. I can't tell what kind of a story it is. I can't hear you. Damn." And smash down the phone on him. [*Laughs.*]

Farris: And then he would have to call back from some quieter place.

Hamburger: And hope to reach someone else.

Jerol Garrison worked several years as a reporter, mainly on the federal beat. He lived across the Arkansas River in North Little Rock. Charles Allbright once told in his Our Town column about the day Jerol's Plymouth turned over 100,000 miles.

Garrison: Well, it was a 1953 Plymouth that I'd bought in 1954 when Sally and I were married. I was rather proud of the car and rolled up a lot of miles on it. Well, one day I was looking at the odometer, and I noticed that sometime the next morning on the way to work it would turn over 100,000 miles. So I said, "Well, that'll be fun to watch that thing turn over." Well, by the time I got to my parking place near the *Gazette* building, I looked down at the odometer—I'd forgotten to look! The odometer had already turned over, and it said 100,000. So, so much for that. I didn't get to watch it. But Charlie wrote a column on it, and it was funny.

John Woodruff: In June, as I say, I passed 36,000 miles of running. On October 1, 2000, I ran my thirty-seventh marathon. Of course, marathons are 26.2 miles each, and on eight of those I've been up and down Pike's Peak out in Colorado. So I tried to keep myself healthy over the years as a journalist, and a lot of times it has come in handy with some of the long hours or whatever is involved with the energy that you really need a lot of times to be a reporter and keep going and going and really don't have time to be tired. That came in handy, and the conditioning helped when on October 1 I did my thirty-seventh marathon, and three days later we found that I had a tumor inside of me, and on October 12, twelve days after that marathon, I had surgery to remove that tumor and some other infected mass tissue that had caused the tumor and then had to replumb as it were. I joked that they used some of the equipment from Home Depot to replumb me, I guess. But we are back up, and it's been about two weeks now since the surgery, and I am walking a couple to four miles a day now, so we are getting back there.

Celia Storey called Roy Reed from the Democrat-Gazette *in August 2005 to gather information for Jerry Jones's obituary. She mentioned that she had just got back from Pike's Peak, covering the marathon, and had seen John Woodruff cross the finish line "running hard." John died in 2007.*

Brantley: My first vision in my mind of Mike Trimble is sitting at one of those old Underwood typewriters with a big tray of Sims barbecue or Ballard barbecue ribs sitting on top of the Underwood and all that juice dripping out of it. I'm not one to say, but Trimble is not a neat eater. And just trying to eat it all before the carton disintegrated. Some was on his shirt and some was on his pants, and he was saying, "This is the best food in the world."

Dumas: What was your relationship with Judge Henley? He was a very serious, unusually dignified, Republican federal judge.

Trimble: It was not close. I think that he had more of a sense of humor than a lot of people gave him credit for, and I think he viewed me with sort of amused disdain. . . . At that time, I had adopted a stray cat, black with a little white on its throat, and I named him "J. Smith" because he was a terrible cat. He was irritable, and I'd feed him and he'd bite me. Just irascible. So word had got back to Smith Henley that I had named my cat J. Smith, and in the hall one day he said, "Mr. Trimble, I understand that you have a cat named J. Smith. Could you tell me why you named that cat that?" And I was trying to come up with something plausible—"First of all, he's black and has a little white spot on his collar. You know, like a judicial robe. Why else?"—because I had been regaling everyone else with what an ill-tempered cat this is, so I am sure he had heard about it. And he said, "Well, tell me more. Why else?" And I said, "He's . . . he's very independent and he's . . . " and I was just kind of stuttering. He said, "Are you trying to say that you have an ill-tempered cat, Mr. Trimble?" "Well, actually, Judge, I am trying very hard *not* to say that." He and I got along, but we certainly weren't close. It was an arms-length-and-beyond relationship.

Richard Portis: Trimble was interesting. We lived together. We had a big old house up on Ridgeway, and it was one half of a huge house that had been made into a duplex. It had a big fireplace, and we looked for a long time for a moose head to put on the fireplace, but we couldn't find one. The trouble was his personal habits were worse than mine. He'd never take his clothes to a laundry, for instance. His shirts would pile up in a corner, and sometimes he would air them out, but then when they got really bad, he'd just go buy some more shirts. And then when the room kind of filled up to a certain level, he'd go back down to J. C. Penney or someplace and get some more. He'd never renew his car license, stuff like that.

Meriwether: [Jim Williamson] was quiet, almost Victorian, in his outlook on life and always appropriately attired. . . . Hugh Patterson used to say, "I had very little to do with the day-to-day operation of the *Gazette*. All I did every morning was go down and find Jim Williamson and turn him on, and that was it. Jim did it from there on." . . . He was the best-dressed guy. He never went out with his suit jacket unbuttoned. . . . He was very much a gentleman. Adored Mr. Heiskell. Adored Hugh Patterson. There is a story, one time, about Hugh and Jim at the bar at the Little Rock Club, and Billy Rector [a real-estate developer] was up there hassling Hugh, you know, about something Hugh had done. You know how Billy was. And Williamson went up and punched him out. . . . Socked him right there on the spot.

Dumas: [Nelson] really put a premium on good copy editors, and we had them. They were free to quarrel and thought of themselves as superior to all of the rest of us at the paper. [Pat] Crow was particularly arrogant. He was a great big barrel-chested, red-headed guy. Crow and I were roommates. The two of us and Chris Kazan roomed together for awhile. We shared a house across the street from Central High School one time. I hated for Crow to edit my copy because if he could find anything at all, he would stand up and yell across the newsroom, "Listen to what Dumas wrote!" and would read some awkward sentence. And, of course, I just blushed. He was fond of doing that. He didn't do it to everybody, but he knew he could do it to me with impunity. Once I had written something about the Marshall Plan—I had covered some speech—and there was a phrase about lifting Europe "off" its feet or something instead of "to" its feet. Crow stood up and read that sentence to the whole newsroom in this booming voice. Forty people were out there listening to him, and he wouldn't sit down. He had to continue to talk about it. All night long he would walk across the newsroom and shake his head and say, "Lift Europe off its feet," and just shake his head. But they were like that.

Pat Crow . . . got a job on the copy desk at the *New York Times* and sold everything he had here. He had an old Nash Rambler, and Crow went out and spent every dime he had buying himself three or four new suits. Since he was going to be working at the *New York Times,* he had to get some nice threads. So he had a couple of new suits and some herringbone jackets for work and got himself a cane and headed off to New York. His car played out on him someplace in Pennsylvania, and he had to junk it and take a train to New York. He arrived there, got up the next morning early, and dressed as nicely as he could in one of his new suits and his new cane and walked to the *New York Times* to go to work. When he got there, pickets were out front. It was the first day of the longest newspaper strike in New York history, the longest strike in newspaper history to that point. So he was stuck in New York. He had a lease for a year on an apartment off Union Square on Fourteenth Street, and he had no money and no job, nothing. Ray Kornegay and John Fleming sent him cash from Little Rock to keep him going. My pay as a private in the U.S. Army was ninety-one dollars per month, and, of course, I didn't have anything to spend ninety-one dollars on, so I'd take the ferry into Manhattan on the weekends. I'd buy Pat Crow a sack of about ten pounds of apples, and he would eat apples all week. Apples and oranges, so he stayed alive mainly through Ray Kornegay and John Fleming [who] kept sending him money so he could pay for his apartment until he got on his feet and the strike was over.

[Eric Black] was a general assignment reporter. He wasn't a real popular person around the newsroom, but Eric was Eric. He was pushy, and he didn't mind going in and telling the managing editor how much money he thought he ought to have or how his stories were not properly handled. I loved him, but he just grated on everyone's nerves around there. He was a Boston Yankee. He had a big black beard and bushy black hair, big unkempt beard. . . . And then left the *Gazette* and went to the Minneapolis *Star Tribune*. He has been one of their stars up there. I think he has done several books, and he's the special projects editor. . . . I think he does two or three stories per year, and nobody dares question him about that. . . . But he got upset with the *Gazette* at the end. . . . He did an expose of some corruption in a labor union. Got some tips on that and spent quite a bit of time and endured a lot of intimidation from some of these bullies from this union. They tried to intimidate him; in fact, he was scared to death when he was supposed to meet the president of this union at the Sam Peck Hotel back in a little dining room back in the back. Sam Peck, you remember—that's where we used to meet all the time. And he had been trying to reach this guy to talk to him about all of the stuff that he had on him, and this guy finally agreed to meet him at this place, and so Eric was afraid. He thought of violence because this guy said, "I am going to bring along a couple of people." And he did, so he wanted me to go along with him, as if I could protect him. You know, I was a six-three and 150-pound weakling. So we met up there, and he did bring a couple of these real tough bully guys with him, and they did try to intimidate Eric about doing the story. They implied that if he wrote that story, he'd be sorry. Well, he did write the story and at some length, and there were some reservations about it at the *Gazette*—I think the attorneys—and it wound up getting rewritten, substantially rewritten, and toned down. And it wasn't the hard-hitting story that he had set out to write. He was extremely disappointed about that. . . . But Eric had the goods on them, and subsequently, the state or federal investigations, they were prosecuted and sent to prison . . . It would have probably been in the late 1970s or early 1980s maybe.

Romance occasionally intruded in the newsroom. Pat Best worked the switchboard when her future husband Eddie Best was a sports writer.

Pat Best: I would occasionally work on Friday night for football, or sometimes I would switch out with Mary Grace for the night shift [on the switchboard], so I got to know Eddie. We did a lot of dating after midnight . . . [I had] heard that the *Gazette* wanted a switchboard operator. I went over and applied to Frank Duff, who was the personnel manager. He hired me. I was fifteen years old. Mr. Duff said, "I don't want to come up there and see a bunch of those reporters hanging around at the switchboard." Years later, I reminded him of that, and told him, "Eddie Best did not listen to you."
Garrison: Did he hang around a little bit?
Pat Best: A little bit. He left a few poems for me to find at six o'clock when I went in. He left them on the switchboard, which was nice.
Garrison: How old were you when you and Eddie married?
Pat Best: Nineteen.

The newsroom could produce varied talents and interests.

Trimble: By and large everybody there was really, really good at their job, and they were more sophisticated than me, better read than me. One time I looked over and Chris Kazan was reading a book, just had it down in his lap, and I kind of looked over, and it was in German, for God's sake. And I thought, "Geez . . ."
Pat Best: John Reed . . . was a very nice young man who came to work at the *Gazette*. I found out that he spoke Spanish. Part of my duty at the *Gazette*, as a secretary, was to take care of the orders for reprints for the photographers. Anytime anybody called and wanted a reprint of a picture in the paper, I handled it. One day I spent a whole lot of time with a woman who could not speak English except for one word every fifteen minutes. I knew that she wanted a reprint order. I didn't know what I was going to do. It suddenly hit me. I looked around in the newsroom, and John Reed was there. I called him and told him my dilemma. I said, "May I transfer this to you?" He was so very nice and said, "Certainly." I transferred it and went out there. He was talking and doing his gobbledygook. I would hear a *mañana* sometimes and *taco* every once in a while. John was a delight, and he handled it for me.

Parker: Richard Davis's parents lived at Little Rock, and he had gone to some fancy university, although I don't think he graduated. He had had polio, and one of his hands was withered. He was hired at the *Gazette* and was assigned to the city "crap desk," writing obits, market reports, and that sort of thing. Among his skills was Greek. One evening, soon after he went to work at the *Gazette,* Richard was on the phone talking with someone about river stages or something, and as most of us did, he was doodling—only his doodling was in Greek. Someone from the Associated Press office passed by and saw Richard talking on the phone and doodling in Greek. By the next evening, the word was out that the *Gazette* had a new side man who took notes in Greek. After some time at the *Gazette,* Richard left and went to New York. There, he contracted some illness and died as a young man.

Bill Whitworth, who eventually became a prominent magazine editor in New York and Boston after leaving the Gazette, *was more than casually interested in music during his early days.*

McCord: I think a big question in your life is that you were always kind of torn between music and journalism, and so is your taking this job when you finished college, is that a sign that you had made up your mind that it was going to be journalism instead of the music?

Whitworth: I knew that I was not a good enough musician to make a career out of it. I could just barely have hung on in some way. Right before I left [the University of Oklahoma], I was promised a job on the Hal McIntyre band. Most people don't know that name anymore. McIntyre had been in the Glenn Miller sax section, and in the fifties and sixties he had a very modern, very good little band. And then after I went to work at the *Gazette,* I was offered a job on the Jimmy Dorsey band, which was one of the early "ghost" bands. That is, Jimmy Dorsey was dead, but a trumpet player named Lee Castle, who had been with Dorsey, was running the band. And then when Stan Kenton was in Little Rock, in about 1961, he asked me about joining the band. I had known Kenton just from running into him a lot, and I had friends on the band and everything, but he had never heard me play and had no way of knowing whether I was a good enough player to work for him. But he asked me if I would be interested in joining this so-called Mellophonium band, which he was then planning. You know, he loved brass. He had five trumpets and five trombones, and then he planned to add five Mellophoniums. This was a horn that, I believe, was sort of invented for him: a combination of a trumpet and a French horn, I guess. He asked me if I would be interested in playing one of these horns. But I didn't think I was good enough to play for Kenton, and I knew that music wasn't going to be my career.

McCord: But you played, though, a little bit while you were at the *Gazette.*

Whitworth: Yes, local stuff. I played with Tommy Scott. I played some of those concerts in the park with my own band, and I played in a band over in Hot Springs at a club where they tried out Las Vegas shows. The Mitzi Gaynor Show was there for two weeks, preparing their Las Vegas show. I would do little things like that.

McCord: But it never was a big, hard decision for you.

Whitworth: It was not. No, because I knew that people who were better than me were a dime a dozen, literally, at this time, all over the place.

Paul Nielsen: Richard Portis was Buddy [Charles] Portis's younger brother, and brilliant, just brilliant. I think Richard left the business to become a doctor. As I recall, the family wanted him to do that. The word was that they hoped that this young genius would not have dirty fingernails like Buddy and the rest of us but would become a professional. Every journalist who knew Richard just mourned the thought of him leaving the business . . . I knew Richard from when he'd worked for the *Pine Bluff Commercial.* It amazes me to think of it now, but Richard Portis had been the bureau chief in Hamburg, in southeast Arkansas, living in a trailer. The mind just spins now at the thought of that much wit and that much insouciance living in a trailer in Hamburg and reporting on the Pink Tomato Festival—and loving it and making the reader love it. Richard was good. And I tell you, at the *Commercial,* we thought the Pink Tomato Festival was important too. It was a part of real life, the way our readers lived.

The Gazette *had a succession of popular columnists, and each had his enthusiasms. Carol Allin, Richard's wife, became manager of the Cathedral School in Little Rock in autumn of 2000. Before that, she lived another life, semi-anonymously, as Allin's "traveling companion," or "TC" as she was called in his column.*

Richard Allin: I never made reference to TC as being a woman until one day somebody questioned, "Is TC a man? Is he traveling with a man?" And I thought, "Well, I better get that straightened out." So I started calling her TC, that's most definitely a woman. And we traveled thousands of miles in every possible way.

Reed: A story about Ernie Deane [the *Gazette*'s longtime Arkansas Traveler columnist] writing letters to the editor, under different names ordinarily.

He'd take an assumed name and send them to the *Democrat* and criticize the *Democrat,* but one letter was published under his own name, and it was a complaint about truck drivers and how they treated other people on the highway. And it was a rip-roaring letter, just taking the hide off truckers as a class, and he wound it up with this sentence, "And if I ever again encounter a truck that says 'Tex and Maxine' on the driver's door, I aim to stop it and cane the hell out of Tex—or Maxine as the case may be."

A stringer is a part-time correspondent not on the regular payroll.

Thompson: Orval Faubus was a stringer for the *Gazette?*
Donald: At Huntsville, yes. David Pryor was the stringer for a while when he and Barbara were up at Fayetteville, when they were going back to school. At one time or another, you know, most people wanted some kind of connection with the *Gazette.* I will tell you another one. It was Marlin Hawkins at [Morrilton]. Marlin was a great stringer, being the "High Sheriff" of Conway County. Marlin would call in—of course he knew everything that was going on in his bailiwick there, and he also understood newspapers and newspaper deadlines, and he knew my first edition deadline, which is what he made sure it would get into his papers up there, were such-and-such a time. I think it was seven o'clock, and he would call in earlier. He would say—say it was a bad car wreck—"I can't get you in for first. I have to inform the families, and I may not be able to do that until second edition deadline, but I will have the families informed so I can give you the names and the details of the wreck in time to get in the second edition paper." All of them understood. They were good. We had some good stringers.

Not all the Gazette *hands were liberals. One was the son of a leading segregationist spokesman, the Rev. Wesley Pruden. Young Wesley was a* Gazette *reporter before his father came to prominence as an opponent of school desegregation.*

Dean Duncan: Wes [Pruden, later editor of the *Washington Times]* was a really nice fellow . . . He was always a good writer. . . . He was almost an office boy when he first came to the *Gazette.* He had a job writing for the state desk. Now and then, he would write a story, and I would hear the other guys talking about it. I didn't pay any attention to it. I read the story, and it was very well done, and I appreciated that. It was only after I got to the *Commercial Appeal* and began working part-time as an assistant city editor that I got acquainted with his copy. He was the smoothest and snappiest writer that I ever came across. . . . I used to see him occasionally on C-Span. He was always dressed in a white suit—linen, I suppose, sort of like a Southern colonel. . . . He was working on the *National Observer,* and I had just begun work at UCA as a teacher in 1967. He came up a couple of times. The last time was about 1971 or 1972. I remember asking him how many countries he had been to while working at the *National Observer.* It was some ungodly number like fifty-five. He had covered some of the strife in Northern Ireland. He had been headquartered in Hong Kong. He had made at least two trips into Vietnam.

The paper sported a few family connections. There were the Patterson father and sons, the Portis brothers, the Douglas husband and wife. Some years after Roy Reed left, his son joined the paper.

John Reed: I got into the newspaper business late. After college, I went to Madrid, and I taught English as a foreign language in Madrid, and I believe I was twenty-six or twenty-seven when I moved to Pine Bluff from Madrid. I didn't have any job skills except teaching English. . . . I went to Yale and got a literature degree. There was a line, I think it was a line in a movie where Sophia Loren was the rich young daughter of a rich Italian man who lost all his money, and she says, "I'll go get a job." And he says, "I've given you an education in the finest schools of Europe; you have no job skills." I burst out laughing at that! That hit home with me. I got a very good education with no job skills. My dad, when I came back to the United States from almost five years in Madrid, was teaching journalism at Fayetteville. I sat in on a few classes of his. I sat in on some classes with Bob Douglas and enjoyed those. And I probably shouldn't say this if there is anybody at the university listening, but I don't think I paid; I think I just sat in. And then my dad helped me get a job at Pine Bluff. He had this child-exploitation racket going where he would send journalism students off to jobs in Pine Bluff and Little Rock mostly, but other newspapers too. It was for students like Stephen Steed and Michael Haddigan, who went to the *Gazette,* guys that never got their degree, but Dad didn't care. He seemed to be the only college professor that I ever knew that didn't care if you got your degree. He would send you out to be exploited by an editor. He helped me get the job at Pine Bluff where Frank Lightfoot, one of my editors there, said, "Yeah, this is the *Pine Bluff Commercial* and graduate school." They knew what they were doing in Pine Bluff. They were just getting young guys, teaching them the business, and then they would go off mostly to Little Rock but also to St. Louis and other places.

Tomfoolery was a Gazette custom. There were always the wits, clowns, and pranksters to provide it.

Richard Portis: Ernie [Dumas] became prematurely bald and started affecting a hat in the newsroom. He would wear it. His desk was pretty close to the door as you walked into the newsroom, and he wouldn't take his hat off quick enough to suit me. And when he did, he would put it in a drawer. I would hide his hat, and Douglas got in on it too. We would hide it in different places. He finally quit wearing it, but he took it in good stride.

Reed: Ernie wanted me to have you come clean on something else that he accuses you of. Something about the furniture at the *Gazette,* his desk and chair and typewriter. . . . It began to disappear one item at a time. Until finally he came to work one day and even his typewriter was gone, and he just had a couple of pencils.

Richard Portis: Well, those things expand. I mean, I've taken blame or credit for stuff I did, but furniture? He doesn't remember the good part. Did he tell you about the letter of recommendation I wrote Alex Washburn trying to get him a job at the *Hope Star?*

Reed: Yes, he did, and he's offered to give me a copy of it to put in the files. In fact this was part of the same story that he told about the furniture. He said that you came up to him and said, "They don't appreciate you here, and if they were up front with you, they would just tell you to leave." But he said then you wrote this letter to Alex Washburn recommending him for a job at the *Hope Star.* He says he's still got a copy of that.

Richard Portis: I really don't think I pulled that furniture job.

While his brother Charles became famous as a novelist, Richard Portis carved out a niche of sorts as a writer of nonsense poems.

Richard Portis: [Jerry] Rush [Sunday editor] would fill in the bottom of this Richard Allin column with little poems sent in by mostly female poets. So I told Rush one time, I said, "I'm tired of reading all that crap. Let me write something for you." I would make up these nonsensical poems, and for a long time, once a week, my poetry would be at the bottom of Richard Allin's column on the front page of the Sunday section.

Reed: Was that the beginning of your poetry career?

Richard Portis: That was the beginning of it and probably the apex too. It was all downhill from there. . . . I had different names, but there would always be three women's names. I guess looking back on it, they didn't give you much room. You couldn't write much, and most of the time I would try to put the word *gossamer* into the poem. It would just be like a lot of modern poetry that they say is not supposed to make sense, but it would just be strings of nonsense syllables.

Reed: How hard was it to write one of those poems?

Richard Portis: It would only take me a matter of seconds. One of the easiest things. . . . If it required any effort, I wouldn't have gotten into it in the first place.

Hamburger: Jimmy [Jones] used to invite us—he said, "You got to come over and try—I am going to make my special." So I get to his house, and I say, "What are you making?" He said, "My special recipe, creamed corn." And he would have left about six, and I was supposed to sort of close down the state desk. And it is nine o'clock and I think, "I am starved," going to this dinner at the editor's house. And when we get there, Jimmy's stirring this yellow mess on the stove [*laughs*], going, "Yes, this is an old Jones family recipe. It's going to be a little while. Have a drink. How many fingers of scotch?" And it didn't matter what you'd say, you'd just get a tumbler full of whiskey. And I don't remember anything else that he made. I think it was just creamed corn. I got absolutely blotto by the time it came in. I could barely get up from the chair. [*Laughs.*] And I think Trimble was there and a couple of other people from the newsroom. He said, "Jimmy's whole plan is to serve dinner around midnight. We're so drunk all we can do is exclaim over it." But he later said, "Isn't it good? What do you think of the texture?" [*Laughter.*] He cared more about his creamed corn than he did a story. I think Jones was a quite a good cook. I think it was very good corn. We might have had some barbecue with it . . .

Ernie [Dumas] got me in terrible trouble, to his great delight. There was a Judge Means whom I had reported on who was up for some kind of—I think . . . there was some investigation by the state senate of this judge. And his sister, I think, not his wife—his sister or sister-in-law, Fritzy, was the official nurse for the state capitol. . . . She had been there forever, and she was sort of an adored figure by the legislature, and completely harmless, except when you got on the subject of her brother. When he was in trouble, she would lobby everybody and go nutty-crazy, and she didn't want anyone—you weren't supposed to talk about him. If you said anything offensive to her brother, she'd whoop and holler. So I'm going over to the capitol—I didn't go over there very often, at this point. Dumas says for this story there's one person you want to interview, and that's the nurse over there. She knows a lot about this. "Really?" He said, "Yes. She knows about the case." And he's completely poker-faced as he describes this. So I go in and there. I say, "I want to ask you what you might know about anything." And she starts hollering, and she's treating some legislator while I'm in there. He had a "boo-boo," as she called it. He had a blister, and she was putting a Band-Aid on his blister. And she starts raving as she gets the Band-Aid on him. And she is shouting and carrying on. And I remember Dumas was out in the hallway. He was listening, because he knows that this stuff is going to echo. And the legislator comes out and says, "Ernie, you gotta stop that boy!" [*Laughs.*] Ernie says, "I can't stop him. He's a real ankle-biter!" [*Laughter.*]

Thompson: Did people get fired at the *Gazette?*

Donald: No. I don't ever remember any. In fact, one guy was in a witness-protection program, or else he was, he was something weird. He got fired when they found out about him. That is the only guy I ever remember getting fired.

Gazette people were not popular in much of Little Rock after the 1957 school crisis when many citizens thought the paper was part of the Communist conspiracy. As a result, the paper's newsroom employees clung to each other during those tense days. After-hours parties became an institution.

Reed: I was never a binge drinker, but the *Gazette* had a few of those. At the parties, you could count on two or three of these. Mainly, they were photographers that were falling-down drunk. Literally, falling-down drunk. There was a famous night when Larry Obsitnik, the chief photographer, fell into a tub of ice-cold beer.

Ed Gray: Mike Trimble was one of the best writers around. . . . He was funny and gregarious and a fine writer. He would have incredible Christmas parties. He lived at a place called the Ridgeway House. It was at Ridgeway and Lee. A bunch of those people lived there. Mike was a bachelor in those days. Somebody said they went to a Christmas party at his house, and then the next year they went to a Christmas party there, and there were the same dirty dishes!

Hamburger: Mike also had trouble because they had great parties at his house . . . And the party got out of hand, and he was celebrating. . . . The party was so successful that they took all of his furniture out of his home—I think he told this—and they put it out on the lawn and built a bonfire. He organized it, but they, you know, can't remember. Maybe they didn't have power and they needed the heat, I don't know, but all the furniture was gone the next morning, and Mike woke up on the floor.

Julia Jones: I need to say a few words about the parties because they were pretty famous and had been for a long time before I ever heard of the place. I had gotten to know Pat Trimble, and it was her brother Mike Trimble who had the party house at that time. He and George Carter had something like a fourth of a big, old house, in a nice, old neighborhood. Their apartment had the living room of the original house. So he had a good room to have parties in. I don't know why their landlord didn't throw them out because there were a lot of parties. We didn't miss a holiday. They had birthday parties, and we celebrated the arrival of someone at the *Gazette* or someone's departure. It wasn't just a matter of opening the doors. We made plans and bought food and cake and stuff. We always had Christmas parties. . . . at Mike's. We always ended up singing along with Peter, Paul, and Mary [a musical group that was popular in the 1960s]. And I remember "Old Stewball Was a Race Horse." We listened to it so much that we sang with it, that we could do all the harmony. That was fun a thing to do. The important thing about this was it was a community; we all knew each other. If we didn't work together, we were on the same floor. And we look at it now, it was all really innocent fun. It was just a friendly thing to do. We didn't tear up anybody's house. Nobody ever got into a fight. Nobody ever made off with somebody else's wife. Some of us would borrow a bedroom and take a nap. . . . I remember when Max Brantley came to the *Gazette* we had a whole new kind of party. Max celebrated the Chinese New Year. And he would find a restaurant, check it out, and order up a six- or seven-course meal. And people would sign up and pay him, and he would deal with the restaurant. It would usually be some nice little family restaurant, and they wouldn't have a liquor license. We'd roll in with big coolers with plum wine and sake and Chinese beer. I imagine after such a party somebody posted a note by the cash register, "Do not accept reservations from these people." I do remember one time that there was a bunch of us standing at the Officers Club over on the east side, and we had a drink. We were just talking, and I looked back over there, and Max had put his glass eye in his drink. . . . Then we went to one of the bars where there was a band or some music, and we were all out there on the dance floor moving around, and suddenly—this happened several times—Max and Mike Trimble would both leap up into the air and fall on the floor on their bellies and kind of writhe around. They called it "The 'Gator." They only did this in bars because these are two pretty big guys, and there wouldn't be room in somebody's home. I don't know how they made it to work the next day.

Donald: I can remember one time, in fact, this would be, this was in the days when the Arkansas Power and Light Company and the Arkansas Electric Co-ops and so forth, as you remember, used to give these great Christmas parties. And one of the best ones was the AP&L party down at the Lafayette [Hotel], and they would have Betty Fowler on piano, and shrimp. Of course, those newsroom characters would go anywhere where there was food, free food and booze. Lot of booze. And, of course, it went on way into the night because they tried to let everybody [come], including, at that time, a lot of people in the newsroom worked late into the night to get the paper out. And I can remember standing there overlooking the party, and Nelson said, "Leroy, would you run back down to the paper?" The hotel is, what, two blocks from the *Gazette?* "Would you run back down to the paper and see who is in the newsroom?" And I said, "Sure." I went back there. There was one poor old—this was on a Christmas—one poor old soul was in there, editing the whole paper, laying it out. And I went back and I told Nelson, I said, "Nelson, nobody's down there in that newsroom but Deke Parker. Everybody else is up here." And he said, "Okay. Deke can handle it."

Linda Pine: Betty Turner as library director would cook up this twenty or thirty pound ham. . . . You could pay three dollars and kind of eat all you wanted, and she would do that, or you could bring something. So there would be this monster spread. . . . And I remember Jerry Dean's rum balls. He would make these balls that were just unbelievable. And then people would make salads and that kind of thing. So we would have a big Christmas buffet. I remember it up on the reference desk where you came in there would be this monster, monster ham.

Anne Farris: We'd go to dive barrooms, but this place, International Bazaar, was cosmopolitan for Little Rock. It was nice, the décor was nice, and they actually had international food, Middle Eastern mainly. They had these paper-lantern lamps that hung low over each table. Bob Douglas, a former editor, was at the University of Arkansas and periodically would come back, especially during the "Save the *Gazette*" days. He just was always scowling about the paper lanterns. Deep down inside he was a puppy dog, really a great man and a great writer. But he was always grousing, maintaining this image of a hard-nosed guy. He said, "I don't understand why you go to a bar that—who can drink under a paper lantern?" He just thought that the place was too nice for journalists. But we didn't seem to be too discriminating. In fact, we were there so much, they erected a plaque and put it in the bar with a photograph of all of us huddled around a table. There must have been twenty to thirty of us, and we're all raising our glasses in the air. The plaque said, "This table belongs to the *Arkansas Gazette.*" We're immortalized in the

International Bazaar at least. . . . We had great parties. Stephen Steed was notorious for his ridiculously over-dressed New Year's Eve parties. And he had a collection of tuxedoes he had bought at thrift shops that were the most god-awful things you've ever seen. One was lime green, and another one was purple with velvet lapels and a spangled cummerbund. He had a different one every year. The women would put on tiaras and long dresses with white gloves above our elbows. Everybody would get ridiculously over dressed and show up at this New Year's Eve party, and we partied way into the night. We'd all end up going and having breakfast somewhere in our ridiculously over-dressed costumes.

Donald: Hugh [Patterson] was a big partier, and, a lot of times, they would wind up at Hugh's house, much to Mrs. Patterson's chagrin because she would have to go in and either tell them to go home or tell them to go find a couch to sleep on.

Thompson: Did [the parties] continue during the Gannett years, or did that stop then?

Donald: No, by then, some of the new people coming in, and the younger people, doing their own thing. I don't know what they did. I am sure they did, but the old guard had begun to go their different ways, so, you know, that kind of ended that. You didn't have the crew that would sit in the bar at the Officers Club every afternoon any more and solve the problems of the world.

Death came occasionally to the Gazette. *Some of the paper's most valued and promising talents died too young.*

Reed: Tell about Frank.

Richard Allen: Frank, my brother? . . . Well, you know, it's just absolutely heartbreaking. We were playing a touch-football game down in Allsopp Park, and Eric King and probably Robert Shaw and some of the others from the paper. He had a stroke. He collapsed and died. He was twenty-seven years old. Of course, it was just completely devastating for the whole family. But he was, I think, a very talented journalist already at that age and very committed to working very hard and would have been an excellent journalist, whatever he wanted to do there at the *Gazette* and whatever else he would have done. . . . November the second of 1965.

Dumas: [Ernest Valachovic] died right before the general election in 1968. He was a great beat reporter because he had a disarming way about him, and he got to know every secretary at the capitol. And that was kind of his philosophy. . . . The key to it was knowing who the career people were, the people who had been around for years and who were going to be around, who actually ran the government, ran all these various agencies, and to know their secretaries and the file clerks and everybody else. So Val made a point in all of these agencies to go around and flirt with all the women and get to know everybody around, particularly all the deputies, the people who were career people. And they were helpful always to him. They knew where the files were and would tip him on things and kept him abreast of things so that during that period after 1957 when Faubus put out the word that nobody was to cooperate with the *Arkansas Gazette,* Val continued to beat the *Democrat* day after day after day because he had all these connections. . . . He was a terrible writer. He couldn't spell. His sentences, his stories were frequently disorganized. He had everything there. He had all the information there, but nearly everything he did had to be rewritten. And Shelton was happy to do that . . . Shelton ordinarily was irritated with people for their flaws in their writing, but not Valachovic because he got all the facts. And Shelton would sit down and rewrite it or give it to Jerry Jones or somebody to rewrite most of Valachovic's stories. Because I remember sitting with Valachovic everyday and the common thing all day long, Valachovic would turn around and say, "How do you spell *accommodate?*" And I'd say, "A-C-C-O-M-M-O-D-A-T-E." And he'd say, "No, it doesn't look right." [*Laughter.*] . . . But he was a great guy, and I loved working with Valachovic. Valachovic was always there early in the morning. He always beat me there. Only one time did I come to work ahead of Valachovic and that was the last day. I'd gotten there one morning and Valachovic wasn't there. He was usually sitting there drinking coffee and making telephone calls, reading the paper in the capitol pressroom. And so he didn't come to work. So an hour passed, and I got to worrying about him, so I called him at home. And he picked up the phone, and I said, "Val, Dumas. I was just worried about you." And he said, "I'm just in a lot of pain, a lot of pain. I don't have time to talk. Sorry, it just hurts too much." And he hung up. And an hour later, Shelton called and said, "Ernie Valachovic is dead." He had died of a heart attack. Apparently they had called the doctor, and the doctor had told him to take some Tums or something, that he had extreme indigestion. Anyway when they finally got him to the hospital, he was dead. And he was about forty-five or something.

5

The Newsroom

Thick with Smoke, Excitement, and Tomfoolery

The decline of American newspapers began when they put carpet on the floor of a newsroom somewhere. A publisher who had been in too many corporate offices decided that his paper should be spruced up—civilized—and that carpet in the newsroom was a good beginning.

The Gazette newsroom in the 1950s had a hardwood floor that predated the memory of everyone except that of the Old Man himself. You could scuff it and abuse it and pitch pennies on it. You could throw cigarette butts on it, usually without setting fire to the trash and paper lying around. All that changed when carpet was installed. After that, inevitably, came computers, and typewriters disappeared. The Teletype machines that carried the wire news followed the typewriters, and there went the comforting drum beat that soothed the spirit as the daily deadline drew near. The newsroom went silent. Raised voices were shushed, and tobacco smoke was banned, and page design went modern, and syntax went haywire, and fifty-word leads became stylish, and run-on sentences stole in. It all started with carpet on the newsroom floor.

Margie Snider: You could smoke at your desk—because I smoked. You just put your cigarettes out on the floor . . . I remember hearing when the *Gazette* was remodeled or something and they put carpet on the floor. That that caused a big uproar. People were really upset about that.

Tish Talbot: It was loud . . . This was the days before computers, and there were always typewriters clacking. People were hollering at each other. Everybody smoked. There were always cigarettes put out on the floor. You know, somebody would come in with a sack of barbecue sandwiches and throw them across the room like softballs for supper.

Bob Douglas: The newsroom was as Spartan an office as you ever saw. They brought in some new desks, which were orange crates. There was a strange-looking old desk, culled from some source, an old roll-top desk that some reporter used up against the wall with a bunch of books on the Arkansas statutes, about to fall down. [*Laughter.*]

Roy Reed: They literally had orange crates? Are you kidding?

Douglas: No, no, I am not kidding.

Reed: Did you have a desk?

Douglas: Had a crate. . . . Mr. Heiskell, who held the title of editor—which he never relinquished until he died—had an office, if you could call it that, in the corner of the newsroom . . . It was more a cage than an office. Some kind of wire contraption. . . . It had a door, but he left that open. And he'd sit in there, reading editorials mostly, I guess. I don't know what he read. He read a lot of newspapers. But he didn't keep—he was way behind in his newspaper reading because there was a stack of old yellow newspapers all over the place. . . . Hot as hell, and no screens on the windows. Naked light bulbs. And at night, in the summer—and this was in the summer when I went there—about July, a terribly hot summer, bugs would come in through those windows. The paste we had was old flour paste, to paste up pieces of copy, and bugs would get into that and also get into our hair, wherever they wanted to go. But it still was the most exciting place in the world as far as I was concerned. Still is. Still would be. . . . As far as I know, they [Allsopps, part-owners and business managers] never came upstairs. I understand that one of them came up once, one of the Allsopps, and asked if we needed anything in the newsroom. They were just a shambles, living in a shambles, working in a shambles, and Count Dew assured them, "No, nothing, not a thing in the world." [*Laughs.*] They had some extra money after some kind of tax rebate . . . Heinie Loesch was there a long, long time. I remember before the strike they didn't actually do any remodeling, but they moved in a few chairs, and Heinie Loesch lost his box. And I ran into him in the restroom, and he actually had tears in his eyes. He said, "I sat on that box for thirty years, and I come in and it's gone."

Margaret Smith Ross: Nell Cotnam told me that . . . they'd open a desk drawer and there'd be a mouse in it and some of them became kind of pets. They even gave names to some of them.

Charles Portis: They're pretty sad places [now]. Quiet, lifeless. No big Underwood typewriters clacking away. No milling about, no chatting, no laughing, no smoking. That old loose, collegial air is long gone from the newsrooms. "A locker-room air," I suppose, would be the negative description. We wore coats and ties, and the reporters now wear jeans, and yet they're the grim ones.

Jerol Garrison: My first memory of Bob Douglas was in 1958, '59, '60, along in there, when he was standing up all day at a big table editing the wire copy that came in, and as the day wore on, he would have a big stack of wire copy that was spiked over the sides of his table, maybe two spikes. A real steel spike probably six inches tall that you slammed the copy down on.

Reed: And to be spiked meant that was not being used. . . . More copy would be thrown away than would be put in the paper in any one day.

Garrison: Yes, that's true. Probably three-fourths of the wire copy that came in got thrown away because it wouldn't fit or they had duplication—the *Gazette* had both the AP and the UPI wire service, and sometimes they would use just one story instead of trying to put the two together.

Introducing computers in the newsroom was traumatic for many.

Diane Woodruff: The problem was you came in in the afternoon and you had a deadline to meet. You didn't have time to learn to use the computer there while you were trying to get your typing done. What became very simple and routine pretty quickly was new and foreign and frustrating. And I think too, I think we were sharing a terminal. I think we had to switch off there in the beginning. I don't think everybody had a terminal to start with. One of the most frustrating things that happened to me was . . . there was an amendment, and it changed the makeup of the Pulaski County Quorum Court . . . And I had written my story, had done interviews for weeks. And this was the pre-election, the primary-election story. And I had about 104 inches of copy in my story in that computer. And I didn't, I don't know, I didn't have it backed up and lost it. And had to rewrite that whole thing. [*Laughs.*] That was terrible. . . . We had metal desks and very functional looking chairs. And we had a phone. You had a phone partner; we had one phone between us with the two desks that sat side by side.

At midcentury, there was a sort of universal dress code for newsrooms. Charles Portis described the one at the Memphis Commercial Appeal, *where he worked after leaving the* Gazette. *It was in the style book.*

Portis: Those little booklets, you know, telling you how things were done there—spelling quirks, that sort of thing—at the beginning of this one, there was a general edict that went something like this: "The employees of the *Commercial Appeal* will dress and conduct themselves as ladies and gentlemen at all times." Well, yes, a good policy, all very Southern. I approved, but it was hard to dress as a gentleman on fifty-seven dollars a week. Even then.

Every newsroom had a contingent of copy boys. No girls then, only boys.

Jerry Dhonau: The copy boy did just about everything anybody wanted done, particularly, the city editor, Bill Shelton. One of the things you did was go down to the bus stations and pick up copy that was sent from stringers around the state. There were three bus stations—one at Markham and Louisiana, one at Markham and Main, and there was one at Sixth and Broadway. So, you had to make the rounds of the bus stations. You'd carry copy from the newsroom back to the composing room. You would fill in on the switchboard too when the switchboard operator, Mary Grace, was gone.

Doug Smith: You would slam your story on a spike and yell, "Copy!" and a copy boy would come get it and take it over to the city editor.

Bill Simmons: My first day on the job, the other copy boys took me down to the basement to show me the hideout place. I never went there once they showed it to me, but it turned out that it was apparently a hideout place where the copy boys could disappear when they didn't want to be found. They showed that to me as sort of an introduction to the club.

Reed: Let's talk about dictating stories without first writing them at the typewriter. For people who don't know anything about newspapers, they probably have no idea how difficult that is.

Jerry McConnell: I had to do it . . . in sports because there was so much of the sports news that was going on at night. So we were always facing deadlines, and if I were out of town or something, then I had to do it . . . The only way you could get your story in was call and dictate it to somebody back in the office. You wouldn't have time to sit down and compose it and make that deadline. It is difficult to organize your thoughts. I know a lot of people who would say, "Well, I couldn't sit down at a typewriter and write, you know, fifteen paragraphs in an hour." We have to do it in fifteen minutes sometimes. So you had to be practiced in it and skilled in it and had to have an organized mind.

Jim Bailey: If you tried to sit down and write a twelve-, fifteen-, twenty-inch story on your typewriter and then pick up the phone and read it, it wasted a lot of time. So before my first season was over, I might sketch out a little lead, a little outline on the typewriter, but essentially I just started picking up the phone and dictating. There was no other way to go . . . The really tough night [at a basketball tournament] was the first one, with four games, one after another, with about fifteen minutes in between. One phone. Two papers, us and the *Democrat.* So an old friend, Joe McGee of the Conway *Log Cabin,* who, being with an afternoon paper, wasn't in any hurry to file . . . So when a game was winding down, I would get up from the press table, go down around the end zone and—the office we were going to was actually underneath the stands on the opposite side of the gym . . . Well, I'd stand there at the edge of the court long enough to get the final score, and then I would go down, get on the phone—even before the officials got to the dressing room—start dictating, [and I'd] leave Joe to pick up the box for me. Well, here would come my competitor, and he'd stand there, and, of course, he was nervous. The other game was about to get underway. Here comes Joe and he'd hand me the box, and I'd read the box, and, probably maliciously, I'd sit there and chat an extra minute or two, "How's everything going with the high school tournaments? How's Northside?" And this guy, the other guy, would be going crazy. And just as the other game was getting underway, "Okay, better go. I'll see you," and so I'd slam the phone down, and he would jump on it. And he would reappear out on the court about the middle of the first half of the next game. The funny thing is that we did that five or six years in a row, and he never seemed to remember from one year to the next.

McConnell: One of the big, and difficult, jobs of the *Gazette* sports department was our effort to report on every high school football game played in the state of Arkansas. Our goal was to have at least a short story on every game played . . . For several years, we basically relied on part-timers from outside the staff to help take the games and write them . . . We would call journalism or English teachers in local high schools, ask for their recommendations, and urge them to mention it to their students. This is how we came up with people like Robert Shaw, Bill Simmons, Harry King, Collins Hemingway, and others who went on to exemplary careers in journalism. But we never had enough of them . . . At any rate, the *Gazette* hierarchy finally decided that the only way to get the job done well and expeditiously was to ask or require the regular news reporters, who usually finished their day by 7 or 8 p.m., to come back at 9:30 or 10:00 on overtime and take calls and do the rewrites. This was not necessarily greeted with elation by everyone on the news staff.

Ernest Dumas: When I went to work there as a reporter in 1960, on Friday nights for years and years and years a lot of us on the general assignment staff, and even after I went to the capitol, we went down on Friday nights and wrote up those high school games. You'd get about two hours overtime.

McConnell: One of the problems we had was that some of them took out their aggravation with a little horseplay, like making up nicknames for some of the high school players they wrote about. I remember particularly that Mike Trimble always seemed to have a lot of nicknames in his stories, which might read something like this, "James (Big Train) Smith scored four touchdowns to lead, etc." They were frequently nicknames I'd never heard and was pretty sure had been made up, so we had to discourage this activity. I think we decided we'd better leave out all nicknames, right or wrong ones . . . I also recall that we put a lot of effort in our attempt to get all the district tourney results and that it irritated me that the *Democrat,* an afternoon paper, would have all the same scores the next day, and I knew they were just taking them out of the *Gazette.* So one time I started making up scores and putting them in the paper. I'd make up a name of a team that sounded plausible, even though it was nonexistent, and run the score in our final edition . . . The idea was not original with me. I think I heard about it from the Kansas City papers, where the morning paper ran a college basketball story that reported: "The South 68, Will Rise Again 54," and the afternoon paper picked it up verbatim.

There was always a strain of daring among reporters.

Eddie Best: We were real proud of the fact that when it snowed, we got to work. We figured out a way to get there. We had an old black 1963 Rambler, four doors, and it had lots of room in it. It was heavy and wonderful in the snow. We would plan beforehand when we would know the weather was going to be bad. We would get it out, park it at the curb, head it downhill, and we would have our snow crew ready to ride with us. Sometimes we would knock over garbage cans on the way out. Sometimes we would almost slide into the ditch. But we got to work.

Most reporters at the Gazette covered beats—the courthouse, the city hall, the schools, etc. A small but energetic minority were on general assignment, poised to jump on any breaking story at a moment's notice. Reporters' hours were staggered and flexible to accommodate the flow of news.

Diane Woodruff: You went to work when the news of the day, when it was happening . . . Most of the trials and things didn't usually start until about ten o'clock . . . We had pressrooms there in the county courthouse, or over in the federal post office building there was a pressroom, and if you weren't working and covering something, you were in there during the day rather than over in the newspaper office until after five or five thirty in the afternoon and working then into the evening.

Garrison: Well, now, how did you juggle your home life with reporting? I mean if your husband John was covering North Little Rock and you were covering the county courthouse or the federal court, so how did you? Did you have much home life? Did you and John leave work together sometimes, or did you go home and then John would come in later? How did that work? What's it like to be a husband and wife reporting team?

Woodruff: [*Laughs.*] Well, it worked out really well. I guess John was there late more times than I was, for the reason that a lot of his council meetings and board meetings met at night. Certainly, every other Monday night was the city council meeting. He was never home on a Monday night. And then, a lot of others, he would have a late afternoon meeting. And, really, it would push him later into the evening routinely than I seemed to have, but because both of us were covering beats, our morning schedules were pretty flexible. So that was good. But that's why I left the *Gazette*. Because after Michael was born, one of us needed kind of a regular schedule we could work around day care.

Garrison: And Michael was born in 1978?

Woodruff: Yes. And I went back to work in the spring of 1979, so I was there a year. And what I did during that year was, I worked in the office. I was there, and I had an office general assignment position. And that was the best way that they could figure out to give me an assignment that would try to work around the hours. But one of the things I was writing were the city obits, and they would come straggling in late. And so a lot of afternoons you'd be wrapping up a bunch of obits, and I'd be watching the clock, doing that, and then trying to figure out how to get across town and pick Michael up.

Garrison: Did you ever get there late and they had closed the door and Michael was on the inside and you couldn't get in?

Woodruff: [*Laughs.*] No. I don't think I ever. Cut it close a lot of times, but they never set him out on the doorstep.

Many people used the Gazette *as a quick reference library.*

Donna Lampkin Stephens: And the phones would ring off the wall. And people would call with the strangest questions. I swear, one time I answered the telephone, "*Gazette* Sports." And some woman said, "What's the capital of California?" And I thought, "Why are you calling the sports department to ask that?" . . . If you wanted to know something, you would call the *Gazette,* even if it is "What's the capital of California?"

The Gazette *carried an injuries list that rivaled the Razorback football team's.*

Harry King: Orville actually issued an edict: anybody that got hurt playing could be fined. It wasn't always me. I was on crutches two or three different times.
McConnell: Playing touch football?
Harry King: Yes. And we played softball out there at UALR. I think it was Robert who said, "The birds stopped singing," when Darrell Mack and I ran together, chasing a pop fly out over second. . . . I knocked James Thompson over a fence out there at Allsopp Park. He was lying there at the bottom of the fence, and he was half conscious. "James, throw us the football." Portis got three or four stitches in his mouth. Lightfoot cracked a rib or something.
McConnell: Didn't Ernie Dumas do something?
King: He still blames me for—we were playing out at UALR, and he had his arm raised to throw the ball, and I hit him up under his ribs. It punctured his lung.

The Gazette *was uncommonly slow to add women in the newsroom. World War II, when men were scarce, provided an opportunity for a few, but after that it was years before women were hired in any numbers.*

Reed: How was Nelson to work for?
Martha Douglas: Well, you know, I was kind of brash, and so I didn't take him very seriously. He was kind of crusty, and I think probably he'd pretend being tough.
Reed: Did Nelson ever give you any indication that he saw women in the newsroom in a different way from men?
Martha Douglas: It was pretty obvious somebody saw it that way because there were only two of us in there [Martha Douglas and Matilda Tuohey].
Reed: I once heard Nelson say that he didn't think the newsroom was any place for a woman. Did you know that he had that attitude?
Martha Douglas: No. He never said that to me. And I don't think a woman's presence was really a problem for the guys. I mean, I didn't see them necessarily clean up their language or anything. You just learned to close up your ears if anything bothered you. Besides, the place was so noisy, you couldn't

hear a lot anyway, with all the Teletype machines going . . . It never did occur to me that I was competing with guys. I just knew I was getting paid less.

Reed: Was that okay?

Martha Douglas: Well, what could you do?

Reed: Of course, it was not just women. There were not any black reporters. . . . I've heard Ozell Sutton talk about the liberal *Arkansas Gazette* and, with some derision, point out that the *Arkansas Democrat* hired him as a black man years before the *Gazette* ever hired [any black reporters].

McConnell: For years and years there was a law. Well not a law, but it was a common practice to bar women from the press box [at football games]. Women were just not allowed in the press box. The way they finally got in the press box was they ran out of men Western Union operators. They could not send the story. They did not have enough men to punch in the stories, so they started letting women in the press box then. That is how women— that is what finally broke the ban on women in the press box.

Julie Baldridge: When I first came, I was expected to make coffee every day in this huge pot. I had to carry it all the way down and around the hall to the women's restroom, which was, of course, way off from the newsroom. And I don't drink coffee, never have. I dutifully made coffee for about a year for that whole . . . It was a big newsroom coffee pot, forty-plus cups that used to sit sort of behind Bill Shelton . . . I finally just said, "I am not going to do this any more," and there was all this grumbling about me being uppity, and I said, "No, no, I just do not drink it. If I drank it, I would make it." . . . I did it for a year before I finally got my courage up. . . . I never felt resented to be in that room as a woman. I never felt that. The times were just chang- ing; they were different then . . . I think I got all the respect that they felt for me, and I heard every reservation that they had. In another setting, I might have been treated more courteously and undermined in other ways. At the *Gazette,* I never felt that my career was in jeopardy or that my path toward a higher salary or toward a better job was jeopardized by my gender. Any reser- vations that anyone had about women were pretty much personal as opposed to occupational. And they would say it right out loud. That is as bad as it ever got, so I never had to be worried about being passed over or disrespected behind my back.

Under Orville Henry's editorship, sports became a strong suit at the Gazette. *And nothing was more important than Razorback football. Unlike many other states, Arkansas had no professional football team. The Razorbacks filled that niche.*

McConnell: There was a time when I went along with Orville and some others sometimes too to cover the Razorback games, the football games particularly. But I would go along to do the sidebar, and we might have somebody else . . . Orville always wrote the game story, and I did a dressing-room story. Usually go to one or the other dressing room. It might be Arkansas's dressing room or it might be the other team's.

Reed: What did you do during the game?

McConnell: I sat in the press box and took notes and kept track of the game. I guess sometimes I was helping Orville funnel his copy to whatever source. When we first started, we sent our copy by Western Union. They still had Western Union operators in the press box.

Reed: You mean you would actually tear off a piece of copy and give it to the operator?

McConnell: Right. Orville would write his, or I would write it on a typewriter, and then take that sheet of paper and hand it to the operator, and she would keyboard it in and send it back to the *Gazette* . . . Orville was not a touch typist and neither was I. I was a two-fingered typist, but Orville, there is no telling how fast he could go.

Reed: Do you still use the two-fingered method on your computer?

McConnell: Yes, I do. I always told people I could type as fast as I could think with two fingers.

Jim Barden: I sat by Bill Lewis. Bill was an incredibly fast writer and typist. We would have typing races when there was nothing to do. [*Laughter.*] I mean, we'd sit around and see who could type—I never beat him. Talking about competition, the staff was very competitive about everything and on everybody about everything. Any mistakes were—people were constantly on top of each other and made fun of—maybe not good but well deserved. I remember at one point there was going to be a [contest over] who was the worst speller as far as their copy went, and I think it was between me and, again, Bill Lewis, who had disdained ever looking at a dictionary. I would go to the dictionary, and Bill never bothered. He used to say that wasn't part of the writer's job. It was the editor's. . . . The editors were supposed to correct his spelling. I believe that Bill Lewis was the worst speller by one or two words during the week of the competition. He beat me out by one or two words. But he never consulted the dictionary.

One of the thrills of newspapering was the deadline pressure.

John Brummett: One morning Jimmy [Jones, the state editor] got me out of bed and said, "The Allied Telephone Company in Harrison has blown up. . . .

So I went up and spent the day just looking around and talking to people, trying to figure out what the ramifications were. I remember just walking the square at Harrison, trying to see just how far away things were destroyed. It was an extraordinary thing. The Allied people flew back about six thirty, and I strolled back in that office about seven. The deadline is seven thirty. Jimmy says, "Damn it, why didn't you call?" I said, "Jimmy, the phone company blew up. I didn't have a way to call." [*Laughter.*] One thing I am, and that is fast. I knocked that story out. . . . The most fun I had was having to write on deadlines: a big story like a tornado or going to the capitol and, say, something came up at four that afternoon. You are working the phones and getting information. You are writing and have to get it done by seven or seven thirty. That was what it was all about.

Dumas: Those are the best stories too. I look back on those type of things, and the best stories were the ones I did under pressure. If I've got a lot time to polish, it just comes out stiff.

Brummett: The energy in that place, when the deadline is approaching and Bill Rutherford is getting a little nervous on the copy desk. The beat reporters start coming in. There were not a lot of editor meetings, like there came to be later. Whatever you got, that's what got put in the paper. It was sort of a reporter-driven culture. You get it, and it could be something that you didn't advise the desk of earlier. But they got it in somehow. It was tremendous energy, great fun.

Dumas: From five to eight o'clock it was the place to be in.

Brummett: Yes. I was smoking in those days. Some days I would have three to four cigarettes going at a time, sitting back there trying to knock out those stories. I was loving it.

Newspaper people keep strange hours. They report for work at all hours of the day. On a morning paper, only a few editors show up before midmorning. A substantial force gets there in late afternoon and stays through the evening. A handful are there until about three in the morning.

Garrison: When I first went to work at the *Gazette* [as a reporter], I came to work at two thirty in the afternoon. That was the first two years, and I would cover the federal beat, try to get in a little supper, and then cover a night meeting and get off after the night meeting, along about 11:00 p.m. After two years, my hours began whenever I felt I needed to come on. Usually, I would report in about ten in the morning and leave about eight or nine at night. The hours varied depending on the news load. I would be going to work on a schedule that kept me away from morning traffic and coming home on a schedule that kept me away from the evening traffic. So, that part I thought was great. . . . I didn't turn in overtime. During the legislative session, I would ask for some extra time off in return for working long hours. And that would give me a three-week vacation rather than a two-week vacation and enable us to take some trips out west.

Making a mistake was always embarrassing for a reporter, but getting a name wrong was especially bad.

Garrison: I can remember that shortly after I came to the *Gazette,* I got a name wrong. [A. R. Nelson, the managing editor] came over to my desk where I was working and told me that there was a man named Jack Pickens, a major building contractor who had an office in the *Gazette* building, and I somehow got his name in the paper as Jim Pickens. And Mr. Nelson came over and said, you know, his name is Jack Pickens. . . . I was very embarrassed by it. I probably hadn't been there but about two months.

Newsroom equipment tended toward the retro, both in quality and quantity.

Garrison: There would be two desks and one phone. And sometimes you just would have to wait, maybe thirty minutes while a neighboring reporter was finishing up the use of the phone. Usually, beat reporters—who weren't there during the day—shared a phone with a general assignment reporter.

Reed: What kind of typewriters did you have?

Garrison: Well, they were Underwoods and Royals, the way I remember it. And they sometimes worked and sometimes didn't. And they were not always in the best of repair. I remember on the city desk—it may have occurred after I left there, but Jerry Jones accidentally knocked Bill Shelton's typewriter to the floor. It broke, but was still functioning. Shelton was still using it. The *Gazette* went to computers a year after I left there, in 1973. And I remember the reporters telling me about this wonderful machine, that when you were writing, you could go back in and insert a phrase or a sentence somewhere in the paragraph you had already written, and you didn't have to tear out the copy and cross it out in pencil. It was just right there—you'd make the change right there on the machine. I was notorious for having trouble getting the first three paragraphs written, and I would rip it out and start again with a fresh sheet of paper. And then I would go on from there, and then frequently, if I made some more mistakes, more than I thought was acceptable, I would tear out that much of the story and then start over and then I would paste the two pieces together when I got through.

Reed: There were paste pots around just for that purpose. . . . Then there was the row of Teletype machines over against one wall.

Garrison: And they clacked away all day long and all night long. . . . Pat Carithers would be going in there, ripping off the articles as they came in over the Teletype machine.

Reed: Can you describe the sound of the Teletype machines?

Garrison: It was like someone typing into a magnifying amplifier that made it louder, and the typing never stopped. It was constant, clackety-clack-clack.

Ken Danforth: Smoking was particularly perilous because computers hadn't been invented and we worked purely with paper. And the paper baskets would fill up by 7:30 p.m. After that there was no attempt to throw paper into the paper basket. So you would be wading through paper as you walked through the newsroom. And in addition to editing copy, I had to write headlines, and I had a box of continuous copy paper folded in this box. . . . We had to know how to count headlines. Uppercase *W* and *M* was two; uppercase *I* was one. All the other uppercase letters were one and a half. Lowercase *i, l, t,* and *j* were a half a count. You had to go through there counting them. So you would type it out on one of these rolls of paper and see if it fit. If it didn't, you would rip it off your typewriter and throw it away—throw it on the floor—and then start over. . . . The slot man, the news editor of the night—Bob Douglas, if you were lucky—he would look through the story deciding mentally where he might put it, whether it was front page or inside.

Anne Farris: So there was no meeting of editors, as there is today, to decide what would go on the front page?

Danforth: No, not at all.

Farris: It was all one slot editor who would make the decision?

Danforth: Yes, that was it. . . . After supper the managing editor would go home. There were no meetings. . . . There was a really good editor named Pat Carithers who ripped the wire copy . . . Pat stood up at a big slanted desk, and he was masterful at putting together pieces from the AP and UPI and putting them together into a coherent whole. Cut and paste. It wasn't a term of art then. It was just what you did. And that would be the story he would put in. But the stories from the police beat and from the state desk, they just went into a two-tiered tray in front of the news editor, Bob Douglas. And the honorable thing to do would be to take the top story, not to rifle around in there looking for something short. Why do it anyway? You're working eight hours. But some guys liked to do that. So you would take the story and go through there with your pencil, a big, black copy pencil, marking paragraphs. Paragraphs might be there, but you still had to mark them. Doing transpositions, maybe moving a paragraph higher. You might see something that wasn't clear, and it couldn't be fixed with pencil editing, so you would type it out, cut the story in half, and stick your insertion in there. We had one police reporter. You had to totally rewrite everything he wrote. He was good at getting the cops to talk, but he couldn't have written the legend on a Safeway bag. But the stuff was there, so you had to do that. And then writing the head, and then you'd put it in the news editor's in-basket, and he would go through it and send it to the composing room. What I suppose is lost today is that the composing room—maybe I should say for people who don't know about newspapers—this is where the type is put together and the headlines are assembled. It was just a few paces away from the copy desk. . . . And we had one guy back there who was particularly sharp. He wouldn't worry about minor transgressions. If he saw something he thought was going to embarrass the paper or something bad, he would come out there. And he would go to Bob, or my initials would be on it, and he would go up and say, "Hey, what about this?" And invariably we were grateful for it. It wasn't like he was a busybody. He would make good catches. But you could go back there, you could go through this steel door in there, and there was all this hot lead back there and the composing tables and uppercase and lowercase display heads being set. It was right there. We really had a community of people putting out the paper. And I liked that a lot.

Farris: And how quick a pace did you all have to work? Was it heated?

Danforth: Very, very, very quick pace, a lot of pressure. We'd work hard and then we'd play hard. As soon as they said the first edition was put to bed, it was out the door.

Farris: Yes, until it was ready for the second edition?

Danforth: Yes. There wasn't too much to do with the second edition, but we were very careful with the city edition.

Martha Douglas: My most vivid memories are election days, you know, and election nights. It was just organized chaos, as you remember, during elections. Everybody knew what they were supposed to do, and you had deadlines and you met all of those. And it was—if somebody from the outside were looking in, they'd think, "This is the most disorganized place I've ever seen in my life," and yet all of us knew exactly what we were supposed to do. It was fun. The next morning was not such fun because if you had to come in to work early, you'd been up a pretty long time. It was pretty tough.

Reed: And the next day with all those tables of votes.

Martha Douglas: Oh, yes, all the boring stuff, you know, dull, boring stuff.

Reed: And then you'd have to analyze it and so forth. James Warren, do you remember him on election nights? . . . Bringing in sandwiches? I never knew where he got them.

Martha Douglas: They weren't very good either.

Reed: No! [*Laughs.*] Do you remember the story, was it being told when you were in the newsroom, about an election night years before when a governor of Arkansas had the presumption to walk upstairs into the newsroom and Fred Heiskell threw him down the stairs? . . . It was always told to illustrate the fact that the newsroom was a working place, and it was not a town gathering spot as some people would like to have made it, and also to illustrate that even the governor couldn't just come barging in uninvited. . . . I think it also helped that this particular governor was not well liked by Fred Heiskell and the *Gazette* staff.

Donald: They rigged this kind of strange gizmo that moved copy from the copy desk to the back shop. . . . It was, that is the best you could call it, was a contraption because what it was, it was done with pipes and a belt. And it ran from the copy desk up a pole to the ceiling, and then it traveled across the ceiling and then back to another copy desk back in sports, and it was still traveling around. It made more noise, and then, somehow or another, it would go over the wall, back into the back shop, and drop off in a basket back there. This was copy. Instead of having copy boys running, they would stick it on this gizmo. The thing never worked right, and paper copy was always falling off here, falling off there, and, eventually, when they changed the news room, incidentally, when they did some redecorating, they found about half the copy had fallen down in the wall itself. So it never got into the back shop.

Dumas: There was a copy editor named Ray Kornegay, . . . an elderly fellow who was a wonderful copy editor and a wonderful old guy and a great storyteller and just a rabid leftist. Ray was about sixty-five, I think, when he went to work there. And he was always in a towering rage. But he hated that conveyer belt. The noise just drove him crazy. And every day I thought he was just going to climb up there and rip that thing out.

Jordan: If you remember, Ray was there the day that it broke or that night. It was real close to deadline, and that broke, and that thing started whipping around and whipping him [*laughs*] with that broken conveyor belt. Ray jumped up on it with his pocketknife and cut it and just started whipping it and cutting it. [*Laughs.*] . . . He was cutting it, and it cost about eight thousand dollars or something. [*Laughs.*] They almost fired old Ray over that. . . . The copy editors in those days, the early days, were wonderful. They were well read. You couldn't slip anything by them. . . . They'd catch you doing something, and that's what Ray did one day. He yelled back there, and he said, "Hey, Jordan!" And I said, "Yes!" And he said, "Let me ask you something, boy." He said, "In the *Arkansas Gazette,* do we apprehend anyone?"

And I said, "Well . . . ," And he said, "Answer my question!" [*Laughter.*] And I said, "Well, I didn't." And he said, "You damn fool! You don't apprehend anything in the *Gazette*. You arrest them." [*Laughter.*] So I said, "Well, thanks." When the copy editors started rampaging, everyone just kind of cowered because they were so, like you say, arrogant.

A newspaper library is called the "morgue." In more trusting times, people came in from the street to use the Gazette's morgue.

Linda Pine: A young man who had been there a year or so longer than I had—he always told the story about one night he was working, and we were open. There was no security guard downstairs. Anybody could wander in up to the newsroom. He was working, and two men showed up at the counter and said they wanted to see what the *Gazette* had written on a guy name John Moore. . . . And what we would do, if we had multiple individuals with the same name, the envelope we would keep the clipping in would have a little distinguishing sentence. So it might say, "John Moore, judge" or "John Moore, mayor of Sheridan" or "John Moore, police chief of Forrest City." So Joey goes back and is looking through all these envelopes, and he says, "[John Moore], convicted of two murder charges," and the guy says, "That's me!" And it was about ten thirty at night, and he is thinking, "Oh, my lord." . . . Occasionally, we had attorneys wander in and want clipping files. We would also get phone calls from individuals . . . It was almost that they believed that the *Gazette* was a state agency and that this information was available to them under the Freedom of Information Act. I mean, it was a public institution. So we would get calls from someone who would say, "I need to know, I need you to look for an obituary. I think my uncle died in 1964." And we would say, "We can't do that, and we don't have a list of this. It's not indexed." And they'd say, "Well, you can't tell me that you're not going to do it. This is a public institution; you can't deny me this information." And we would have to explain, "Well, we're not denying you the information; what we're saying is that (A) we don't have the time and (B) you can't get it in that particular form." But I did, over time, come to realize that the view really was that the *Gazette* was almost like calling Washington or calling your congressman. . . . If you said, "No, you can't see all the news clippings related to the Public Service Commission because you are doing a paper," their view was that "I have a legal right to it." . . . Now, in one particular instance, we did have an attorney come in who wanted something extraordinary from us; I cannot actually remember now what it was. It was going to be a monster research project. And we said we were closed. And he proceeded to just tear us up, threaten us, tell us he was a friend of Carrick Patterson. He was just gonna— we were going to lose our jobs. . . . Carrick Patterson came down and said that if this guy ever showed up again and threatened his employees, he would be booted out and never permitted to come in the building again. Carrick backed us up . . . With most of the reporters, many of them would come back just to visit. They enjoyed us. We were a lively lot. There were your occasional arrogant individuals. We did have one reporter who came back and actually asked us how to spell *apropos*. And we told her, A-P-R-O-P-O-S. And they didn't believe us. And when they went and checked it in the dictionary and turned around and said, "I can't believe you stupid people would know how to spell."

Pat Best: One thing about the *Gazette* building . . . it was never locked. I mean twenty-four hours, it was never locked. I would go in in the mornings sometimes, and there might be someone asleep in the restroom. There would be a woman asleep in the ladies' restroom asleep. She obviously came in off the street. It happened many times, more than once for sure. . . . Everything was dark except for my office. Even the hallway down to the other door, all of it was dark. Nobody was on that second floor except me, or sometimes the cleaning people. I heard the door open once, and a man came up. He was drunk! He started talking to me. He backed up and pulled out a pocketknife from his pocket and opened it. He put it between his two fingers and said, "I am so good with this knife. I could stand right here and throw it and hit you right between the eyes." Anyway, he didn't throw it. He did go away. At that time I immediately called circulation. They were the only other people there. Some of the circulation guys came up and looked around. I told my mother, who—I didn't know at the time—told my daddy. It was still dark outside. The next door that I heard open was my daddy coming down the hallway. He looked all over that building. The man obviously left. He just came in out of the cold or something, just like everybody else did who needed a good warm place.

Paul Johnson: The thing that I think that all of us who were there in that era remember is the old wooden floor. Parquet. I guess it was oak. It seemed impervious to wear. The smell was—Bob Douglas and I were both tremendous cigar smokers at that time. Each afternoon at about four thirty, Bob and I would send a copy boy out. There was a tobacco shop on the ground floor of one of the banks there on Louisiana Street, I guess. He would buy ten cigars for Bob and ten for me, and over the course of the evening, we would smoke those ten cigars. [*Laughter.*] Of course, everybody would flick their ashes on the floor. Nobody had ash trays . . . There was always someone hollering, "Copy," to get one of the copy boys.

Nate Allen: I was the copy boy. I changed the paper and changed the ribbon on the Teletypes, and I went and got people coffee. I went and got people cigarettes. But mainly I carried the copy from the desk. You know, you'd pick it up off a spike and take it back in the back shop to the typographer. . . . It was noisy. There were great, big, wonderful, old, noisy, smelly Linotype machines. It was just fantastic to watch that all transferred into hot type. And, you know, you'd bring proofs back, and you'd read them as you go along, and you'd try to find the errors and point them out to people.

Paul Nielsen: I am very fond of recalling that wonderful frenzy of checking the early copies of the paper. We were a U-shaped desk, with seats for maybe six or seven around the outside, and we sat with our backs to a row of windows that fronted on Third Street. There was a space between the backs of our chairs and those windows, and it would end up just hip deep in tear sheets. The shop foreman would bring an armload of early copies up to the copy desk, and we'd start devouring them. Just tearing into them. I think [Richard] Portis was the one who started the process of just ripping the paper apart. You'd tear your page out, scan it down really fast, and then get rid of it. Get it off the desk. Get it away. It was done. Rip out the next page. Finish it. Throw it behind you. Rip out the next page. If you found something, tell Douglas or Carter, and somebody would go running back to the composing room or the presses. And on and on, like sharks around bleeding meat. By the end of this process, all that space right behind the desk would be filled with tear sheets from the paper. Like a pile of leaves in the fall. Ah, it was frantic.

Barden: Well now, one thing about—were there ever any big fights in the newsroom or big disagreements while you were there?

Nielsen: I don't remember anything particularly colorful, except the time Douglas threw me out of the newsroom because I'd been drinking too much. This happened after I had left the *Gazette* to join the *Democrat*. The *Democrat* was an afternoon paper and the *Gazette* was a morning paper, so I was done with my work and the poor *Gazette* folks were working. I was bothering them. I don't remember what I did or said, but I'm sure I deserved to get thrown out.

Richard Allen: The terrific thing was that nobody whistled. You know, it was bad luck to whistle in a newsroom. I learned this from Bob Douglas. Anybody whistles around me in the newsroom, I start screaming at them. [*Laughter.*] It was an old tradition. Do not whistle in a newsroom. I saw Bob Douglas telling copy editors to stop whistling in the newsroom.

Ronald Farrar: Reporters all wore coats and ties. Nobody ever told us to, and I could have easily not worn one over in North Little Rock. But I felt like that this was a certain mark of respect. . . . The copy desk didn't. It didn't matter. Nelson wore a starched, white shirt, brown suit, brown shoes every day. Like a preacher.

Clark: Under the Pattersons we would have Christmas parties with alcohol.

Farris: In the newsroom?

Clark: Yes, in the newsroom. That stopped when Gannett took over. There was no more alcohol then . . . They banned smoking too in the newsroom, I think. . . . When I got there in the early 1980s, there were more than several smokers in the newsroom.

Reporters played pranks on each other during slack periods. Copy editors wrote verse. Some of the limericks were saved by Julia Jones Drury. The authors are anonymous:

There once was a Harv from the Bronx
Who ate cheeses that smelled worse than skonx.
His friends held him at bay,
Then sent him away,
And now he is living with monx.

There once was a looney named Bradley
Whose demeanor was that of Boo Radley.
Too blank was his stare,
Too listless his air,
And his headlines were always writ badly.

There once was a lady named Mazy
Whose knowledge of style was quite hazy.
She used whichs for thats,
And ins for ats,
And claimed nations were driving her crazy.

Julia Jones also remembered the way staffers treated the office bulletin board. When Hariett Aldridge, the food editor, posted a note asking for favorite recipes to use in a food feature, reporters and editors flooded the board with suggestions. Typical was one from Jerry Jones, a jazz enthusiast, with a recipe for "Hot Suet Ralston," to be eaten sitting on the rillarah, *calling up a nonsense ballad by Sammy Kaye. Doug Smith's in its entirety read, "Remove hot dog from package, heat, place on bun, eat." Julia said, "Harriet was so pissed, she didn't even collect them."*

Bill Lewis: The newsroom was a jumble of papers stacked on desks. I did all of my work on an old Underwood [typewriter], which I didn't realize took so much physical effort until we got computers. I'd pound on that thing all day long and come home absolutely exhausted! I didn't realize that it was just the physical effort of pounding on those keys all day. It started out quietly. In the morning, when I got in, there were rarely ever more than two people there . . . But, then, as the day went on, it got noisier and noisier and more busy and so forth, and when the capitol crew came in, that's when it got to be fun to me. One of the things that I loved about newspapering was that it was so unpredictable. I mean, it was a new world every day. You go down there, and I usually had no idea what I'd be doing the next day except for those leftover things that I was still working on. That was just great fun. I really, really enjoyed that aspect of it . . .As everybody else came in, it just seemed to liven the place up with everyone sharing stories and that sort of thing, tales about what went on that weren't news stories.

Fire was a newsroom hazard, but it never spread far.

Reed: Do you remember the night that your wastebasket caught fire?
Tom Davis: I don't particularly remember it. I think the story was that I continued to take care of the copy and took care of the fire later.
Reed: You didn't have a thing to do with putting out the fire. Some copy boy got some water and put on it. I took it to be testimony to your power of concentration. How did it catch fire?
Davis: Everybody smoked then. Cigarettes—three or four packs a day.

There was occasional violence in the newsroom. There was the night when the copy desk chief slugged a star reporter, Ray Moseley, while Moseley was sitting in for an editor on the city desk..

Douglas: Tom Swint kind of had it in for Ray, and some said it was because Ray was going to New York and he resented that. I don't know whether that is true or not, but it was silly, the whole argument. You couldn't even call it an argument. Tom hit him. Tom's a big guy, strong, pretty good hands. He hit him when he was sitting down and had his face turned. Tom wasn't a coward, but it was just—he wasn't a cowardly man, but it was a brutal thing to do. And then he jumped on him when he was down and beat him some more until he was unconscious, got a concussion. And Ronnie Farrar, I didn't see this, but Ronnie Farrar is the one who broke it up.

Ray Moseley: I don't remember the details, but some wire story came out of New York. And Swint came over to me and said, "I think we ought to get some reaction on this here." And I said, "Well, we covered that in the paper yesterday." And he went away, kind of grumbling. And, you know, I wondered afterwards. He may have been right. Maybe I should have done it even though we had already . . . Anyway, I was working away there at the desk, and he came by. There was a coat rack there, and he started putting on his coat to go out to dinner, and I looked up and he gave me a really dirty look, and he said, "Don't you say a word." And he really said it in an angry voice. And I said, "Fuck you, Tom." [*Laughter.*] The next thing I knew I woke up in the hospital because he knocked me out with one punch. I'd had a front tooth, half of it knocked out by a baseball when I was young. He knocked the cap off that tooth. And I was down on the floor, bleeding, I guess, and Tom was on top of me, still pounding away at me. Apparently . . . [Ron Farrar] came up and pulled Swint off me. If he hadn't, I suppose I might have died because people said I was choking on my blood and turning blue. Anyway, I remember waking up for a second in the ambulance taking me to the hospital, and then I was out again. And then I finally woke up in the hospital, and there was a young blond reporter there, Bill Rutherford. I saw him standing there, and I said, "Bill, what happened?" And he said, "I don't know, Ray. I was back in the composing room," or something. And I lay there, and I said, "I remember what happened. Tom Swint hit me." And he said, "Well, I don't know anything about it." Anyway, Tom Swint was asked to leave, I think, after that. I'd already given notice I was leaving. I left the *Gazette* about a week or two after that. . . . He must have hit me pretty well for me to be out for as long as I was. That's probably why I am brain damaged today. [*Laughter.*] I wondered, you know, I seriously wondered, whether I should bring a baseball bat with me when I came to work the next day, but Tom Swint and I never exchanged another word in the time we spent . . . I told my sister about it. My sister was living in Houston. She got so angry she and her husband called up Tom Swint and gave him hell over the phone. [*Laughs.*] . . . Several weeks before that, there was a party . . . and Tom Swint had almost gotten in a fight with Richard Davis there because he had made a sandwich or something and left it, and Richard took a bite out of it. And Swint just went to pieces over it. I guess he was just ready to slug him. I think Bob Douglas pulled them apart.

Alcohol was the invisible presence in the newsroom down through the years. Mostly it went unremarked, but now and then it called attention to itself.

Bob Douglas: Clovis Copeland [a reporter] was a pilot. I don't think he was in the air force. He was in the CAP, Civilian Air Patrol, something like that. And he always had excuses to be late showing up for work. This one [time] he called and said he was in Atlanta and he was rained in, having trouble taking off, and he might be a little late. Well, he was there in about twenty or thirty minutes [*laughs*]. Came in with an old World War I pilot's uniform, one of those caps, and drunk as a boiled owl. [*Laughter.*]

Richard Allin: Also, people drank during the day at the old *Gazette*. The one exception—well, there may have been more than one exception—J. N. Heiskell did not drink on the job, but many, many others did. One or two editorial writers would come in and do their work before noon, because after noon they would be past goin'. I can remember the Sunday editor, Charlie Davis, a guy that I liked very much. Charlie was drinking all the time. I never knew how he put out a Sunday section that looked as well as it did. Then that changed. I mean, now, no one, no one takes a drink in the newspaper business. Or it's very rare.

Farrar: No one drank in the newsroom. They would come to the newsroom having drunk, of course, at times. As a matter of fact, there were a couple of copy editors, I think, that were pretty well liquored up a lot of evenings. There was a little press club right across the street, and sometimes we'd go over there for a beer after work.

Technology was a continuing challenge for reporters.

John Reed: At some point, they gave me a laptop, and I hated that because you had to attach it to these phone couplings. One time I covered the Gillett Coon supper, and I needed [a phone coupling], and [U.S. representative] Marion Berry was very, very helpful. He let me go into his bedroom, I think, where he had a telephone, and fool with my laptop and curse at it while I was trying to get it hooked up to a telephone. It took me half an hour to get my story transmitted. . . . Another time—gosh, that Coon supper is in January or February . . . It's in the dead of winter, and at that time there was actually a pay phone in Gillett, out in the middle of a cornfield, bean fields, and I did this business with my laptop connected to the telephone and this functioning pay phone in the middle of this field, and it was only five degrees. And the wind was whipping around, and it wasn't even a pay phone that went down to the ground. The glass wall only went about down to about knee high, and so on top of having, not having the technical know-how expertise to hook up my laptop, my fingers would hardly move either. . . . Of course now, all the reporters you see have cell phones; they have laptops, just super duper things, and they're used to using them, and I have a laptop at my new job, and it's a lot better. But except for a few occasions of having to mess with a laptop, the technology part of the *Gazette* was pretty easy. Basically it was to sit at my desk in the newsroom on the second floor of the *Gazette* building and type on a word processor. With the deadline pressures we had, with the newspaper war and the constant battle with *Democrat* reporters, if we had had to mess with computers, it would have driven me crazy because guys like Paul Barton [his rival at the *Democrat*] were just bulldogs.

Joe Mosby: I wrote columns sitting on the tailgate of a pickup truck, for instance. I wrote them on picnic tables in state parks. Many columns I wrote in motel rooms at night. My years at the *Gazette* were in a time of technological changes. We still used portable typewriters and got into tele-copiers. They were predecessors to the fax machine. They were cumbersome things you carried around. It took, I believe it was, six minutes to transmit one 8½ × 11–inch page of typed copy. Then we got into the early comput-ers, or I guess you call them computers. They were fairly compact machines made by Texas Instruments . . . In the eighties, I'm not sure of the year, maybe '82, '83, we got compact little Radio Shack computers, Model 100. They were light; they were portable, battery operated or AC powered. You could hook them to a phone anywhere and transmit your material to the home office. Those were very helpful to me. I transmitted stories from all kinds of strange places out in the boondocks. . . . Used a phone line. You'd use a pay phone, for instance—just stop on the side of the road at a pay phone. At times noise from passing eighteen-wheelers would interfere.

Hamburger: We had used the typewriters to write the stories—and we had these newfangled computers in that year, 1977. My friend from [Oberlin College] was there, Eric Black. He was kind of a whiz at those computers. . . . I mean, here I was who had worked hard at the *Gazette,* and I was leaving, and Jimmy said, "I've got one last thing for you to do. Write McClellan's obituary." It was to be about 150 inches. So I wrote his obituary, which started out—I remember the lead was "John McClellan, Arkansas's dour con-servative senator, died . . ." So Eric was showing me—I think I was con-cerned, and when I went through it, I hadn't spelled *McClellan* right, or something. He showed me how you could do a search and replace. Eric came over to my computer as I was just about to turn it in. It was 100 inches. I had it done, and I was doing the spell check and just a final, to make sure all the *McClellan*s were spelled right. So Eric said, "This is what you do if you want to replace." He took the copy and wrote, at the top, "McClellan = asshole," and hit enter, and suddenly it went through the whole thing. It said, "John L. Asshole, Arkansas's conservative senator . . . Asshole, as a little boy . . . Asshole was raised by his parents . . . Asshole, Asshole." So I was gassed. I was supposed to be driving out of town in my Gremlin, and Jimmy Jones was waiting for the copy. I said, "Eric, you fix that right now!" [*Laughter.*] He thought you could fix it—he'd just write the shorthand, so it would just replace it really fast. "Ass = McClellan." So then it disappeared from the screen for a while, and it came back up and said, "John L. McClellanhole." [*Laughter.*] But it didn't just change the *Assholes:* it changed everything. So, "His first committee *ass*ignments . . . " Every time there was an *ass* in this long story, it changed it to *McClellan.* So I made Eric stay late. We were there until—I was supposed to leave that afternoon, but I ended up staying until nine thirty at night replacing all the *McClellanholes.*

Richard Portis: Copy editors were still like printers at that time. They were still kind of a transient, kind of drift in from North Carolina, sit down, and start writing headlines. . . . There was a big horseshoe-shaped copy desk, and in the middle of it was a slot, and all around the outside was called the rim, and everyone had his number-one pencils and a typewriter, and in the middle of the slot there was a big basket, an in and out basket. The slot man, who was the news editor, would put the raw copy from the reporters or wire services on the top, and the person, copy editor on the rim, would pick one up, and he would have on the top listed what size headline and sometimes about whether they needed to be cut down. And you would go through and edit, as an editor does—that is, for grammar and style—and then write a headline. . . . Very little grammar correction at the *Gazette.* There was more spelling correction than grammar. Most of the writers at the *Gazette* were instinctive or educated grammarians. But, oddly enough, some of the best writers were awful spellers. Mike Trimble, probably one of the best writers who ever came through the *Gazette,* couldn't spell.

Reed: I've heard that about [Charles] Allbright too.

Richard Portis: Douglas has always stated that Allbright was a bad speller, but Trimble, he would really butcher them.

Reed: That's odd about Trimble because his mother was an English teacher. . . . But so was Allbright's mother.

Farris: Those people were so much fun. They had a lust for life. Great sense of humor, quick wits, a self-deprecating humor. The talk was shop, the talk was news, the talk was politics, the talk was gossip about other people in the newsroom or the management. We loved it. We just had a great time. They were some of the smartest people I've ever met.

Hamburger: There was one story that I love. . . . This also occurred before I got there and might be apocryphal. But you remember that little sort of roof—you could go through a small door and be out on the roof—outside the newsroom? There was a woman copy editor who used to go out there on occasion and have sex with a lover or various lovers from the newsroom. And the roof wasn't visible to anyone but Hugh. When he was standing up, he could see out there. . . . And apparently he was standing up and saw something that did not appeal to him going on on the roof, and he immediately did what a publisher would do. He called Douglas on the phone and said, "I want you to put a stop to this." And Douglas wrote one of the memos— memos were posted on the newsroom wall in those days when it was mostly male newsroom. Anyway, it just said, "To staff. From Bob Douglas. No fucking on the roof."

6

Stories

Scoundrels, Heroes, and Lesser Species

Any day's Gazette could be counted on for the latest installment in the affairs of the city, the state, the nation, and the world. Sometimes the story was politics or government or the latest doings of Arkansas's always colorful politicians. Sometimes it was disaster—a tornado or an explosion in a missile silo. Sensational murders occurred with dismaying frequency. Civil rights and the accompanying violent resistance came along during the 1960s. Bill Clinton was in the paper almost daily from the 1970s on. There were Razorback sports and colorful prison escapes and fads by college students and feature stories with unexpected plot twists. In later years, there was the ever-present desire to beat the Arkansas Democrat *in the "newspaper war" that the* Democrat *eventually won.*

And, year after year, generation after generation, there was corruption. Bob Douglas, one of the last and best of a long line of managing editors, set up teams of investigative reporters to expose not just corruption but all sorts of questionable practices in government.

Bob Douglas: There's always controversy over the letting of the state printing contracts. Well, I sent Tucker Steinmetz out to the capitol with a calculator, and he spent a lot of time in a dusty old basement to find out how it worked. They were doing it according to a formula, which was as crazy as could be. You and I could go in Allsopp and Chapple and buy some plain white paper for a fraction of what the state was paying for it under its blue book.
Reed: Did Tucker's story make a difference? Did anything change?
Douglas: Yes, it did, except some of the changes didn't work out too well.

There was no reason the state couldn't print its own stuff in a lot of cases . . . And one thing they did was buy a press and do some state printing at the penitentiary at Cummins. They put a press out there. Well, can you guess what happened? Started counterfeiting.

Tucker Steinmetz: We did some things on some of the poverty programs that kind of haunted us for a while because there were some abuses. What with three liberal guys, I was supportive of most of their efforts, but some of the charlatans found their way into some of the poverty programs of the Johnson era. We did some more stuff on that. I did a big thing on state printing contracts, which really resulted in some legislation. One of our poverty program things, about five people went to prison after it was over. So, we had some nice experiences doing all that stuff. They cranked it back up, and Jimmy [Jones] and I were back doing the same old thing together.

At midcentury, Arkansas and other states went through a series of scandals involving insurance and stock frauds. Leland DuVall, the Gazette's *business and farm expert, explained one of them.*

Leleand DuVall: I don't remember how many of those companies there were, just one after another. And there was one—I forget the name, Empire Life or something—out on University, and they started to sell it, which they did. There were two men who started it. And while they were still in the business of selling stock and charter policies, the federal government caught up with one of them and sent him to jail. They came here from New Mexico. One was a used-car salesman, and the other one had a land-development thing on one of the desert spots out in New Mexico. And so they'd been in that promotion, and they put in this insurance thing. And so they sent this guy to jail. And while he was in jail, the one who didn't go to jail stole the other one's interest in the company. [*Laughs.*] So he ended up with all of it. And the jailbird got out; he was livid with rage because he'd lost everything he'd had in it, you know? And he came down to my office complaining about that other crook stealing him out while he was in jail. And so I asked him, I said, "Well, how did you people sell this stock in the first place? What was your sales point? Sell me stock in your company. I'm a prospect and you do the selling." So he started selling me. And it was the most convincing sales pitch you ever heard. I mean there wasn't a way you could lose. He sold a deal that sounded solid. "You know, what you do is you buy common stock and preferred shares, and in ninety days, if you don't like what you've got, they'll give you your money back. Except you can keep the common stock that goes with the package. And they'll give you all your money back. And you know, you just can't lose." Except, when you read it—he had a prospectus there—and when you read down in it, they promise to do that if you make the claim on January the fifteenth or whatever day it was at that time. And if the company has five million dollars in unassigned surplus in their treasury, they pay you out of that. If they don't have the five million in unassigned surplus, why, they don't pay you, you know? [*Laughs.*] They're not obligated. Well, unless you read that you don't know that that's what they're going to do. And it turns out that's the way they sell the stock. I said, "Well, how do you sell that when people can look at that and see that you're not going to make the payment?" He said, "They don't have to do that. They just read down to where it says you'll get your money back if you don't like it." He said, "That's as far as they go." Just get your money back. [*Laughs.*]

When scandal erupted at the capitol, that was Ernest Dumas's territory. He had become the Gazette's *main reporter on government and politics and, in time, would be a major source on Arkansas for traveling national reporters.*

Dumas: One story was the Arkansas Loan and Thrift scandal, which would have been about 1967, '68, '69. The scandal covered the latter years of the Faubus administration. There had been some guys over at Fort Smith, a guy named Ernest A. Bartlett Jr. that had found an old defunct building and loan charter that was maybe thirty or forty years old that had been unused. And he got this thing and made a company out of that charter, not a savings and loan association, and it was not chartered as a bank, but it was some hybrid outfit under some old law. And he was using this, and there were a whole bunch of public officials in on it. The charter was written in the office of the attorney general, Bruce Bennett, and he got stock in the company, and one of his deputies who actually drafted the charter became a stockholder in it. A number of other prominent political figures were involved, Representative Paul Van Dalsem, state Senator Joe Lee Anderson of Helena. This thing operated for three or four years, advertising heavily in western Arkansas, and got a lot of widows and churches to take their money out of savings accounts, church building funds and put them into the Arkansas Loan and Thrift because they were promised a higher interest rate than banks or S&Ls could pay under the law. And so they operated pretty freely for those years, and they would build up deposits quickly of about four million dollars. And then all of a sudden in about 1968, it was shut down. The Securities and Exchange Commission came in, and . . . they went to the federal district court of Fort

Smith and petitioned to close it, put it out of business, and Judge John E. Miller of Fort Smith did so . . . I was making copies of all of these records, and I came back and just wrote stories day after day. And then we found out that what had happened was that they had—the bankers were upset about it because this place was draining off deposits from the banks and S&Ls were upset about it. So what happened was that the state S&L regulator who was also the state security commissioner, a guy named Clint Jones in the Faubus administration, he wrote the attorney aeneral's office, asking Attorney General Bruce Bennett, "Is Arkansas Loan and Thrift an S&L and can we regulate it?" And Bruce Bennett wrote back and said, "No, it is not a savings and loan association, and your office has no authority to regulate this company." The state bank commissioner, Dick Simpson, wrote a letter saying, "Is this a bank and can we regulate it?" And Bruce Bennett writes a letter back to Simpson saying, "It is not a bank. You cannot regulate it." And so the state insurance department says, "There is a thing called a savings and guaranty corporation that has been set up to guarantee assets. Is this an insurance company that we can regulate?" Bruce Bennett wrote an opinion back, "No, it is not an insurance company set up under the statutes, laws of the state of Arkansas. You cannot regulate it." None of these opinions were put out for the public. We never saw them. Those opinions were put in a box and recorded as so. These never made it out into the box, and I just found a copy of them in the files at the Arkansas Loan and Thrift. . . . And so I wrote a long series of stories about it, and all of these guys were indicted. The attorney general was indicted, and the president was indicted, and two people from Booneville were indicted, and there were charges in federal district court. . . . Bruce came up with cancer and lived another ten years and was never tried. . . . Claude Carpenter, the attorney for governor Faubus, he was involved.

Attorney General Steve Clark, one of the state's more promising young politicians, got caught padding his expense account. Anne Farris was the reporter. As a daughter of John Herbers, a New York Times reporter, she had grown up in Washington and knew a corruption story when she saw it.

Anne Farris: I think the biggest story for me at the *Arkansas Gazette* was in 1990. I went to the appropriate agencies to get the filings that they were required to submit to the state on how they spent their office budgets, their expense accounts, and their salaries. And they were all easily accessible because it was public information. When I got the attorney general's information, it hit me like a cold slap. It was unbelievable. It was this very detailed explanation of Steve Clark's expenses that the state had paid for, and they were outrageously excessive, especially for Arkansas. We're talking about constitutional officers who earn twenty thousand dollars a year, including the governor at the time, and here was Clark spending tens of thousands of dollars on meals and travel. He had four-hundred-dollar lunches. . . . He would list the people who he had dined with to verify and justify that it was a state expense. He listed congressmen, federal judges, representatives from other attorney generals' offices. He also listed these very expensive travel expenditures to Hawaii or Washington, DC. . . . So the story went on the front page about how exorbitant these expenditures were, and the next day I walked into the office, and Brummett had a "Return This Call" slip. He said, "You need to call this woman. She called me this morning. Her name is Marilyn Porter. She works for the Clinton campaign, and she's listed in Steve Clark's expense accounts, and she is pissed because there is no way she would ever have lunch with Steve Clark. Here he is running against Bill Clinton! She thinks she's been sabotaged." So I called her up, and she said, "I have never had lunch with Steve Clark. I never will have lunch with Steve Clark." . . . People who are listed were never there, time and time again. I went back to work full time then for a year starting on that day. There was no warning. We launched a major undertaking. There were seven reporters under me, helping make calls to all these people to figure out exactly what was true and what wasn't. I thought, "Well, wait a minute: if there are his expense accounts, there must be other stuff." I wanted everything. I went back to the attorney general's office, and they gave to me everything without question. I got all the telephone calls from his home and from the attorney general's office. . . . They were the actual bills, so I could see every call he ever made from his office phone and his home because he charged everything to the state. It was like he had no personal expenses. The telephone logs were the mother lode. But I got airline tickets and everything that he claimed expenses for. I remember having to carry it out in a dolly. . . . And so we took them all back over to the *Arkansas Gazette,* and the next day the state police went to the attorney general's office and confiscated all of those documents. . . . We spent the next six months writing story after story after story based on these logs. We had to call these numbers, and a lot of the telephone numbers were to his girlfriends. He was not married. He was divorced, and he had all these girlfriends he was calling long distance with state money. We'd call a number, and we would reach women who would spill the story because they were jilted lovers. They would tell you everything. . . . We found eighty-dollar shots of cognac and expensive entrees. It was a plethora of paper. It was a reporter's dream, and I can take no credit for the success of that story because it was just so easy. . . . So we published this series of stories, and the stories prompted him to, within days, hold a press conference and drop out of the gubernatorial race.

Anne Farris was also one of the first Gazette *reporters to cover another rising political star.*

Farris: I was always having to ask Clinton to stop long enough to find a telephone so I could file my story, and he was always gracious in doing that. He didn't have a problem because I'm writing about him, of course, but I filed the story that night about the varying opinions of Clinton: that he was loved and hated. I told about the love-fest breakfast with five hundred people showing up. But then, at the same time, here he was deep in Republican territory where he was scorned, and there was high disapproval from the people I had talked to, in the man on the street interviews. The next day I showed up at the capitol because he wasn't traveling that day. When he saw me, he launched in to me, physically too. He didn't touch me, but his sheer presence—he's pretty tall—caused me to back up against a wall, and he kept pointing his finger toward my throat and screaming at me about how unfair my coverage had been. Now, I take a lot of pride in my objectivity and my ability to pull back from any situation and show all ten sides because that's usually how many sides there are to a story. And in this one, I thought I had been fair. I showed both sides. In fact, it was probably one of the fairest stories I had written. Some previous stories had been pretty isolated to my restricted view of Clinton campaigning and the reception he was getting. So I was proud of the story, and I thought I had been really even handed. But he just tore into me. Veins bulging in his throat, he was red faced and screaming at me about how unfair I had been. "How dare you stray from the campaign trail to talk to these people," he said. He accused me of going out of my way to find people who didn't like him. And I tell you, I'm a fighter, but I also know sometimes it's best to just keep quiet.

So I just was very mute, and I finally said something like, "I stand by my story." I could care less what he said. In fact, to me, it was a compliment. I was doing my job. For him to get that upset, to me, was a confirmation that I had done exactly right. I guess because I was so quiet, he realized how loud he was, and he backed off and regained his composure. And he—this was classic Clinton too because I've had him mad at me for other things before, like when I wouldn't play spades with him. Within just a few minutes, he had calmed down, and he came back to make amends. He said, "Anne, I'm sorry. I didn't mean to do that. Now, we're still okay, aren't we? We're still buddies. Come on, Anne. You know, we're all right." I just thought, "Hey, you know, whatever, you're the one who blew up." I just thought that was so interesting that he could change so quickly. He was so used to the press catering to him, and the *Gazette* has been accused many years since then of being much too favorable about Clinton and not coming down hard enough on him. He was used to the press being his playground, and so whenever there was a piece like mine, it just irked him to no end.

And he's still like that. He never seemed to learn that lesson throughout his administration here and in Washington, DC, as president, that the press is not always your friend. Now he did endure unmitigated and perhaps unprecedented press scrutiny. But he didn't seem to understand that good objective journalism is not all glowing. And he takes it so personally. Both he and Hillary Clinton become very personally aggrieved when the press says anything critical about them. And I just expected them to have a lot tougher skin.

David Terrell: I wish I had the notes Clinton used to send me. I had no idea that he would go beyond the first term as governor of Arkansas. In fact, he didn't for a little while there. I would write things especially in a little weekly column that would anger him terribly, and he would send me these crappy little notes. At the same time, we seemed to have a lot in common in some ways. I remember one day I was coming into the capitol carrying a copy of Barbara Tuchman's book on the fourteenth century, *A Distant Mirror*. And Clinton was coming to work, driving along toward his office, spotted that thing and said "Hey, if you like that, I've got a book for you. Come on up after a while." So I went up there to the governor's office, and he had a book he had just finished. It was this, oh, my goodness, a thousand-page impenetrable tome about some monks in a convent in France in the Middle Ages. It was just hideous. And I couldn't possibly read this thing, so I kept it a couple weeks or three and took it back up to him and told him how great it was. He could probably cite you all kinds of statistics and stuff out of that damn book.

. . . I don't know if he's ever had an original thought, but he is a great assimilator of information. I don't think of him as a particularly original thinker, but I've always underestimated him. I mean, I thought while I covered Arkansas politics, I thought there were two people might be presidential temper. Two characters who might one day become president. Either of them. Dale Bumpers and Jim Guy Tucker. It just never crossed my mind that Clinton could do that. I was not the greatest judge of some things political.

Dumas: Those years covering the capitol in the governor's office, were there rumors then about Clinton's womanizing?

Terrell: Oh, sure.

Dumas: Did you all ever decide to look into it?

Terrell: I didn't.

Dumas: At that time we didn't do those kind of things. We heard that about every governor, every politician, just about, to some extent.

Terrell: Oh, every politician of any stature I have ever known has lived amid rumors about his sex life . . . At that time it hardly even seemed out of the ordinary. Moreover, there was nothing that suggested that what might have been going on was in any way connected to policy or politics.

John Brummett covered Bill Clinton's second campaign for governor in 1980, the year the brash young man lost to the Republican Frank White. Brummett worried about becoming too chummy with the candidate. He and Ernest Dumas agreed that politicians generally were far too easy to like.

John Brummett: As I look back now at those dispatches from the 1980 campaign, I can tell as I read them they are almost boosterism. It's obvious that I am caught up in what Clinton said that day.

Dumas: 1982. Clinton runs again. Did you spend any time with him during the period that he was out of office? Did you talk to him much?

Brummett: Yes. We became entirely too close. Yes, I spent time with him. We did a little socializing, but not much. I was a little younger than he was. I wasn't one of his best buddies, but I spent some time with him. I had dinner with him, had drinks at the Afterthought with him. I would see him on the sidewalk and pull over and say, "Where you heading?" . . . I always felt Clinton's tremendous eagerness to be liked and to be your buddy. I think that is the natural way he is. It is just like my dog, Bubba. He just loves you and wants to come over and be friends with you. But it is always in a simultaneous context of manipulation. He is a gregarious, tremendously manipulative person. . . . You can see him even now. If he could possibly be outside the protective ring of the presidency, you could see him across the parking lot, and he would yell at you. "Hey!" He is just bouncing with eagerness to chat. You just sort of go along with this. This is a superstar politician, and he is really coming on strong here, and, eventually, you realize it isn't all good or all bad. It is just Clinton. That is just the way he is.

Then there was Whitewater, perhaps the most overwritten and poorly reported "scandal" of the era. The story might have been different if the Gazette had still been alive.

Margie Snider: I always thought this Whitewater thing was just the most absurd thing. He wasn't interested in money. I said, "This is crazy." They weren't—Hillary either—they didn't seem to be interested in money or a house or cars or clothes. They didn't care about that.

Dumas: Bill Clinton is running for president and has beaten Sheffield [Nelson] in the 1990 gubernatorial election. Sheffield switches parties in 1990 and runs against Bill Clinton for governor . . . It's a very brutal race, and there's lots of bitterness. So he alerts Jeff Gerth, and Gerth is asking him what he knows about Clinton. It turns out Sheffield has just finished talking to Jim McDougal, and McDougal tells him about Jim Guy Tucker and some of his dealings and this Whitewater Development Company and how Clinton had screwed him. He was going to get him a job and so forth. So he tells Gerth about all of this and arranges for Gerth to interview Jim McDougal. So Gerth gets together with Jim McDougal, and McDougal tells him all. So [Gerth] writes the first Whitewater story, owing to that tip from Sheffield Nelson, and the first Whitewater story is news to the country and probably worth the story because everything about a prospective president's life, I guess, is news. I mean, you ought to know everything you can about him, and this was a tiny episode in Bill Clinton's life. As an attorney general of Arkansas in 1978, he and his wife had gotten into a land deal with Jim McDougal, and they had lost some money. It turned out to be a bad investment, and that's really about all there ever was to the story. There was just no more than that: that Bill Clinton and Hillary Clinton unwisely borrowed a bunch of money and invested it with Jim McDougal in a remote land development and lost their money over a period of years. But, of course, the story becomes much more than that. All kinds of angles, everybody exploring all kinds of angles on that. Ten years later, that's all the story ever was. From the first, Gerth magnified it far beyond what it was worth and failed in that original story or subsequently to tell the other side. Gerth's failing as a reporter was that he did a lot of good leg work, but when he came across something that didn't fit or that diluted his story somehow, he just left it out. I think that's what Gerth has always done. If he comes across inconvenient facts, he leaves them out, so, basically, the stuff he writes, you can say, "Well, yes, that sentence is factual and that sentence is factual, but it's not the truth." Quite often, you'd get things that are not factual. There were a number of instances when he just got things wrong.

. . . McDougal also told him how Hillary had made $98,000 off a $1,000 investment in cattle futures. Gerth called me and said did I know anything about that, and I said, "No, that's news to me. I've never heard of it. . . . That's completely fresh news." He said, "Well, I've pretty much pinned it all down, and she invested $1,000. Jim Blair handled the accounts for her and did most of the trading for her, and she got out of the thing about eleven months later with a $98,000 profit." So I said, "Well, that's a good story." I thought it was a good story, but when the story appeared, it had major errors in it and just left out some important facts. To give you a couple of examples, the lead was that Hillary Rodham Clinton, when she was the first lady, had used an executive vice president of Tyson Foods to help her earn a $100,000 on cattle futures trading. Turn a $1,000 investment into a $100,000 profit. That was the lead, that this Tyson Food executive had assisted her in making all this money. And then the next two or three paragraphs suggested that, as the result, the Clinton administration threw, I think it was, something like $9 million in state loans to Tyson Foods, loans and grants of $9 million to Tyson Foods and that Clinton rewarded Tyson executives with state patronage plums, state appointments, and waived regulations for them. It went on in some detail about Tyson's polluting plants up there in the hills and how the state didn't do much at all. The whole story was the favoritism done [for] Hillary and the payoff for Tyson. When I saw the story, I said, "Well, that's a hell of a story." Then I looked at it and said, "Wait a minute. What's Tyson doing getting $9 million in grants and loans from the state? What program is that? I've never heard of a program like that, particularly for a big company like Tyson Foods getting loans from the state." . . . And so I called the Arkansas Industrial Development Commission to see whether they had any such program, and nobody knew what they were talking about. I read them this paragraph out of the *New York Times,* and they said, "No. We don't have any program like that." I think I called Archie Schaffer up there at Tyson Foods, or Jim Blair, and they said, "We never got any loan. We don't know what he's talking about." So I've forgotten now whether I sent something to the *New York Times* or what, but about a month later, they ran a correction on page two. The correction didn't make any sense. There were actually no loans and grants, and it tried to make some explanation. But Gerth's explanation later was that he was in a rush, and he just made a mistake. And, I think, he first told Gene Lyons [a Little Rock political columnist] that maybe somebody told him that, and he just failed to check it out or something, but nobody knows where it came from.

Reed: And the entire story rose or fell on that particular fact.

Dumas: Yes, the magnitude of the story as a scandal. . . . Also, he talked about how Tyson had always been big supporters of Clinton, that they had contributed all this money to his presidential campaign. Well, of course, what he failed to point out was that Tyson had opposed Clinton until 1992. He supported him in his first race in 1978, and then worked hard against him in 1980. Supported Frank White, gave him all this money and gave money to Frank again in 1982. We had a letter to the editor in the *Arkansas Gazette* signed by Don Tyson, against Bill Clinton, why he should be defeated, a lot of it over truck weights. Clinton would not support raising the weight limits on Arkansas highways, which the industry wanted. And, you know, Tyson hadn't supported him all those years, and the whole poultry industry had been opposed to him. . . . over the years until he runs for president, and Tyson said, "All right. I'll support the son of a bitch."

Reed: In 1992, when the first Whitewater story was written, the *Arkansas Gazette* had been dead for a year. If the *Gazette* had still been publishing, at least the old *Arkansas Gazette* before Gannett took over, what would be the normal routine for an out-of-state reporter coming in to work on an investigative story? Would he go to the *Gazette* and talk with . . .

Dumas: That's typically what had happened over the years. Political reporters, like me and John Brummett, in political season we'd spend a lot of time with the reporters from the big city papers who would always come down. You've done that. A great source is the local political reporter. That's typically what would have been done, and you give him all this stuff, what you know about it.

Reed: Is there any chance the Whitewater story would have turned out any differently if the *Gazette* had still been alive?

Dumas: I think it might have. I think it might have turned out quite a bit differently. The *Gazette* would have been the chief source for all the national media, and there would have been people, not only Gerth from the *New York Times* but other reporters as well, I think, would have gotten an accurate and balanced account.

Reed: What difference did it make that instead they all went to the *Democrat-Gazette?*

Dumas: The *Democrat* had very little institutional knowledge of it. The problem with the *Democrat* was that they were unable to help anybody because there was nobody over there who had more than two or three years experience. In 1992 all the reporters—and that's still the case—about two or three years is the max, and they're gone. There are a handful of reporters who have been around more than two or three years.

Arkansas has never lacked for colorful politicians.

Mort Stern: When I think about Arkansas politics, I remember a [gubernatorial candidate] named Uncle Mac Mackrell. I actually heard him say something to this effect: "All those other candidates are stealing from you. It is time you give me a chance." [*Laughter.*] So help me, I actually heard him say that. I thought, "Did I hear that right?" I kept looking at my notes. "My God, this man tells the truth if you listen carefully."

Bob Douglas: Politics was the big story. The 1948 election was the biggest news. And that was an exciting time, and not just the local races. We had Henry Wallace come to town. Strom Thurmond and the Dixiecrats. I covered both of them. No violence. [*Laughs.*] I think I got a byline out of the Henry Wallace story. There were a few Henry supporters—Communists all [*laughs*]—that picketed the school board. The board wouldn't let them use the school board building for a meeting. So they picketed, and I covered that. It was on a Sunday afternoon. I think I got my first byline that day.

Gene Foreman: Shelton let me cover the Faubus re-election campaign against Jim Johnson [in 1956]. I know I didn't have enough background, and I did not do justice to the story. A lot of things, of course, I know now that I should have followed up on. It is clear, for example, I could have followed up on what was said in off-the-record time with Faubus and Claude Carpenter and Kay Matthews—Carpenter and Matthews were his Ehrlichman and Haldeman. Without betraying the off-the-record thing, I could have reported that they had a stalking horse, that one of the other candidates was in there simply to ask tough questions of Jim Johnson and deflect from Faubus's at-that-time moderate stance on segregation. Faubus positioned himself as the moderate and said to the segregationists and those inclined that way the right things about how "this is not what we want to do." He didn't talk in the rhetoric that he later adopted. . . . He wasn't by background and upbringing a segregationist. He was still a consensus builder. The difference between him and Johnson was obvious. It was also significant that Faubus won, and it reinforced the idea that in 1957, he should have done the right thing rather than what he did. . . . He would not have won a third term if he had simply done the right thing.

Tom Hamburger: There were always these crazy people who were running for office along with—we had this fleet of blow-dried sophisticates—Bill Clinton, Jim Guy [Tucker], [David] Pryor, all about the same age—[Dale] Bumpers . . . And then there would be someone running against them, like Monroe Schwartzlose. . . . Monroe used to give out Grandma Schwartzlose's brownie recipes. His campaign platform was mostly about legalizing gambling in Arkansas . . . He was a turkey farmer from Rison, and he'd get off on these tangents. He was really kind of crazy. And he would follow Jim Guy, who was so overly earnest and self-important. And Monroe always wore his overalls. And he'd stand up there, and Jim Guy would talk about social security and what he had done on ways and means—and Monroe said, "I want to talk about—you gotta do like when you have a sick turkey. You get the turkey, and you've got to do it with an old eyedropper. You take the eyedropper and you fill it up, and you hold the turkey like this." And the crowd would start roaring. And then the timekeeper—you know, the guys got ten minutes to speak—I think this was at Mount Nebo—the guy said, "Time." And Monroe said, "I'm not finished yet!" He said, "I'm sorry, Mr. Schwartzlose, your time is up." He'd say, "I'm not quittin'!" And the crowd starts clapping and carrying on. So the crowd is going, and he says, "See, they're with me!" [*Laughs.*] "Do you want me to finish this story?" [*Laughs.*] And the people shouted, "Yes!" And all the press corps shouted "Yes!" too, of course. And Monroe says, "Now, where was I?" So we shouted, "Doctoring turkeys!" [*Laughs.*] And he goes back to cradling the turkey's neck in his arm and showing the eyedropper. [*Laughs.*] You'd just laugh, and tears would be rolling down your cheeks.

. . . [Then there was another guy.] Toughy [Chambers] had been to the clerk at the courthouse. [Mrs. Chambers] says, "No, he didn't file for governor! You've got the wrong number, sir." [*Laughs.*] So Dumas looks at it again and called back. "Mrs. Chambers, this is Ernest Dumas. There is a Toughy Chambers. You live at this address, right?" She says, "Just a second. [*Spoken to someone in the room with her:*] Toughy, this man says you've filed for governor." And then you hear her say, "Well, did you do that?" [*Laughter.*] "When you told me you were going to the store, you went to the state house and filed for governor?"

Farris: [*Laughter.*] He hadn't even told his wife!

The Gazette's *longtime cartoonist George Fisher virtually built his career around caricatures of Orval Faubus, the state's longest-serving governor.*

George Fisher: Another [popular cartoon] was Faubus addressing the legislature . . . And everybody in the audience, including the galleries, including the people sitting behind him, including the microphone, including everything—the pictures on the wall—all looked like Faubus.

Dumas: Including a mouse . . . peeking out.

Fisher: From a hole down below the platform. The mouse had a nose like old Faubus.

Dumas: Another enduring metaphor of Fisher cartoons was the "Old Guard Rest Home." When did you first do an Old Guard Rest Home? How did you get the idea?

Fisher: Do you remember when Paul Van Dalsem [representative from Perry County] was finally defeated? The lion of the legislature was finally defeated. It occurred to me—and I don't know why it occurred me—that there should be a place for him. And how about all the rest of them that went the same route that he did? So I showed the old porch of an old house, a post–World War I vintage house. I showed these old guys sitting on the porch, Orval Faubus and Bruce Bennett, Mutt Jones, and Marion Crank . . . And they were sitting on the front porch, looking down the pike. Here came somebody carrying suitcases, a big, hefty man, carrying suitcases, and he looked beaten. And they were saying, "It looks like it might be . . . Yes, it is. It's old Paul." And I didn't have to label Van Dalsem because everybody knew it was Paul Van Dalsem. That was the first one. The Old Guard Rest Home series got to be such a big hit, I thought I'd keep drawing them . . . I guess I did about a hundred Old Guard Rest Home cartoons. They became everybody's favorite. During the post-Faubus era, Faubus was on the porch, and he was the head Old Guard, the first Old Guard. In history the people who surrounded Napoleon when he came back from Elba were called the Old Guard, and that's where I got the idea for the Old Guard. There are a lot of old guards around everywhere in politics. Anyway, that was the first Old Guard Rest Home, and Faubus, who is, of course, on the porch, is Napoleon . . . During the years, they kept adding new members. When politicians get defeated, they have to have someplace to stay. A politician has to have a place to stay and a room to sleep in and some people around him who understand him and share the same thoughts that he has. The Old Guard was the proper place for all these people, but they have to share the same philosophy, more or less, as Orval Faubus because he was the first one in the home.

Governor Faubus professed to believe that the Gazette *always portrayed him in an unfavorable light. He used to say that the editors routinely discarded good photos of him and used those that made him look ugly or ridiculous. However, there was one famous picture that he liked. Years after the 1957 school integration story and after the worst of the bad feelings between him and the* Gazette *had faded, Rodney Dungan of the photography staff snapped a picture of the governor walking toward him at the dedication of a river ferry. His hat was pushed back, and he was smiling broadly and carrying a pennant in one hand and a cigarette in the other. Faubus had the cigarette airbrushed out and used the photo repeatedly in his campaign advertising—to Dungan's chagrin.*

Rodney Dungan: How that picture was done is a pretty decent story. Leroy Donald and I were already in the car. We were going to travel through the silica mines. Faubus was coming, and we were waiting on him to get to the car. I looked out the window and saw this thing. I didn't even have time to set my camera. It is a little off angle and into the sun. I leaned over Leroy's lap and shot it through a car window.

After Faubus, the state's politicians took a turn for the bland. But they still entertained.

Doug Smith: Well, Rockefeller went in. It was the "Old Guard," as they were called under Faubus, that he had left, and Rockefeller had beaten the last of the old segregationists, Jim Johnson, so it was race. And improving race relations was a very big thing. I remember when Martin Luther King was killed, Rockefeller stood out on the front of the capitol steps with a bunch of black ministers, singing "We Shall Overcome," and he was very much into that kind of thing. He had been a member of the NAACP and admitted it, which was kind of surprising in Arkansas. Just a few years before, they had been trying to outlaw the NAACP and people like that. And he made a big point of appointing blacks to public offices.

Dumas: [Dale Bumpers] knew everybody. And the most astonishing thing was his memory. Bill Clinton is the only person I've ever known who is better at this. We were someplace like Conway, and we'd gotten out and he'd hopped out and hit Wal-Mart. He never missed a Wal-Mart. . . . He'd shake every hand in a Wal-Mart and across the parking lot. And he'd tell them who he was, and he'd ask, "What's your name?" He'd always ask everybody what their name was. So I think we were in the supermarket line or something in Conway. And we were going through the line and he shook hands with this woman. And he said, "Wait a minute. Now, aren't you Mrs. Hunkapillar? I met you over at—What are you doing here? I met you at the Wal-Mart at Forrest City last week." And she was just—you could just tell—she was just transformed. She was going to vote for Dale Bumpers for the rest of her life.

I remember that general election of 1970. And it was the night before the election. And we were on an airplane coming back from Fort Smith. . . . I remember because Tucker [Steinmetz] and I were just terrified. The plane was bucking around through the sky and there was lightning all around. And so Bumpers disavowed his remark early in the campaign that he had once challenged the parting of the Red Sea, that it was a kind of a myth. . . . Well, Bumpers—we were coming back—he said, "No, no. The parting of the Red Sea really happened!" [*Laughter.*]

The Arkansas General Assembly was home to a particularly rambunctious collection of politicians.

Gene Prescott: My first assignment for the *Gazette* was, I believe, Larry sent me to the legislature. Well, I'd never been to the legislature. And I went to the House. Nobody filled me in or anything like that. And darned if while I was in there, Paul Van Dalsem and another legislator got into a fight over the microphone. [*Laughter.*] And I walked down the aisle, and I shot three or four pictures. I remember we were shooting 4 × 5 Speed Graphics. And I thought, "What kind of job have I got into?" [*Laughter.*]

Michael Haddigan: Now, the quality and the character of the legislators . . .

Carol Griffee: My experience was with the Virginia General Assembly, where just to serve is considered the highest honor. You could hear a pin drop in the Virginia senate or the house, and if you spoke, you could be thrown out . . . In the 1973 session [of the Arkansas General Assembly] I'd go home every day with a headache from the roar of the noise in the Arkansas house chamber. I also watched [Guy] "Mutt" Jones in his little red cowboy boots climb up on his desk at the rear of the senate chamber. He was wild and wooly, I mean. And the 1973 session in the house ended in a fist fight! And I'm the one who got black and blue from it because my seat for WEHCO Media was right at the end of the press box on the house chamber floor, and when Julian Streett and Jodie Mahony came down and were heading for Buddy Turner, who was the speaker, Boyce Alford got up to stop them, and the state policeman came down the other aisle, and Boyce threw a punch! [*Laughs*] My colleagues scrambled over me to get out to get a better view of the action. I got the worst of it all!

The legislature meets every two years except for special sessions. It occasionally embarrassed the state in those days.

Dumas: In 1981 the legislature passed a law that required schools to teach creation science if they taught evolution.

George Wells: And it outlined in the law very specifically what should be taught, including things like the flood of Noah, and that sort of thing. And the ACLU [American Civil Liberties Union] filed a lawsuit in federal court. It was assigned to U.S. District Judge William R. Overton. We started receiving attention from all over the world. We had reporters come in from England, France, and all parts of the country . . . It was marked by some strange things. [Attorney General] Steve Clark wanted to try to make a point that there were a variety of explanations for creation, even though the scientists say that creation itself is not necessary to understand evolution. So he brought in a scientist from England—Dr. N. C. Wickramasinghe. He was an associate of Sir Fred Hoyle, a world-renowned astronomer, and he tried to explain Hoyle's theory of how life came to earth. He said it was probably in the form of something like a virus and came in on meteors. Another witness was a professor from a Baptist seminary in Dallas. He made all the headlines because on his cross-examination by the ACLU lawyer he said that he believed in UFOs [unidentified flying objects], and he thought that they were satanic manifestations. Of course, everybody grabbed on that. I was the only one who noticed, I think, that during his testimony he also said, "Of course, the law is religion," which just shot the bottom out of the state's boat right there. I mean, he was their expert on religion, and he said, "Yes, the law is religion."

Dumas: That was the bedrock issue. "Is this law the imposition of a government religion?"

Wells: Right. That was how the ACLU framed it. That's how it was decided. And, of course, Judge Overton struck down the law in January of 1982. It was the second time Arkansas had been the legal battleground over evolution. The Supreme Court struck down the anti-evolution laws in an earlier Arkansas case. By that time, however, only Arkansas and Tennessee had such laws on the books.

Local government made the news regularly, none more gaudily than in North Little Rock, Little Rock's neighbor across the Arkansas River.

John Woodruff: One of my favorite stories is probably one of the shortest ones in the *Arkansas Gazette*, where former Mayor William F. Laman, who used to get put out every once in a while with different reporters, ordered all the city employees not to talk to reporters. And I found this out not by Laman but from a city employee. So our story went to the effect of—it was only about a paragraph long. It said something to the effect that "Mayor William F. (Casey) Laman ordered city employees not to talk to reporters," and with a comma there, "a city employee told a reporter."

In 1971, I had to miss a city council meeting . . . The young reporter who was sitting in for me wanted to know if it was normal when one alderman, Paul Duke, grabbed another alderman, John O. May, and hauled him up, literally carried him up the stairs, and threatened to throw him off the balcony of the city hall onto the marble floor below . . . I told the reporter, no, that didn't happen at each city council meeting. That was rather unusual, and we needed to report that one alderman hauled another one up the stairs and attempted to throw him off the balcony. The North Little Rock City Council meetings did have a history of a lot of turbulence. In fact, the city clerk, Jackie C. Neil, who is now deceased, got caught because of the placement of her desk between, I believe, the mayor and an irate person in the audience. I think she got caught between them in a fight and was the one that ended up being struck. During the time I covered city hall, one of the prevailing jokes was that they would check you for weapons on getting into the city council chambers, and if you didn't have a weapon, they would give you one so you could defend yourself.

Roy Reed had his own experience with weaponry there.

Reed: Laman's Furniture Store [in North Little Rock] was like a government in exile. It was a hotbed of intrigue, people coming all hours of the day. They were conspiring with Casey [Laman] on how to overthrow the government across the street. . . . Following a tip from Casey, I wrote a story about some minor scandal like replacing the screens on the windows of city hall without bids, or something of that caliber. . . . The story mentioned an alderman named Joe Donnell, a powerful member of the city council. The day the story appeared in the *Gazette,* I had a call from Donnell asking me to come to his house, a few blocks north of city hall. I did, but with some trepidation. I knew he was going to remonstrate because there was no way that he was going to like the story that I had written. I was prepared to be told the other side of the story with some emphasis. I got there, and he had one of his coworkers on the city council, a man named Dallas Bobbitt, another old Missouri Pacific [Railroad] worker, also a member of the city council, in the living room with him. They asked me to sit down, and I took a seat in an arm chair in the living room. I thought it was kind of interesting that both of the men were standing up and never did sit down. After a few words of taking me to task on this story, the first thing I knew, Joe Donnell came across the room and was all over me, whaling away. As the police reports used to say, "So-and-so had been beaten about the head and the ears." I sure was beat about the head and ears. I couldn't get out of the chair even if I had had the wit to fight back. . . . Bobbitt was there purely as a witness. One of them called the police. In a very few minutes a patrol car pulled up front. Joe told them that I had come out there and caused trouble. He demanded that I be searched for a weapon. I was carrying, as I always did, a pocket knife about 2 to 2½ inches long. The police duly noted that I was armed with a pocket knife. That went into their report. I had some scratches and bruises around my head and my shirt. I was pretty much a mess when I left there. I drove straight to the *Gazette* newsroom. I walked in, and Bill Shelton, the city editor, took a look at me and said, "Good God, what happened to you?" I told him, and he immediately assigned another reporter, probably Bill Lewis, to write a story about this incident. It had the opposite effect of what Donnell might have intended. I think he might have wanted to intimidate me into laying off these stories about malfeasance at city hall. Instead, it emboldened other people to call me up and tip me off to other things that were going on. The story ended sadly. It turned out that Joe was in bad health, which I did not know. In about a year, or less, he committed suicide with a shotgun . . . Years later, when I was covering the White House and other exalted branches of government, I got a fair amount of mileage out of being able to boast that I was the only newspaperman [in Washington] who had ever been beaten up by an alderman.

Martha Mitchell, a native of Pine Bluff, was the wife of John Mitchell, attorney general under President Richard M. Nixon. Mrs. Mitchell became famous for her telephone calls to the press passing on secrets embarrassing to the Nixon administration. She played a significant role in bringing down the president— and in bringing down her husband, who was sent to prison for obstructing the investigation of the Watergate break-in. One of her more sensational phone calls was to the Gazette. *She was sore at Senator J. William Fulbright.*

Jerol Garrison: John, you had a phone call one time, I believe, from another famous lady. Would you tell us about it?

John Woodruff: I was working the police beat one night when I was gathering up my materials, ready to leave. It was right at midnight, time for me to close up, and I was the last person on the city desk. I kind of shut it down and told the news editor to go ahead and close out everything . . . I gathered up my materials and was ready to leave when the phone rang . . . and this person wanted to know if she could dictate a letter to the editor. I told her we didn't do that sort of thing. She had to write it and sign it. The conversation went on like that. She was very insistent. Finally, she said, "You don't realize who you are talking to, do you?" I said, "Well, ma'am, it really doesn't make any difference because we have a policy on that. You need to write your letter and sign it before we get it in the paper." The conversation went on and on like that. I began to realize that what she was talking about were some of the events going on in Washington, DC. She was very knowledgeable, and I thought, "Whoops, I may have somebody on the phone here," and I didn't realize who I had. I said, "I'll tell you what. I'll take your letter, and I'll give it to the editor." She said she would tell me who she was then. "Just to show you I am being honest about it or whatever, I'll take your letter and then you can tell me." She dictated a short little letter asking that the *Gazette* should crucify, that was her terminology, Arkansas Senator J. William Fulbright for voting against the [Harold] Carswell nomination by President Nixon to the Supreme Court. Fulbright had voted against it. She was just livid about it.

It was Martha Mitchell. After she dictated the letter, then she said, "That's signed Martha Mitchell, wife of the attorney general." I nearly swallowed the telephone that I was holding. I told her we could get that in the paper probably not as a letter to the editor but as a news item, but we had to verify the telephone call. She gave me the White House number, and I called the White House, and they wouldn't connect me with her, so I couldn't verify it. In the meantime, we had decided to hold the presses because this, of course, involved a national person and a celebrity even. In the meantime, Mike Trimble, one of our reporters, happened to be drifting through to see if the first edition was out and stopped over and saw what was going on, and I had him go over and get my tape recorder out of my desk. We began tape recording the conversation, or were going to if she called back. She did call back. We thought we had lost the whole thing because we didn't have verification, but she called back and wondered why I hadn't called. I told her I called, but the White House wouldn't put me through to her phone. I said, "I still don't have verification." So she finally broke down, literally, I guess, because she— at times in our conversation, which was quite extended, she would at times cry and at times laugh. We had a lengthy conversation. She gave me the Mitchells' unlisted telephone number, so when I was able to call that number, the White House put me immediately through, and I was able to confirm that it was Martha Mitchell, the wife of the attorney general.

In the meantime, Mike Trimble started writing the lead to our story about Martha Mitchell, wife of the attorney general, calling and asking the *Arkansas Gazette* to crucify J. William Fulbright for his vote against the nomination of Carswell to the Supreme Court . . . We held the presses, and it made front page. I promised a fellow associate [Kay Patterson] that I would play tennis with her the next morning about seven o'clock. We put the paper to bed with that story on the front page. We all gathered at one of our apartments and kind of talked about it and joked about it and listened to that tape recording that I had of the conversation. We went to bed. I got a couple hours sleep and went to play tennis. When I got back to my apartment from playing tennis, the phone wouldn't stop ringing. I had newspaper calls from my office and around the world, really: United Press International, Associated Press, ABC television. ABC interviewed me later in their local studio, and I told them about the conversation. After the national news of it got out, Martha Mitchell denied that she ever called the *Gazette*. She finally fessed up that she had talked to a reporter, but that we had called her. But I had that tape recording, and in the tape recording she also said on it, quoting Martha Mitchell, "The reason I called you was that I wanted you to" so-and-so, you know, write this letter or crucify Fulbright for his nomination opposition. So she finally quit denying it, and then later on one of our other reporters interviewed her. Of course, Martha Mitchell was from Pine Bluff, Arkansas, and that's why she was calling the *Arkansas Gazette*. Somebody—I had it second-hand that she actually meant to call the *Democrat*, which was not the liberal Democratic newspaper that the *Arkansas Gazette* was. She forgot about that or whatever and called the *Gazette* instead.

Reed: Were you news editor, or night managing editor, when Martha Mitchell made her famous phone call to the *Gazette*?

Douglas: Yes. I had gone home. It seemed like every time we had a crisis, I was home in bed with the flu or strep throat. I had strep throat the day Robert Kennedy was assassinated and got out of bed and went to work. But I had to go home early because I wasn't feeling well. Somebody called me; she said, "John Woodruff"—who was a North Little Rock reporter working late— said, "John Woodruff has Martha Mitchell on the phone." Well, the only person in that newsroom or in that whole staff who would've talked to somebody who did not identify herself, who called in at one thirty in the morning, was John Woodruff. She identified herself finally as Martha Mitchell. Anybody else would have hung up long before. . . . John liked to talk, and so did Martha Mitchell.

Reed: So you had to handle this story as editor from your home in your sickbed?

Douglas: Right. And tell them where to put it and check the headline and all that. . . . It was a one-column head, italics to give it a little more—we used italics a lot for stories that were a little offbeat. Italic headlines attracted a little more attention. That's the only spot we had for it on page one. That's about the play we would have given it anyhow. . . . It was over near the lead story. It was on the right hand above the fold.

The civil rights movement came to Arkansas during the late 1960s and early 1970s. It was sometimes dangerous for reporters.

Wayne Jordan: We had another riot at a school in Marianna. The state police came in as they always did to make sure that people aren't killing each other and calming down everybody. So it was the next morning after that night. I'm eating breakfast at the local restaurant. As customary, I had a sports coat on and a tie. There was a group of farmers over there, and they are discussing the events of the night before and the day before. They were very upset that they were under almost martial law with the state police in there . . . There's one farmer, and he was standing up, and there's seven or eight others there, and he kept looking over at me. I'm sitting in a booth. So he walks over there, and he says to me, "Who are you!?" I said, "I'm . . . I'm . . . I'm Wayne Jordan." "What are you doing in town? What are you?" And I said, "Well, I'm here [*laughs*] covering the . . ." "Covering? You're a reporter, aren't you? I knew it. I told the boys over there you were a reporter. Who are you reporting for?" "Ah, *Arkansas Gazette.*" Boy, he hit the back of the booth, and I thought, "Oh, he's going to hit me." He said, "I want to tell you something right now, boy," he said, "I ought to snatch you out of that booth right there and take you out and whip you." He said, "I would if I didn't have so much respect for Orville Henry. Yes, I'll tell you what, boy, I hate your paper, but we love Orville. He gives us the information we need to know about the Razorbacks. And if it weren't for that, I'd thrash you, boy. I'd put you out there, and I would whip you like a yard dog." I'd come back to the *Gazette* after these kinds of things and grab Orville and hug him.

Hamburger: There was a school desegregation fight going on in Eudora. . . . Why they were—maybe it was a busing issue. They had to call out the state police. . . . It was a little bit scary. I got there at night, and there were still a lot of teenagers on the street. And there were a lot of cops, state police cars out. I wrote a sort of a story about the town, what the atmosphere was like. And I quoted some racial epithets from some of the kids. . . . I got there late, after dark, and I had to file by ten o'clock or something, so I only had a couple of hours. I was out on the street interviewing people quickly, and there were some outspoken black activists and some outspoken white kids and, you know, put it together and the story was done. But I remember the next day I got this call. . . . It was the first really, really angry call I'd had as a journalist. I had had some tough and angry calls, but this one, this guy was threatening to break my legs and . . . Oh, and he started it, you know, by saying, "You have ruined the reputation of our lovely town." And I thought he was going to complain that I had overdrawn the conflict. He said, "You ain't nothing but a nigger lover." Then threatened to break my legs.

Threats to reporters sometimes came from unexpected quarters.

Tish Talbot: One time I had a *Gazette* assignment with Larry Obsitnik, our chief photographer, to cover a speech by Nelson Rockefeller, who was then running for president as Republican here, and it was put on by the Republican Party. I had been warned about half an hour ahead of time that some people were going to disrupt the speech. These were people who were members of the Communist Party in Arkansas, and they were going to disrupt the speech. So I told the chief that we needed to sit close to the front, and we needed to be in a position to get some good pictures when it happened. I didn't know whether to believe these people or not, but just in case. And, sure enough, they came in, and they started turning over speakers and—nobody was hurt except the chief and me. We both got run over [*laughs*], and I got hit with a night stick from the security guard. [*Laughs.*] . . . I was poised to jump and go with the people who were, you know, where the news was. I got between them and the security people [*laughs*] and got bruised up a little bit.

Dumas: [Keith Moyer, the editor] told Bob Lancaster, who was kind of a feature writer on the state desk, to pass the word along, go out and find just a down-to-earth, ordinary old guy, or people, to write about and write some features. So Bob struck out and went down to south Arkansas, and he found this guy named Ora Golden. And Ora was living in his car, and I think the car was not running, but that was where he was living. So he interviewed this guy, and it was a long interview. And this guy tells all these tales. I mean, everything in the world has happened to this guy. He just had one stroke of bad luck after another, year after year after year after year. Just incredible things happened to him. Now, sooner or later, you began to disbelieve most of this stuff. This guy's just got such horror stories to tell about himself. I mean, he's just been impaled on spikes and bitten by rattlesnakes and shot at and fallen off a bridge. Everything has happened to him. And he's been through a couple of wives and all kinds of things. And then he's obviously kind of crazy as well. Well, Bob relates all this stuff kind of matter-of-factly. It was a long, funny piece. . . . So Bob wrote this thing, and it was a huge piece that ran in the *Gazette*. And a lot of people just thought, "What in the world is the *Gazette* doing running this huge piece about this no-account bum?" And then one day, Bob got this call. And it was from the current husband of Ora Golden's ex-wife. And he calls up—and this was a pretty rough character himself—and he's going to "whip Bob Lancaster's ass." In fact, he just may "goddamn it kill him" because he's written about all this stuff that this lying Ora Golden's done. He's just a terrible, good-for-nothing liar. And he's going to come whip his ass. So Bob tries to defuse it, and said, "Well, why don't you get her to tell her side of the story?" And so they finally had some meeting, and Bob is kind of—he's pretty scared that this guy's going to come shoot him or whip him or something. But he called me and said, "Look, if we get a letter to the editor from this person, will we run it?" And I was in charge of the letters, and I said "Okay, if it's going to save your life, we'll run this letter. We don't care about having you shot to death here." So she wrote this letter, and the letter is as good as his stuff. I mean, she starts telling terrible things about Ora Golden and then the terrible things that had happened to her. And even worse things had happened to her. I mean, it's a medical miracle either one of them was alive. [*Laughter.*] And so it's a bitter, nasty letter, but I kind of edited it up a little bit and pretty much ran it as is.

A straightforward news story sometimes turned into a saga.

Leroy Donald: [Joe Hildebrand] was the "Outlaw of the Ozarks". . . . He lived up, actually, I guess, you would call it Booger Hollow. And he had been down in the jail for various and sundry reasons. I think he held up some people on the highway on an overlook up there, and he was just kind of a wild kid, nineteen. He was down there in the prison farm, and he would just get out every now and then, and they would catch him and send him back to prison. Well, he got out one time on a furlough to go home and see his sick daddy and got in some sort of trouble with a branch of the family and ran off with his wife's cousin, or something like that. And Joe just didn't realize it was time for him to go back to the prison, so they wandered around through the Ozarks at the time and . . . made a national figure out of him. They had cops and helicopters and dogs chasing him all over the place, and he really wasn't running. He was just wandering around up in the hills where he was home. It got to be a real—it was a front-page story. They finally caught him and sent him back down to the farm.

Reed: Finally, there was so much pressure on the sheriff's office there to catch this guy that they had organized manhunts. It got to be a huge thing. They even wrote a song about him, "The Ballad of Joe Hildebrand." *Life* magazine did a feature on him. They finally found him. I believe he was under the floor of his girlfriend's house.

The verb "to hunker" became a running story.

Douglas: There was a hunkering fad, guys sitting on their haunches and talking like they used to do in country towns. But some of the boys—I think they were fraternity boys—started a hunkering craze at the university, and [Patrick] Owens wrote about it and had some pictures. Spread all over the state. *Life* magazine ran a four-page spread on it. I think I got that one out of the wastebasket and put it on page one.

Disasters, natural and man-made, were covered fully.

Ken Parker: I think the high point of the *Gazette* staff during the ten years I was there was the tornadoes in March of 1952—Judsonia, Bald Knob, and all that—I was assistant state editor at the time. Ralph Leach, the state editor, . . . [called] to say there had been a tornado at Dierks. He and Gene Prescott were going down to cover that, and he wanted me to come in and fill in on the desk while he was gone. Well, on the way from Conway to Little Rock, I found out there had been a tornado at Mayflower, so I stopped off and got notes on it. I came on in, and when I got to the state desk, the phone was ringing, I answered it. [It was] someone reporting a tornado somewhere else. And before I could sit down, I had three calls from correspondents reporting tornadoes, and, of course, Leach and Prescott were in the wrong part of the state. They were in the right place at the time they were sent, but it was the last place that you needed a couple of staffers at the time. But that night there were tornadoes in Tennessee, Kentucky, all through this part of the country. Gene Fretz set up a tornado desk, and he was coordinating all tornado copy. I was handling the Arkansas tornadoes. Gene and I were probably the only two people in the office who had any idea what everybody was doing and what was going on. Everybody was working. "Whatever you want me to do, I'll do it." And I've thought several times since that Jim Meadows, for instance, went to Judsonia and got a byline on a story that moved on the AP A-wire. Pretty heady stuff. Dean Duncan was at Baptist Hospital, counting injured as they were brought in, which was pretty grunt-type stuff. Carroll McGaughey was at some HAM operator's house in Sherwood, getting what he could from the HAM radio. No one ever complained, "Well, why didn't

I get to go to Judsonia?" or "Why am I being told to do this?" It was "Whatever you need me to do, I'll do it." And that was the weekend that Douglas MacArthur made his triumphal return home [to Little Rock]. . . . Sam Harris was in the pressroom at the MacArthur deal. One of the national reporters said, "Well, you must have had a hectic time around here. How many people did you have covering tornadoes?" And Sam quickly counted up the number of people we had actually out in the field, and he said, "Three." And the guy said, "You did all that with three people?" And Sam said, "Hell, there were only three tornadoes."

Dumas: They were retrofitting one of these Titan missile silos in central Arkansas, and I think, maybe, they were converting them to liquid fuel from solid fuel or whatever, and there had been a fire down in one of these silos where all of these private laborers were working, and the upshot of it was that there were fifty-three or sixty-three men who were trapped in the silo, suffocating, who died down there. You were with the *New York Times* and came flying in for that. . . . Probably what had happened was that one of the workers way up high had dropped a wrench, and it might have fallen and snapped a hose or something and some gas leaked out, and there was some kind of fire, and it almost instantly consumed all of the oxygen in the silo, which was closed off and could not get the lid off. It had a concrete lid on top of it and so everybody died. Sometime in the night they got down in there to retrieve all of the bodies.

Bill Lewis: It was about probably six thirty or seven in the morning. I was still in bed, half asleep, and I heard this big boom. I got up and went to the backdoor, which was the side of the house that faced town. I saw sort of a pink puff of smoke in the clouds up there. I knew it wasn't a natural cloud. It looked like something that had just happened. I didn't know what it was, so I went back to bed, and the phone rang almost immediately. It was Shelton. He told me an airplane had exploded over Little Rock and said, "Get on it." So I spent all day covering that story and going from place to place. The wreckage fell in such a scattered area that it kept popping up everywhere. You'd think you'd gotten the main story, and then there it would be some other place . . . There was one survivor, Lieutenant Smoak . . . He was at the old Baptist Hospital, and we went out there to see if we could interview him or find out what the situation was as far as he was concerned because he was the only survivor. We were in an anteroom to the room where he was, and one of the other reporters was John Robert Starr [Associated Press]. They came out and said, "Well, he is really, really badly burned," and he was. He was burned all over his face and just everywhere. They said, "We really would rather you didn't talk to him now. Come back sometime later, if you agree to that." I said, "Fine." John Robert said, "No way! We're going to talk to him regardless." So we went in and talked to him for maybe five minutes. But, you know, that was one of those instances where I thought there should have been a little humanity, you know? There should have been some consideration for the guy. . . . The pilot of the plane was Harriet Aldridge's husband, Captain Herbert Aldridge. She came to [A. R.] Nelson and asked for a job, and he gave her one. She was assistant to Millie Woods [the food editor] for quite a few years [before becoming food editor]. I think she learned a lot about food on the job, and it was sort of on-the-job training because she had never worked for a newspaper before and had never done any serious writing, as far as I know.

Murders of all kinds found their way into print. Besides the usual grudge slayings and Saturday night brawls that ended in shootings, there was an axe killing by a berserk son and a spectacular matched pair of murders that stirred up a political circus.

Chuck Heinbockel: Tommy Robinson was sheriff, and he was an outlandish kind of character, and he was always getting into confrontations with other politicians, and in criminal cases there would always be something going on. They would be high-profile cases just because Tommy Robinson was affiliated. And the biggest one was the Alice McArthur murder case, and that intertwined with some other murder cases, but that was just a huge case. . . . The two schools of thought were that basically Tommy Robinson was taking the philosophy that Bill McArthur [a Little Rock lawyer] had arranged to kill his wife, Alice McArthur. At first there was an attempt on her life with a car bomb that was unsuccessful, and then she was shot in an execution-style manner by some people who brought flowers to her front door, flowers bearing a note saying "Have a Nice Day." From all this Tommy Robinson had deduced that Bill McArthur was the likely suspect. And there was a woman who had apparently murdered her husband, a woman who Bill McArthur defended, that Tommy Robinson got very close to, Mary Lee Orsini, and, apparently, he believed, or found it useful to believe, what she was saying about her relationship with Bill McArthur, which was basically that Bill McArthur wanted to get his wife out of the way so that he could hook up with Mary Lee Orsini. Those of us at the courthouse, who had interviewed Mary Lee Orsini and followed the murder case involving her husband, thought that she was kind of zany. . . . It was a soap opera, and I think in Mary Lee Orsini's mind, she loved the idea of being involved in a soap opera. . . . She just wanted to be the evil heroine of a soap opera, manipulate people around her. You could see that in the criminal cases involved that she was having a good time manipulating these people, these hit men, to go ahead and kill Alice McArthur without getting paid, and then getting Tommy Robinson to follow her line, her storyline, on the case. . . . It was one of the craziest times, and, really, one of the things that I look back on and regret is the rise of Tommy Robinson and how he would play us as a newspaper of record. I mean, he would say things that were so dramatic and so newsworthy, you felt that you couldn't ignore them, but, in some ways, it seemed like the responsible thing to do was that every time he came up with something outrageous was that you had to go ahead and deconstruct it. You know, that you had to do almost an analysis piece immediately afterwards to show where he was off on a tirade or his emotions ran far away from where the facts actually were. So it seemed to me that it was crying out for a different kind of journalism to respond to him because by the normal rules most of his utterances were newsworthy.

Laurie Karnatz: This prominent Arkansas family—his sister was president of the school board, father was a judge. One of the children wasn't very mentally stable. Everybody knew it, but no one talked about it. . . . I was at a restaurant around the corner from the *Gazette* when I got the phone call. This middle-aged, or sixty-ish, not-very-stable brother had apparently attempted to decapitate his father in the kitchen with a meat cleaver. When it didn't work, he dragged his father, who was about eighty-two, outside to the barn where he finished the job with an axe. He went and got the big family turkey platter and put his father's head on it. He placed it on the front yard and just sat on the front porch until the family came home. I got to write a couple of really good stories about that. Then the whole thing, as was normal for east Arkansas, just kind of disappeared, just like the brother. He got put away and that was that.

The Gazette *starting covering sports seriously after World War II. The coverage eventually concentrated on the University of Arkansas at Fayetteville, far in the northwestern hills, where all the teams from soccer to baseball were called the "Razorbacks." None got more attention than the football team. The sports editor, Orville Henry, was on top of the story from the beginning. Henry had come to the* Gazette *as a high school boy in 1942. He was sports editor from 1943 until he left in anger at the Gannett Company and joined the rival* Arkansas Democrat. *His reputation among sportswriters was nationwide.*

Jim Bailey: How did you persuade the paper that the main sports story was a couple of hundred miles to the north?

Orville Henry: The only thing everybody in Arkansas agreed upon, not as much then as a little later, was the Razorbacks. And in all seventy-five counties you had people in power who really were Arkansas, mostly University of Arkansas, lawyers . . . They sent for me one day and said, "Mr. J. N. wants to see you." So I went in, and there sat this man, and he said, "Mr. Henry, this is Mr. Gordon Campbell, and he wants to visit with us about something. He thinks that, in this time of growing sports interest, we should do more to support the Razorbacks." And so I said, "Sure." And he said, "Well, he wants to take you up to Fayetteville for this last game this year." . . . This is something that occurred in the off-season of 1943 . . . [Campbell] was general manager for Aetna. He was kind of a big mover and shaker around town and a big member of the Little Rock Country Club. He was head of the [game] officials' association because he had been an official in Illinois. But Gordon was a going Jesse, and almost nobody could say no to Gordon because he wouldn't leave them alone. You know, he is the person who got the stadium built [War Memorial Stadium] . . .

Bailey: The upturn started in 1946 by going to the Cotton Bowl, but the real breakthrough came in 1954 when they went to Cotton Bowl again. It wasn't long before the game stories started running on the front Sunday page . . . I know after 1954 it was always on the front page for about twenty-five or thirty years.

Change came even to Razorback football.

Donna Lampkin Stephens: No woman had ever been in the Razorback dressing room. But Paul Borden and Jim were very firm about that—I was going to be writer there, so I was going to be treated just like the rest of them. Originally, in 1990, they brought players out to me. They did not let me go in the locker room after the game. You know, you're on a deadline.

Garrison: Were these Razorback players or opponent's players?

Stephens: Now, opponents? I could go into the dressing room whenever I wanted to, but the University had a rule that no women were allowed in our locker room.

Garrison: That's weird, that you couldn't do it for the Razorbacks but you could do it for the opponents.

Stephens: I remember they had me write a first-person piece about what it was like to be in the locker room, and I think I made a joke that all their teeth are straight and I know what color eyes they all have. But the players were fine. In fact, there was something like I had covered opponents' dressing rooms and the opponents had won more games, and the Razorback players were begging me to come in and do the sidebar because it seemed like I always covered the winning team, as it turned out.

Jerry McConnell: There were three interviews that I did that I really had immense fun with. One of them, Ted Williams; one was Dizzy Dean; and one was Brooks Robinson. I interviewed Brooks more than once, and, of course, he was a Little Rock boy. . . . I had known his mother. She worked in, I believe, the secretary of state's office, so I had met his mother when I was covering the state capitol. So when Brooks went to the majors, she would call me and say, "Brooks is coming home. You want to talk to him?" I said, "Sure." . . . Then Dizzy Dean came in one time, and that may have been the funniest interview that I ever did. . . . He had given three different birthplaces when he was in the major leagues, pitching for the Cardinals. He had listed his birthplaces as Lucas, Arkansas, and Holdenville, Oklahoma, and someplace in Mississippi. . . . So somebody asked him, "Why do you give out three different birthplaces?" Dizzy said, "Well, when I first came up here, they said the press is going to be around interviewing you, and you ought to be polite and careful with them. They are always looking for something new. So I just gave them a new birthplace." I said, "Okay, where were you born?" He said, "I was actually born in Lucas, Arkansas. My family was itinerant farmers. We just traveled around, you know, picking crops and working different crops. One time we took off with a couple of horses and wagons. There were quite a few of us. We took off with couple of horses and wagons going to Texas to work in the harvest down in Texas. We got down there and one wagon got a little ahead of us. A big train came along, and it took a long time for that train to get past. When the train finally got past, the other wagon had gone on. It was not anywhere in sight. You know we did not see each other for two years?" . . . He said, "You know, times were really hard. That is how I built up my arms. I used to go out and throw rocks at the squirrels in the tree trying to kill these squirrels." He said, "Eventually, they told me I was going to have to start throwing left-handed. I was throwing so strong right-handed, I was tearing up the meat." . . .

I interviewed Ted with some trepidation because he had the great reputation of being tough on the newspaper guys in Boston. He just did not get along with the newspapermen in Boston at all. I had, you know, really some concern. He was just as polite as he could be, talkative and friendly. Never had a bit of trouble with him or getting any information out of him. . . . [I asked him] about Brooks Robinson, and he said, "Oh, the greatest third base-man that I have ever seen." At that time, I believe the Oriole shortstop was one of the Latin American players. It might have been Aparicio. [Williams] said, "There is not much sense hitting the ball on the ground to that side of their infield." He said, "You are not going to get it through there."

Brooks told me a story that I find very interesting. Later it was kind of confirmed in a way. He said that Ted Williams's last time at bat in his career was against the Orioles. He had a home run. It was toward the end of the sea-son. He said the Oriole pitcher threw him nothing but fastballs. He wanted to at least give Ted a chance to get a hit. He was not just deliberately saying, "Here, just hit it," but he was not throwing a bunch of junk and a bunch of curves and everything. Ted hit one out of the park, and Brooks said Ted called this pitcher up that night and thanked him. He said, "I appreciate you giving me a chance to get a hit in my last time at bat." Well, it turns out, that is not an unprecedented thing in major league baseball.

Joe Mosby: A reader called me and said there was a Little Rock woman who was going to try for the world scuba-diving record. This would be in late 1987. . . . She was forty-three years old, which is kind of unusual for an ath-letic endeavor like that. I talked to her on the phone a little while, and I wrote a story on it for the next day's paper. The sports editor at that time was Paul Borden, who had been brought in there by Gannett. Borden came to me the next day and said, "Joe, we had a meeting this morning, and we want you and the photographer to go down to the Bahamas and cover this woman's scuba-diving event." So I listened to him a little bit slack jawed. . . . We flew to West Palm Beach, got on a boat, went out to Bimini. We were on the boat six days. . . . The record was 330 feet; she intended to dive to 335. She went down so fast she went past that and went to 345. . She got the world record . . . This was on a Sunday, right before Christmas, about December 20 or 21. . . . I had already written a story on the computer, but I needed to transmit it to the *Gazette*. . . . There was a fellow sitting there on the dock, and I said, "I need to find a telephone." He said, "Mon, it's Sunday. No phones on Sunday, mon." . . . So I walked down this gravel road in the dark, for half a mile, to this police station. . . . There was a police sergeant sitting at the desk there in a British-type uniform with a starched white shirt and big shoulder boards. I said I needed a telephone to send a news story to my newspaper in the states. He looked at me for a minute. He said, "Sure, mon," and reached under the counter, gets the phone, sets it up on the counter there. I con-nected my laptop to the phone and transmitted the story to the *Gazette*. . . . The sergeant listened to my conversation, and when I got through and hung the phone up, he said, "That lady dove 345 feet?" And I said, "Yes." And he said, "One tank or two?" Meaning air tanks. And I said, "Two tanks." He kind of looked at me and said, "She's some woman, mon." And, I said, "Yes, she's some woman."

Feature stories usually don't cause much commotion. But now and then . . .

Dumas: There's this great catfish restaurant at De Valls Bluff, Arkansas, called Murray's. I suspect most people in Little Rock or central Arkansas, at one point or another, have been to Murray's. It's down on the banks of the White River [in] this little ramshackle house. I think it, maybe, started off as a railroad car, and things have been kind of built on so that now it kind of rambles. . . . When you are walking through it, it's kind of rocking a little bit. It's kind of unsteady on its base. It's run by this black guy named Olden Murray. Everybody loved to go eat catfish at Murray's. And Trimble thought it was the best place to eat in Arkansas. He loved to go to Murray's. So he went there once to write a feature about it. And he told Murray's life. Murray had been—used to work on boats on the Mississippi River. And he had suffered some kind of injury working on the boat and had been disabled. And so that's kind of when he retired and started this little restaurant. At any rate, he told about a day in the life of Olden Murray. And here was this guy getting up early every morning and doing all this and that and all the chores he did all day, and it was obviously a lot of physical labor getting the catfish and doing all this work. So it was a beautiful piece of work by Trimble.

There was a guy who had formerly worked at the *Gazette* whose name was Bill Shadle . . . And he had left the *Gazette* and taken a job with the Social Security Disability Administration. And so he picked up the paper that morning and sees that story, and he calls Trimble, who had been his seat mate there at the *Gazette* for a while. Shadle said, "Well, I read this piece about Olden Murray. Is all that true?" And asked him a whole bunch of questions about—"Oh, yes, yes," and he went on and on about it. Shadle said, "Well, I just hate to hear that because," he said, "he's been drawing 100 percent total and permanent disability for twenty years, but yet you describe these long activities he does every day, seven days a week." And so Trimble said, "Oh, well, you know, I was hung over that day," [*laughter*] "and I might not have heard everything just right."

The upshot of it was they went to Murray and said, "With this article as evidence, you owe us twenty years of disability payments," which came to some huge sum of money. And, of course, Murray didn't have any money. He still lived hand to mouth, but I think he really couldn't dispute that he actually did some work. So they cut off his disability payments, and they lodged, I think, a formal petition for him to repay all of this. And so, I can't remember whether Mike was responsible or Murray himself did it, but they got Bobby Fussell [the bankruptcy judge]. Bobby Fussell was a big Murray's fan, [and] he took up Murray's cause. And filed a bunch of pleadings with the Social Security Administration. The Social Security Administration were going to start proceedings against him and foreclose or whatever. So Bobby's final order was he just called up and said, "Okay, Murray's Catfish House is yours. Just come get it. It's yours. It belongs to you folks. Murray can't pay it, and he'll never be able to pay it. And he has no money and no other assets and so just come get it. You can take possession whenever you like." And so there was silence for a while, and finally, he gets a call back and says, "Well, let's forget about it. He's not going to draw more benefits, but let's just forget about it."

So after he gets that, Murray tells Fussell to "Bring your friends over and let's have some catfish." So Bobby leased a bus, one of those big, giant buses, and we all got on, including Trimble, who had never been back there since he caused so much trouble. Trimble went with some trepidation. It had been about year or more, maybe a year or two years preceding. And so we all loaded up and went over to Murray's, and he took us back to a big, long room back there. There must have been twenty-five of us. Jack Meriwether, as I recall, and a whole bunch of others. And we had a massive catfish feast. He brought out tons of catfish and slaw. And I bet there were ten different vegetables. Fresh okra, fried, turnip greens and mustard greens and hushpuppies and potatoes and just endless—he brings out all these vegetables! Then he brought out catfish. Then he brought out crappie. All this fried crappie— which is illegal. [*Laughter.*] So we had all kind of—we couldn't talk about that. We had the crappie. And then when that was all over, we were all just stuffed. We were just dying. Everybody was about to split. Then he brought out these hot chocolate pies. And so we all dined on chocolate pies. And Trimble had to get up and make a kind of confessional there and formal apology to Murray, and he told Murray had it gone to court, he was ready to perjure himself and stand up in court and say, "I made every word of it up. I never met Murray. I've never talked to him in my life." [*Laughter.*] "I made it all up."

Mike Trimble: I do not know exactly what Fussell did. I suspect he may have enlisted the help of Dale Bumpers's office because Dale Bumpers was also a big fan of Murray's. In fact, when I was getting the information for the article, I had called Dale Bumpers's office in Washington and was speaking to his secretary, trying to get a hold of Bumpers himself, and she said, "Well, what's the nature of your call?" And I said, "Well, I'm calling about Murray's Catfish Place." And her response was, "Oh, my God, it didn't burn down, did it?" [*laughs*] which was everybody's fear, because it was a fire trap, and indeed it did burn down later on. So everybody at Bumpers's office was familiar with Murray's, and I think Fussell may have enlisted his help, although I do not know. . . . I used to say that De Valls Bluff had more great restaurants per capita than any other city in the world, because it had that wonderful pie shop, which split off from Craig's Barbecue. The pie lady got mad at Mr. Craig and moved across the creek. But you had Craig's Barbecue and Murray's and that wonderful pie shop all in that same little-bitty town.

Some features were such inspired foolishness that it was surprising to see them in the "Old Lady," as the paper was sometimes called.

Dean Duncan: We got word through the Associated Press that a part–Cherokee Indian—it seems like he had an Irish name. His nickname was Pushmataha, who was one of the exalted leaders of the Cherokees in the days of old. . . . I joined this guy up at Morrilton early one morning. He had a string of boats. He had been a fishing guide at or near Tulsa, Oklahoma. The thing that caught our attention was this AP story saying he planned to become a fishing guide at Batesville. He was quoted as saying the fish up there were tremendous. We decided it was a lark and would cover this oddity. He had two boats in the water. In the second boat that was being towed by the big boat, he had a couple of smaller boats . . . He was accompanied by his wife and daughter, who was about thirteen years old. It took us two days. Back then there was no dam system, so the Arkansas River consisted of various pools. You could get your boat stuck in the sand and have to push it to the next deepest pool to get it floating again. At certain places—I put this in the story—he would direct his daughter to march ahead of the lead boat in shallow water, and when she would sink, he would know it was safe to proceed. [*Laughter.*] An unusual system. . . . This fellow had a lot of medical doctors as clients in the Tulsa area. His name for the lead boat was "Coronary Thrombosis." John Fleming suggested that I arrange to spend the night at Toad Suck Ferry so that I could write, as a dateline, "Aboard the 'Coronary Thrombosis' off Toad Suck Ferry." [*Laughter.*] I don't think I have seen a better dateline. . . . I went up to a liquor store at Palarm and called in my story. The next day we proceeded into Little Rock. . . . We knew that there was going to be this fireboat with the mayor of North Little Rock [Ross Lawhon] in it. He had what looked like an Indian blanket around him. I think he had head feathers on. There was this North Little Rock boat shooting water into the air, like it was a big New York reception.

The Gazette *had begun to relax after World War II. A lighter tone was allowed. Mort Stern was a master of the genre. The price of coffee was going from a nickel to a dime, and that inspired Stern to mimic the hard-boiled detective style.*

A well dressed man leaned up against a Little Rock coffee bar last week, obviously trying to shake a caffeine hangover. He said, "I'll take the usual, Josephine," as he plunked a dime on the counter, "And make it straight." "No cream, huh?" was the bar attendant's answer. "That's it," replied the welldressed man in a hoarse tone. It was easy to see that he had something on his mind, so I emptied my saucer and moved along side of him at the bar. "Want to talk about it, fellow?" I asked. He sizes me up and replies, "You're a reporter, he muttered." He took a stiff gulp of Java. "All right, I will tell you something if you won't use my name. They are playing right into the hands of the teetotalers," he blurted.

A talented writer could turn a ho-hum story into a bright feature. Here's the lead paragraph of a story by Doug Smith about a mock trial at the local law school.

"Watching lawyers become lawyers is a little like watching crocodile eggs hatch. Fascinating in its way, but frightening to consider what the creatures will become."

National figures occasionally came to Arkansas.

Garrison: [President] Kennedy came to Greers Ferry Dam and dedicated the structure in 1963 on October 3, 1963, just six weeks before he was assassinated. I covered his speech that same day at the Little Rock fairgrounds. It was a sweltering hot day and beads of sweat were falling off my forehead onto my notebook as I was trying to take notes. Fortunately, I noticed a White House stenographer taking down the speech, and I asked him if I could get a copy of it. And he said, "Well, if you'll go out to Little Rock Air Force Base, why, in about two hours, we'll have this transcribed and you can get copies." So, after the ceremony and the festivities, I got in my car and drove out to Little Rock Air Force Base and didn't have to wait long and got a copy of the speech. It really saved the day for me because I had crummy notes and I didn't have a tape recorder, and I was grateful for that copy.

After the Gannett company bought the Gazette, *the paper occasionally dropped the ball.*

Sean Harrison: The biggest story that I ever worked on didn't get much play in the *Arkansas Gazette,* and I was frustrated. I felt like I didn't get a lot of support from the newsroom or from my editor to pursue this more and to put more into it. It was about military suicides. There were some very questionable suicides. It all came about from a call I received one morning from some couple in rural White County. . . . Their son had died in a very questionable, so-called suicide. He was in the navy. After I published the story about the strange circumstances of this so-called suicide, I started getting calls from other parents. They were saying, "That is a lot like what happened to our son. I want to tell you about it." I started trying to get some answers from the Department of Defense. I tried to go through all the normal channels. I started getting stonewalled. More strange cases came up. I did some follow-up for the *Gazette,* but I was never really released from having to answer to this central Arkansas section and my duties to cover White County to pursue what looked like a really interesting story. I followed it even after the *Gazette* shut down, when I went to work for the Donrey Media group covering the capitol. I eventually collaborated with the *Philadelphia Inquirer* about it. They did a very fine job on it, and I got a little reporting credit on it. They even did a four-part series and put it up for nomination for the Pulitzer Prize. It didn't win. . . . I never got to the very bottom of it because we kept hitting a wall called, "That's a matter of national security." . . . Some of these suicides were murders that were covered up simply because the military couldn't afford that bad PR. They needed to keep their funding coming and their recruiting going, and these kinds of black eyes they couldn't afford. There was certainly shoddy investigative work on the behalf of some of the military investigators.

Gannett was sometimes willing to spend money to cover a faraway story. It sent Deborah Mathis, formerly a local television personality who had joined the Gazette *as an editorial writer and columnist, to the Persian Gulf because Arkansas had a disproportionately large number of soldiers in the first Gulf War.*

Deborah Mathis: I always came down into the newsroom all the time, even when I was upstairs, so I was just making one of my little visits down to the newsroom one day, and Moyers jumped out and said, "Hey, you want to go to the Persian Gulf?" Just like that, and before I could even think, I said, "Yes!" And then, of course, I'm thinking, "[Gulp!] What am I doing? I don't know anything." . . . We did get somebody from the Little Rock Air Force Base who was a public-relations person there with the squadron to meet me at the Abu Dhabi airport, where I almost got arrested right away because I was tired and irritable, and when the guy made me open up my suitcase to go through everything—"What is this?" he said. I pulled it out and put it right at his face like a gun and said, "Blow dryer!" I was really hostile and threatening to him, and kind of cussing under my breath and everything. They are used to women being very deferential, and there I was traveling around with my head uncovered—lots of swagger and attitude. I kept having to remind myself, "This is not the western world. You can die here." . . . We ended up great friends, me and all these troops. I mean, they saw that I wasn't one of those who was coming over trying to write them into trouble, and that kind of thing. I stayed there with them. I stayed on base with them. I slept with them. I pitched tents with them. I did road sorties across the desert. I saw a herd of white camels running down the—I mean, did all those things with them, and stayed up all night. I drank, cussed with them, and smoked. They let me hold their M-16s and their M-35s. They took me out on patrol with them and stuff like that. I became one of the guys . . . I wrote about how, when the shooting started—I left right before the actual firing began, okay? Before the first bombing. I wrote that when it began, it may be over quicker than you—the Iraqi, the most vaunted Republican Guard, or whatever—and the average Iraqi soldiers may give up quicker than you think because, based on what these soldiers have told me that they have seen, they are famished. They are cold and hungry. They will give up. They will surrender quickly. . . . But what was really funny was one day I was speeding up Markham trying to race home for lunch or something like that—speeding, I know. A cop pulls me over and I'm thinking, "Okay." I'm already getting out my license and everything. I don't fight with them. I just tell them, "How fast was I going?" And I turned around, and he just routinely said, "May I see your license, please?" And he just kind of reaches down to see, you know, some shoulders—and he looks up, "Oh, Deborah Mathis! You're a war hero!" [*Laughter.*] That took me to no end. I thought, "I am no more a war hero, baby, than the man in the moon, but you know what? You gonna let me out of this ticket, I'm gone." He sure did.

When the competition with the Arkansas Democrat *grew fierce,* Gazette *reporters sometimes found themselves outnumbered on a story.*

John Reed: [The newspaper war] was a lot of fun. It was frightening at times to pick up the paper and see how much copy they expended on stories. I think they had more of a news hole, at least they devoted more space to stories they really liked, but that made us a little sharper because it made us pick and choose what was newsworthy. I can give one example. Some time during my career there the records of the Razorback Foundation, which is a private fundraising arm of the athletic kingdom up at Fayetteville, were opened. It was decided that all of their records would become open to the public, and Scott Van Laningham and myself drove up to Fayetteville the day before they were to become public, got a hotel room, and these lawyers and big shots with the Razorback Foundation were going to open them up to the press at nine the next morning in the offices of the McIlroy Bank. And so Scott and I went across the street at nine and tried to look at these records. Well, there were four or five *Democrat* reporters. We recognized most of them, and there was just me and Scott for the *Gazette*. And there was a room full of records. There were probably fifty boxes, and each box was just full of receipts and memos, and everything, you know. Scott and I picked a box, and at least four *Democrat* reporters—each [of us] picked a box and started going through it. The records were not in any order. There was some stuff about Eddie Sutton, the basketball coach. There was some stuff about whoever the football coach was at the time. It was just a hodgepodge of stuff. Everybody is scrambling through, taking notes as rapidly as they could record whatever seemed interesting and newsworthy, and during the first coffee break, Scott and I had a little discussion. It's like, you know, they're going through a whole lot more boxes than we are because there's just more of them, and they're taking notes like crazy, and we made a decision we weren't going to beat them on just covering this stuff. We had been through quite a few of these boxes, and it's like there is no rhyme or reason to it. It's just going to be pure luck if you see a story. So we just wrote about the work of the Razorback Foundation and how it interacted with the athletic department, chose a few receipts to show what the records revealed, and it was not as exhaustive a piece as the *Democrat* had, but I think it was better reading because we recognized that there were going to be no smoking guns in there. But there was a lot of very interesting stuff. Eddie Sutton would charge the Razorback Foundation for everything. There were receipts in there for coke and gas that Eddie Sutton collected from the Razorback Foundation on the way back from a recruiting trip—you know, twelve dollars' worth of stuff—and I never would have known that had happened. There were receipts for steak dinners for the entire football team, and I cannot remember how much that cost at Coy's, the big steakhouse up there, but it was a huge amount of money. It's just like a little awards ceremony, but just seeing the numbers of steaks eaten gave you an idea of just how many steaks a football team can eat. It was pretty impressive. But it seemed that the

Democrat had more space, and they would have these big, big long stories. And our editors did a good job, I think, of making us—just old fashioned journalism—making us pick what was important, answering the questions, getting the important stuff in the top of the story, and just cutting out the verbiage and not relying on background paragraphs too much.

Most of us started our reporting careers by writing obituaries. Ernie Dumas finished his the same way.

Dumas: My last day as a reporter would have been about the second week of January 1979. Bill Clinton had just been sworn in as governor. And so I went up to take Jerry Neil's place [as an editorial writer]. Jerry Neil had died the previous fall. And my last day as a reporter, I went to the capitol and had written everything, and I was cleaning out my desk there in the newsroom. And Bill Shelton, the city editor, came over and said, "Is this your last day?" And I said, "Yes." And he said, "Well, what happened to this?" And he tossed me this old carbon of an assignment he had given me a couple of years earlier. It was what we used to call "As Time Allows." Up at the top it said "ATA," and that meant, "As time allows, do this." And it said, "Do a Faubus obituary." And as usual on those kinds of things, I'd stick them in my drawer, and sometimes on a holiday, or whatever, and nothing going on at the capitol, I'd do these assignments.

But here was one that was going to take a ton of time, to write a Faubus obituary. You know that was something that was going to take a week or a couple of weeks, maybe, and so I'd never done anything with it. And Faubus, I think, was back out at the Baptist Hospital that week. He'd had a pacemaker put in, and I think he was back out at the hospital with some irregularities or something. We'd had a little story about it. So Shelton said, "Faubus is back out at the hospital. If Faubus dies and we don't have an obituary, the headline is going to say, 'Faubus Dies, Dumas Fired.'"

And so I kind of blushed because Shelton just never—you know, I think he was kind of joking, but Shelton usually meant everything he said. So I thought, "Oh, shit. I guess I've got to do this." So I called Elaine and said, "I'm just going to get a bite to eat here, and I'm going to work tonight." So I stayed up there all night long and went back to the microfilm and read microfilm all night long and got all the resources I could about the '57 crisis. There were a couple of books about it. And got all of Faubus's files down, pulled all the files. And read that stuff all night and stayed there all day— stayed up all night Friday night, all day Saturday, worked on it. I went home

Saturday night and got a few hours sleep and came back down and worked all day Sunday on it and finally finished it. And it was a mammoth obit. They rolled it down the aisle in front of the city desk. . . .

And, of course, Faubus had a career after that. That was 1979. He came back, and, you know, afterward, he divorced his second wife, Elizabeth Westmoreland, and got back into politics, ran for governor again in 1986 or so, and was in the Frank White administration, so he had quite a prolific career after that. And so, about every three or four years, I'd dig this thing out and splice in some more stuff to get all the new stuff in. And so, by 1991, when the *Gazette* closed, it was an even longer article because I had written probably another thousand or two thousand words.

So that afternoon, the computers shut down at twelve, and they had the big thing down in the newsroom and told us the *Gazette* was closed and to clean out our stuff. So I was up in my office cleaning out stuff, and Max Brantley called and said, "Do you know where that Faubus obit is?" And I said, "No, I guess it's in the computer stored someplace." And he said, "Well, I can't find it. It must be on a disk someplace." And so he said, "Well, I don't want the *Democrat* to get their hands on it. So I want to get it killed before they come in and take over." So he said he'd talk to one of the wombats who were our main computer specialists there. And he told me later that he had found somebody, and they had found the computer tape, and it had been killed. It had been thrown away. I, of course, had printed out a copy of it and took it home with me and had it at the house. So in 1994, Faubus died. And the next day the *Democrat-Gazette* had this big front-page obit. That was the lead story in the paper, and it went all the way down the right side, and inside it just filled up page after page of the paper. And I didn't read it. And up at the top it said, "By the *Democrat-Gazette* staff." And that night, Doug Smith called me and said, "Was that your obit in the *Democrat* today?" "No, no. Max killed that." Well, he said he had mentioned it to Max and Max thought it read familiar. Both of them thought it read like me. And so I went back and picked up the paper, and it did sound awfully familiar. So I dug out the old obit that I had written. And, sure enough, it was. There was my obit. So I called Doug back and said, "Yes, that was my obit." And so the *Arkansas Times* did a little blurb on it. You know, they write these little press columns, usually attacking the *Democrat-Gazette*. And it pointed out that the *Democrat-Gazette* was claiming credit for this obit that its staff had not written but that had been written by this old *Gazette* staffer. And about a few weeks passed and I go down for a little luncheon, a Society of Professional Journalists banquet. Griffin Smith, the editor of the *Democrat-Gazette,* was there. He was the speaker. And after he speaks, he spots me and calls me over and said he wanted to apologize for that obit. He said, "I assumed you didn't want your byline on it, but I personally edited it, and when I left there, I left instructions that there was to be no byline at all on it. But when I picked up the paper the next morning, somebody had stuck that line on there, 'By the *Democrat-Gazette* staff.'" And so I said, "Oh, Griffin, it doesn't make any difference. I was just happy to see it in the paper." And he said, "Well, you know, we had every right to publish it because we bought the paper and we had every right." And I said, "Oh, sure. I realize that. I don't have any problem with it. And I didn't ask the *Arkansas Times* to write that. I'm happy to see it in print." And I told him the story about how it came about. And so months passed. And I picked up the paper one day, the *Democrat-Gazette,* and see a full-page ad that said, "Prize-winning Newspaper." And it said that the *Democrat-Gazette* had won first place in deadline news reporting from some national organization for the Faubus obit. . . . First place in deadline news reporting. It took something like—how long?—fourteen years to write that story!

Bill Shelton, a few years out of service as a World War II pilot, was one of the nation's best city editors. He was jovial company away from work, but in the newsroom he was demanding, stern, and sound in his judgment. Reporters called him the "Great Stone Face"—behind his back. [Photo by Larry Obsitnik, courtesy of the *Arkansas Democrat-Gazette* and Special Collections, University of Arkansas Libraries, Fayetteville.] (MC 1280) Box, 92, File 514.

Larry Obsitnik's photo of the 101st Airborne paratroopers rolling into Little Rock became a lasting image of the 1957 school desegregation crisis. [Courtesy of the *Arkansas Democrat-Gazette* and Special Collections, University of Arkansas Libraries, Fayetteville.] (MC1280) Box 11/7 Image 441.

J. N. Heiskell, editor and a chief owner of the *Gazette* for seventy years, wrote his editorials in longhand. He specialized in one-paragraph essays and bristled at having them referred to as mere column-fillers. [Photo by Larry Obsitnik, courtesy of the *Arkansas Democrat-Gazette,* and Special Collections, University of Arkansas Libraries, Fayetteville.] (MC 1280) Box: D3, File: D555 & D 558.

Executive Editor Harry Ashmore wore his authority lightly. He enjoyed slouching around the newsroom, but when he sat down to compose an editorial—sometimes after three martinis at lunch—his words were unfailingly eloquent. [Photo by Larry Obsitnik, courtesy of the *Arkansas Democrat-Gazette* and Special Collections, University of Arkansas Libraries, Fayetteville.] (MC 1280) Box D3, File D738.

Police Chief Gene Smith, who was known as a fearless cop, halted angry, hurriedly assembled segregationists before they could reach Central High School on August 12, 1959. The school board, taking opponents by surprise, had reopened the city's high schools early after having closed them the previous year in a futile attempt to avoid or delay integration. [Photo by Larry Obsitnik, courtesy of the *Arkansas Democrat-Gazette* and Special Collections Division, University of Arkansas Libraries, Fayetteville.]

Rodney Dungan of the *Gazette* photography staff shot this picture of Governor Orval Faubus after the dedication of the Guion Ferry on the White River. Dungan and Leroy Donald of the reporting staff were already in their air-conditioned car. Dungan got off a single shot through the window glass, leaning across Donald's lap. He was amazed when he developed his film and saw that he actually had a picture. The photo became perhaps the most famous image of Faubus. The governor air-brushed out the cigarette in his hand and used the picture in several reelection campaigns, to the consternation of the *Gazette's* anti-Faubus readers. [Courtesy of the *Arkansas Democrat-Gazette* and Special Collections, University of Arkansas Libraries, Fayetteville.] From the Margaret Smith Ross Papers (MC 1587), Box 66.

Governor Faubus facing reporters and photographers and backed by members of his administration. He held numerous press conferences during the fall of 1957 to defend his calling out the National Guard to block the desegregation of Central High. [Photo by Larry Obsitnik, courtesy of the *Arkansas Democrat-Gazette* and Special Collections, University of Arkansas Libraries, Fayetteville.] (MC 1280), Box 9, Folder 1, J174.

George Fisher, for many years the best-known political artist in Arkansas, drew this cartoon to be published on the *Gazette's* last day. The paper was suspended before it could be printed. He then drew it live on KARK-TV. The eagle's weeping drew tears from old staffers and from countless readers. [Courtesy of Special Collections, University of Arkansas Libraries, Fayetteville.] From the George Fisher Collection (MC 1495).

William E. Woodruff, who founded the *Arkansas Gazette* in 1819, brought his press to Arkansas Post by riverboat. He was a native of New York but quickly established himself as a leading citizen of the Arkansas Territory. Arkansas Post, a thriving community of mainly French settlers, celebrated the *Gazette's* first issue with a grand party. A local business contributed a barrel of whiskey. [Courtesy of UALR archives & Special Collections] From UALR Photo Coll., J. N. Heiskell Individuals, William E. Woodruff.

7

Harry Ashmore

Harry Scott Ashmore was a South Carolinian. His newspaper career began in the 1930s at the Greenville Piedmont *and the* Greenville News. *He left his hometown to work two years at the* News *in Charlotte, North Carolina, then won a Nieman Fellowship to Harvard University. World War II interrupted in 1942. He served in Europe as an officer with General George Patton's Third Army.*

After the war, he became the editorial writer for the News, *a job held before the war by W. J. Cash while he was writing* The Mind of the South. *Ashmore was hired as executive editor of the* Gazette *in 1947. During the next twelve years, as the civil rights movement swept the South, he and his friends Ralph McGill of the* Atlanta Constitution, *Hodding Carter Jr. of the Greenville* Delta Democrat Times, *and a few other Southern editors earned national reputations as leaders of progressive thought in the former Confederacy. Only a handful of earlier Southern editors, such as Henry Grady of Atlanta and Henry Watterson of Louisville, had achieved similar national standing.*

Ashmore's book The Negro and the Schools, *a study funded by the Ford Foundation in the early 1950s, laid out in plain language the unequal treatment of black children in the segregated schools of the South. Advance copies were given to the justices of the Supreme Court. According to Chief Justice Earl Warren, the book influenced the Court's decision ordering school desegregation. It was published the day before the decision was announced, May 17, 1954.*

Ashmore's career changed dramatically in September 1957. His one-time friend Governor Orval E. Faubus called out the Arkansas National Guard to block the desegregation of Central High School in Little Rock. Ashmore denounced the action in a series of eloquently written front-page editorials. There was a strain of poignancy in the ensuing feud. Ashmore had helped elect Faubus and had supported the governor's progressive policies during his early years in office.

For years after the school crisis, Faubus would lambaste Ashmore and the paper as integrationist tools of a dictatorial federal judiciary.

The paper won a Pulitzer Prize for its coverage of the school story. Ashmore won another for his editorials on the constitutional crisis provoked by the governor's action. At a dinner given by the city's leaders to celebrate the paper's prizes, Ashmore, already known for his wit and presence at the podium, began his remarks by recalling an anecdote about Watterson, the turn-of-the-century editor of the Louisville Courier-Journal. *Someone had once asked Watterson what he would do when he retired. He replied that he intended to lie in bed all day drinking bourbon whiskey and reading his own editorials.*

Ashmore left the Gazette *in 1959 to join the Fund for the Republic in Santa Barbara, California. He was concurrently editor-in-chief of* Encyclopedia Britannica *and divided his time between Chicago and Santa Barbara. He wrote numerous books on civil rights and the South, including a well-regarded history of Arkansas. He died in 1998 at Santa Barbara. According to his friend Sander Vanocur, the former television correspondent, he spent the last evening of his life entertaining friends at Vanocur's dinner table with one story after another, then went home and died. They scattered his ashes on the Pacific Ocean off the coast at Santa Barbara.*

Jason Rouby, a copy editor, recalled the night the governor sent National Guard troops to surround Central High School and what happened when Ashmore was told about it.

Jason Rouby: I had written the headline and the subhead for the main story: "City Quiet on Eve of Integration." George Stroud [another copy editor] went home for dinner, like he always did, and called back to the *Gazette*—this must have been at eight at night. He said, "I don't know what's going on, but there are troops around Central High. You'd better find out." . . . Somebody called and found out that Governor Faubus had called out the Arkansas National Guard . . . Someone asked, "Shall we tell Harry Ashmore?" . . . Finally, I think it was Ken Parker and I who said, "We've simply got to call Harry Ashmore! This is big! We've got to call him." And Harry Ashmore by phone immediately said, "Stop the press!" Just like in the movies. I had never heard that before in thirteen years of newspaper work: "Stop the press!" And in the first edition, probably the central Arkansas first edition, there was a boldface lead paragraph saying that troops had been called to Central High. . . . Harry Ashmore came down and heard what had happened. He made a few phone calls. He sat out in the city room, and he sat at the typewriter and wrote the front-page editorial that said this is no longer a case of integration; this is a case of constitutional rights—states' rights versus the federal government. And that's the editorial that won the Pulitzer Prize for him . . . That's what impressed me more about Harry Ashmore than anything I ever knew about him before or after. And it was remarkable to be there that night to see history being made.

The editorial said in part, "Thus the issue is no longer segregation vs. integration. The question has now become the supremacy of the government of the United States in all matters of law. And clearly the federal government cannot let this issue remain unsolved, no matter what the cost to this community."

Ashmore talked about his early years and changes in his thinking during interviews with Roy Reed while Reed was researching a biography of Orval Faubus.

Roy Reed: Harry, how did you become a liberal?

Harry Ashmore: I don't know that I am a liberal. I'm a moderate—I'm a [*bleep*] immoderate moderate. [*Laughs.*] Growing up in South Carolina, I think the South has always had—the stereotype has never been a perfect fit. I'd say that there was always in the South a substantial number of white people who believed in justice for blacks and who believed in fairness for blacks. That didn't mean that they wanted them to marry their daughter or [*inaudible*] support social integration . . . I had become by the time I got to Harvard [on a Nieman Fellowship] convinced in my own mind that this old segregated pattern would not hold much longer. I didn't know how it was going to end, but due to—the demography was changing so rapidly. The cultural standards were changing. The old segregation society depended on being isolated, and it wasn't any longer. Everybody was moving around, and people were moving off the farms to the city. The courses I took up at Harvard were really intended to explore—as best I could with people up there—what kind of changes to expect. I was determined to go back south, and I thought—I was correct in this—[that] this was going to be the biggest goddamn story. If I'm going to stay in the news business—it's coming. It might not be right here yet. Of course, shortly after the war, Truman came out with that Civil Rights Commission report, and that really put the shit in the fan. Well, then I got back from Europe at the end of the war in Europe and was ordered back to the Pentagon . . . Nobody ever heard of me, and they couldn't remember who the hell had issued the orders to bring me back or what I was going to do. So they said, "You're entitled to rest and recreation. You can take three weeks and then come back. By that time we can figure out why you were ordered back from Europe." So I went up—my wife was staying with her mother . . . I picked her up—now, this was the spring [and] it really wasn't warm enough to do it, but . . . we went out to Nantucket. The place was practically deserted because the summer was over. My wife still talks about this. She was pissed off. I picked up . . . the two-volume [Gunnar] Myrdal report, "An American Dilemma." I took the goddamn thing out to Nantucket [and] spent my rest and recreation two weeks reading "American Dilemma," which confirmed a lot of notions that I already had and did convince me that this system was not to endure. By the time I got out of the army and went back to Charlotte —which I did directly and then went back to Greenville—I became editor of the Charlotte *News*. I succeeded W. J. Cash there. He had been the editorial page editor before—he was dead by that time. I never knew him. The *News* was an enlightened paper. Again, you could stand for justice. You could stand for gold supply. You could fight for improved schools for blacks—not desegregating them but teachers' pay and all that kind of thing—and generally improving the standards for blacks. We cracked down on police abuse cases and clear cases of miscarriage in court, and that kind of thing. I think we had a general approbation list, and there was a hell of a lot of people didn't like it. They considered us as kind of a half-ass liberal—but at least you weren't unrespectable. If you crossed the line in anything that they called "social intermingling of the races," that was absolutely taboo, and you would either have to leave the South or shut up.

Reed: Some people say that the enlightenment came during the college years . . . You went to Clemson, didn't you?

Ashmore: Clemson's campus is the former plantation of John C. Calhoun, and the founding father was Governor Pitchfork Ben Tillman, who actually set the damn thing up. The land was left by Clemson, who was John Calhoun's son-in-law and who had inherited the plantation . . . The most distinguished graduate ahead of me was Strom Thurmond. So Harvard thinks that I was in a hotbed of insurrection. I was [a Nieman Fellow] in 1941 and 1942. I was there at the time of Pearl Harbor. I didn't finish the year.

Reed: You had clearly begun to think about the race issue by then.

Ashmore: Oh yes, I had thought about it a great deal. As a matter of fact I had been writing politics. I had been through some political campaigns. By that time I was convinced, as I say—I had also spent enough time in the North to know something about—I had gone up and done a series on the

"Deep North," comparing the working-class people . . . The unions and the northern press were attacking the terrible conditions in the cotton mills in the South because all the cotton mills were moving South . . . I never thought that I was actively out there crusading for change. It was rather that I thought change was going to take place, and I wanted to prepare myself to deal with it. I knew damn well that any newspaper editor or newspaper reporter in the political heart of the South was not going to escape this question very long. I could see it was bound to come.

Reed: What were you doing at the *Gazette* during this period, 1954 to 1957?

Ashmore: I think what we were doing—and to some extent consciously—was trying to prepare our readers to face the fact that there was going to be change and that it was going to happen in any case and get ready for it. It was probably a good thing. We were not talking so much about social justice. I've said . . . if you look at places in the South that had newspapers that followed, that took the position the *Gazette* did when the showdown came—as in Louisville, Nashville, and most of the North Carolina cities—you would find that it wasn't so much what they said when the thing happened as what they'd been saying before. They had been consciously trying to prepare public opinion that this was not the end of the world—that it wasn't going to mean your daughter would have to get married to a nigger tomorrow morning. So, I think we were trying to do that. Also, we were very strong supporters of Harry Truman in the Dixiecrat rebellion [of 1948]. We led the fight against the Dixiecrats [in Arkansas]. Ben Laney was the governor, and I actually debated Ben Laney on a statewide network, and we were arguing party loyalty. For God's sake, lets don't split the party on this issue . . . We were arguing about this change, [and] the South can't secede again.

. . . And I felt strongly that the burden and obligation of the newspaper was to try to alert the citizenry as far as it could, try to prepare them for the transition. So we were willing to support any kind of a compliance if the court came down. I then took for some practical reason making law and order the issue instead of segregation, saying there isn't any option and we stand for law and order, we've got to have an orderly procedure, and then follow. . . . And I was convinced right up to the last minute that Little Rock would avoid the trouble that we had. I thought that it would go in the pattern of North Carolina and Tennessee and there would be resistance in east Arkansas but that there would be compliance and it would be slow, it would be gradual, but they would start moving . . .

The big department-store people stood with us. That was kind of the acid test because they were threatened with boycotts, secondary boycotts. They

were under pressure to pull their advertising out. And the *Democrat* was trying to get it. And we never did lose any significant amount of the department
stores. At that time we must have had 75 or 80 percent of it. And in fact, that
was one of the things that enabled us to get through, and it was very critical
with national advertising too. As long as we could hold the department-store
stuff. So Hugh and Jim Williamson [business manager] and those people
worked on that very hard.

Reed: Here in Arkansas, we had the leading paper, a paper of enormous influence, taking this reasonable stand and saying get ready for this. We had a governor whose inclination was probably along the same lines but who
essentially kept silent. Now, I'm tempted to believe that if the governor had
joined the *Gazette*, and added his voice—

Ashmore: I think that's possible. I don't think we can guarantee it, and I think
that Orval—whether right or wrong—made his decision essentially on his
reading of the political situation that he couldn't be elected for a third term.
He had the third term tradition to overcome.

Reed: Why didn't some of you leaders in Little Rock make it your business to
see that this fellow [Faubus] did the right thing?

Ashmore: I don't think that I ever could have been thought of as a leader in
that sense. I think we were trying to maintain a standard to which the wise
and just could repair. We were trying to prepare people for this change, and
we were on the editorial page and the reporting . . . Your question is a proper
one. Why didn't I follow up personally if I felt so strongly about this and try
to persuade Orval? There's another reason that's quite revealing . . . When I
went [and] took a year's leave for Stevenson in 1956 and went with Adlai [in
his campaign for the presidency], shortly after I got up to Chicago, Orval, of
course, was then governor. [Senator] Bill Fulbright was a strong supporter of
Stevenson's. [He] had Stevenson come down for a duck shoot at this damn
place in south Arkansas . . . Orval was there, and I did everything I could to
put him together with Stevenson. It turned out that we didn't persuade
Orval. Orval went with Harriman . . . Well, that may have convinced me to
some degree that I really didn't have any real influence with him.

Reed: I guess what I want to hear you say—I'd like for you to assure me that
this was not simply an extension of this class problem that we were talking
about earlier. That Orval simply didn't appeal to you.

Ashmore: Well, I don't think that's true. I really don't think that's true. I never
had any adverse reaction personally to him at all. You know, he wasn't the
kind of fellow that I'd like to have sat around with all night drinking whiskey,
but I certainly had nothing against him, and I didn't dislike him. I certainly

had no feeling of scorn for him until he began—actually, I really got personally outraged.

Reed: But were you ever aware after Orval became governor that he felt that
the Little Rock establishment held him in contempt [and] that he felt resentment toward the establishment?

Ashmore: I don't think I was aware of that until about the time it all blew up.
Prior to that I don't think I was aware of that. I don't think that I felt he was
being scorned. I don't think he was, particularly.

*In the 1954 gubernatorial primary, Governor Francis Cherry made an issue of
Faubus's having been a student at Commonwealth, a left-wing college near Mena.
The suggestion was that Faubus might have been a Communist or Communist
sympathizer. The college became an explosive issue in the campaign. Faubus tried
in vain to explain it away, saying at first that he had been on the campus only a few
days, then having to back down from that. As he became desperate, Ashmore and
some other Little Rock friends came to his defense by drafting a statement that
turned the tide in Faubus's favor.*

Reed: Tell me about the Commonwealth College speech that I have always
heard you wrote for Orval.

Ashmore: John Wells [a conservative journalist and political activist who had
formerly worked for the *Gazette*] was running the Cherry organization—he
was doing the hatchet work for the Cherry campaign. I don't think John but
somebody with the Cherry campaign came in to see me and said they were
going to put out a handbill with this Commonwealth College story in it. We
were nominally supporting Cherry with no enthusiasm. I said, "Let me tell
you something"—this is Joe McCarthy time, you know—and I said, "We
have all heard that goddamn story. We've got that damn story in the files over
here, and we know he was at Commonwealth College, and I'm not going to
tolerate that kind of smear. I'm just going to warn you that if you do run this
goddamn thing anywhere, or anybody else publishes it or an ad—" First,
they wanted an ad, and I said we won't take that. "And I want to tell you
something else, if you run it, I'm going to have a front-page editorial denounc-
ing Cherry. It's absolutely outrageous." So they circulated an ad down in
Little Rock, and I denounced Cherry duly. Well, the thing came out and
Orval panicked—just completely fell apart. He issued a flat denial that he
had ever been to Commonwealth College. It was absolutely absurd on the
face of it. This was very late in the campaign. This was in the last two or three
days before the runoff. So Ed Dunaway [a lawyer] and Henry [Woods, a

lawyer and along with Dunaway a Faubus supporter] and I then went out to my house, and we put the speech together. I did most of the writing, and we hacked it out in the afternoon.

Reed: How did he handle that? I mean, how did he get around the denial?

Ashmore: It took some pretty fancy footwork. I think what he said was that he had been misinterpreted. He didn't say he had been misquoted—I think that is the usual wile, isn't it? [He said] that what he intended to say was that he had been there a very short time and, when he found out what was going on there, that he left and that he had no further connection with it ever. That's what he intended to say, but somehow it got to be a denial that he had ever been there . . . I didn't have any doubts that he had been there. I don't know how active he was. Of course, it made so much sense. If you could know old man Sam Faubus [Orval's father], he could send him to a college like that, hoping by God it would make a Christian out of him or make a Wobbly [International Workers of the World] out of him, anyway. So, Orval's story was—which I accepted for the purposes of the speech—that he had gone there and stayed just a few weeks. He was deliberately vague whether it was two weeks or ten days. Obviously he was trying to cover his ass from what the hell was going on. I think it's probably true that he didn't stay there. The biggest lie he told was [that] he left because they were practicing free love and that deeply offended him. Now you talk about a preposterous lie.

Reed: You mean that was out of character with Orval?

Ashmore: Well, I would think it would have been out of character with any hillbilly eighteen years old—a horny boy coming down out of [*inaudible*] being deeply offended by free love and all this loose morals [*laughter*] around the college. I worked around it in the speech, and then we went on the attack against Cherry for using this dreadful thing . . . A poor boy down from the mountains trying to get an education [who] realizes he's gotten in the wrong place and left . . . I've got that terrible book he wrote that he autographed to me—"To my old friend Harry [*inaudible*] favors." . . . My recollection is that everybody including Orval thought he was beaten. You know he had just edged into the runoff . . . It was a stupid thing for him [Cherry] to do.

Ashmore was a hero to the Gazette's *young reporters and editors, partly because of his wit and his eloquence with the language. Many stories were told by and about him.*

Mort Stern: Ashmore was a lot of fun . . . A new book came out called *The Indoor Bird Watcher's Guide* [by Helen Ferril]. It caricatured all types of people as birds. So I did a bunch of such sketches of people at the Gazette. And the bird that looked like Harry I named "the Offcolor Tailspinner" because he was a master of such tales.

Reed: One day a neighbor lady was out in her yard and noticed that Barbara [Ashmore] had a ladder up, cleaning out the gutters on her house, on Barbara's house. And the neighbor lady, I gather with some indignation, said, "Mrs. Ashmore, let me ask you a question. What does *Mr.* Ashmore do?" And Barbara said, "He *thinks*."

Bob Douglas: Mr. Heiskell named Harry Ashmore executive editor and put him over the newsroom as well as over the editorial page. . . . He [Heiskell] wanted a different kind of paper after the war. He wanted to catch up. And Ashmore was a great newspaperman. He was great to work for . . . [Ashmore] really came to prominence in 1948, through the editorials he wrote about the governor's race. The *Gazette* had never endorsed a candidate for anything. It had a policy against endorsement. Well, we didn't endorse one that year, but Harry took out after Jack Holt [a leading candidate] because Jack interjected the race issue into the campaign. So he pretty well blasted him, and that hadn't been done before.

Reed: Ashmore lived and breathed politics. What did you make of Ashmore's being involved in politics, his extracurricular activities?

Douglas: I would have preferred that he not be, but Harry could do it, you know. It certainly didn't affect his objectivity at all. He liked for things to come out his way, but if they didn't, he wasn't going to tell you to make it come out like he wanted.

Reed: He worked for Adlai Stevenson in 1952.

Douglas: Yes, in 1952 and 1956. He wrote speeches for [Governor Sid] McMath and for Orval. Wrote the famous speech that Orval gave, so he was an activist. He was a great newspaperman and a lot of fun to be around. A great talker, had some great stories, and a darn good newspaperman. What he did for the *Gazette* can't be overstated. He had a difficult, big, bold sort of mold in his head of what kind of newspaper it could become. Oh, it had always been a solid newspaper. Harry supported the newsroom. He was a champion of the newsroom . . . The only time I can remember Harry being upset about anything and saying so—in 1957, I remember a straight news story—I think a round-up on the legislature, and it had one sentence about Faubus. It said, "Following the Governor's own peculiar liking. . . ." Well, that was not objective, and he was really very upset about that. He was the most objective man I guess I ever knew.

Reed: I wish I had known that and had bounced it off Orval Faubus before he died. Faubus might not have believed me. He always figured Ashmore was his sworn enemy, that he went out there in the newsroom and directed the reporters to write biased copy against him.

Douglas: Yes, that is what a number of our readers, of course, thought. They believed Faubus. It was total nonsense. There was never anything like that.

Reed: Did you tell me that story about him being out at the Little Rock Club one day during the Central High crisis?

Douglas: Herbert Douglas, the bartender, the black bartender, . . . a legendary figure, he would put Harry's drinks on the tab of some arch-segregationist. [*Laughs.*]

Reed: The other story also involves Herbert Douglas and Ashmore, who having been in there with two or three visiting newsmen, had already had two or three martinis under his belt. As they were leaving, Harry tells the others to go on, and he stops at the bar and tells Herbert Douglas to make him another martini. And while the man is mixing the martini, Harry said, "You better make it a double. I have to go back and write an editorial."

T. Harri Baker: You mentioned the view among the anti-integrationist group that Harry Ashmore was standing there in the newsroom directing news.

Reed: Harry Ashmore did spend quite a lot of time in the newsroom because it was his job. He was not just the chief editorial writer of the *Arkansas Gazette;* he was also the executive editor, which meant that his responsibilities were for the editorial page and the news coverage . . . He was in and out of the newsroom all day long. That was his job. He felt at home there. He was an old newsman, and he loved being around things that were happening . . . He was a presence in the newsroom but not at all in a way that his enemies liked to think. First of all, he didn't believe in slanting the news. He felt the story as the facts had it was interesting enough. They didn't need to be slanted. They were not slanted . . .

I would see him over at the telegraph machines reading the latest wire stuff coming in from around the country. I have seen him, after a spirited conversation with some of the other editors and obviously thinking it was an editorial idea, look at his watch, realize it was close to the deadline, . . . [and] sit down at a typewriter in the newsroom and commandeer some reporter's typewriter and dash off an editorial. He could do it in minutes. He was a very fluent writer.

8

1957

The Gazette's *biggest story during the last half of the twentieth century was the desegregation crisis at Central High School. The Little Rock School Board, led by Superintendent Virgil Blossom, had proposed to comply with the Supreme Court's 1954 desegregation decision by moving nine black students from their all-black school to Central in the fall of 1957. On the day they arrived, they were turned away by Arkansas National Guard troops called out by Governor Orval E. Faubus. After weeks of court appearances and after a day of serious rioting that threatened to get out of hand, President Dwight D. Eisenhower sent federal troops to quell the trouble and enforce desegregation.*

The story made national and international headlines for almost a year. Faubus, exploiting his stand against "forced integration," won the third of what would become a record-setting six terms. The Gazette *won two Pulitzer Prizes for its news coverage and Harry S. Ashmore's editorials. The prizes came at a heavy price. Segregationists tried to mount a statewide boycott of the paper. Thousands of readers cancelled their subscriptions. Faubus used the* Gazette *as a whipping boy almost daily.*

The governor emerged from the conflict as the new hero of the South's massive resistance. Segregationists bent on preserving the Southern way of life—white supremacy, that is—took heart from the events at Little Rock. Since the Supreme Court's school decision three years earlier, they had looked for a leader. Here, apparently, they had one. Never mind that he had once attended a left-wing college, that his father had been a card-carrying Socialist (almost no one knew that at the time), that he had developed a reputation as a social progressive, and that he was even suspected in some quarters of being an integrationist. Faubus became the man of the hour in the Deep South, a leader for Dixie's last stand.

There remained a few other last stands after Central High. Blood was shed in some places. Two men died in the struggle to integrate the University of

Mississippi. A lot more died in the long effort to secure African American voting rights in Alabama, Georgia, Mississippi, Louisiana, and the Carolinas. The simple right of a person of color to buy a cup of coffee in a five-and-dime store cost more bloodied heads. Martin Luther King was assassinated for the cause of racial equality, but he was only the best known of the many victims of murder, arson, and assaults on common decency. Finally, toward the end of the 1960s, massive resistance was quietly put to rest, virtually unnoticed, almost unmourned.

But in Arkansas in 1957, feelings ran so high against Ashmore and the Gazette *that it became unsafe for its carriers in parts of the state. An angry crowd blocked the road at Clarendon one day and refused to let the* Gazette *truck pass. Leon Reed, the* Gazette's *circulation manager at the time, described how the driver persuaded the crowd to disperse.*

Leon Reed: He explained to these people, "Now, folks, I just got a company here that hauls papers. That's how I make my living. I don't know what your complaint is. I'm not interested about your complaint. All I'm going to do is, I'm going to back this truck up about a block, and when I come through here next time, I'm going to be going forty-five or fifty miles an hour. Please don't be in the way." He backed up, and he started driving the thing forward. [*The crowd parted.*] Someone asked the driver later, "Were you going to go all the way through with it?" He said, "We'll never know, will we?"

When 1957 hit, we lost thousands in circulation in thirty days. People were knocking on doors. Neighbors didn't want the paper being delivered. [*Laughs.*] We got the hell kicked out of us pretty good.

Pat Best, the switchboard operator, fielded many of the angry phone calls.

Best: It was frightening sometimes, believe me. Every call was usually—if we could get the calls through, they were usually cussing the *Gazette.* Everyone was upset and angry with the *Gazette.* They called us everything. Threats came constantly. They were going to come and kill us. They were going to come and bomb the switchboard. We had ten lines, incoming lines. At that time all you had to do was to go to a pay telephone and dial Franklin 4-5081, put the phone down, and walk away to tie up our lines until the telephone company was able to physically go out and put the receiver back on the hook.

Charles Allbright was a popular columnist for many years. He worked for the Gazette *off and on from 1955 to 1991 as a columnist, an editorial writer, and a reporter. Years later, he still remembered how it was when the paper was under siege in 1957.*

Charles Allbright: I think we all got very, very close at that time. We knew we were right, and we also knew we were in some sort of peril . . . I would get calls: "Allbright, stay out of this," from people I didn't know. And being met out back at the alley, maybe, by some, you know, burly folks. "Stay out of this. Stay out of this." . . . I went out there one day, at Central. There were, by police estimate, two thousand people in the street between Fourteenth and Sixteenth Streets in front of Central, and they were really restless because nothing had happened all day. And, at that time, the *Arkansas Gazette,* the *New York Times,* and *Time* magazine were reviled by the people in that street. And, with nothing happening, they were looking for something to unload on. There is a guy over here, an author that I knew and a professor at Arkansas Tech, Francis Irby Gwaltney. And he said—I will never forget this—he pointed at me and said, "Well, there is a *Gazette* guy right there." . . . And I will never know why he did that. But I have never been more frightened than I was at that moment. . . . I thought, well, here it is. I had some notes and pencil, and I just dropped them, and I freed myself up to do whatever. And back over here somewhere, I was tapped on the shoulder, and it was a major in the army, and he was in uniform, and he announced, "This man is going with me." And he got me out of there, and I don't know what would have happened. But mob psychology is a fierce thing.

Ray Moseley in later years dodged bullets all over Africa and the Middle East. He covered the Iranian Revolution, the Rhodesian Civil War, and the first Gulf War for the Chicago Tribune. *He was first baptized in abuse in Little Rock. In 1957, he was one of the* Gazette *reporters on the scene at Central High almost every day. On a typical day, he might find himself hectored in the daytime in front of the school, then again in the evening at a segregationist rally.*

Ray Moseley: I spent a lot of time during all of this going to these White Citizens' Council meetings. This guy, I think his name was Amis Guthridge. Guthridge was always very friendly to me. I think he had a sense of playing to the press. I remember going to one of these meetings one night, and they had some guy there from Mississippi. And he started talking about some incident, and he said, "Are there any reporters here? If so, I'd like to go off the record." And I stood up and said, "I'm from the *Arkansas Gazette,* and my paper's policy is if this is a public meeting, you can't go off the record." People started screaming or shouting, "*Gazette* scab! Throw him out!" [*Laughter.*] I felt pretty uncomfortable. As soon as that meeting was over, old Amis Guthridge rushed up to me and said in a very loud voice, "Ray, I think you were absolutely right!" [*Laughter.*] I think he was afraid they were all going to pounce on me.

Robin Woods Loucks, a daughter of Millie Woods, the food editor, was a junior at Central High that fall. She later worked in the Gazette *library. She remembered the reaction of some white students when she befriended the black students.*

Robin Woods Loucks: When they finally were allowed into the schools, Terrence Roberts was in my algebra class . . . He came in and was absolutely shaking with fear. The teacher assigned him a seat right by me, and then she called the class back to their books and said, "Please open to page . . ."—whatever it was. And he didn't have a book. I expected one of the guys in the class to share his book, as they would have done normally because girls wouldn't share their book with a boy. Nobody did, so I pulled my chair close to his and shared my book with him.

Reed: Did that seem to calm him down?

Loucks: I think we both sat there and shook for the remainder of the class. [*Laughs.*] . . . Not all of the white students but a certain element of the white students behaved very badly. They followed me home that day and cussed me and threw stones at me. It was about a mile walk to the house. I went in and threw up, and I got—I promised myself on that walk that I would not turn and look at them. I didn't want to let them know how terrified I was . . . But I did not realize how badly [the black students] were treated. I did not realize, for instance, that Ernest Green—in gym class they urinated on his uniforms. Things like that. If you have to deal with that every day, that would make life—the anguish I felt was only a tidbit in comparison. And I know how much it affected my life, literally. Even today, I don't think it will ever go away.

The city's four high schools were closed the following year after a citywide election on the question of whether the voters were for or against total integration. Predictably, they voted to close the high schools rather than fully integrate them. All the high school students, white and black, had to miss a year of schooling or find a school somewhere else. Robin Woods was one who had to make other arrangements or simply drop out.

Loucks: I was one credit short of graduating, so I took the Scholastic Aptitude Test [SAT] and went on into UALR [University of Arkansas, Little Rock]. But I was in no way prepared for college at that point. I dropped out, and it took me ten years to go back. In the interim, I tried to just completely erase that year. It took me ten years to even start thinking about it. It is called going into a state of denial. But it also—it made me realize that we were really not a very civilized people.

The Gazette's *huge press stood exposed behind a large plate-glass window on Louisiana Avenue. It must have been a tempting target for the paper's enemies.*

Reed: Did you ever worry about that plate-glass window?

Leon Reed: Yes, yes. During the integration period, I thought maybe we ought to board that up before somebody goes crazy and throws a brick in. I thought better of it. That would be admitting something and we aren't supposed to be afraid of anybody.

Gene Foreman: There's a great camaraderie, particularly during 1957–59 period when we were "Fortress *Gazette.*" Everybody out there was gunning for us. Faubus would denounce us at every turn. The Citizens' Council, Reverend L. D. Foreman—no relation, I might point out [*laughter*]—was the chairman of the "*Gazette* Ad, Too Bad" campaigns of the Citizens' Council. They were trying to drum up a secondary boycott of the advertisers of the *Gazette,* so it was all-out economic warfare against the *Gazette.* Basically, we knew we were right. Great camaraderie, great sense of liberal approach to politics, quite different from what existed beyond the *Gazette's* walls.

Photographers covering the story were too noticeable for comfort. Rodney Dungan tried to become invisible one day.

Rodney Dungan: I remember one day that I slipped into the school. I was pretty young looking back then and had a crew cut. With my 35mm camera that I hid in a girl's books, I went in one morning as a student. I walked through the bayonets and all the troops and everything else. I got in there and the black kids were late that morning. I wanted that picture of the black kids in school. They were late that morning, and when the bell rang for classes, I didn't have anywhere to go. I went into a restroom and, of course, they caught me and marched me promptly out. Two soldiers down those long Central High steps and back through the lines and told me, "Don't come back!"

Gazette reporters felt the hostility at Central High and beyond. Patrick J. Owens recalled an incident at Pine Bluff where he had been sent to cover a protest rally against integration.

Owens: Along came a car, and I was sitting in the phone booth . . . and somebody reached out a hand from his car and just took my notebook.

Citizens who stood up to Faubus and the segregationists found themselves under scrutiny by the state police.

Farris Wood: Enter Orval Faubus. Also, here comes the White Citizens' Council, which is just a front for their Mississippi buddies, the Ku Klux Klan. They moved into Little Rock en masse, so Orval had all this "proof" that all this violence was going to take place if he didn't call out the National Guard and stop the integration. Beverly [Wood's wife] belonged to the Women's Emergency Committee, as did several of our friends. We talked about it before she joined it, and I said, "I guarantee you, we're going to be under observation for weeks and weeks to come." Sure enough, we had the state police go into the grocery store with us and everything. Right on the heels of World War II. I mean, goddammit, the guns had not cooled off hardly! It was scary. It really was. We had a virtual police state in Arkansas. The *Gazette* became the focal point of it. The *Gazette*, to my knowledge, never one time said they wanted to integrate anything. We said, "We are a nation of laws." But that's not the brush they painted them with.

Bob Douglas: It was a tough period to go through. I never felt like I was in any physical danger. It was just unpleasant. Any time you were out in public and somebody knew you worked for the *Gazette*, you were vilified.

Reed: It was commonly believed around town and among the segregationists that Harry Ashmore stood in the newsroom every day and delivered orders on how to distort the news in favor of integration. In turn, Harry got his orders from the Communist Party, USA. That was widely believed. I was having coffee at Paladino's Cafe in North Little Rock, while I was still on the North Little Rock beat, and having coffee with somebody from the city hall. Another man who was a friend of this other fellow, a well-known businessman in North Little Rock, joined us for coffee. Before I knew it, we were talking about the *Arkansas Gazette* and its role in the Central High crisis, which had already occurred at that time. To my absolute amazement, I heard this otherwise responsible businessman referring to Harry Ashmore as a Communist. The man obviously believed it, that he was a Communist.

Bill Lewis: Faubus said that he had gotten information that there had been a run on the gun shops, the pawn shops, and so forth, and that people were stocking up on weapons. The most logical thing on earth for a city editor is to say, "Check it out. See if it's true." So Shelton gave that assignment to me, and I called as many pawn shops and gun shops as I could find, and not one of them said there had been a rush on anything. The next day, Faubus was asked about that, and he said, "Well, that was written by an agent for an integrationist newspaper." [*Laughs.*]

Jason Rouby: Carol Channing sang, "I'm just a little girl from Little Rock" in [the theatrical production] *Gentlemen Prefer Blondes,* and she got booed in New York. That's how bad it was. . . . We did not have an industrial plant come into Little Rock from 1957 until the Jacuzzis came here in the early 1960s because of the reputation of Little Rock, which had been imposed on this community.

Foreman: Ashmore, who really stood tall during this time, was a visible target. Mr. Heiskell, who risked his family fortune, was more in the background, and fewer people knew who J. N. Heiskell was and his importance. But Harry was the villain for the people on the other side.

Ashmore was interviewed several years after he had left the paper and gone to the Fund for the Republic in Santa Barbara, California. He wrote a number of books on civil rights and the Little Rock story before his death in 1998. In one interview, he reflected on Orval Faubus, his friend-turned-enemy, and on his own change of attitude toward the race issue.

Ashmore: I think Orval was fighting back against Pappy [Sam Faubus, a race liberal and a Socialist Party organizer in Madison County]. He wasn't going to do what Pappy tells him to do. And my sense of Orval has always been almost total absence of total conviction about anything. There was an expediency. He was like [the first president] George Bush—whichever the hell way the wind is blowing. An element . . . [is] the class aspect of this and the resentment against Ed Dunaway and me and the town of Little Rock and the fact that Orval was an outsider. . . .

I told Virgil [Blossom, school superintendent] that Daisy Bates's real great protest was the fact that this was a goddamn segregation scheme. And that's the way he saw it. . . . That was a part of his delay, that was to get Hall High built so all the well-to-do people's children like mine would be going to Hall, and so they weren't with the poor folks. Now, Orval always made a great point out of this. This is the one thing I give Orval. This is the old populist point of view: you're putting it on my people; you're making the poor folks integrate. All those Cadillac brigade out in the Heights doesn't have to . . .

Mr. Heiskell was an interesting case. The old man was a real civil libertarian. He was a real free-speech man. He didn't want them to be shut up, and he certainly didn't want anybody lynched. He didn't want it to become violent. Well, I think Mr. Heiskell was one in his generation who believed that, certainly, blacks should be treated fairly and be treated decently. This was a part of the gentlemanly tradition. He didn't consider desegregation either desirable or necessary. He was able to convince himself that you could achieve racial justice, social justice, within the limits of a segregated society. I suppose I started out accepting that proposition pretty much too.

. . . I remember Hugh and I went to see Old Man Heiskell down at the *Gazette,* and it could have been a Monday morning because it was a holiday, but I remember there was practically nobody there. This was about nine o'clock in the morning. We went in there to tell him that the shit was going to hit the fan. Apparently Hugh had been talking to everybody, and I'd been talking to people, and we were pretty damn sure that he [Faubus] was going to make his move by that time. And I remember we told the Old Man, and I said, "Well, of course, the position you have to take is to support the school board. But I can't make that decision. It's your newspaper and costing you the money," and made the point that we would stand absolutely alone. We already knew the *Democrat* wasn't going to support the school board and the damn chamber of commerce and everybody else—Hugh had been talking to him—were going to run out. And the Old Man said, "Well, I won't let people like that take over my town." And he stood firm thereafter pretty much.

. . . I think I told you about talking to Daisy Bates back when I was doing the Arkansas history. And we were talking about this. She said, "Well, hell, I knew what Orval Faubus was about. He wasn't really against me and the black people. I told Ed Dunaway, 'He's against you and the people in the Heights, and I'm going to have to pay for it.'"

Foreman: Harry would respond to some of the letters, very rarely, but one letter said, "It's all right for Mr. Ashmore to desegregate Central High School. He does not have to rub shoulders with blacks on his golf course." And Harry says, "Madam, I have been accused of many things but never before of golf." [*Laughter.*] One letter that we published but he did not respond to was, "When I read Mr. Ashmore's editorials, I was so angry that I called the *Gazette* and said, 'Stop my subscription immediately.' But you didn't stop it immediately, and you kept sending it and in the last two weeks I've continued to read your paper and in that time I've lost ten pounds. Send the paper two more weeks." [*Laughter.*] I remember some of the milder ones saying something like, "The slimy communist editor of your filthy red rag. . . ." Harry was the guy they loved to hate.

Bob Douglas: Ashmore and J. N. Heiskell and Hugh Patterson were towers of strength. Ashmore was very persuasive, but Mr. Heiskell deserves an enormous amount of credit. Because he was not—Mr. Heiskell was not an integrationist. He believed in segregation. He was the son of a Confederate colonel. But he was for obeying the law and hated mobs.

Doug Smith: Well, I think, well, I guess I think you would just have to give credit to Mr. Heiskell, who, as you know, back in the twenties when they had the big lynching in Little Rock, he thundered against that, and that was a time when newspapers in Jackson, Mississippi, and places like that—they didn't condemn lynchings. If anything, they apologized for them. But he was—the stories are that friends of his had to have an armed guard around his house, so I think he and his son-in-law, Hugh Patterson, also, I think, were more enlightened than a lot of people at that time. Of course, in the '57 crisis, I think now everybody recognizes that Mr. Heiskell didn't really, or the *Gazette* didn't really, come out for integration. They wanted to obey the law. That was really what they were saying. They didn't come out and say, "Blacks and whites are equal. . . ." It was mainly the thrust to just say, "This is the law of the land, and we have to obey the law of the land." But that was much more than most Southern newspapers were willing to say at that time about school integration. So, I think, yes, I think, the family. And then they got Harry Ashmore, who was a liberal, to run the paper—they brought him in. He was gone by the time I got there, incidentally, but he had been, they called him executive editor, so he was over the editorial page and the news side of the paper both. And he had a great deal to do with setting the tone of the paper, particularly in the crisis years. So, I think, just a combination of some unusual individuals.

Fred Coger: There was a mob of "foreign" reporters, foreign to us, mostly, not foreigners actually, but "outsiders," reporters from major newspapers, networks, columnists. We had people in all the time. I remember network reporter Sander Vanocur broadcasting or taping a report, at least, from our newsroom. There were lots of others. Dorothy Kilgallen was there, among other big-name columnists. It was a circus in a lot of ways. Those people all relied on the *Gazette* and its staff and library for basic facts, and they came there and not to the *Democrat* because of our reputation. I do not think very many of them spent much time at the *Democrat*. But they were in and out, in and out, and Mr. Ashmore, in spite of being very busy, took all the time needed to brief and help any and all of those people and entertain them into long night sessions of drinking at whatever that little club was over there [The Press Club]. They had a grand time. Ashmore was a great guy with a story.

Not everyone at the Gazette thought its coverage was fair. Even in the newsroom, which was thought by outsiders to be a hotbed of integrationists, some were critical of the paper's coverage.

Charles Rixse: When I was working with the *Democrat,* I thought [the *Gazette*] was highly overrated, as you usually do when you are working against good competition. When I went to the radio and TV station, I was able to step back and look at what everybody was doing, and I suddenly realized that, although they had a definite liberal bias, they were an exceptional newspaper, really exceptional. As far as coverage of the Central High crisis, I really felt a lot of respect for the *Democrat.* [I think] they did better job of it than [the *Gazette*] did, but [the *Gazette*] got the awards for it.

McConnell: Do you remember anything in particular about the coverage?

Rixse: Well, they [the *Democrat*] reported accurately, or fairly accurately, things that were going on that we just didn't bother to write about. I don't think people reading the *Gazette* got as accurate a feel for what was really going on around Central High as the people who read the *Democrat.* Although I can't say all that *Democrat* stuff was accurate.

Jerry McConnell: Why did you leave the *Gazette?*

Rixse: Well, I was very disillusioned by the way the Third Estate conducted itself during the Central High crisis. I was taught that your first duty as a journalist, as a newspaper person, was to report the facts in a fair and unbiased way. In no instance should you try to control or manipulate whatever was going on to suit your own particular purposes. That is not to say that I was not ever accused of doing exactly that because I am sure I was.

Wes Pruden: And there were times in the coverage of the desegregation thing at Central High School when [the *Gazette*] didn't play fair. I knew it at the time, and looking back I know it now. The segregationists were painted as unredeemable rednecks who were ignorant and stupid, and some of them were. There's no question a lot of them were, but not all of them were. And, you know, it was a time when if you—a lot of the press, and the *Gazette* I would have to include in this—if you quoted a black person, they spoke like an Oxford don, perfect syntax, perfect grammar. The white segregationists were quoted as they spoke . . . My father [The Rev. Wesley Pruden, president

of the Capital Citizens' Council] read the *Gazette* every day. He never cancelled his subscription . . . My poor mother, whose life was shortened by that
whole episode because she had extraordinarily high blood pressure, and that
was at a time when there was very little way to treat it. She died young. She
was only fifty-nine when she died, and I really think the Central High thing
shortened her life. I can remember on several occasions my mother would be
reading the paper, and she would be crying because there would be references
to my father she thought were unfair. I remember one time—she wasn't crying. She was just kind of angry, and my father said, "What's the matter?" And
she said, "Oh, this old *Gazette!*" He said, "Well, what are they saying?" So
she read a statement. She said, "Listen how they quote you," and she read it.
My father said, "Well, that's what I said." "Well, I know, but they didn't have
to put it in the paper." [*Laughter.*]

Robert McCord: There were a lot of people those days, Ken, who, as you
know, said, "Well, the *Gazette*'s news columns are just as bad as the editorial
page. They're so wrapped up in this thing that they're distorting the news,"
what have you. I'm sure you heard that probably every day. Was there any
basis to that?

Ken Parker: I can truthfully say that in ten years at the *Arkansas Gazette,* no
one ever told me to write a "policy story." It was always write the story and
write it accurately and fairly. During the strike, for instance, the bus drivers
and people like that were pretty hostile toward the *Gazette,* but then as they
started having their own strikes, they realized we were covering them fairly,
and they changed their attitude toward the paper. We always felt that if you
had both sides angry with you, you probably were doing a pretty good job,
and we succeeded in that a lot of times. Even during the 1950s, I think I had
a pretty good relationship with Jim Johnson, Amis Guthridge, and some of
the other segregationist leaders. They knew that the paper didn't agree with
what they were doing, and they probably knew that I didn't agree with them,
but we were always fair with them. I think they recognized it, whether they
would say it or not.

Some saw a strain of hubris at the paper.

Foreman: One thing that troubles me a little bit in retrospect is the feeling
that we were better than they were. I have tried over the years to be more
egalitarian. We may not agree with our public, but they are our public. I'm
not sure there was the kind of respect that I would like to see our [*Philadelphia Inquirer*] staff show, but then again it was a difficult time, and some of

the things done by the "Segs," as we called them, were really dumb. But there was a feeling that we were one level intellectually and the rest of the state was pretty much below us. There's one quote that the *Gazette* people treasured that had been said about the *Gazette* maybe ten, fifteen, or twenty years earlier. That is, "[The *Gazette* is] one of America's most literate voices in one of America's most illiterate states." That was even trotted out and used purposely in the *Gazette* just before and after it was sold to the *Democrat*. It's a sort of thing that I don't think we should do. It may make us look good, but it makes your readers look bad, and that's what troubles me about it.

The Gazette *was open to a charge of hypocrisy during the school crisis.*

Foreman: The *Gazette* had segregated obituaries, and segregated various other news columns. There was not a whole lot of remarking about that. Some of us, I think, as time went on into the late 1950s and 1960s, started murmuring about, "Isn't it time we did not have a separate obituary for Negroes?" But it was not until Mr. Patterson, Hugh Patterson—some masseur at some athletic club he went to talked to him as he was giving him a massage: "Mr. Patterson," or "Mr. Hugh, don't you think you ought to not . . . ?" And so Hugh—I remember he came to the city desk, and I think he said to Shelton, "Why don't we just stop having separate obits for Negroes, and just have one." You need to document that, but that is my recollection of how it changed. Various other people wondered why we continued to do this. The so-called Southern traditions were pretty well imbued, and they died hard.

Gerald Jordan: Did the subject ever come up even in the Press Bar, that maybe we ought to have somebody black—or at the time it would have been "Negro"—working or reporting on the story?

Foreman: I don't recall it being discussed.

Jordan: Were you aware of what the *State Press*, Mrs. Bates' paper . . .

Foreman: Not very much. I think that's worth noting here. Our view of that, which was not very smart in retrospect, was that you were put off by the amateurism of the Negro press and put off by its advocacy. Obviously, the advocacy was what it was about, but it took me a long time to recognize how important the black press was in the civil rights movement. At Memphis, last fall at APME [Associated Press Managing Editors], the woman who is the publisher of the *Baltimore Afro-American,* talked about how the white press, the mainstream press, did not understand how this big crowd was going to go up there at the Lincoln Memorial in 1963, when Dr. King was going to be there. It was a stunning surprise, the huge crowd. But she said, "That's what we did, we passed the word. The white press," which I was guilty of, "was not paying attention to us." We discounted the influence of L. C. and Daisy Bates's paper. Of course, outside of Ozell Sutton, who worked some for the *Democrat,* there were no African American reporters at the time.

Jordan: When did he start? Was it 1959?

Foreman: No, it was before all this happened. I'm not sure he was still there when the Central High thing occurred. He was an oddity, a Negro reporter. While the *Gazette* people were very liberal, none of us thought that maybe we ought to have some black reporters. That seemed not to have entered anybody's mind

Even those who disliked the paper's editorial stand depended on its coverage of the Razorbacks and other sports stories. And there were other well-liked features such as the Arkansas Traveler column.

McConnell: Of course, one thing we have not touched on is the *Gazette* during the integration crisis and sports in the integration crisis. As you know, the *Gazette* lost a lot of circulation, a lot of advertising because of its editorial stance and everything. I had covered enough sports statewide, and I used to cover conventions, you know, and meetings of all—I didn't just cover games. I covered all their political meetings and everything else, you know, sports and everything. I got to where I knew coaches all over the state in basketball and football. I had any number of people come up to me during this time and say, "Jerry," this particular one in eastern Arkansas said, "you know, we don't agree. I don't agree with your editorial policy, but I still take the *Gazette* just because of the sports, but I think you ought to know that." I said, "I know a lot of people who do that." I had a great number of coaches come up to me and tell me that.

Leroy Donald: And so I would make frequent trips out into the state, sometimes with Ernie Deane [the Arkansas Traveler columnist], just covering the chamber of commerce meetings. I guess Ernie and I were just kind of stupid because we didn't think anybody was going to hurt us. There was some feeling that if you got out in the state, that you could be in some trouble . . . But Ernie and I both would just jaw with anybody and get along with them. We started going out there, if nothing else, to just be at the meetings, like chamber of commerce meetings or even ribbon-cuttings and things like that. Of course, Ernie Deane was doing the Arkansas Traveler column and, I think, played a great role in bringing the *Gazette* back into the mainstream of the Arkansas scene. I think he played as much a role as Orville Henry did in covering the Razorbacks.

Faubus relaxed toward the Gazette *and its reporters near the end of his tenure in the governor's office. He moved back toward the progressivism of his youth. In his later years he flirted with right-wing politics, but before he left the governor's office, he had begun to quietly cultivate black support. L. C. Bates, whose wife Daisy was head of the state NAACP, became a behind-the-scenes adviser.*

Dumas: I think he liked Valachovic quite a lot and wished he did not work for the *Gazette.* . . . In one of his efforts to come back into politics—I think it was either 1970 or 1974—it was a big evening rally right before the election at Heber Springs. And he was speaking out on the back of the courthouse square in Heber Springs. And I got there late, and there was a crowd, eight or nine hundred people gathered out there on the back, and he had a little platform or something, or truck, up there, and he had gotten up and was speaking. And I kind of was out in the crowd and under a tree or something, and he got to reminiscing about his life and his career in the governor's office. And he talked a little bit about the *Gazette,* how the *Gazette* had worked so hard against him. But he said, "But, you know, I always liked the *Gazette.*" And he said, as far as news coverage, it was the best newspaper in Arkansas. It always told things fairly. And he said, "Now, the editorial page is another matter." He had a lot of grievances with the editorial page, but he always thought the news side treated him fairly, and their reporting was accurate and balanced and fair.

Reed: Do you remember a conversation that you and I had with him one evening at the governor's mansion?

Dumas: He had beaten Winthrop Rockefeller in 1964. He invited all the press who had covered him to a party at the governor's mansion. He had never done anything like that before. So we all went out there. And Faubus said some reminiscences for a while, and everybody began to filter out. And you and I were kind of close to the door right at the end, and I think maybe by that time you and I might have been the only ones there. And Faubus was at the door and kind of asked, "Come back." And, as I recall, we went back in the living room for a couple of minutes and chatted. And he started talking about his—he was kind of boasting that he was the real Southern liberal, that of all the Southern governors, he was the most progressive of the Southern governors. You had Leroy Collins of Florida. You would bring up another of one of these, and he'd say, "Well, yes, but . . ." And he'd talk about all the great things he did for poor people and improving state benefits for poor people and the state hospital and getting rid of the snake pit that the state hospital . . . and starting an employees' retirement system, a retirement system for state employees, and getting benefits and improving benefits for teachers and working people and workers' compensation. He had a litany of all these fairly progressive, liberal things that he had done. And then you had to do the—raise the obvious question, "But, Governor, what about . . . ?" And to my recollection, you were obviously going to ask about '57, the calling out the troops in '57, and I don't know whether you finished the question or what, but my recollection after all these years was it went something like this: he said, "Well, you can't do great things unless you are in office. You can have great ideas about things you're going to do and run and never get them done, but if you are going to get things done, you have to hold office. And you have to trim your sails to the wind." That's a phrase, I think, he used. "You have to trim your sails to the winds and you gain office and you get things done." And that was his kind of justification, I thought, the strongest I think I'd ever heard him make, kind of acknowledging that he did it for political reasons in 1957 and not because he heard that there was going to be violence. And he talked about the effect that Eugene Debs and Norman Thomas had on . . . Sam [Faubus, his father] and also on Roosevelt. He said if you go back and look at what Roosevelt did, there wasn't a fresh idea in all of it. He said it was Norman Thomas and, mainly, Eugene Debs, that Eugene Debs was talking about a system of universal social security. It was Eugene Debs who talked about all of these things, and that years later Roosevelt adopted these things. And he said, "That's how these things work." People with kind of radical ideas, and then generations pass, and then it becomes acceptable in a crisis to do these kinds of things.

Reed: There was one other thing. I must have gone back home that night and typed up some notes on that conversation because I came across those notes on that old yellow newsprint that we used at the office. When I did the Faubus book, I came across this note. It was over a page long, maybe two pages, about the conversation you and I had with him, and what I remember from those notes now is what he had to say about his father being a member of the Socialist Party, or not saying about it. Do you remember we tried to get him to tell us that Sam had been a member of the Socialist Party? We'd been hearing that. And he dodged around the question. He never would answer. But Orval, that night, talked all around that. And we went away, in my memory of it. We went away from that conversation convinced that, yes, his daddy had been a Socialist and that he stopped just short of telling us that. Yes, but he still wasn't ready to because he was still in office, and he wasn't ready to damage his future prospects or whatever. He just wasn't going to talk about it at that time. But he came awfully close in part of the

conversation that was done about Debs and Norman Thomas and the social-
ism he had learned at his daddy's knee. I had wanted him to say, "Yes, my
daddy was a Socialist," but he wouldn't do it.

*Years later, Faubus did tell Reed that Sam Faubus had been a leading organizer of
the Socialist Party in northwest Arkansas. He had kept Sam's party card and the
charter of the Madison County chapter.*

9

Gannett and Be Damned

The Gannett Company, Inc., bought the Gazette *in 1986 and promised to respect it and maintain its reputation as one of the nation's best newspapers. It did neither. Instead, it systematically set about making the oldest paper west of the Mississippi into an imitation of* USA Today *with its splashy color, tasteless photos, and page-one stories designed to titillate instead of inform. That was Gannett's way of competing with the* Arkansas Democrat. *The national chain with "deep pockets," as its officers put it, set out to bury the smaller rival and turn Little Rock into a one-newspaper town. They turned Little Rock into a one-newspaper town, but not by burying the opposition.*

Gannett was not the only corporate villain in the American newspaper business during those years. Dozens of other chains followed the same route, dumbing down their "product," as they offensively called their papers, to accommodate the basest tastes of the readers. They paid constant and cloying attention to Wall Street. Stock prices and quarterly profits drove editorial decisions. If anyone in the upper management of one of those newspaper giants thought that informing the citizenry was more important than ever-ballooning profits and craven subservience to the stock market, he never let on.

A few metropolitan dailies and national newspapers bucked the trend. They included the New York Times, *the* Washington Post, *and—at least until Rupert Murdoch, the transplanted Australian media baron, bought it—the* Wall Street Journal. *Overall, though, it began to appear by the end of the twentieth century that the golden age of American newspapers had faded.*

In Little Rock, Gannett's contribution to the general decline is a long, dark, and depressing story. Among the reasons for the failure are the company's arrogance, its hubris, and its stubborn, insistent, breathtaking ignorance about the newspaper it had bought and the state it had served for 167 years.

Reed: Something you said a minute ago reminded me that one of the criticisms that I've heard repeatedly about Gannett was the lack of institutional memory that they brought to the state of Arkansas. They brought in people in most of the top management positions from faraway places . . . Was that a valid criticism?

Aubrey Shepherd: Oh, certainly. As an example from the sports department, there was a young man sent in to be the sports editor . . . He was having people clean out the photo files that went back one hundred years or so, and they were just throwing these photos in the trash. And sports had Razorback and all other college sports and high school sports and national sporting things. They had a photo file that was pretty massive and just wonderful to anybody who had a little knowledge of the past.

Charles Allbright: They had a lot of wine-and-melon-ball retreats, the Gannett people did. . . . And they started calling the *Arkansas Gazette* "the product." Now, "the product"—Michael, do you hear me? The *Arkansas Gazette* is not "the product." So we all began to total up how much time we had before retirement.

Deborah Mathis: Gannett's way of doing things is under cover of darkness. You'll go home on Tuesday, and sometime Tuesday night planes are crossing in the air, somebody is coming in, and somebody is leaving. The guy leaving —it's kind of like the whole White House turnover. The whole crew has moved in there and removed every strand of DNA from that person, and the new guy is there. You don't find out until you show up Wednesday morning, and they're saying, "We have a new publisher," or "We have a new editor," or whatever. That is Gannett's paranoid way, thinking that people are going to trash the place. They don't understand people. They don't understand people, despite the fact that Gannett, year after year after year, won some big award for its benefits policies, being one of the best companies to work for and everything. Yes, its paper and its theory and its policies are great, but they don't understand. The corporate giant does not understand human beings . . . Craig Moon [publisher] wanted to be involved in all these meetings, and I never liked Craig Moon, and I know he's still alive, that I may work for him, probably not now, someday. But I thought that he was not good for the *Gazette*. I thought he was very good for Gannett but not good for the *Gazette*. . . . They used to have these little citizens' meetings and stuff— prominent people from the community would be invited, sometimes in groups, for lunch, sometimes individually, to come in and talk about what can the *Gazette* do to make you—it was the beginning of this new "please the public" bullshit journalism that's still practiced now, which I am completely opposed to because I believe in a certain arrogance that is healthy and righteous for the press to have. But, anyway, this was the beginning of that news-you-can-use, please-the-public, focus-group-driven kind of thing, which is the Gannett mantra . . . The paper was being tampered with, just top to bottom. It was embarrassing.

. . . People were rebelling. So I went in, unbidden, to Craig Moon one day, and I said, "I am from the streets of this city, and I know how people think. . . . You don't need to fix this thing because it's not broken. . . . You really need to leave this alone . . . You don't need to make these cosmetic changes. People in Arkansas like—familiarity does not breed contempt here. They want the content. They are not going to be bamboozled. Please don't come here thinking we're a bunch of yahoos that aren't going to get it."

I will never forget. He looked at me like, "Oh, it's so cute of you to come in here." He didn't say that, by any means. He said the right things, but everything about him was so patronizing. I walked out of there absolutely furious and knowing that it was hopeless. And, sure enough, they just continued to mess with the paper until they had killed it . . . And so you have a company that really likes tin soldiers, people that all march in straight lines, ultimate conformists, yes men, company men, that kind of thing. That's what's rewarded. Anything that is kind of different or out of line, whether it's the paper itself or a manager at the paper, is kind of repelled by the Gannett white-blood-cell system. The Gannett immune system attacks anything that's different. So the *Gazette* had to conform and be kind of like the *USA Today–*influenced prototype or something. You look at all the Gannett papers, and they're all baby *USA Today*'s.

. . . So they saw [Walter Hussman] and said, "Okay, we need to go into Arkansas, kick that guy's butt, and take all his stuff. Spoils go to the victor. Take his whole kingdom, in other words . . ." It wasn't simply between two newspapers. This was the whole kingdom they were after, and that's why they went in there. They're used to winning. They almost always win. They can big-foot their way through almost everything. . . . So they thought, "Okay, we're going to steal their thing. We're going to do everything they're doing, plus some new stuff, and everybody's going to love us, just the way everybody loves *USA Today*. They're going to love us, and they're going to drop those guys, and we're going to come over here, and they're going to have to surrender, and we're going to take everything they've got." . . . It blew up in their faces. They didn't expect somebody who—normally, they can defeat you, if no other way, with their deep pockets. They didn't know they had a kamikaze pilot against them. They didn't know somebody who'd say, "I will die before I surrender."

Donna Lampkin Stephens: Gannett really tried to talk about all the wonderful opportunities I would have as a woman; they really wanted to stress that. But the longer that Gannett owned the paper, and I am sure my thoughts are colored a little by the way it ended, but it really became, "Oh my God, what are you doing to our paper!" The impression that we had was that these outsiders were coming in and thought we didn't know how to run the paper, and they were going to show us how.

George Wells: They didn't know Arkansas. They didn't know the market or the people, and they didn't understand the institutional value of the *Gazette* to Arkansas. So they were going to make a Gannett paper. Reporters kept getting all this negative feedback from people who were loyal to the *Gazette*. We'd go in and tell the editors, and we'd be ignored. In the end, my conclusion was they took something that wasn't broken and fixed it to death.

Jerry Jones: Gannett took over the paper. Well, we had more people, more editors from all over the country, and less news. That is what happened. That was our downfall, and they realized that too late in the game. Of course, the *Democrat* under Bob Starr stuck with what the *Gazette* used to do best of all—that was cover the news. Every day, day in and day out, whatever it was, we covered it. But Gannett was more on soft news, they thought, and they tried to find what they thought people wanted to read instead of telling them what happened the day before—giving them the daily news. That was our downfall.

Ernest Dumas: [Walker Lundy, the first Gannett editor] didn't think government should be covered much. He didn't like government news—state government news, federal government news, the court news. He thought the *Gazette* devoted far too much to that kind of stuff, which was boring—that we needed more kind of lighthearted feature stuff that young people might like who were bored by public affairs. He didn't like public affairs. And he loved movies. He thought he'd love to have instant movie reviews. He thought that was a priority. The day a movie came to town, he wanted a review in the next day's paper, and prominent movie reviews.

Wells: I remember when this TV actress, Clara Pella, died. She had been the one who said, "Where's the beef?" We put that on page one.

Dumas: Lundy thought she was an important figure in American culture.

Doug Smith: Lundy thought that there was too much space given, and may have been correct, that the readers didn't want all this hard news stuff about government. I remember Pat Carithers, the wire editor, telling me one time that Lundy said he didn't want to see all this Middle Eastern news. People in Little Rock weren't interested in the Middle East. He claimed he liked both the hard news and the soft news, but he certainly seemed to devote more to features. It just became a flashier kind of paper. The *Gazette's* old makeup had been very conservative, and it probably could have used some change, but a lot of the people didn't like the changes that were made.

Keith Moyer: Well, there was a strong feeling, and I think that even Craig [Moon, the last publisher] felt that the newspaper had swung a little bit too far [under Gannett], . . . a little too driven by the graphics and the art, and had gotten away from some of the solid, day-to-day that the *Gazette* had been known for forever. And we had both wanted to bring it back to more of a middle ground . . . As I read some of the accounts of how things were at the *Gazette* in the final days—frankly, in the final days, we had one of the finest [newspapers] in the country down here.

Walker Lundy, the first editor of the Gazette *after Gannett bought it, had years of experience as an editor at various papers—the* Tallahassee Democrat, *the* Charlotte Observer, *the* Fort Worth Star-Telegram. *He brought to the* Gazette *a conviction that newspaper writing needed to be lively, that it was no longer sufficient just to recite facts. He came to that conviction while working as a reporter at the* Detroit Free Press, *where he became city editor before moving on.*

Lundy: Most of my bedrock beliefs about journalism—what a newspaper ought to be—were formed in the years at the *Free Press.* There was a very talented group of people there, and I learned to do a lot that I had not known to do before . . . Everything I had done up until that point was kind of . . . "emphasize the reporting"—didn't emphasize the writing. The *Free Press* emphasized the writing. When I first got there, they started kicking stories back to me because they just weren't interesting. Nobody—that had never been an issue before. We didn't need to be interesting as long as we had all the facts there. The *Free Press*—that was a competitive market there looking for news. And the *Free Press,* before anything else, wanted to be interesting, and it seems kind of fundamental in the year 2001 to be talking about that, but that was like—I just remember them saying, "You know these stories— you know, it's all there. It's just not interesting." And I would go home thinking, "Well what's that got to do with it?" And I finally came to understand.

Adam Weintraub: Was somebody in particular who was the . . . advisor of that viewpoint?

Lundy: Yes. There was a guy, Kurt Luedtke. He was the editor of the paper. While I was there, he quit the business and went to Hollywood and became a screenwriter and wrote *Absence of Malice* and won an Oscar for *Out of Africa.* He was a very interesting guy.

Weintraub: What were your first impressions of the [*Gazette*], other than the fact that it was better than the competition?

Lundy: That it was . . . very traditional. Without a lot of energy. It looked to me like it was a paper put out by staff that was kinda back on its heels . . . I remember early on that the *Democrat* out-hustled the *Gazette*. I don't think I said this at the time, but in hindsight the paper was kind of, "We're the *Arkansas Gazette*. We don't really have to out-hustle anybody." It kind of rested on its laurels. I remember, near the end, somebody doing research there came in, and we were talking about the paper. And he said, "What's the hallmark of this paper?" Several people spoke up right away and said, "It's the oldest newspaper west of the Mississippi." I was shocked. "Is that what you're selling to readers?" And everybody started realizing, "Oh, yes, that's a nice thing to say about a paper, but I'm not going to read you on account of that." The paper sort of gave off that kind of flavor. The other thing that was true—this one is still going on—Gannett had tried to, you know, put some zip in the paper. We had been giving instructions to the people who were there to sort of do that. They didn't have any practice at it and weren't very good at it, and they were trying to carry out somebody else's vision. So they frequently missed. The story that was in the revisionist history attributed to me—it allegedly happened on my watch, but it didn't. It happened before I got there. There was some story involving cheerleaders in spandex, and I don't remember what the story was about. I just heard about the spandex and how that got on page one and what a shock that was . . . And my agenda was a pretty simple one: just to be interesting. I did not find page one often to be very interesting . . . But one of [the] things I was told that I still remember is when I went in there, this was an Arkansas newspaper, and what Gannett didn't want was for me to . . . I felt like my marching orders were to do the best I could with the people who were there. And that would have been fine, if what I had wanted to do is keep the paper exactly what it was. The problem with keeping it exactly what it was, which a number of people wanted, was that clearly was not a winning strategy. If you looked back over recent years—had that been a winning strategy, Hugh Patterson never would have had to sell the paper and the *Democrat* would not have survived. And when people would argue with me about the new direction, I would say, "Well, that is a new direction. If there's some other new direction you want to go in, let's talk about that. But we know the old direction has not been successful." I think there was a critical mass of journalists who didn't believe that, who wouldn't accept that. And most of the friends they had, who were the intelligentsia of Arkansas, didn't believe that. They liked the paper the way it was.

. . . I'm not sure in hindsight even when I got there if—if it were still possible to win the battle. Hugh Patterson may have gotten the best deal of all out of this. Because he got his money and got out. I think there's a—this is an unanswerable question, but there's a pretty good chance that the battle was done for when Gannett bought the paper. There were just too many things that just weren't going to work.

. . . One of the things that Gannett had done was starting with the color photographs on the front page of the newspaper. . . . And I remember being astonished to hear opinion from readers who complained about color photographs. That is to say, "God did not mean for there to be color photographs in newspapers." One of the people that I met in the community, through my daughter—she was a member of the intelligentsia, they being college-educated, smart people. And she complained about the color photographs. She complained, but it was in the form of a question: "Why do you have color photographs?" I said, "Well, because the world's in color, and all the newspapers are in color. And because we can, and it looks better than black and white." I said, "For example, is your TV at home black and white?" And she said, "Yes." That should have been the tip-off for me.

Gene Foreman: [Gannett] trivialized the *Gazette*. When the *Gazette* finally died, it was as if somebody had been on life support, brain dead, for ten years, and then they died. . . . The finality that the *Gazette* was now dead was very painful, but it was also mixed feelings because it wasn't really the *Gazette* that died. That happened to an alien paper with all that color and trivial stuff on the front page. A lot of us in the business know that in spite of all the gimmicks that have been trotted out over the past thirty years or so, efforts to stanch circulation losses, the *Gazette* always did what the *Gazette* thought was important. Some of the stories may have been too long and kind of wandered, but the paper's overall coverage was solid. It fulfilled the reason why people picked up the paper, to read about something that happened in Little Rock, North Little Rock, and the rest of Arkansas. They knew the *Gazette* was going to have something on it.

Bailey: Walker Lundy came in as executive editor. The first thing he did was spend several weeks interviewing all the staff members and people who had been there a number of years, like Ernie Dumas, Jerry Dhonau, Doug Smith, Max Brantley, Jerry Jones. He apparently thought we were all old mossbacks. You know, satisfied, entrenched mossbacks. His idea was that everybody ought to be clamoring to move on to a bigger paper. And, of course, the kind of people I'm talking about were the backbone of the *Gazette*, people who had so much pride in the *Gazette* they never had any idea of working anywhere else. Lundy called me in, and he said, "What do you do?" I told him, "I cover baseball, football, whatever's in season, write columns." "Well, how long have you been doing that?" "Oh, twenty-five, thirty years"—however long I'd been there. "Well, what would you like to do?" "Just what I'm doing." And he got a similar response from all of us old settlers. He couldn't cope with that.

And after Gannett had been operating the paper about a year, they sent off a bunch of pages to editors on other Gannett papers for evaluation, critique or whatever. And some fellow in White Plains, New York, critiqued about a month's worth of sports pages. He didn't like the way we were doing things, but the silliest thing he said—and this is, as best I can recall, this is verbatim his little notation on the page—"The outdoor page, the fishing, the wildlife, looks okay to me although I didn't read it." Read it? Somebody was supposed to read it! Some critique . . . And then Lundy was swept aside, and they brought in Keith Moyer. He was the last one. He went down with the ship. He said he wasn't a newsman as such. He was a manager. I don't know about manager, but I know he wasn't a newsman as such.

Shepherd: Joe Mosby wrote a column about an outdoorsman, a significant citizen of his area, near where he lived in Conway, a man he had known for many years, and the guy was an outdoorsman and significant in other ways to Joe. Joe wrote a column about the man's death, not about his death, but what he'd been, what he'd meant to people, and so forth. Interesting column. This young man from Gannett said, "Well, you can't run Joe's column. You can't put Joe's column in the paper." I said, "What do you mean?" He said, "He doesn't have the cause of death." Well, I started trying to explain to him. I said, "Well, you know, our obits don't necessarily have cause of death. Many papers refuse to run cause of death. They don't think it's a significant part of it. Maybe in a news story if you died in an accident or something, but cause of death is not necessarily part of an obituary either." Well, apparently, this young man had been somewhere, and they said, "Always put cause of death in an obit." And he saw this column, which was a personal opinion column that would have a photo of the author, the outdoor editor. He thought it should have cause of death in it, and he was not going to allow it to run. Well, finally, he got tired and went home, and I ran the column. [*Laughter.*]

Douglas: [Lundy] led the paper one day with a kid who was dying of leukemia or something. A four-column headline. Leading the paper with a two-column picture close-up of him. Of course, those stories go in the paper, but lead the paper with something like that? That was just an example. And I kept hearing these stories from horrified staff members about the decisions he would make. So bad that even Gannett fired him.

Leroy Donald: Gannett came in and, once again, made the mistake of think-ing it knew everything and that it, Gannett, owned the paper, when the paper belonged to the state of Arkansas. But Gannett put a lot of money in there, and we all made a lot of money off of them, and they gave us a lot of benefits, so we couldn't holler too loud. But it was a strange operation. . . . They always had meetings. They had meetings to talk about having meetings, and you would look around, and there would be twice as many people in an editors meeting as there would be reporters out trying to cover things. . . .

They would send teams out. I remember one instance when Walker Lundy sent a team over to Oklahoma to a church where a kid was cutting up all the time, and they were having a big fight in the church as to whether to tell the kid he couldn't come to church. For some reason, we sent a team of people over to Oklahoma to cover this story, which didn't have anything to do with Arkansas. That was the type thing Gannett did. . . . He was big on movies. For some reason, he just went to every movie there ever was. And I think it was the first of the Superman or the Batman movies—I can't remem-ber which one it was that made such a big splash. And he held the presses and had a special reporter . . . to go out and cover the . . . first showing in Little Rock of *Batman* or whatever it was. . . . And then he did the one about the flying saucers of north Arkansas, and nobody was ever sure what that was all about. And he did a whole front-page story on people seeing flying saucers. It was just out of the blue. It wasn't even during the flying-saucer craze.

Thompson: And did people stand up to him and ask him?

Donald: Well, we tried, but it was like dealing with Jell-O. Some of them, like Pat Carithers—he really just ate their lunch every time he opened his mouth about them. He just said, "You know, you all are the biggest bunch of fools we ran into in our lives." They didn't like any of us. They wanted to get rid of us anyway. . . . They no more had any concern about the state of Arkansas than the man in the moon. They just said, "Well, this is the way we are going to put out this paper. And that is the way it is going to be."

Paul Johnson: I came into work one day, and there was an *AP Style Book* on my desk, and there was a note that said to start using this. That was really kind of a major departure for those of us who had taken a certain amount of pride in the fact the *Gazette* didn't do things the way that every other news-paper in the United States did it. All of a sudden, we were going to look—essentially, as far as the way we wrote, it was going to be exactly like every newspaper in the United States. . . .

There were other changes. People who had been doing their jobs for many years or a generation were replaced by people from outside of Arkansas. They weren't bad people, but they had no real understanding of Little Rock or Arkansas. They had no institutional memory of why the *Gazette* was an important institution. The Central High School crisis that had been the annealing fire for the *Gazette* was something many of them had no idea that it had ever happened, much less that it had happened to the people who were working there with them. For a while, it was kind of funny that young reporters would be brought in from outside and they would say, "Did something happen here in 1957?" We would say, "Yes, something happened here in '57." Or they would say, "Why haven't we had any stories about this guy named Faubus?" It was a traumatic time for those of us who had been there for awhile.

John Woodruff: I remember one of the editors was astonished that one reporter had been on a beat for so long. He asked me how I could stand that or whatever. . . . They cut me way, way back, I remember, like a city council meeting that may run a column and a half or two columns sometimes was cut back to like three to six inches. It was almost to the extent, "The city council met last night, a lot of business conducted and was adjourned."

Richard Allin: To my mind the Gannett people were a ruthless bunch. They hired people who knew nothing about Arkansas. None of their top officers had the slightest idea of Arkansas history. And Arkansas does have a considerable history. They knew nothing about that. Gannett cheapened our paper. We were a gray, good newspaper. The news that was supposed to appeal to people eighteen to thirty-four started getting preference in the paper. We did Spandex on the asses of cheerleaders at UALR. In the first staff meeting that we had with Lundy in the features department, he described to us one of the best features that he liked so much. In another newspaper a fellow had taught a cat how to shit in the commode indoors. "What you do," Lundy said, "is you put Saran Wrap over the toilet and put some of the cat's kitty litter in there, and then you do this, and then you do that." That's what he considered to be a wonderful feature for a newspaper. All of us declined to write that. But that was the inspiration that he left us with. I will say that he didn't like my column very much, and he didn't like me very much. And I didn't like him. . . . Gannett took this paper and destroyed it. They destroyed it, and they started the first day destroying it. They made it a cheap rag.

A rumor got out in the newsroom that Charlie [Allbright] and I had accepted [job offers from the *Democrat.*] I learned this after the fact. It was such a flaming rumor that one day an emergency meeting was called of the upper staff of the *Gazette.* I mean, it became crucial. They wanted to keep us. They couldn't let us go. They decided it would be wrong for the *Gazette* to let us go. Everybody was panicked except Charlie and me, and we didn't know anything about it. We had no idea until Mr. Moon came into our office and said, "I want to talk to you guys." He was the new publisher. He took over after Bill Malone had been retired. He said, "We really want to keep you." He offered us the most outrageous raise in salary, free parking, plus a $10,000-a-year bonus for staying with the *Gazette.* Charlie and I just sat there open mouthed, shaking our heads. Everybody else knew we were gone, and Charlie and I didn't know anything about it. We hadn't discussed it. We had both made our decision to stay at the *Gazette,* and that was it. We were not going to the *Democrat.* And here he came in and dumped this bunch of money in front of us. He gave us a contract. So we were rolling in dough. We made more money than anybody. . . . We enjoyed more money than, of course, we were worth.

Dumas: Carrick [Patterson, J. N. Heiskell's eldest grandson] was one of the unsung and largely unappreciated heroes of that struggle. . . . Most people came around eventually to the recognition that he was a very good newspaperman. He made a great contribution to bringing us into the technological age but, beyond that, he knew what made the *Gazette* a great newspaper and especially what made it a valuable institution for the state, and he wanted to keep that. . . . Carrick was the editor when Gannett took over, and the suspicion was that he wouldn't last long simply because he was a Patterson. Regardless, he never tried to endear himself to the new owners. One instance in particular stood out. Michael Gartner, I think, had been editor at Des Moines, but by 1986 he was doing a stint as what they called a "news executive" with Gannett. I think they supplied Gartner with two or three copies of the *Arkansas Gazette,* and he wrote a scathing critique of the paper for the company, which was circulated at the *Gazette* so that all of us could see our shortcomings. Basically, Gartner said the *Gazette* was a dull newspaper that devoted far too much energy and space and emphasis to government news, government process, state government developments, the legislature, local planning commission meetings, that sort of thing. The Gannett formula then was light features, television and entertainment news, lots of sports, and generally just breezy, colorful, and short stories. Oh, they loved short stories. They didn't want stories jumped from page one to an inside page. I think Gartner wrote a critique that he thought the Gannett bigwigs wanted to hear. Carrick wrote a blistering response to it, point by point. He didn't think the *Gazette* ever was or ever should be the kind of paper that Gartner envisioned. And he didn't think Gartner knew anything about the *Gazette.* He was not diplomatic about it.

Now, being on the editorial page, I was never a part of the news meetings or the big planning sessions, but Max Brantley and others told me he was the same way there. Gannett sent a "transition team" down to help the *Gazette* plan the new directions in which it was to go. Carrick was not a team player. Everyone else realized pretty quickly, intuitively, that you had to keep differences of opinion to yourself. Carrick may have realized that too, but he didn't keep his opinions to himself. It was pretty clear that they were going to have to find a way to sidetrack Carrick. He was marginalized pretty soon, and they brought in Walker Lundy, who had left his previous paper unceremoniously and eventually would leave the *Gazette* the same way. Lundy never wanted to see a planning commission story in the *Gazette*. On the other hand, he wanted instant movie reviews. I think Carrick was prophetic. All the changes they brought about in the *Gazette* after he was shoved aside unsettled our readers. There was a big change in attitudes about the *Gazette,* both among many of our old franchise readers as well as the broader public. We went from being the most respected newspaper in Arkansas when Gannett arrived to being a paper that was viewed as less comprehensive than the *Democrat* in nearly every area. By the way, Gartner had an unhappy time at NBC after that and then bought the paper at Iowa City, Iowa, where he won a Pulitzer Prize for editorials that focused on the importance of such things as local planning commission actions.

Carrick Patterson: We had some feelers from people we'd never heard of and people who had been printing some suburban newspapers and turned out to be not really able to appreciate what was going on with the *Gazette*. . . . And nothing ever came of that. Well, finally, the Gannett people approached us. Al Neuharth, the head of Gannett, was kind of at the end of his career. He managed to convince us that he was now looking for respectability, that they were going to get some papers that they could be proud of having, papers that would have a new feeling of quality. And they demonstrated that by getting the Des Moines paper and the Louisville paper and convinced us that they—or at least made a strong case to us—that they wanted to do that at the *Gazette,* that they had no interest in changing the nature of the *Gazette,* that they merely wanted the prestige of being associated with that kind of paper, and that they would lend their vast economic resources and also their resources in advertising and promotion and so forth. And so, it was the only game in town at that time. Of course, the clock was very loudly ticking on how long we could survive without the infusion of capital. . . .

I didn't have a whole lot of respect for them as a chain. I didn't have much respect for the way they ran their newspapers. But, either naively or for whatever reason, I thought that going with Gannett, with the assurances we'd been given, was better than shutting the thing down. . . . It literally was Gannett or nobody at that time. There was no other choice. . . . There was an alternative: you could shut down and just be a central Arkansas newspaper and not go through all the expense of having the newsprint, transportation, and everything that you had to have to circulate papers in Fayetteville, where, after all, your core advertisers had no interest in advertising. . . . But the problem with that was you still needed to provide the bloody printing press. See, that was the rub: the darn printing press had to be bought. You had to go offset so you could do the color and stuff. I mean, there just was no other way.

[Gannett] brought in a man named Bill Malone, who was actually a native of Arkansas, to be the publisher. And, indeed, they did give us some resources in terms of capital in advertising and circulation and that sort of thing, but, as it also turned out, about that time Al Neuharth left for good. He left his post as chairman of Gannett. It turned out, the people who were left there were not of his same point of view about keeping the *Gazette* the way it had been. And they started bringing in people asking us to do things a certain way, and I resisted. I resisted very strongly because I thought we'd been assured that that wasn't going to happen. And they did it in kind of subtle ways. They called them "contests" among all their papers, and you were graded on certain things. And what it turned out you were graded on was not anything that we thought was anything that contributed to the newspaper's merit. So we got low grades. . . . Like how long your average story was, how many stories you had on page one, how neat your weather map was, whether you had daily color comics or not.

And they'd do silly things. Malone decided that we, by God, would have daily color comics. The way the press worked, you could only have one color page devoted to comics. You couldn't have all three comic pages be in color. So he said, "Well, you know, comics are so popular and everything, we need to have color comics." I said, "Fine, but we can only have one page of them." He said, "Well, you'll just have to cut it back to one page then." . . . So I said, "We can't do that because, you know, which comics are you going to cut out? People are used to all these things." "Well, why don't you make them real small, where they will fit on the page?" I said, "Well, no, we've got a lot of older readers. We can't do that. We tried to make the obit type smaller from time to time. We tried to do something with the stock market and every time, we couldn't do it, you know, because the older people are, you know, very important to us as readers." Well, you can't do any of that. Okay, so we ended up with one page of color comics and two pages of black-and-white comics, and, I mean, it was incredible the expense of it to do. We had to hire people to, literally, color those things every day and to go through all the mechanical problems of separating the color plates and everything to make the darn thing work, and it was just stupid.

Well, they decided, by God, we were going to have a Monday business section, for no reason but that that was just kind of a fad in the country at that time. There wasn't any advertiser interest. There wasn't particularly any reader interest. Oh, we came up with a pretty good Monday business section, but it was just more newsprint being put out. There was no advertising to support it, and staff resources being spent on it that could have been used for news that was actually of more compelling and more vital interest to the readers. But they said, "Well, you don't have to do the Monday business section, but we are not going to give you any resources to do anything else. So if you want any resources at all, it's going to have to be for the Monday business section." Okay, fine.

About that time, after we'd been fighting little stuff like that and having visiting firemen come in and give us ideas and notions, they decided that they'd have this Michael Gartner, the editor who had been in Des Moines, whom they'd inherited in Des Moines, and who had moved up to their corporate level. They decided they'd show him a week of *Gazettes* and have him write a critique. And he wrote a critique that I just thought was—the technical newspaper term is "chicken shit." [*Laughter.*] He criticized the front page. He criticized the little In the News column that we had on the left-hand column, which was a little briefs column. He criticized the weather map. He criticized the river bulletin, which is the thing we ran that showed the different flood stages of the river. The river was vital. It was vital information for agriculture and that sort of thing. He didn't understand that. Five or six pages of just nit-picking stuff, ignorant, shoot-from-the-hip stuff, I mean, and I say "ignorant" just because he didn't know the state of Arkansas and he didn't know what we were trying to do. Nobody asked what we were trying to do. They just said, "Oh, this is bad; this is bad; this is second rate; this is amateurish; this is . . ." We weren't used to people talking to us that way.

And I reacted very strongly. I wrote a very, very strong letter back, and the phone started ringing from Washington, and I was told how bad a mistake I'd make if I didn't show more tact. Another time I went to a national Gannett meeting in Washington, and they had the editors of *USA Today* there, and they were talking about how wonderful they were. And they were talking about their daily process of putting out the paper and that they were going to find the one story that they thought they wanted America to talk about that day, and they would put all their resources behind that. They would have a page-one thing about it, then they'd have a sidebar, and then they'd have editorials about it and op-ed. On the day I was there, there was some prizefight that was to take place. And I got up in the meeting, and I said, "You know, that's very interesting what you're doing, but don't you think it shows a little contempt for your readers, that you decide on this frivolous thing, that it's going to be the big topic every day?" And they sort of looked at me like, "Well, what's your point? Of course, that's what we're doing. Yeah, yeah, we have contempt for our readers, sure we do."

Well, that wasn't popular for me to sass them like that. I mean, my name was put down in a book somewhere, and so Malone, the publisher, had me in and said, "You know, this isn't working. You've got to go." So I said, "Well, I don't want to go. Why don't you let me go up and work on the editorial page?" So I did that for a while, but that wasn't really viable long term. I had some fun writing editorials for a while, but—so I had an opportunity to go to work for an advertising agency, so that's what I did [in] 1988. . . . They went through several editors, and one of them was very much into wanting every day a story about some sort of heroics on the front page. There should be some hero on the front page. Of course, you know, there isn't always a hero story. [*Laughter.*] So when you are in a position of trying to create something like that, you end up doing some pretty ludicrous stuff. And they did.

Hugh Patterson: You can't imagine just how intense that was for the last two years before we finally sold the paper. You know, I'd wake up and try to fathom just what we could do and all. But I had, of course, a pretty good opinion of what Otis Chandler had done with the *Los Angeles Times,* and I thought, perhaps, that could be a good kind of outcome or that the *New York Times* was a potential owner or . . . and then when Gannett indicated interest, it was after they had acquired a couple of bigger papers, including the *Courier-Journal,* and Al [Neuharth, Gannett's board chairman] had said that the *Gazette* would be another jewel in their crown. And I thought it was at a time when Al, really having fooled with all these smaller papers and running them on a kind of a formula basis, was really trying to achieve some distinction in the good paper field and what not. But, of course, about the time our deal went through, he decided to vacate the chairman job and turned it over to John Curley. And that was a disappointment to me.

From then on, their judgment in who to send in and how to try to deal with the thing was just flawed in just about every respect. The man they sent in to be publisher had been a circulation manager over in Memphis at one time, and just had no concept of the editorial strength of the *Gazette*. Then the later ones tried to put it into the local formula edition of *USA Today* and that kind of business, and it was just—and I called Al a couple of times and said, "I just don't know what to think because they are making every mistake you could make. They are offending people. They are offending the intellectual people from the university. I attend these meetings and they come cry on my shoulder, and there's nothing I can do."

I went up to their headquarters at one time and thought I was setting up just a private meeting with Curley, but he brought in their man who was nominally in charge of a certain group of larger papers and all. And so I said to John that I really thought their selection of people was really unfortunate because they just did not comprehend what was happening in their own organization. And I think this man is just not the right choice, and you have the opportunity, I think, for some other people, like Joe Stroud [editor of the Detroit *Free Press,* an Arkansas native and former *Gazette* employee] for example, who had indicated an interest and all. And so John said something that suggested that, you know, my view was pretty harsh, and I said, "Well, now, look, John. I've been around this track for quite a while, and don't take me for a fool." Boy, he almost hit the ceiling. And I said, "Now, calm down. Settle down. And let me tell you, I am not here as your enemy. I am here as your friend." And he said, "Well, I'll tell you, we're undertaking a survey of opinion, and we'll see how that comes out." Well, I learned after about six weeks that their opinion survey had apparently just revealed exactly what I had been telling them.

Reed: You talked to the *L.A. Times,* the *Times-Mirror* people—how interested was the New York Times Company?

Hugh Patterson: Well, not that interested. They, I think, recognized to a greater degree than some what an undertaking it was, and by that time the *L.A. Times* had made the decision to go for the *Dallas Times Herald* and the *Denver Post* and had made a mess of both of those things. . . . And then the Knight Ridder people and what not, but they were not—they were realists, you see.

Dumas: When Lundy went to work there, were you there that day when we assembled in the newsroom and Bill Malone announced, "Here's our new editor, Walker Lundy"? . . . And Lundy makes a little two-minute little talk and said, "Any questions?" And Chuck Heinbockel, who was a business writer, asked the first question, "Can you tell us something about your management style?" And Lundy said, "Yes, I can. Let me sum it up this way: I know how to fire people, and I don't mind doing it." It was a stunning remark!

Jerry Dhonau: I think [Malone] was ticked off for a number of reasons, among them that I had resisted his entreaties that we not endorse in the '88 presidential race. The editorial board did not take a formal vote, but there seemed to be a consensus that we wanted Dukakis, though not enthusiastically.

Dumas: His wife had been on George Bush's staff. . . . I have a recollection that we had all met about it, and Malone had wanted us to endorse George Bush, and there was no sentiment for endorsing George Bush. . . . Lundy was at the meeting down in the publisher's office where we talked about that, and Lundy probably expected to vote for Dukakis himself, but he was trying to push it over into the no-endorsement thing. We were all saying no. We didn't take subtlety very well, and they were trying to subtly influence us to do that. And we wound up writing the endorsement of Dukakis, and it sat there for a good long while, did it not? [Malone] wanted Lundy to look at it, pass on it, and Lundy disappeared in Florida. Lundy went to Florida, and days and days passed. The election was creeping up, and Malone did not want us to run that editorial, but he did not want to order us not to. Lundy disappeared, and Malone couldn't get him on the phone, apparently.

Dhonau: And I told him, "Look, if we run this editorial at all, it's going to have to run this Sunday because it's the Sunday before the election." He never then told me, "Don't run it." When he didn't say, "Don't run it," it ran. Although Walker was gone and, obviously, Malone didn't want it to run.

Dumas: I had the impression that that's when he soured on Lundy as well. I think he thought Lundy ducked out on that. Of course, he later fired Lundy. And they brought in Craig Moon as the publisher. Moon had been at Fort Myers, Florida. Moon brought in as editor Keith Moyer. So Moyer became the editor and was over both news and editorial.

Dhonau: You know, these guys, Moon and Moyer, just disappeared sometimes. They were going on golfing vacations at Walt Disney World in Florida. They were both golfers, and I guess that's what they were doing. They would just go out and let the paper run itself. . . . I had a hard time even talking to Moyer sometimes, just pinning him down and talking to him. We should have some communication. You talk about this as maybe an omen or an indication of what was in their minds. But that January of '91, I decided one day to go down and try to talk to him, pin him down on some things we should talk about. And we talked for a while, and that was when the real dark things started descending. He made not-too-thinly veiled suggestions that our editorial policy needed to change, that is, become conservative, and that we needed to reflect the views of the railroad worker in North Little Rock.

Apparently, they had done reader surveys or something, and he had some interviews that showed that we were just out of sync. I was aghast at that. But it was clear that he didn't care. All he cared was doing what the bigger boys wanted to do. I just flat resisted that. I knew that if we did that, the game was up, that this was no longer the *Arkansas Gazette*. We were not going to do that. I expected from then on that they were going to relieve me for resisting that.

About that time they must have been negotiating the sale. I sensed that. Later that spring—it was May, I'm not sure—Moon was shifted to Nashville, and the hatchet man came in. As the publisher, Moe Hickey had the reputation, deserved the reputation, as the hatchet man. A friend of mine at the *Denver Post,* where Hickey had been, couldn't stand the guy, and the damage he had done to the *Denver Post.* When the word got out that Hickey was going to be our publisher, a pot of black carnations arrived to me. This was my friend out in Denver. He had heard the news and was offering his condolences because Moe Hickey was coming in to do us in. He was right. I knew something was going to happen. A real chill settled between him and me.

The crowning blow came in August. Moyer and Hickey wangled lunch with Clinton. Maybe it was the other way around, I don't know which, but, anyway, they had lunch with Clinton. As a result of that lunch, word was sent to me that we were to have an editorial telling Clinton, encouraging Clinton to run for president. Virtually endorsing him. That was almost a direct order. I turned that one down too, saying that the editorial board doesn't do that and never has. The *Arkansas Gazette* has never done that, never told somebody to run or not run. We had been over this, by the way, in '88. They wanted to curry favor with the next president for Gannett. It wasn't put that way, but it sure sounded that way. Anyway, I thought the traditions of the *Gazette,* and you did too, I think, was that the editorial board should prevail. That's the way it should be. That's where the decision should be made. In any case, I've forgotten the tenor of our emails back and forth, but I refused to do that.

[Moyer] stormed up, in August, I think, and threw open the door and shut it and started just really raising hell. "Why won't you do it?" I tried to explain to him that you don't do these things, that the *Arkansas Gazette* doesn't do these things. It didn't make any difference to him. It was clear that he was getting orders from Hickey, who, obviously, was trying to curry favor with Clinton because of Gannett and the presidential possibility. We had extremely sharp words, and, at the end of that, I expected it at any time. Of course, it was only a few weeks later that the paper went down anyway, so it became academic.

Robert McCord: All of this meant mostly that we had to have study groups. They would go out and interview just the man on the street. Most of these people, I always thought, were people who didn't even read newspapers, but they would ask them, "What would you like to see in the newspaper? Would you like to see more stories about movie stars or about NATO?" You can imagine the kind of answers they got. It was just, I thought, so idiotic. Well, Mr. Moon insisted that this be done, and we had to make the changes in the paper accordingly. The news department just had a fit. So, you know, I think we might have been close to winning, but Mr. Moon didn't see it that way. What was Mr. Moon thinking about? Mr. Moon was thinking about his career with Gannett, not about the *Arkansas Gazette*. That is the last thing that he was thinking about.

So one day I was walking in the building. And out comes Mr. Moon, a bit overly dressed and carrying a briefcase with him that was about this thick. I never saw him with a briefcase before. I said, "Craig, I need to talk to you about something." I have even forgotten what it was, but he said, "Well, you talk to someone else about it. I am leaving town for a few days. You talk to somebody else." That was the last time Mr. Moon was ever in that building. Of course, typical of Gannett style, he told no one. I guess maybe he told his secretary, but nobody else knew it. He was on his way to Nashville, Tennessee, to become the publisher of the *Nashville Tennessean* and also the manager of the biggest *USA Today* printing plant that they had. You are talking about a promotion. I mean, there is no telling how much money he makes over there . . .

There was going to be a meeting at 1:30 p.m. Everyone went, of course, and you know what happened. Hickey walked in and, I timed it, talked for twenty-seven seconds. He said, "The paper has been sold, and the *Arkansas Democrat* will take it over today." That's about all he said in his twenty-seven-second speech, ending with, "If there are any other questions, you can take it up with the personnel director, who will now take over this meeting." He walked out of the room through 150 people crammed in there and then downstairs where he had a limousine waiting for him . . . He got into the car, went to the airport, and never came back to Little Rock, Arkansas. . . . I found out that Moe Hickey had shut down newspapers in two other cities. The reason for secrecy was that they didn't want any other bidders fouling up the deal. The story was that they paid him one million dollars for that four months that he was here. That was the story. He did a beautiful job of it because he sure fooled a lot of people.

The person who might have been able to explain Gannett's handling of the Gazette *was Al Neuharth, who left the position of board chairman of Gannett shortly after the company bought the paper. In the ten minutes he allowed her for an interview, Anne Farris tried gamely to get an explanation. Here's most of what he had to say.*

Al Neuharth: If we'd had any reservations, we wouldn't have done the deal [to buy the *Gazette*].

Anne Farris: Well, right. But I think initially in all sorts of deals there might be some problems or reservations even if they go through.

Neuharth: That is correct. In all business deals there are pros and cons.

Farris: Can you exemplify some of the pros and cons?

Neuharth: No, I would just simply tell you that obviously the pros outweighed the cons, so we made the deal.

Farris: Did you ever feel at any point that it was a mistake to buy the *Gazette?*

Neuharth: No.

Farris: Well, I wonder if you had made any sort of—I don't know if *promise* is too strong a word, or indication or commitment to the Patterson family that the *Gazette,* under the ownership of Gannett, would retain the editorial direction that the paper had taken in the past?

Neuharth: I'm sure we would not have done that, but I am equally sure that we told Hugh Patterson that we had admired the editorial philosophy and positions that he and his editor, Harry Ashmore, had taken through the years and that since we admired that, there was every implication that we would try to continue along those general lines . . . You have to remember that at that point I was supervising nearly one hundred daily newspapers, a lot of television stations, and radio stations. And no one who runs a corporation that size can or should pretend that he or she can get into details or specifics. He or she should set general goals and then hire the right people to try to make those goals work. And so, in the case of the *Gazette,* I told John Seigenthaler and John Curley and Doug McCorkindale and others that our goal should be to make sure that the *Gazette* won the war in Little Rock. And then they had to figure out [*laughs*] how to do that.

Scott Stroud: My father had conversations with them about becoming the editor [of the *Gazette*]—the thing he had always wanted to do. He had a meeting in Little Rock with John Seigenthaler, who seemed intrigued by the idea. I think he would have been the right guy for that job . . . I think my dad told the folks back at Knight Ridder in Detroit, and then he never heard another word about it. They didn't call him and say, "You know, I don't think that will work." They brought in some regular corporate guys. The sad thing about it is that I think my dad knew what the *Gazette* needed . . .

I am less bitter than wistful about that. I think that had Gannett seen the value of having an Arkansas guy who knew the state and who was also a serious journalist who understood the middle ground between the two extremes, the *Gazette* would have had a different history. My dad was emotional when the *Gazette* went out of business. He cried about it. He wrote a column about it. His prediction was—and it has come true to some extent—that Arkansas politics would lurch to the right. It would be less enlightened and sort of more lunk-head conservative instead of thoughtful. Conservative is one thing, but thoughtful and having an interesting dialogue—a newspaper is an important part of that. The *Democrat* hasn't done it, partly because of its history of credibility problems. That has a big impact on a state. It is not just a newspaper going under. The *Gazette* had something to do with the kind of politicians that represented Arkansas. The Dale Bumperses, the Bill Clintons, the David Pryor folks who weren't the run-of-the-mill conservatives. I have always wondered what would have happened.

Wayne Jordan: I think, if you will remember, they found out that we were doing a lot of things right. We were well thought of by the readership. But Lundy said, "But the thing is we need to get more reader input. We need to interact with the reader more and find out what they want." I jumped up, and I said, "Mr. Lundy, we don't need the reader to tell us how to put out this newspaper. They have trusted us for 150 years around here to provide them with the information that we know that they need. So we know what to do to keep the people of Arkansas informed. What they expect of us every morning when they get up to have their coffee is a product that's going to inform them of what they need to know to get through that day." [*Laughs.*] He said, "You are an elitist! You're an elitist!" I said, "Yes, damn it, I sure am!" [*Laughter.*] . . . No, he didn't like me.

David Terrell: I worked in chain organizations, and they are unable because of certain inherent flaws in the way they operate to duplicate that kind of spirit and that kind of product, and they're not interested in it, anyway. They're driven solely by profit. I worked in a Scripps Howard organization over in Memphis. We tried hard, and it's a good, solid sort-of-okay newspaper, but it can never be a great newspaper, nor could a Gannett newspaper ever be great. They don't know what the term means in that organization.

Many Gazette *people were resentful that they were not allowed to publish a final edition. Some blamed Gannett. Others blamed the new boss. Walter Hussman was a third-generation newspaper owner. His grandfather, Clyde E. Palmer, had acquired a string of south Arkansas papers and his father, Walter E. Hussman Sr., had expanded the company's fortunes by farsighted investments in cable television. Young Hussman had persuaded his reluctant father to move into the Little Rock competition as the underdog. The company bought the money-losing afternoon* Democrat *in 1974 and soon converted it to a morning paper. Hussman lost many millions of dollars—he too had deep pockets—before humbling Gannett and forcing it to sell the* Gazette *to him in 1991. He explained why he could not afford to let it publish a final edition.*

Walter Hussman: One of the things we couldn't do was accept the liability of buying the *Gazette* and operating it for a while. If you buy assets, you don't take on any liabilities. You either buy assets or you buy the stock in a company. You can buy the stock and you take on all the liabilities. But we didn't know what their liabilities were because we weren't privy to them because the Justice Department wouldn't let us see any of their financial statements and contracts. Anyway, the people got mad at us—people like the *Arkansas Times* —"Well, the *Gazette* didn't publish a final edition." The *Gazette* could have published a final edition. Gannett could have operated the paper one more day and let them do that. But I was not willing to buy the *Gazette* and operate it for a day because if I had bought the *Gazette* and operated it for one day, I would have been buying the stock in the *Gazette,* assuming all their liabilities, and not knowing what those liabilities were. I was only willing to buy their assets.

Reed: If you'd elaborate just a little more on that fine point. If you had operated it for a day, you'd have been obligated to take their liabilities, not just their assets. Why is that? How is that?

Hussman: Well, if someone had come in and said, "You operated the *Gazette,* so you owned the *Arkansas Gazette* as an entity, so you assumed the liabilities. Even if you only had them for twenty-four hours, you have them. And now we're going to sue you." We had a defense against that. We said, "We never operated the *Arkansas Gazette*. We never published a single edition of the *Arkansas Gazette*. We published the final edition of the *Arkansas Democrat,* and the next day we published an edition called the *Arkansas Democrat-Gazette*.

Reed: And this was part of your satisfying the bankers that you knew what you were doing?

Hussman: Right, and satisfying the bankers that we weren't picking up any of their liabilities.

When the Gannett managers let the Gazette's *celebrated sports editor Orville Henry slip away to the* Democrat—*apparently because they never understood his value as the state's foremost sports authority—many people suspected that the newspaper war was almost over.*

Orville Henry: I called Jack Stephens and asked—I said, "Jack, would you do me a favor?" He said, "Why, sure." . . . I said, "I think that I can make a deal with Walter Hussman that would be good for me, and I've got to get out from the *Gazette* because under Gannett it is going to go under." . . . And I said, "All I need is for somebody he trusts to call Walter Hussman personally and to tell him, 'If you want Orville Henry, you can get him immediately if you will pay him a fifty-thousand-dollar bonus and give him a contract. This would be a three-year contract, and he will sign for as long as we want.'" . . . We sit down at ten o'clock, and I said, "Walter, did Jack make you aware?" And he said, "Yes." Best visit I ever had at the *Democrat*, ever. And it was over, and they brought in our lunch. . . . And, finally, I walked over to the *Gazette*. And I remember walking down the hall toward [publisher] Bill Malone's office. First, I went to my old desk to get two or three little things that I felt like I had to have, and Lundy saw me. He turned against the wall with his head just like that. . . . If I'd left the old *Arkansas Gazette,* there would have been some wrenching things. You know what I thought about? Those marble steps to the back way of the city room, which is to our office. I ran up and down those things three at time for many years, and I always claimed that they—over fifty years they had worn, then they turned them over, and I wore them out the next.

There was something about the Gannett people, a kind of unearned swagger, that nettled the old Gazette *hands.*

Max Brantley: Al Neuharth came in in his sharkskin gray suit and drove up in his gray limousine and told us all they were there to win the war. I was there, and then there was a session at the Capital Hotel as well. Of course, Neuharth took a limousine between the *Gazette* and the Capital Hotel, which were a block apart, which told us a little something about their operational standards. But, you know, I was at that point so fearful about the *Gazette*'s future that I wasn't necessarily depressed by the news. Although Gannett didn't have the best reputation in the world, I knew they had deep pockets. I knew that we didn't. I knew that, over time, Hussman, inevitably, with the antitrust suit won, could do anything he wanted to in this market, and he clearly demonstrated that he was willing to do it forever. The thought that somebody was coming in with unlimited money, I thought, well, better that than going out of business. I preferred to be optimistic although they brought a retinue of Gannett overseers who made everybody a little bit nervous by the way they were looking around. John Seigenthaler came over from Nashville. He was the publisher of the Nashville *Tennessean*. And they brought up an editor from the Jackson newspaper. They brought up a woman who was, I think, publisher in Monroe or Shreveport at the time, and various others, and they assessed every department of the newspaper. Went out to eat with a lot of people, spent time with everybody, and read the paper, and they basically formed an operational plan. They were also saying who they thought deserved to stay and who needed to be replaced. It became clear that that was part of the process that was at work. We were assured that the *Gazette* team was going to stay in place, including and up to Carrick Patterson, but, you know, I don't think anybody really believed it.

One thing that was reassuring: John Seigenthaler was a very reassuring character. He agreed that one thing we needed to do was be as big a newspaper as the *Democrat* was. And to have more news reporting. He is a news man at heart, and a lot of things *Gazette* people had wanted to do for years, start state bureaus, for example, he said, yes, and that was, in fact, something that happened very shortly after the Gannett plan was put in place. They did begin spending money on opening state bureaus. That was a good thing. And beefed up the staff considerably, improved the pay, improved the benefits.

Dumas: The Gannett team came up with a plan, and they decided—I don't know how long it was—that Carrick had to be fired.

Brantley: Well, they booted him over to the editorial department. They said they would let him keep working there, be in charge of the editorial page. It was a safe move for him because he had no constituency on the newspaper, which is sad in a way because, as years would go by and people would choose people to villainize, sometimes they would villainize Carrick. If anybody didn't deserve to be a villain, among old *Gazette* loyalists, it was Carrick because he opposed the sale, he was brought up under the old traditions, and he got moved aside quickly because he stood up for them. But the fact was that he never was able to bring many people around him. That is why he wasn't able to survive.

Many years have gone by. Many regrets have been felt. Many second thoughts have pushed into many minds.

Lundy: If I knew then what I know now, I think I would have gone in, and I don't know whether this would have been successful. I think I would have gone in and said our model is going to be the *New York Times*. We are not going to have color. We're not going to spiffy it up, but we're going to be the very best producing this kind of newspaper. The reason I'm not sure that would have done it for us is the *New York Times* is not the best-selling newspaper in New York City, and it's not a paper that appeals to the masses.

Joe Mosby: One reporter from the *Democrat* stopped me and asked if he could ask me a few questions. . . . He asked why the *Gazette* closed. And I told him, "Because Gannett never knew the meaning of the two words at the top of the front page: *Arkansas* and *Gazette*."

10

The War

Mr. Hussman's Paper

The Arkansas Democrat, *an afternoon paper, habitually lagged behind the morning* Gazette *in circulation, revenue, and reputation during the middle years of the twentieth century. That was typical of afternoon papers around the United States. The evening television news shows had seriously eroded their circulation. Walter Hussman knew the risks of buying a newspaper that was struggling to stay afloat. He recognized the challenge. But he had some ideas, and along the way he found others. The* Democrat *always had some good reporters and editors. But it had problems that even the best reporters and editors couldn't solve.*

Paul Nielsen: The *Democrat* was not a well-organized paper. . . . The composing room more or less put the whole paper together. . . . There was also no copy desk under the old *Democrat.* The system was that as soon as assigning editors wanted to send copy to the composing room, why, they just sent it. There was no central organization, no universal copy desk.

David Terrell: There was a lot of craziness in the newsroom. We had some editors who were overworked and underpaid dealing with some terribly young writers and with some older ones who were difficult. There were people around with problems with alcohol and problems with this and that—kind of a crazy, hectic, very fast-paced place to work. It seemed our opportunities for news in terms of time got squeezed a little further every month. Our deadlines were short. Nothing much happens before nine in the morning. And we were a p.m. paper. With a noon deadline, we had three hours of generally a slow news day to cover breaking news. So we were at a great disadvantage against the *Gazette* in that way, and we hustled a lot. We took a lot of pride, I think, in what we did.

The Democrat's *prospects changed dramatically in 1974 when the Hussman family's WEHCO Media, which owned several television stations and south Arkansas newspapers, bought it from the heirs of the late K. August Engel. Walter Hussman, at age twenty-seven, became the publisher. The Little Rock newspaper war was under way. Here, in his own words, is how he won it.*

Walter Hussman: I had this business degree from Columbia University. Back in those days I was anxious to use a lot of the ideas I had learned. I had used some of it in our business. But what was really exciting to think about was turning around a business. We had turned around the *Camden News*. It was a very small business, you know, but that was really exciting. And I thought it would be great to turn around a larger newspaper. I said, as long as we're in the business of journalism in Arkansas, then the ultimate would be to have a newspaper in Little Rock. You know, that's the capital of the state. That's the center of the state, the largest city in the state. That would be a wonderful thing if we could own a paper there, and if it could be a really well-regarded . . . And we had a high regard for the *Arkansas Gazette* as a newspaper. My dad read it every single morning. And when I went to New York and lived up there a couple of years, I subscribed to it by mail and read it every day . . . My dad said, "This is a well-packaged newspaper. It's got a lot of good in-depth reporting, high story count," a lot of attributes that were positive about newspapers. He said "You know, if we buy the *Arkansas Democrat*—it may have gone down too far. We may not be able to turn it around. And we may not be able to succeed with it."

It was losing money. It wasn't losing a lot of money, and it had been profitable several years prior to that. And it had been profitable for many, many years, so it had lost money only four or five years by the time we bought it. And turning it around also meant moving it back into the black—making money and reversing the advertising and circulation trends and getting those on the upswing. We said, in three years we'll do that. So the hope was that we would be able to turn the paper around. And we knew that was going to be difficult, but in the early 1960s the *Democrat* had about the same daily and more Sunday circulation than the *Gazette*. Part of that may have been the aftermath of 1957. But still, the *Democrat* had a very strong circulation base within the retail trade zone which was the twenty-six-county area. Anyway, yes, being an afternoon paper, we realized, was part of the challenge.

. . . So when we bought the newspaper the first thing we had to do was work on this union organizing attempt because we were a nonunion operation. We perceived the newspaper unions with all their archaic work rules as an obstacle to improving the newspaper. It was something that was really holding back the *Democrat,* and we were going to try to convince the employees that they didn't need to belong to unions, that we had good healthcare plans, a profit-sharing plan, and lots of benefits. And, over time, hopefully, we'd become a nonunion operation and a more efficient operation . . . There were four unions . . .

Well, the first thing I did after we bought the *Democrat* was that I went around and talked to various people who had been at the *Democrat* but who had left. . . . And they said, "Man, have you got problems in your circulation department!" The circulation manager played golf about three afternoons a week and would even wear his golf shoes into the newspaper office. [*Laughs.*] The average age of the advertising staff was sixty-six years old. That might be a politically incorrect thing to talk about nowadays, but, you know, advertising in certain ways, is a younger person's game. People need a lot of energy to get out there and hit the streets, and we just didn't have a lot of younger people to do that.

Anyway, circulation turned around. We sold it better. We delivered it more efficiently. Advertising turned around. We brought in a lot of new ad salespeople. We brought in a new ad manager. We got a new circulation manager. And, all of a sudden, with new ownership, and also an ownership that had decades of experience in the newspaper business, the employees and community perceived us differently . . . They thought, "They've operated newspapers for decades. They know what they're doing. Let's give them a chance." So a lot of people in the business community in Little Rock started advertising with us.

I made Bob McCord the editor, and Bob started doing a good job editing the newspaper. We had a lot more interesting stories in the paper. And we started running some color, which the paper hadn't done in a long time. But it dawned on us that as we went on month after month there in 1974, that something was wrong. I remember coming back from [a] trip, and Paul Smith [business manager] said, "We had a twelve-thousand-inch gain in advertising in September." It was fantastic to have a twelve-thousand-inch gain. But every month I looked at the profit-and-loss statement, and the more business we did, the more money we lost. And I thought, "This is crazy. Something is wrong with this picture." And it turned out that our operating expenses—mainly because of all the union work rules and restrictions—we couldn't make money by bringing in more business. It just didn't make any sense. . . . From 1975 through about 1977, most of the unions decertified. Eventually, all . . . The members themselves said that they no longer wanted to be represented by a union. And what happened was our losses started getting less and less. We were still losing money. We lost money in 1974 and up through early 1975. But then, once we started really focusing internally, our losses started shrinking. And we had reduced the losses down to a fairly small amount by 1977.

But what had happened—while we were focusing internally, the *Gazette* was just getting stronger and stronger, gaining more advertising, gaining more circulation, and we were losing market share. I think when we bought the paper, we may have had 65,000 daily circulation, and maybe by 1978 we were down to around 56,000. And the *Gazette* during that time had grown from 116,000 to 126,000. They were continuing to gain market share on us. Anyway, soon, 1977 had rolled around. We had accomplished great things, I thought. We had been able to show that we could turn around circulation and advertising. We had shown we could reduce our losses. We got our production and operating costs—labor costs—down from over $100 per page down to around $20 a page.

A dramatic improvement internally, you know. But we weren't making money. So my dad reminded me, "Hey. Three years are up." So my dad was seventy-one years old. So we sit down and start talking about it, and he said, "I think it was a valiant attempt. It was a good try, but we're still losing money, and we've lost market share. It's time to come to grips with that reality." And at that point we decided that it hadn't worked, and we'd try to get out of this investment . . .

Of course, it was clear to most people that afternoon newspapers were having major problems in 1974. By 1977 no one wanted an afternoon newspaper [*laughs*]. And it was better to sell the *Democrat* back when the former owners had owned it, but once an experienced newspaper operator had come in and operated it for three years, and now they wanted to sell it. Well, that made it more difficult to sell. So we thought, "This thing is going to be tough to sell. Maybe the best way out is to do a joint operating agreement [JOA]. And let's not make any bones about trying to get a good financial deal or the best deal or whatever. Let's just try to get out."

So I called Hugh Patterson and set up an appointment with him to talk about trying to do a JOA. I had a couple of meetings with him . . . just the two of us, one-on-one. I had known the Pattersons. Ralph Patterson [Hugh's younger son] had gone to the University of North Carolina where we both were in college, and we even rode back to Arkansas once together. And I've stayed with the Pattersons in their home. Back in those days we were just a family that owned some small newspapers down in south Arkansas [*laughs*]. Anyway, I told Hugh, "We got into it for laudable reasons. We wanted to have a voice in Little Rock. We had been in the newspaper business for years, and we hoped to make money. We haven't been able to. We had hoped to be more competitive with the *Gazette,* and we haven't been able to do that successfully. It's time for us to recognize that, and we're willing to do a JOA. We're willing for the *Gazette* to be the dominant newspaper, and the *Democrat* to be the secondary newspaper. We're not asking for fifty-fifty or anything like that. We will agree to whatever terms you think are reasonable."

He got back in touch with me and said he didn't really think they were interested. I thought, "Gosh! You're not interested? Just about everybody would be interested in eliminating the remaining competition." [*Laughs.*] And I couldn't believe he wasn't interested. So I told my dad, "They're not interested. We've got to make them interested. Let's come up with a proposal, an offer he can't refuse." So that's what we did. We came up with this offer that basically said, "Look, we'll distribute the paper wherever you want us to distribute. If you want to distribute the *Democrat* in Pulaski County only, we'll distribute in Pulaski County only. If you want to deliver it Pulaski and Saline County only, or if you want us to deliver it in Little Rock only. Whatever you decide is our geographic boundaries, that's okay. We'll be the afternoon newspaper and you be the morning paper. You be the only Sunday paper if that's what you want.

So I went back and said, "Here's what we'll do. We don't get anything until you earn as much as you made last year. You'll get 100 percent of the profits until you get that—then we'll split $600,000 fifty-fifty. And then you get 90 percent and we get 10 percent." And I thought, "That way he's guaranteed—he'll always make as much as he did last year, and that will address that concern." His response: "Not interested." So at that point, I went back to my dad and said, "Gee. They definitely don't want to do this JOA." And we thought about it and thought, "Why don't they want to do the JOA?" And we thought, "Patterson probably perceives that we're about to go out of business. He had good reason to believe that. And if we go out of business, then he is better off than if he has to share 10 percent or $300,000 or whatever." And we said, "So what do we do now?" So at that point, what we said is, "Well, we need to find out how we close the newspaper."

We didn't want to talk to any attorneys in Arkansas because there was a concern about word getting out. We talked to our Washington attorneys that we generally used for FCC broadcasting and cable TV, so we could keep it very confidential. I just started thinking, "Is there anything else we could possibly do to revive and resuscitate the *Arkansas Democrat?*" So I started on my own doing a little investigating, and I thought, "Who has ever been in the shape we're in today? And if they have been in that shape, have they ever made a comeback?" So I started doing some research, and I discovered a paper over in Chattanooga [Tennessee] that had been a distant-number-two newspaper. In fact, it had started out as a shopper: the *Free Press.* It eventually passed the established morning paper over there, and it was an afternoon paper. And it had started out with far less circulation. And I thought, "Maybe I ought to go over and talk to those guys."

So I went over there and talked to the owner, Roy McDonald. "What did you do? How did you accomplish that?" And he was very inspiring. He was telling the story of how he had done it. He started asking me a lot of questions. He started saying, "Yes, you know, you could do a lot of these things in Little Rock. It might work. It might just work. So we went down to Dallas. The *Dallas Times Herald* had switched their state circulation from afternoon to morning. They were an afternoon paper, and they had started publishing a morning edition. And they had had a lot of success doing that.

We said, "We could go to the major retail advertisers and say, 'Look, you operate in Tulsa. There's a joint operating agreement in Tulsa. If you run an ad in one Tulsa paper, you pay seven dollars. If you run an ad in both Tulsa papers, you pay eight dollars an inch.'" So it's a no-brainer. They ran in both newspapers in Tulsa. With these alternatives, they forced the advertisers into both newspapers by making it uneconomical to run in only one paper. We said, "Well, we don't have a joint operating agreement in Little Rock." The *Gazette* didn't want to do one of those. "But we can make the economics the same. We could say, we'll just charge you a dollar an inch if you'll duplicate your *Gazette* ad in the *Democrat.*"

We heard about this newspaper in Winnipeg, Canada, that had gone to free want ads. So we went to Winnipeg. We flew up there, . . . and they said, "It's incredible what happened when we started offering free want ads. About 15 percent of our classified advertising was transient ads, and about 85 percent was commercial accounts." Every place we went was a two-newspaper market. And they said, "So we gave up that 15 percent of our revenues when we went to free want ads. We just forfeited it. But the amazing thing is—" They had about 70,000 circulation. Their competitor had about 130,000— not exact numbers, but close. And they said, "Within about three or four months, we went to 90,000 circulation. And the really amazing thing was our classified revenues went up." I said, "How did your revenues go up after you lost the transient ads?" And he said, "Well, all of a sudden, now we had all these free ads. We had all these bargains in the newspaper. People were looking for the bargains. So all of a sudden the auto dealers started saying, 'Hey, there's a lot of readership over there. Let's start running some ads in that paper.' They ran ads, and they got good results. And they ran bigger ads."

From Roy McDonald—put out a bigger news hole with a big emphasis on local news. *Dallas Times Herald* published a morning edition outside their city zone. Winnipeg—do free want ads. Duplicating the big retailers' ads was an internally generated idea. We didn't find anybody who had come up with that idea. Running more color on the front page. And, at that point, we started thinking about this as an overall marketing plan.

Reed: Was any thought given at any time, or was it even an option, to just sell the *Democrat* outright to the *Gazette?*

Hussman: We talked about that with Hugh Patterson. He said, "I might be interested in buying the paper." And we said, "Well, okay. How do we do that?" And he said, "First of all, you need to create a public monument to the fact that you've been a failure." I thought, "Okay, a public monument. Do I need to go build something down here in the Metro Center Mall?" [*Laughs.*] I didn't really know what he meant. And I guess what he was trying to say there is that we not only had to admit to being a failure but we had to convince the Justice Department that we couldn't sell the newspaper to anyone else. And if we could show them we couldn't sell to anyone else, then he would take it. That gets into federal antitrust law. But then we thought, "Well, if we did that—if we've got to do that in advance of him telling us what he'd pay us for it, then how do we know he'd pay us anything?" [*Laughter.*] So maybe if he said, "Well, I'll pay you XYZ if you'll go do that," we might have sold it. But he said, "No, no. First you've got to go prove that you've been a failure and create a monument to your failure." So we really didn't think that was a viable way to proceed.

Anyway, we came up with this plan. I went to see my dad and mentioned that I thought that this was something that we ought to try. If we did, it was like, "We can try this for ninety days. [*Laughs.*] And if it isn't working, we can say—or we can try it for six months. We don't have to set a time limit of three years on this." This was 1978. And I said, "To do it, we really need to convert to a morning publication out in the state." And that seemed to be the most dramatic thing we were considering doing. But part of the plan was to double the size of the newsroom and get more local reporting and start covering the same stories the *Gazette* was covering. I said, "It's going to be costly, but it might work. And if it works, then we can resuscitate the newspaper." Anyway, that's what we did. We came up with this plan to do this. He gave me the go-ahead to start the morning edition. So we started our plan in December of 1978, when we came out with the free want ads.

Bob McCord told me, "You know, you need to get somebody in here who would really believe in this, who could think they could really challenge the *Gazette* and really put out as good a newspaper as the *Gazette.*" [Hussman hired John Robert Starr, former bureau chief of the Associated Press in Little Rock, as editor.] The first year, 1979, we increased the news hole 60 percent. We went from about fifty people in the newsroom to about one hundred. And we started running color every day. We intentionally tried to publish a few more pages than the *Gazette* every day. If they published a forty-page paper, we'd publish a forty-two-page paper. . . . So that way we could call ourselves Arkansas's largest newspaper. That was sort of a stretch. We weren't the largest in circulation, but we were the largest in page count.

Bob [Starr] had a lot of common sense. He was a very down-to-earth, common-sense kind of person. He had really good news judgment. He realized that even though we were doubling the size of the news staff, we didn't still have the resources that the *Gazette* had. We really had to stretch a dollar. We had to get the most out of our people. There was dead wood, and he was trying to clean out the dead wood and trying to get more productive people who would write more. So in that sense he was great. And he also bought into the concept. He believed that we could do this, which was a lot at the time. So I was really pleased with him and what he was doing. Then I was at the [*laughs*] grocery store, and I picked up a copy of *Arkansas Times* magazine, and there's [a cover photograph of] Bob Starr squatting on the newsstand with a knife in his teeth saying, "I'm Bob Starr. I'm declaring war on the *Gazette.*"

And, you know, I saw that, and it really shocked me. He didn't even tell me he was doing that. And that—first of all, that worried me. He did this, and he didn't tell me he was going to do it, you know? And I thought, "This is—no, no, this is not an alley fight or a knife fight. We're not out to kill the *Gazette* or maim the *Gazette*. We're trying to compete. We're trying to save a dying newspaper. This is not a message we want to convey." I remember thinking—I was out jogging right after that, and I thought, "Maybe I need to fire Bob Starr. This is crazy. We've got this guy, and he's almost the perfect person for it, but then he goes off and pulls some stunt like this. He might do something else like this. But if I fire this guy—he's been there less than six months or a year—it hadn't been very long that he had been there—then who am I going to get?"

Anyway, we had a pretty serious talk. "This is not good. You shouldn't have done this," et cetera. He was sort of contrite about it. Anyway, I didn't fire him. It was probably a good thing that I didn't, although my first instinct was to do it, because I think he was very helpful to us in trying to continue to improve the newspaper and trying to catch the *Gazette.*

And I also had concerns about news versus opinion because my father had taught me, and I really believed there needed to be a significant separation, a complete separation of news and opinion in the newspaper. Well, here's the managing editor writing an opinion column. So that kind of crossed the line. That worried me. That always worried me. That never stopped worrying me. But, you know, what happened was his column got so incredibly popular, and we would do readership surveys, and it was one of the most popular things in the newspaper. And then it was kind of, "Well, how do we get rid of this thing if we wanted to?" [*Laughs.*] So, frankly, it's a little easier to do something like that if you're the only newspaper in town than you are if you're a struggling newspaper that's trying to make a comeback. You need things that attract reader interest. And he did attract a lot of reader interest. And a lot of times I would disagree with him, but I thought, "Well, that's okay." I don't have to agree with him. He's not the editorial page. I expect the editorial page to agree with me. I thought he'd be too caustic. He was a more caustic kind of guy than I was. I sort of came to realize that and understand that.

. . . We didn't say, "Hey, the *Gazette* is liberal. The ownership of the *Democrat* is conservative. We think they're wrong. We want to advance our conservative agenda. That's why we want our newspaper to be the dominant newspaper in Arkansas." This was more of a business proposition. We were more conservative. We did disagree with them, but that was not the driving force behind the ownership. Now, it may have been a factor in marketing. And I'm sure it was among some readers because we would hear that from people. "We're glad we finally have a conservative voice that we can read in the morning. We really didn't like an afternoon newspaper," or something like that.

So our circulation was going up. But we started losing more money. We had lost more money in 1979 than we had ever lost. In fact, it drug our whole company into the red. We lost, I guess, $5 million in 1979. That's a staggering amount of money to lose. I mean, by 1977 I think we lost $500,000, and that was down from maybe a million our first year. So we really started getting the losses back down where they were more reasonable, and all of a sudden—but, you know, my dad was like, "Good grief! Look at the amount of money we're losing." My mother would say, "Look how much money we're losing." I'd say, "I know! It just makes you ill to see that much money being lost. But look at the circulation. It's going up. Look at our advertising. It's going up. We're really having to force-feed this thing to resuscitate it. We don't have a big enough share of the market to be able to profitably operate because we've got to add on enough expenses so we can go out and cover those same meetings the *Gazette* is covering—so we can have those delivery routes in Crossett and places where the *Gazette* delivers. And those are going to be unprofitable to do for now."

Reed: For the benefit of future historians who might be reading this, it might be a good idea to explain how it's possible that your circulation was going up, your ads were going up, and you were still losing money.

Hussman: Because you had to add on so much additional fixed cost in order to compete with the *Gazette*. As I say, you know, to staff all the meetings you're going to have to make, you've got to pay that reporter to go cover that meeting. You aren't going to necessarily generate any revenue off covering that meeting, but as you cover it consistently and people recognize that, they say, "Hey, that's a little different than what I read in the *Gazette*. I'd like to subscribe to the *Democrat*." So there's a lag there. You have to add the fixed costs first before you can start covering those costs with . . . new revenues.

Anyway, there were a lot of dark days there when I had that same thought: "I don't know if we'll make it." Anyway, what happened after the first full year, 1979, was the reality of how much it was costing. We said, "We can't continue to lose this amount of money. We've got to get our losses down. Circulation is still up. Advertising is going up. Great. But this is just too much to lose, so we've got to raise our prices." We had to start getting more revenues—we just didn't have the money as a company. We were a smaller company than the *Gazette*. Our whole company was a smaller company than the *Gazette*. That's one of the myths that's been perpetuated, that we were a much bigger company than the *Gazette*. It's really not true.

Reed: You mean, in money figures, they were a bigger company than—even though you had the cable and all going?

Hussman: Right. So we were able to raise prices. By the time the *Gazette* sued us in 1984, we were up to $18 million in revenues. We had taken our revenues from $5 million to $18 million. That's why our share of revenues had gone up, because our revenues were going up faster than the *Gazette*'s revenues. The *Gazette*'s revenues still went up while we were competing with them, but they weren't going up as fast.

Well, we had our first profitable month—what happened was when we started raising those circulation prices and were raising the advertising rates, our losses started coming down. So I said, "Well, this has a familiar ring. We've been through this in the mid-1970s. [*Laughs.*] We got in and streamlined things. But now our losses were coming down because our market share was going up. We've got an efficiently run newspaper." So in 1984 we made our first profit. I think it was in April. And I think we made, after interest and depreciation—I think we were still paying interest on note—we had to pay for ten years—and I think we made $14,000. So we took that $14,000 and divided it by three hundred plus employees we had, and everybody got a check for about $42. [*Laughs.*]

The lawsuit came in December of 1984. The lawsuit lasted until March of 1986. Of course, the *Gazette* sued us, saying we were trying to drive them out of business using predatory pricing, et cetera. And, of course, it was a jury trial, and the jury verdict was that, no, we had not violated any antitrust laws, and we won resoundingly. . . . Hugh Patterson and the *Gazette* found some really high-profile attorneys for the case. Our attorneys were Williams and Anderson. Well, it was Phil Anderson. He was at Wright, Lindsey and Jennings at the time. And Phil is a great attorney, but Phil also had a great passion for what we were doing. He had been our attorney since 1974, for twelve years by the time the trial came. And Phil—not only was it a case—he absolutely was convinced that we were right, that what we were doing was procompetitive, not anticompetitive, that it had increased competition between the newspapers in Little Rock. It hadn't diminished competition among the newspapers. So I think the fact that he felt so passionately about it helped. . . . So someone expressed the opinion that maybe what the *Gazette* wanted to do was win in the courtroom what they had not been able to win in the marketplace. So when they sued us for between $30 million and $133 million, our net worth at the time was, I think, $30 million or $40 million. And, of course, any judgment is tripled in antitrust. If they had won a judgment, then we wouldn't have been able to pay it. We would have had to file bankruptcy or sold our companies, or we could maybe have settled the case by agreeing to close the *Arkansas Democrat*.

So we entered into this credit agreement with our cable TV company and the agreement with the bank was that "Okay, as long as WEHCO Video has this credit agreement with the bank, you can't take any money out of WEHCO Video and ship it over to the newspapers. It's got to stay in WEHCO Video." So we didn't have access to any of the cash flow, revenues, profits, or anything from our cable companies back in the 1970s, probably not until it was in the 1980s. In 1983 the cable TV company finally paid off all their debts. So, basically, when we bought the *Arkansas Democrat* in 1974, it was really our newspapers—we had access to revenues and profits from our newspapers but not our cable TV companies. And then in 1978 when we decided to challenge the *Gazette,* we still didn't have access to the cable TV funds, either. In fact, in 1980 the cable companies owed more money than they had ever owed. They owed over $5 million. And then the prime rate went to 21 1/2 percent. My mother said, "We're paying a million dollars a year in interest!" I said, "I know we are! It's staggering!" [*Laughs.*]

. . . By 1983 we had paid off our cable TV debt. I remember after Gannett bought the *Gazette,* we had access to our cable TV funds. I remember thinking if we hadn't had the cable companies helping, it would have been difficult against Gannett. But when Gannett bought the paper, that changed the dynamics because obviously they were not buying the newspaper to have one of two newspapers in Little Rock. They were buying the newspaper to have the whole Little Rock market. So at that point we said, "Oh, this is not going to work, trying to sit here and make money. These guys are going to try to kill us [*laughs*], and we've got to respond." We're now in something that we really never had when we were competing with the *Gazette.* We never had a circulation war. We really were mostly competing for advertising. We were mostly competing journalistically. We were competing for readership, but it wasn't a circulation war. . . . Of course, if you do that, it's a bloodbath. It's just red ink everywhere because now you're cutting back into that circulation price, and there's no profit margin as there is in advertising. You can cut your advertising rates 25 percent, and you can still make money. But you can't do that in circulation.

Anyway, we said, "Okay. We've come all this way. We've made all this progress. Now they're selling to Gannett. Gannett is going to force the issue so there's only one newspaper in the market. What are we going to do?" So we had to come up with a new strategy. One was to gain circulation as fast as we could. And we said, "You know, this is going to be terrible financially. We've got to forget about the financial part. We've got to dive back into huge losses again." I remember May [*laughs*] of 1987—boy, I think we lost maybe a million dollars in one month. We had never lost that much money. It was just—it made me sick. I was driving, and I just started beating on the steering wheel. I thought, "This is terrible. I can't believe that this has happened. We've gained all this market share, and now we're losing all this money. I don't know if we can afford to lose the kind of money we're losing. Maybe we're going to lose all we have gained just because maybe they can outspend us." We weren't so worried about being outspent, but maybe they can do things in circulation that would force us to lose so much money that we can't stay in the competition.

But, you know, it was really interesting. One of the things we did—we sat around and we scratched our heads. We sat over there in the conference room, and we said, "What can we do to compete against these guys? We can say we're Arkansas's largest newspaper. That's what we've been saying since 1978, since we published two more pages or four more pages than the *Gazette*. They can take that advantage away from us tomorrow. They can publish ten more pages than we publish on any day." So we changed. We dropped "largest" and we were "Arkansas's newspaper," by deleting the largest. And we said, "That's sort of what we came up with. The only thing they can't take away from us is that we're locally owned." We said, "Well, that's a great comfort. We're locally owned. Most people could care less who owns the newspaper. They just care about the paper." And we said, "Well, maybe so, but it's an advantage, and we've got to use it for whatever it's worth."

How can we beat them on free want ads? The only way we can beat them is on service. Okay, how can we beat them on service? Well, let's see. Somebody calls up and wants to place a free want ad. We need to make it more convenient for people to place a free want ad. We need to open up—instead of at eight in the morning, we need to open up at seven in the morning. And instead of closing at five in the evening, we need to close at seven in the evening. And we need to start taking free want ads on Saturdays so it's more convenient. When people are at home, they think about placing an ad. They'll call us on Saturdays.

Reed: You say that your losses were greater than ever. How big did the losses get during that competition with Gannett?

Hussman: You know, we've never disclosed our losses, but I will tell you that the *Gazette* lost $108 million. . . . I can tell you that our losses were significantly less, but they were in the tens of millions of dollars. They were huge. They were horrendous. And, really, they were bigger for us than they were for Gannett because Gannett was such a bigger company.

Reed: They had an entirely different way of thinking about newspapers, as I saw it. I'm a reader and an old newspaper man. And suddenly the sober *Arkansas Gazette* becomes, well, flashy. How do you compete against that?

Hussman: Well, easily. [*Laughs.*] That was the best thing that ever happened to us, really, when they started doing that . . . it didn't even look like the *Gazette* anymore. It seemed like a totally different newspaper. Well, as a result, maybe readers would now consider taking the *Democrat*. Gannett did for us what we couldn't do for ourselves by changing the *Gazette* so fundamentally that it put those readers in play where they would consider reading our newspaper. If Gannett hadn't changed the *Gazette,* I don't know if we would have ever caught them in circulation. But they ran on the front page the mayor of Eureka Springs in a bubble bath, you know? And it just horrified *Gazette* readers. It horrified me. I was a *Gazette* reader. I thought, "This doesn't belong on the front page of the *Gazette.* I've been reading the *Gazette* all my life! This doesn't belong there." And I always picked up the *Gazette,* and I would say, "Whether I agree with those editors down there or not, this is what they think is the most important thing that has happened in the last twenty-four hours in the world, and in Little Rock, and in Arkansas." And whether I agree with them or not, this gave me a guide to the news. Or even if I totally disagree with the editors down there and the way they play the news, it still gave me a guide. It's a valuable thing to have that.

The changes just disoriented readers. They would say, "Well, what's important anymore? I can't pick up the *Gazette* and tell what's important anymore." And, of course, the *Arkansas Times* ran that cover story called "Mellow Journalism," and they had Walker Lundy on the front. He was the editor brought in, and he instituted a lot of this feature-oriented copy. And it was a total disaster for them. It was a huge benefit for us. . . . We just went more to hard news than before. We said, "If they're going to forfeit that field, we're going to take as much of it as we can."

Reed: Even the Gannett people now acknowledge that they handled things poorly here. When did they start seriously thinking, "We're going to sell the paper"?

Hussman: I think what happened was that when we passed the *Gazette* in circulation on Sunday, in the first quarter of 1990, it was the first time in thirty years that the *Democrat* had more circulation than the *Gazette.* And I felt that if we could ever pass the *Gazette* in circulation, it was over because I felt like Gannett's only hope was to come in here and drive their circulation so it far exceeds ours, and if they couldn't do that, it was hopeless for them to have the only newspaper in town. So that's why the circulation was so important. So when we passed them in circulation . . . on Sunday—they were still ahead of us daily—Sunday is the biggest advertising day of the week. So we had a party. We said, "We've got to celebrate."

So we had a party for over a thousand people. We invited all of our advertisers. We had it down at the State House Convention Center and had a big band and a big outdoor dinner. We wanted our advertisers to celebrate that they helped us get where we were. But I think that also sent a message. "Gosh, these guys at the *Democrat*—" We really wanted everybody to know we passed them in circulation. Sometimes it's hard to get that message out to ad salespeople if you run an ad. So we kind of drove the point home with the party. I think that's when they [Gannett] must have started thinking about it.

. . . I think it has worked out well. Of course, it's sad to go from two newspapers to one newspaper. Obviously, newspaper competition is great. It really keeps people on their toes. Competition is great. It's great in the newspaper business, and it's great in every other business. Would Little Rock be better served by competition? Probably so. Most markets would. Is newspaper competition realistic in America today or twelve years ago? No. You can look—it has been a steady decline. The world has changed, and there are lots of other ways people get news. Television has gotten much more dominant. Direct mail—we still don't have Kroger's advertising in the *Arkansas Democrat-Gazette.* They go with Advo here in this market. So the loss of competition is sad, but it has worked out well for us. It has worked out well for the community too, I believe, because I think we publish a quality newspaper. We pumped a lot of money into the news operation. . . . Ten years later we were spending more than double what we were spending when the *Gazette* closed. We have won lots of national journalism awards. I feel like we publish a real quality product, journalistically. We still serve the entire state.

. . . We have tried really hard to have a balance [on the editorial pages]. Of course, we had John Brummett, and John Brummett was certainly more liberal than most of our local columnists. We tried to keep John Brummett, and John Brummett left us. . . . Gene Lyons, who obviously disagrees completely with our editorial policy [*laughs*], Gene is somebody I've really depended on to make sure he stays in our pages because I think we do need balance. And, actually, I've even encouraged and allowed people who write for our newspaper —if they want to write an op-ed piece and disagree with our editorial policy, we give them the freedom to do that. We routinely run letters to the editor that are critical of our editorial policy or even critical of me personally.

. . . We hired Paul Greenberg to become the editor of the editorial page, which we felt was a coup for us. He's really a great writer and a great thinker. And when we did, I told him that we will sit down and talk about various issues. I said, "Ultimately, if we disagree, I think the editorial policy needs to reflect the ownership of the paper. But I know from visiting with you that we really agree on most things." Actually, what I did was I sat down and I read thirty days of the *Pine Bluff Commercial.* I read every editorial he wrote for thirty days. And then we met. I said, "I'm going to give you a lot of latitude on how you operate the editorial page and op-ed page—what columnists you want to run, what syndicated cartoons, the letters policies, and things like that—as long as we allow criticism of ourselves, and basic good journalistic standards."

Reed: Yes. Let me ask about a specific issue. Were you comfortable, I guess would be the word, with Paul's commentary through the Clinton years—on the Clinton presidency? He took a lot of heat for this. What about you personally?

Hussman: Well, I've known Bill Clinton since before he ever ran for office. I met Bill Clinton back in 1974. I think the first time I met him was in Hot Springs, and I sat down and talked to him for a couple of hours in Hot Springs. And I felt like we disagreed philosophically, you know, mainly on the role of government. He was very optimistic about what government could do and how government could help. And probably [*laughs*] my attitude had been shaped by my dealings with the FCC, that the government really was a problem [*laughs*]—to deal with them. Anyway, we sort of disagreed on that. So, you know, when Bill got into politics and was attorney general and was governor, we generally disagreed with a number of his policies, but it was all based on policy and what his policies were, and it was more of a politically philosophical difference. And there were always lots of rumors about his character. And we just never really thought that was something that we really needed to delve into, and it appeared to be a lot of rumors. Anyway, I guess that's the way our newspaper editorialized Clinton.

When Paul became editor of the editorial page, he had some fairly strong opinions about Bill Clinton's character. He felt like he had some real character flaws, and one of them had to do with honesty. And, in fact, he told of an experience where Bill had basically not been honest with him. He told him something that just absolutely wasn't true, and he knew it wasn't true. I guess Paul felt early on that the character problem was not just your usual character problem; it was a major problem for somebody who was going to be governor or president of the United States or whatever. So, really, I think if you went back and someone read all our editorials, they would see that's where the questions about Bill Clinton's character started—after Paul became editor of the editorial page. So I think that Paul has probably proven that he was correct in being concerned about his character, you know, over time. But we have taken a lot of heat for it. A lot of heat. And it's been a very unpopular position in Arkansas to take. People in Arkansas still generally like Bill Clinton. A lot of people don't, but a lot of people do, and I think a majority do. And there was a lot of pride in the fact that somebody from Arkansas was elected president. If you're in the newspaper business and you say what you believe, people are going to get upset with you from time to time. They have, they do, and they will.

Reed: How significant was it that Orville Henry came to work for you?

Hussman: I think that it was very helpful. I think it was more helpful to us that he made the switch from the *Gazette* to the *Democrat* than it was that he brought his content to the *Democrat* because, by the time he made the switch, Orville was probably not at the peak of his career. Those years had been earlier. But he still did have a following, and there were people who probably started reading the *Democrat* because Orville was in there. So I think that helped. But it certainly gave the impression to a lot of readers that, "You know, gosh, I haven't been reading the *Democrat,* but maybe I need to be reading the *Democrat.* Even Orville Henry has moved." It probably helped us as much from a business standpoint as it did as a journalistic standpoint.

. . . We don't make as much profit as we could. We don't make as much profit as Gannett would make if they had ended up with the newspaper in this market. But, you know, there are two ways to reach economic value, two ways to reach economic value in owning a common stock, in owning a business, in owning a house, in owning anything: one is the current income you take out of it, and the other is the market value. So some people buy common stocks that pay no dividends, but the stock keeps going up. And they get their return that way. Well, I don't get as much current income off the *Arkansas Democrat-Gazette,* or our company doesn't, in profits, but I think I have a far more valuable newspaper with 71 percent penetration than, say, the Jackson *Clarion-Ledger* [a Gannett paper] that's got 44 percent penetration. I may never monetize or put that economic value in the bank and write a check on it, but it's there.

Meanwhile, at Third and Louisiana . . .

A number of missteps and lapses in judgment at the Gazette *marked the beginning of the end, but not all came from inside the paper. Some people date the final decline to the day that Little Rock's biggest department store, Dillard's, cancelled its advertising over what some saw as a petty grievance.*

Brantley: I guess you could say Max Brantley single-handedly lost the newspaper war. . . . It turns out it was a more complicated story than we know. But certainly, I'm directly responsible for the triggering event. . . . One thing that I did know, because I was the son of a stockbroker, was that there was a vast amount of public information available on publicly held corporations that they were required to file with the Securities and Exchange Commission. At that point, in the eighties, in Little Rock, they didn't provide any of that information to newspapers. They didn't talk to newspapers, and Dillard Department Stores certainly didn't . . . I called my mom, who by then worked in my dad's stockbrokerage office, and I said, "I want you to buy two shares of Wal-Mart, Dillard, Arkla, and several other major Arkansas publicly held corporations in my name, so I'll be on the mailing list when they mail the proxy statement out every year. Because the proxy statement has great stuff about when they raise executives' pay and give them stock-appreciation rights and those sorts of things."

So, my very first year to get a Dillard proxy statement, it so happened that the proxy statement that year indicated that they had fired the previous accounting firm and had hired a new one and were in a dispute over—I don't know the figure—$26 million sticks in my mind. But there was a tax-accounting dispute, and I think the bottom line was that maybe there was going to be an additional charge against them for taxes because of some accounting error or something. So there was this little arcane bookkeeping dispute. So I brought the prospectus in to work. I was a city editor, and I gave it to Chuck Heinbockel, who was then our first, or second, business editor. He wrote a little story about what was in the prospectus, and it was no more or less than what the prospectus said, and that Dillard's, of course, wouldn't comment. They don't ever comment about anything. We went to the news meeting that afternoon, and Lundy asked what everybody had. It was a slow news day. Nobody had much of anything. And I said, "Well, we got this little business story out of the Dillard's prospectus, which nobody else will have," because nobody else was messing with that stuff then, "about this charge against earnings, and, you know, it's a little something." He said, "Well, put it on page one." I don't even think that was necessarily bad. It wasn't that big a business story, but a slow day, and, I mean, who knows? They put it down at the bottom of page one, maybe a two-column headline on it. The next morning, about midmorning, it seems, the people started scurrying around, coming in from the publisher's office and the advertising department, and said, "The Dillard's ads aren't here. Have they been jerked?" or something. Before the day was out, it was clear that Dillard's had pulled their advertising from our newspaper. Without, to the best of my knowledge, without directly telling anybody why. They just did it and didn't pay calls to the publisher or anybody.

The other thing that happened was the *Democrat* the next day ran a very prominent story—it may have been on page one—saying that our story was all wrong and quoting Dillard's people as saying it was just some terrible story. I still say all of that is BS. Our story was correct. It was in the prospectus. Perhaps it was a minor story and not of great interest, and I can plead ignorance to that, but they never came back. And that was the end. That was the end of Dillard's advertising in the *Arkansas Gazette*. It was a chunk. And

despite efforts that included the head of the entire Gannett corporation coming down and trying to pay court to Bill Dillard Sr., nobody would give them
the time of day.

Dumas: Not too long before that, we, the *Gazette,* had written stories about
his grandson.

Brantley: Well, I had a role in that too. And that I have absolutely no apolo-
gies about. He had a grandson who was a troubled kid, who stole a car to go
joy riding one night and was what they call "cutting doughnuts" in people's
yards in west Little Rock. He happened to drive into the yard of an old fellow out on Hall Drive, I think it was, and was turning some doughnuts. A
guy who was a pretty good marksman pulled a rifle out of his closet and shot
the kid, didn't kill him but wounded him, stopped the joy ride. It was a big
story, and we played it on page one and interviewed everybody we could. By
anybody's standards, it was an obvious, big news story, and we reported
exactly what had happened. My recollection of the *Democrat's* coverage of the
story was that they didn't mention that the car was stolen until the last paragraph of the story, I think. And they downplayed the Dillard connection.
The story was just warped in any number of ways. A normal newspaper
wouldn't have handled it that way. They handled it with the maximum dis-
cretion toward the Dillard family, which was typical of later coverage they did
in the business section. John Robert Starr had a writer, Becky Moore, who
wrote an advertising column in which she criticized some Dillard's advertising, and he told her, "You will never do that again or you will be fired." They
took good care of the department store.

Lundy: Dillard's department store was in a dust-up with the IRS. The IRS
claimed that Dillard owed them [back taxes and late fees] in the amount of
$22 million, but it could be a different number. It was a big number. . . . And
there really was no disagreeing. It was clearly a page-one story, so we put it
on page one. Well, unfortunately, that morning Bill Malone was supposed to
go see Bill Dillard who, at that point—he was in his seventies but still real
active. And Bill Malone was to present Bill Dillard with some kind of award
from the Chamber of Commerce or something. So Bill shows up at Dillard's
office at nine o'clock with a little plaque, and Bill Dillard threw him out of
his office, not physically, but ordered him out of his office and was carrying
on and was just having a fit. And said he would never advertise in the *Arkansas
Gazette* again. So Bill Malone went back to his office and called me over, and
he was still shaking. He'd never been yelled at by a guy that rich before. I
said, "Well, I hope he calms down," and Bill said, "Yes. I do too." Well, he
never calmed down. So he pulled the Dillard's ads, and Dillard's, at that time,

was not only the number one department store in town, it was the number two and three department store in town. You can't run a newspaper in Little Rock, Arkansas, without the Dillard's ads.

. . . After about two weeks . . . Bill Malone called me over to his office and said, "I've just talked to somebody who has talked to somebody at Dillard's." It was sort of a back channel of communication with them. "And they said that if you'll pull [Heinbockel] off the Dillard's beat, that they'll consider coming back to the paper." I said, "But he didn't do anything wrong," and he said, "Be that as it may, this is what they've done." . . . I said, "Well, unless I can come up with a good reason—and I don't have a good reason—I can't do that." And so he said, "Well, I want you to think about how. . . ." I'll remember this conversation until my last breath. He said, "I want you to think about the jobs of the six hundred or so men and women in this building and how important those jobs are and how important you think the continued existence of the *Arkansas Gazette* is. I want you to go home this weekend and think about all that. And come back Monday and tell me what you're going to do." He hadn't ordered me to remove the guy. I went home, and I did think about it all weekend. It's your classic ethical dilemma. Certainly, I'd never been in a place where the odds were that high. So I came back Monday morning and said, "I thought about it all weekend. I can't take somebody off the beat if they haven't done something wrong." So he said, "Well, okay. I'll tell him." So he got word back to him. And I don't know whether they would have come back to the paper or not because, I mean, it was a single person's decision . . . But they never did come back, and that was the beginning of the end. It was not immediately but some months later that they would lose Bill and brought in Craig Moon. And Craig was absolutely certain that we could get Dillard's back. He was very confident. I was happy at the thought because I wanted them back too. He made several trips over there and got nowhere.

Dumas: The loss of Dillard's advertising also had some additional fallout because other advertisers followed Dillard's.

Brantley: There were advertisers who wanted to be where Dillard's was because that generated traffic, they thought, for them, and without them, it clearly had an impact . . . We later found out that there were other events. There was simmering unhappiness, and I don't know at what stage it occurred. It had to have happened before then. Walter Hussman had gone to Dillard's and demonstrated to them that we had advertisers that got advertising rates that were, per inch, lower than Dillard's, who was our biggest advertiser and should have had the most favorable advertising rates. Now the lower rates were on, as I understand, what we used to call "standby" advertising. They were ads that could be put in the paper, in the city edition, say, in space that developed unexpectedly or something. You couldn't dictate placement and day of publication and that sort of thing. Whatever it was, that rankled Dillard probably more than anything. But, by timing alone, it was pretty clear that the story was the last straw.

Hugh Patterson: [Hussman's] big move on Dillard [department store] had been to offer [that] if Dillard ran the same advertising in the *Democrat* that they were currently running in the *Gazette,* he would run it for a dollar an inch. And his advertised rate at the time was about seven dollars and a half an inch. Ours was about nine and a half an inch. . . . [Hussman] had been able to sustain some losses on the unusual profits that he was beginning to make on his television franchise, a cable franchise situation in a number of smaller towns. And at that time he was profiting from those operations to the extent of three or four million dollars a year. Well, at one time he finally bragged that he had gotten his losses on the *Democrat* down below his income from these other sources and what not. Well, then as time went on, his profits from the cable just compounded, and it got to where he was getting $15 million. But he was so determined that he would prevail in this market that he was willing to throw all that away. His family was terribly upset over it. And it was during that time that he came to me with the proposition that if we would enter into a joint arrangement that we could make all the determinations regarding coverage, rates, days of publication, that sort of thing, if we would just subsidize his news operation to the extent of three or four hundred thousand dollars a year or something of that sort. But I didn't want to have a thing to do with Hussman. I just disapproved of their outlook on life to begin with. . . . They had cut corners every way they possibly could have over all the years, in the operation, with suppliers, machinery, people. We'd get the reports on those things, so I just didn't want to have to be involved in it, and I didn't think we had to be. I tried to persuade Walter that he could make adjustments of his own in the operation, that he could just decide to go after them and limit his circulation and all to try to develop more retail business and what not and at least be reasonably profitable.

Reed: Did he consider selling the *Democrat* outright to the *Gazette?*

Hugh Patterson: We never approached that because at that point my investigation indicated that it was not possible legally for us to acquire it. . . . And then, of course, the acquisition of control by Hussman has led to a politicizing of the paper in ways that I don't even think conservatives appreciate. . . . We tended to run the columns of the people whose views we appreciated and, of course, emphasized the *New York Times* writers, Tony Lewis and the others. And I think it's unfortunate that the *Democrat* has not kept a representative number of those good writers. And then, I don't know why they feel that they have any obligation to continue John Robert Starr's dribble. You know, Starr claimed to have been responsible in large measure for the *Democrat* dominating the field. Well, I don't think it had anything much to do with that. I think that it was Hussman's largesse to Dillard that did more than anything else.

Meriwether: I remember the day that Walter came over to offer a joint operating agreement to Hugh, and essentially the offer was "I've been here for X years now, . . . and I'm not making any progress, and you're a strong competitor, and I'd like to offer the community an alternative voice. Let's combine through a standard JOA [joint operating agreement]," and Hugh said, "Well, I'll get back to you." Well, Jim [Williamson, business manager] counseled against it, saying, "Hussman can't do it. There's no way he can. We've gotten our strength up now, you know. This is good and that is good and this is good, et cetera." And the *Gazette* had, after all, spent years competing with August Engel, you know, the meanest man in the world, and then "the boys" —I never heard them refer to Stanley [Berry] and Marcus [George] [nephews and heirs of K. August Engel, the *Democrat's* long-time owner]. It's always "the boys." So Jim counseled against the joint operating agreement. Leon [Reed, circulation manager], on the other hand, counseled to take it and run, and I just kept my mouth shut. I mean, why get in it? I don't know that I would have gotten in it anyway. . . . Hugh felt like he had, very much had, the upper hand, and he was the strong competitor, that he had so much of the upper hand that Hussman's was just an impossible task. That the *Democrat* wouldn't last that much longer anyway, which was a miscalculation, a legitimate, honorable miscalculation of how much money Hussman had and how his father had pretty well decided that it was time to let the boy do what he wants to. . . . [Hugh] could not imagine the strength of commitment that was there. . . . "They can't last," they reasoned.

Reed: There's something about this guy, Walter Hussman, that makes people want to underestimate him. What is it?

Meriwether: I sat in an airplane one time coming back from a meeting, and Walter and his daddy were behind me. Peggy [Meriwether's wife] and I were sitting in front of them, and Walter was laying out for me and his daddy a scheme of how he was going to take over the *Arkansas Gazette*. And he said, "Here's how I figure we could do it if we really want to do it." And he pointed to the profits here and the profits there, and I had no idea what he was talking about. I assumed it was the cable company, you know, this, that, and the other, plus other assets that they had, television stations or whatever. And I think what he was doing there was trying to soften the old man up for the idea, bite it one shoe at a time. "Now if we could afford to cut the family dividend back a little bit . . ." Well, about that time Gail, his older sister, sued him, you know, and it got where she couldn't find a lawyer. But that's why people underestimated him. He is the most self-effacing, nicest guy you ever met, friendly. . . . He not only is willing to pay salaries, he's willing to buy newsprint, he's willing to beef up here, there, and yonder, and he's willing to give free classifieds, and he's willing to throw the newspaper, and he's willing to go after it, and he knows how to spend the money, and he knows how to make it. The prize is to get the franchise. That's the prize. And he keeps his eye on that goal, and he goes for it.

Carrick Patterson: [Hugh] had seen that the afternoon paper in those circumstances never did do very well and was an economic drain on the joint operations. And, of course, there was a lot more competition than just the other newspaper. The broadcast was becoming very, very aggressive as competition, less money to go around and costs were going up significantly. Newsprint had soared. All the new equipment that you needed to be competitive, time-wise, the computers and then the huge expense of keeping the presses up to date. It was becoming really obvious that you needed to be going into offset printing to compete, in terms of being able to print color and that sort of thing. There were incredibly huge expenses that needed to be made just to sort of stay up with the industry and to be competitive. So he turned down the offer for the JOA for those reasons.

And so, Walter Hussman, to his credit, said, "Okay, instead of just giving up, I have myself the economic resources to put into this, to try to make a go of it. Despite the real economic realities, I will make the decision to subsidize this operation and to do whatever is necessary to do to make it viable." He was an immensely wealthy person with other newspapers and oil and broadcast interests and had a good deal of money. And I wouldn't be a bit surprised—although he'd never said this, certainly, to me or maybe to anybody else—if he didn't have just a little bit of ego tied up into it, as far as being turned down on the joint operating thing. That may or may not be true. I don't know, just speculating on that.

In any case, they decided to take some really dramatic moves to make the *Democrat* competitive. They shifted it over to morning publication, which absolutely had to be done if they were going to compete. They subsidized the circulation practices and the publication practices by offering the biggest advertisers below-cost rates. They did a general-circulation, weekly throw-away section. They threw the paper away for free on Wednesdays to every-body in the circulation area. They started giving away classified advertising to noncommercial people for free. Very, very costly things to do. They were swimming in red ink. But, overall, they could afford to do it. Well, the com-petition, the economic competition situation changed dramatically because, although the *Gazette* was profitable, it was by no means lavishly profitable.

. . . What we did was try to fall back on what we thought we did best, which was putting out a good newspaper. But that wasn't enough to keep the advertisers, for instance, totally loyal to us. They're driven by economics. If you have a chance to buy advertising for a dollar an inch versus fifteen dol-lars an inch, you're going to do it. I mean, that's just the way it is. And they also did a pretty good job over there at the *Democrat* of identifying interest-ing things to report on. They didn't do as good a job of covering the tradi-tional news of record, perhaps, as we did, but they covered for that to some extent by having, you know, interesting stories about what people were doing and what was going on and that sort of thing. So, to say it was totally eco-nomic competition is wrong, but that was the key factor, the economics. Despite the fact that the *Democrat* itself was not successful. . . .

They established a personality for themselves that they had not had, through the writings of John Robert Starr, the managing editor. And with all that they had a nice little thing going that certain people really, really liked. And, of course, the *Gazette* had never been universally popular among the people of this conservative Southern state. You see, being a liberal newspaper was something that, you know, earned the paper a lot of respect but also a lot of resentment. But the economic power that they [the *Democrat*] had kept mounting. And in our opinion their activities violated the law. Our opinion was that selling below the cost of producing was illegal. And we tried to get various enforcement agencies, such as the attorney general's office and the antitrust division of the Justice Department, and so forth, interested in tak-ing action on that. And we were never successful. So, finally, it became obvi-ous it couldn't go on that way, that we would be driven out of business. So we filed a lawsuit in federal court asking that they be enjoined from selling things below their cost of producing and so forth. And after a lengthy trial, we lost the suit. They did a much better job of presenting their case than we did of ours. We simply didn't do a good-enough job. And after that, there was no question of our being able to survive economically.

Well, it was clear that if the economic competition went on like that, that we would lose, that we couldn't afford—the paper would be bankrupt; the

family would be bankrupt; all the three-hundred-plus people who depended
on the paper for their livelihood would be out of work. And that wasn't something that we were willing to accept even for the ego of owning it for ourselves.

McCord: Hugh Patterson told me that he wanted me to help win the newspaper war because I had worked for Walter Hussman for three years and supposedly knew all of his ins and outs. I said, "Well, I will be glad to advise."
Months went by, and he never asked me anything. So, finally, I went down
to his office one day and told him I wanted to take him to lunch. I said, "You
know, we never have talked about . . ." He said, "Oh well, we have got this
'newspaper war' under control, and Walter is not going to last another six
months. We are just doing fine." I told him I knew he thought that but that
all indications to me are just the opposite. I told him he should copy the free
classifieds, "against the door" delivery, and all the other things that Walter
was doing. It seemed to me you have to fight fire with fire. He said, "Bob, no,
that is not the . . ." Well, I pestered him some more, and we had lunch at
least one other time.

Leon Reed, the long-time circulation manager, was the one who was
advising Hugh. He and Hugh were very close, and I liked him too. I had
known him for years. We went to lunch, the three of us. I started in again on
what I thought they ought to do. I thought we ought to give prizes and give
free papers away to get circulation. I tried to anticipate the next step Walter
was going to take. Finally, I said, "You know, I think we ought to go back and
think about a joint operating agreement so we can keep the two newspapers
alive." Well, they just laughed at that. They just said, "No, no. Bob, you
worry about things that we have under control." I said, "Well, it doesn't indicate that we have. The figures don't indicate that we have." "Well, we know,
but he is going to run out of money. We just don't have to worry about that.
We are going to win this war." So that was kind of the way it was.

One of the worst mistakes, in my opinion, was firing [Bill] McIlwain,
[managing editor]. He got to stay there only one year. He is one the of the
best newspaper men that I ever worked for or ever will. Everybody in the
industry sort of agreed with that except the people at the *Arkansas Gazette*.
They were clannish and didn't want an outsider coming in there and being
the boss. . . . Of course, there's no way to prove it, but I have sometimes
thought that if McIlwain had stayed, things might have ended in another
way—a joint operating agreement or maybe even the defeat of the *Democrat*.
McIlwain redesigned the paper, made it look much better. He also hired
some more people, and they were good people. He made the paper livelier
than it had been. The op-ed page was really his idea.

. . . While I was still at the *Democrat,* Walter talked to Hugh, and Hugh had quickly dismissed the idea [of a joint operating agreement]. He was naturally resentful of the Hussman chain moving into *Gazette* territory and turning the *Democrat* into a morning paper. In my last months at the *Democrat* I had said this to Walter: "I am not going to do this if you don't want me to, but I have known Hugh Patterson for a long time, and I will go out and talk to him about the possibility of a joint operation." Walter, at that time, would have resumed afternoon publication and allowed the *Gazette* to be the Sunday newspaper. Hussman said okay, so I went out to Hugh's house. Of course, he was very cordial to me as he has always been. He and I had been among those who worked to create a chapter of the Society of Professional Journalists in Little Rock. "Bob," he said, "I am just not going to do that. This young man came to town with his daddy's money, and he thinks he is going to win. I don't think he will. The way they came up here, I don't feel obligated to bail him out now." I said, "Well, you know what the end of it is going to be." He answered, "Yes, I know what the end of it is going to be. We are going to win."

Of course, it would be easy to look back and say, "Well, maybe that would have worked, maintaining two dailies in Little Rock." But if you look around the country today you see these joint operating agreements are not surviving. Only a very few. And frankly, I don't know how much longer the situation would have survived here. People are no longer reading newspapers as they used to.

George Wells: There was one thing about the preparation for this trial that I found impressive. I had a conclusion in my own mind and told maybe a few friends, that this was probably the most important commercial trial in the history of Arkansas because the loser was probably going to go out of business, and that would leave us with only one newspaper. That's just the way I felt about it. I went to Carrick Patterson, who was the managing editor then. I said, "Now, this case is too important to screw up by managing the copy." So he sent out a memo that more or less said that I could write whatever I wanted to, and if there was a space problem, come to him. And nobody fooled around with my copy, more than just normal editing things. The *Democrat* reported this thing—it read to me like it had been written by the *Democrat* lawyers every day.

Dumas: I think anybody who wanted to judge the two newspapers at that time—the quality and professionalism of those two newspapers at that time—should go back and read the developing accounts of that trial by those two newspapers. At the time, I thought it was remarkable that the *Gazette's* coverage was thorough, that all the bad points for the *Gazette* were there for everybody to see, and you got a straightforward account of the trial. And I think anybody who read that might have anticipated the result of that case. But if you read the *Democrat* account of it, damaging points for the *Democrat* never showed up in the paper. I thought it was the most one-sided coverage I had ever seen of a case that kind of spotlighted the paper's professionalism. It seems to me that that's the kind of case where you should really set out to prove to everybody that you're fair. They didn't do it, and the *Gazette* did in that case. And that's kind of tooting our own horn, and that's obviously coming from someone who is, I guess, biased about it. We gave, I thought, extremely thorough coverage to that case. I mean, there were long, long, detailed accounts every day. The *Gazette* was, I guess, not an entirely sympathetic institution, and the owners were not entirely sympathetic to their, in effect, working-class jury, probably people who couldn't understand what's wrong with selling your product as cheaply as possible or giving it away.

Wells: The thing about it is, I don't think that Hussman was that appealing to the jury either. Here again, it's a subjective thing, but I think that the jury said, "Why are they taking up our time fighting over something in court? Just let them go at it and the best paper will win or something." In jury selection, it was revealed that several of these people routinely did not read either paper or any paper. And if they had read anything about the lawsuit—several said they had, but they couldn't remember anything.

Dumas: So the jury was largely made up of people at the end who did not read newspapers. It was a condition of being on the jury, I guess, that you had to not be a devotee of either newspaper.

Brantley: When I read—first in the *Democrat,* not in the *Arkansas Gazette*— before the trial that Hugh Patterson, who had brought the antitrust suit on the grounds that he was being run out of business, had taken $400,000 out of the company in the preceding year, in the form of a dividend, personally, I thought, "Son of a bitch." That was a lot of money. I mean, it's still a lot of money, but $400,000 fifteen years ago was really a lot of money. I was assistant city editor, making $25,000 a year, maybe $26,000 a year. As interviews done by *Spectrum,* which was then an alternative newspaper in Little Rock, proved after the trial, there were jurors like the guy who rented buckets of balls out at a golf driving range who said, "Man, you're not being run out of business. You're making $400,000." Of course, the *Democrat* lawyers hammered it and hammered it and hammered it. The suit was premature, and it's easy to fault Hugh Patterson for filing the suit when he did, but the fact is he said, "I could wait until I'm losing money, or I could file it now." I'm not really second-guessing it. He was still the dominant newspaper in terms of revenue at that moment, despite what the *Democrat* had done.

Dumas: After losing the suit, all of us for the first time began to realize maybe the *Gazette* was not going to last forever, that we really were vulnerable. Until that point, most of us thought there is not really any way the *Gazette* is going to go down the drain. At that point, we began to realize.

Brantley: Oh, I did, and by that time, I was nervous. See, I had done a tremendous research project on the newspaper leading up to the antitrust case, in which I was closeted in a room with Hussman newspapers from around Arkansas. I added up their news hole and added up their column inches and looked at their percentage of news column inches and prepared a long document for our lawyers on what my assessment of the Hussman newspapers were. It was going to be a strategy of, "Hey, if you let these guys win, they are just coming in here and buy the market, and they are going to turn the newspaper to crap." That was going to be a defense strategy of some sort. They never really got into it, but part of my memo was highly cautionary because I said that, "You can say that about Camden. You can say it, to a lesser degree, about El Dorado, but the Texarkana paper is not a bad-looking newspaper, and it has a pretty good-sized news hole, and it is an attractive newspaper." It was winning a lot of secondary prizes in the contest then. That project made me nervous. It made me exceedingly nervous. I also could see a company that had immensely successful newspapers in other places and clearly could carry on a fight for a long time. I was nervous from the late seventies on and got more nervous with each succeeding year.

I hated not responding to stories. I hated just being silent when they would break some story or cause some public stir. Finally, we took them on. On one famous story late in the tenure, Bob Wells did a story that finally showed that one of Mike Masterson's most famous investigations, which led to the conviction of a man for bludgeoning a teenage boy on a parking lot, was based on perjured testimony by a medical examiner.

John Robert Starr had been the Little Rock bureau chief of the Associated Press in earlier years. When Hussman made him editor of the Democrat, *Starr immediately launched an aggressive campaign to overtake the* Gazette. *He needled and attacked* Gazette *people in his column. He sent reporters to dig up minor but eye-catching scandals in local and state government. He soon had few friends and little respect from newspaper people outside the* Democrat, *but his tactics were effective.*

Robert McCord: The *Arkansas Democrat's* editor was Bob Starr, who had always disliked the *Gazette.* The story is that this happened because the *Gazette* wouldn't put Starr's byline on Associated Press stories that he wrote that the *Gazette* printed. For the *Democrat* he wrote a daily column filled with name-calling and criticism of the *Gazette* and those who worked there. People like to read that sort of thing. If the *Gazette* wrote a story one way, the *Democrat* always wrote theirs another way. . . . And there is no question that he played a big role in their winning the newspaper war. There is no doubt about it. He deserved much of the credit.

Dumas: So, they bring in Starr, and we have what became known as the newspaper war. How did that affect coverage at the *Gazette?*

Brantley: Well, there were a lot of different effects. I remember a lot of them pretty clearly. I remember, rest his soul, Jimmy Jones, who knew Hussman as a scion of the Palmer newspaper family, which ran notoriously shoddy newspapers in small towns, and Jimmy wrote him off as of no concern. I remember he and Tucker Steinmetz went to the news conference at which the purchase had been announced and asked a lot of tough questions and talked about their newspaper's reputation. It was kind of lording it over the new kid on the block, you know. I don't know why, but that made me nervous. I am a pessimist, I guess. I didn't know that much, but I didn't discount any of it. I do remember Shelton saying . . . in the beginning—he kept a list of what they had and what we didn't have—"We have got to beat them on everything. We have got to have everything they have, and we have got to have more. We have got to have more details. It is not just that we have the story but that we have a better story." Shelton responded to it exactly in the proper way, I thought, which is to match up, day by day, the papers.

Well, it became quickly impossible to do that for the reason that, over a fairly rapid period of time, Hussman made the commitment to publish the biggest newspaper in Arkansas, that is, the most number of pages, and beefed up his staff. The *Gazette* never, never, never, in the Patterson era, made the commitment to newsprint expenditure that Hussman did. And even if we had covered the same stories, even if we had done the same thing, we had no place to print them. It got worse and worse until the late eighties. There were times—this wasn't really in the early era, but in the beginning of the Gannett era—I sat down and counted the column inches in the *Democrat* of local news versus the column inches in the *Gazette* one Saturday morning, which is a pretty good news day, typically. I had been so frustrated because we had so many stories that we had to cut into briefs or throw out entirely or save on leftover, and they had something like, I think, five hundred column inches of local news in the paper, maybe more than that. That is five or six full pages of local news, which is a pretty good amount of local news, and we had about a hundred and ten. They had five times the local-news column inches we had, and I thought, I don't care how bright your writing, how good your editors, how smart you are about context: you are not going to beat anybody with that. More is more. And that was the story from the beginning of the newspaper war, and it was awfully frustrating through the years to work there . . .

We had a superior staff—there's no doubt about that. It didn't instantly happen overnight. One of the important decisions they made too was to place a big emphasis at the *Democrat* on investigative-style reporting. That was not Shelton's strength. I remember it distinctly, being a Sunday city editor, the day that Mike Masterson began a series for the *Democrat* on irregularities in the state medical examiner's office. They weren't disposing of organs properly. They were filling corpses with sawdust. A grisly, awful story. I tried to work up a follow to that story, and, in fact, we printed something. Shelton wasn't very happy that we had done that. I'm not sure that the thing to do in the face of a big, multipart investigative effort is to try and get some spot news, and that may have been a mistake on my part, doing that. But we usually ignored them. That was the end of it on the medical examiner. We chose not to follow it at all, for whatever reason. Ultimately, the medical examiner lost his job, and whether the story was right or wrong, they had written something that had a direct effect. I mean, they were responsible for removing the medical examiner from office.

That would become a pattern of their kind of work, which is to pick on particularly public officials, because you can't libel a public official. You have got the FOI [Freedom of Information Act] as a tool to get a lot of information, and they don't have a natural constituency. They can't call in an advertiser to put pressure on your publisher. Public officials are, by some, supposed to be very powerful, but actually they are some of the most pitifully weak people in the world if you decide to pick on them. They had a pretty good run of finding people. Public officials are human; they have their frailties. They had a pretty good run of finding those sorts of people. Invariably, when they would find one of these cases, we wouldn't follow it. They would make news, and TV stations would pick them up, and people would be talking about them, and we would be silent on those stories.

And we were not really generating those kinds of stories ourselves. Journalism was more about being a recorder of events that occurred rather than seeking things to write about. That is not entirely true, but I think, day to day, the mindset was more like that. I don't think you can underestimate how valuable that was in making the *Democrat* a talked-about commodity in town, particularly among other public officials, who were notoriously chicken. You write a word about a public official in the paper, and it gets them nervous. They start shaking about it. In that news is inevitably mostly about public officials, that target group was really affected by what the *Democrat* was doing. Starr reinforced that through his column. He was the managing editor assigning these stories, and then, lest anyone miss the point, he would follow up with an opinion column that made it very clear what the point was, which was a break in journalistic tradition that journalism professors can argue about. It is viewed as somewhat unethical in the trade, although I kind of practice it here now in our weekly, so I don't want to be too hypocritical about it. In any event, it made for a pretty potent one-two punch.

Shepherd: John Robert Starr was a very mixed bag for people. He was domineering and rude to some people and maybe frustrating for people to work with, but he was aggressive, and he had a mission, and his mission was to outdo the *Gazette*. And the people who got caught up in that with him made it a competitive thing and made the *Gazette* try and do more than it had done. It wasn't necessarily right, but Starr, many times, had reporters out digging up information before the *Gazette* considered it important . . . If you're an editor, in many places, you must have some idea of a mission. You want to cover your community or your area of coverage fairly. Starr wanted to control the state of Arkansas. He would have liked to control the world if he could. . . . Many a night I wondered how he could leave the building and walk to his parking lot without an armed guard because I knew how many people he had offended that day, how many important people had called him to chew him out.

Cottingham: I detested [Starr], and I did not get along very well with him. I will give one example. Leslie Newell Peacock and I were copy editors. We started about the same time. She was then just Leslie Newell at the *Democrat*. She was an excellent copy editor, intelligent, well educated. But her brother was Frank Newell, and he was a Clinton appointee, I believe. I am trying to remember the sequence of events. I think to the PSC [Public Service Commission]. At any rate, this was 1979, and Starr and the *Democrat* had launched sort of a vendetta against Clinton and his appointees. Frank Newell's name came up somehow. The *Democrat* opposed him. He was a liberal. Leslie, being a very frank and honest person, was at a newspaper party around this same time and told someone at the party that she thought the *Gazette* was a better paper than the *Arkansas Democrat,* which, of course, was true. But it got back to John Robert Starr, and he fired her. I was very upset because the talent pool at the *Democrat* was not deep, and she was very gifted. It seemed very unfair to me. I was very young. I went into his office and said—he had heard I was upset. He called me into his office, and he said, "I hear that you are upset that I fired Leslie." I said, "Yes, I am. She is good. We have a lot of idiots. I think it is unfair." He said, "Disloyalty is like a cancer. You have to cut it out." I was very nervous and insecure, and my voice trembled. I said, "Okay, fine. That is your position. You are the boss. I understand you can do what you want, but you may as well know that I am going to have a going-away party for Leslie. She is my friend." He said, "I think that is a shitty thing to do." I said, "Why?" I left the office and went to the coffee room and cried . . . It was kind of a third-world banana republic at the *Democrat* under John Robert Starr. We went ahead and had the party, and all the good people who had any character came from the *Democrat,* and all the butt-kissers didn't come. It was one of the best parties we have ever had, and I did not get a raise for a year.

Later, when I was a general assignments reporter—we are talking probably 1982—Starr told me that I didn't get a raise because I had supported Leslie but that he admired me for moving from the copy desk and showing some gumption and becoming a reporter and also for being loyal to my friend. And after that I started getting raises like, you know, ten dollars once a year. I expected to be fired. My husband had to be physically restrained once from beating up John Robert Starr. Damon Thompson and Bob Sallee—you can verify this. It's too complicated, but he had pissed Omar off. Omar was a Golden Gloves boxer and state champion. It's not a good idea to piss Omar off, although he is a very gentle person. Once he gets pissed off, it's no holds barred. He was angry about Starr and the way he had been treated on a story and took his glasses off. He was going to go whip John Robert Starr's ass, which would have killed him probably. Fortunately, he was restrained.

[Starr] was a very shrewd man, like Walter Hussman, very shrewd. He was a demagogue. He played to the baser instincts of the populace. He played to the baser instincts of the reader. He was very astute, very manipulative. I don't think that he honestly believed some of the things he wrote, but he thought that readers would like them. He pandered, but he was insightful. He had a sense for what readers wanted. He was dishonest. He was a coward. He had a chip on his shoulder. What's the term I want? He played to a kind of class consciousness in Arkansas where he portrayed the *Gazette* as the "paper of the elite" and the *Democrat* as the "scrappy paper of the working man." That was very clever and effective.

Leslie Newell Peacock: After John Robert Starr came, things got sort of calculated, and there was a real political agenda. He used to brag about that. He said, "We are kingmakers. We make or break people." I can't remember the political figure—he said, "I have put this guy in office." That's just really how he talked. And the mood was pretty crummy . . . I left the *Democrat* because I was fired, because everyone knew how I felt about the *Democrat,* that I had never really had much pride in the product, so I was not loyal to the paper. My brother had been nominated to the Public Service Commission and had served on the PSC, and Bill Clinton was defeated before my brother's nomination was confirmed in the senate. This was Clinton's first term. . . . The *Gazette* was carrying front-page stories about how [Sen.] Joe Ford was not going to bring Frank [Newell's] name up for confirmation on the PSC because he perceived my brother to be proconsumer. It was front-page news because it was about political maneuvering. The *Gazette* understood the story. They got it. They got what was happening. The *Democrat* didn't get it. Their reporter was really at sea. He didn't really understand what was happening. So he was coming to me and saying, "Can you help me? Can you get me your brother's phone number?" I said, "It's in the phone book. Why don't you call him?" He said, "Can you tell me about your brother? How does he feel about this?" And I said, "You know, you could really ask my brother those questions." I remember he came up with a story that was about five inches long. That was the best he could do. I didn't feel sorry for him because I had never been a reporter myself. I know that can happen.

I was making fun of the *Democrat's* effort about the story at a party, and news about that got back to Starr . . . So I went into Starr's office and said, "What do you mean firing me?" He said, "I don't have to talk to you about this." I said, "But I want to know." He said, "You are a spy for one thing." And I don't know what that was all about. I said, "Well, I certainly am not a spy." . . . He said, "You trashed the paper at a party. I know all about it. You're out of here. You're gone." He said, "I'm getting rid of people who don't like this paper. I'm not going to have them around." I said, "Well, if you do that, you're going to have a really tiny staff." I was pretty hot.

John Reed: John Robert Starr and Meredith Oakley would write about us by name in their columns, and that was not any fun. . . . Meredith wrote about me by name and Starr wrote about my dad by name, and then Starr was always writing about the *Gazette,* and it is people you knew. And I guess it hit home the day I picked up Meredith's column and saw my own name in Meredith's column as having done a poor job. I can't remember exactly what she said, but it really made me mad and upset me because I had scooped their reporter on a little political story, and it was their way of fighting back. I can't imagine what some of the big names at the *Gazette* felt like routinely being excoriated by John Robert Starr and by Meredith Oakley. Because you know the *Gazette* at that time was at the height of the war, and we took pride in not responding in kind. We went out and covered the news.

Wood: I was walking down the street with Gene Herrington [a former managing editor of the *Democrat*] years ago. We were talking to John Robert. We encountered him walking out on the street. He was rubbing his hands together and just dying laughing. He said, and I quote, "I've got those stupid people on the run over there. They've got the best newspaper in the state, and they don't even have sense enough to know it!" He said, "Every move I make just scares them to death. They run and change something!"

The Democrat-Gazette, *as it became when Hussman bought out his rival, surprised more than a few Arkansas newspaper people. The new editorial page was predictably conservative. Led by Paul Greenberg and operating with the new boss's blessing, it was the opposite of almost everything that the liberal* Gazette *page had been. But the news pages were not easy to classify. The paper continued to run large amounts of national, international, and local news. The news hole was larger than in many other papers of similar size. Hussman also continued to publish it as a statewide newspaper, even though the expenses of circulating it in the far corners cut into profits. Some thought they detected a conservative bias in some of the coverage, and there were days when the paper made questionable decisions on where and how big to play certain controversial stories. But on the whole, it compared favorably to any number of other metropolitan and state-capital newspapers. Not many former* Gazette *hands were willing to offer it any praise. But Scott Van Laningham, a star on the* Gazette's *political beat, found that the passage of years had softened his view of the old rival.*

Van Laningham: It's not easy for me to acknowledge this. My guess is that Hussmann is putting out a better paper right now than Gannett would have. Painful to say, but I think it needs to be acknowledged. He has not drastically shrunk the news hole. They're still covering national, international, and, for the most part, state news . . . I suspect Gannett would have shrunk the news hole, increased the prices dramatically to try and recover their thirty million quickly. I think Hussman has always had the longer term vision of this war.

Even Walker Lundy, Gannett's first editor of the Gazette, *who was roundly criticized for some of his decisions, conceded afterward that in the newspaper war the big corporate army had been out-generaled.*

Lundy: Walter Hussman was very sound. That's what it took, and Gannett wasn't. And, you know, he used to go around town saying, "The difference is if I lose, I lose everything I own. If they lose, they get transferred," and he was right. And if there's anything that people from Arkansas love, it's an underdog. And he played it well . . . I think the story of the victory of the *Democrat* and the defeat of the *Gazette* in Arkansas, even though I was on the losing side, I think is a really fascinating story. And I love the thought that if it happened on the eastern seaboard, there would've been books written and movies made and doctor's theses because it is a classic story of David and Goliath. David whipped Goliath . . . And the only the thing I regret is that I was so close to it in the process that I wasn't . . . able to see what was happening.

David Petty, the Gazette's *managing editor when Gannett bought it, thought the big company might have won the war if it gone at it differently.*

David Petty: Everybody has great hindsight now that it's over. But the war would have turned remarkably different if all that would have happened is if Gannett would have allowed us just to continue as we were doing. If they had just let us keep operating the way we were operating, not adding any staff, not doing anything but just continue to put out a solid newspaper, and then not worrying about whether we might go $100,000 in the red by the end of the next year, or $200,000 or $300,000 at the most. That kind of an approach would've won because Walter was losing money at the *Democrat*. That was fairly common knowledge with what they were doing that they were losing money. And it was the prospect of losing it for an extended period of time that was frightening. But what happened was we began to escalate the losses. An awful lot of people came in with an awful lot of ideas. I think I started thirteen new sections.

One man, a veteran of both papers who had retired to the comfort of his little hometown of Sheridan and was thus in a position to say to hell with it all, summed up the war this way.

Lancaster: Well, I think all that's irrelevant. I think there are only one or two facts about the newspaper war that mattered at all. One was that you had, on the one hand, a publisher who was willing to spend any amount of money, to destroy any of his holdings and his own bank account and go out and beg on the street if he needed to in order to destroy the other paper. And on the other side, you had a newspaper company that had no sense of its own publication's history. It was not willing to lose money forever just to be able to stay alive. And when you have that kind of ferocity on one side and that kind of indifference on the other side, then it's obvious who's going to win. Could it have turned out any other way? I don't think any improvements at either paper would have made much difference. You got a berserker on one side and a bottom-line wuss on the other. Who's going to win?

11

The Last Days

The last issue of the Arkansas Gazette *was published October 18, 1991. A photograph on page one showed fresh flowers someone had left on the grave of William E. Woodruff in Mount Holly Cemetery. Woodruff published the first issue of the* Gazette *November 20, 1819, at Arkansas Post. When it died, it was the oldest newspaper west of the Mississippi River.*

Max Brantley: Everybody in my family cried when the paper came in that morning.

Mark Oswald: My son was at daycare, which was the Montessori School at Twenty-first and Main in an old house there, and there was another parent who came up to me and said he wanted to thank us for what we'd done over the years. That was when I lost it. I didn't do it any other time, this guy coming up and just saying how much he appreciated what we meant to the state and the city and all that. I just lost it right there.

The Gazette, *which covered everything of importance, missed the story of its own impending doom.*

Ernest Dumas: Moyer [the editor], I guess, instructed Brantley, "We're not going to write about this story. Nothing is to appear in the *Gazette* about it because it is a rumor and good newspapers don't write rumors. That's all this is." And so, the *Gazette* remained silent on it, until some point when it was everywhere and the *Gazette* finally had to write about it, and it was really right toward the end before the *Gazette* ever acknowledged it in its pages. At that point, Max, I think, just did it on his own and risking firing by Moyer, but by that time Moyer didn't give a damn.

. . . Everybody was going to be without a job in a few weeks anyway. But we started, after that, after the rumors went around and the stories. We talked to Bill Alexander, who was a congressman from east Arkansas, and Alexander did a little snooping in the Justice Department and told us, "Yes, it's true. The sale is pending and the Justice Department is evaluating the sale under the antitrust law." And he confirmed for us that it was true. He had some sources there in the Justice Department.

We wondered if Witt Stephens would buy it, and I think maybe somebody even—and I don't know whether I did or somebody talked to Witt because, you know, he had owned some part of the *Gazette* at some point and sold it . . . But Witt wasn't really interested in it at that point. . . . But we talked about employee ownership. We kind of talked around the idea of whether the employees could do it and gave a couple of examples, Kansas City, where the employees bought out the paper. And so we—I've forgotten the sequence of events, but there were about six of us who kind of got organized: Max Brantley and Scott Morris, Anne Farris, Scott Van Laningham, Mike Arbanas . . . I called John Norman Harkey [a lawyer] at Batesville and talked to Harkey about what we could do. We wanted to find a way to block this thing, tie it up somehow. And Harkey said, "Call Walter Davidson and tell him I said to call." So I called Walter Davidson, and so he became our lawyer in this thing and filed something with the Justice Department, saying we were exploring ways to buy the *Gazette.* And Scott Morris or somebody ran into Harry Thomason [the Hollywood producer from Arkansas] at the Dallas–Fort Worth airport, Love Field, someplace. And he was asking about the *Gazette,* and he expressed an interest that he'd like to be an investor. I mean, he couldn't buy the *Gazette* himself but that he'd like to be an investor. He had some cash, and he didn't want to see the *Gazette* fold, and he'd be willing to take some risks. So he kind of threw in with us, and so we wanted somebody to kind of evaluate the *Gazette's* financial position.

Brantley: Harry Thomason did come into the picture, a friend of the Clintons, an old Arkansas boy, successful TV producer, who, with his wife [Linda Bloodworth], had done the fabulously successful *Designing Women.* He was a very good friend of Hillary Clinton's. He came in because of his liberal political leanings, I think. He is something of a windmill charger too and joined in our meetings, footed some of our legal bills in the end. Through the connection with Hillary, I believe, he won for us a curiously worded commitment from Wal-Mart for some sort of advertising presence, which the *Democrat* took pains to call somebody else at Wal-Mart to get them to deny. At that time, Hillary was on the Wal-Mart board, though I believe she was the conduit for that announcement. David Pryor, I think, tried to intercede at Dillard's and so did B. Finley Vinson, who was a friend of the Dillards and a banker in Little Rock, with no effect.

Dumas: And so Walter Smiley—I've forgotten how Walter Smiley got involved—but Walter Smiley became a kind of advisor to us, and we managed to get all the stuff from the Justice Department. He was an accountant and founded Systematics and made a fortune. Built Systematics and sold it to in 1988, 1990, I guess it was, to Alltel. And so he was kind of a financial consultant. Mostly, I think he kind of started his own financial services business and was something of a progressive, he thought. And so he kind of threw in with us, or we approached him and he agreed to look at the stuff. And so he looked at the books on a confidential basis from the Justice Department, the *Gazette's* books, and told us, "This thing is hopeless. There's no way the *Gazette* can make it."

So we were talking about what about if we, the *Gazette,* cut it back and made it a Little Rock paper. Just do a Little Rock paper and cut out the rest of the state and all this vast expense of having a statewide newspaper. And Smiley just continued to tell us, "This is hopeless. You can't do it, and you should abandon it." . . . We had these big rallies and so forth. And there was some talk about a *Gazette* employee buyout. Obviously, we couldn't have bought the *Gazette.* Even talked about using the pension fund to buy it, or part interest in it, but eventually after a couple of months or six weeks or so of this kind of stuff, Smiley talked to our lawyer, and our lawyer told us that it had been suggested to him that this was all frivolous, that those of us at the *Gazette* were not serious about buying the *Gazette* and that it was costing Gannett and Hussman millions of dollars, that we had already cost them millions of dollars, like both papers were losing tons of money, to the tune of twenty to twenty-five million dollars a year. So every week was maybe a million dollars lost by the two and that we were liable, ourselves, could be sued by Hussman or by Gannett or both and that we might have some liability, but at any rate, that didn't matter because we didn't have any money anyway. But, finally, on Thursday afternoon, we told Walter Davidson to tell the Justice Department that our proposition had fallen through. So he faxed the Justice Department a letter late Thursday afternoon.

The end was chaotic and wrenching.

Dumas: And so we came back to work on Friday, and at noon the computers all went dead and the sale was final, I guess, about midafternoon. We were told to pack our belongings and get them out of the building by five o'clock. And they piled boxes in the downstairs hallway, so we went down there to get boxes. And they had security guards surrounding the building and all the entrances and all the exits who watched what you brought out. And so a security guard tried to—I had my chair. I had had some back problems, and I had bought an old cheap chair at the budget furniture place a couple of years earlier, so I was wheeling my chair out of the building and a security guard tried to stop and make me take my chair back in. So I kind of exploded, "This is my goddamned chair and I'm taking it back home."

The next Monday I realized that I had my—the *Gazette* kept a big file for each of us, so you had all your bylines. They kept a byline file for every reporter, everybody who worked at the paper, so it occurred to me the next week that I might need something if I applied for a job . . . So I asked if I could go back in and get my file, my own personal file from the library, and was told I could not. Somebody said check with Walter Hussman. I called over there and somebody checked with Walter Hussman and came back and said, "No, no *Gazette* employee will be allowed in the building." But I tried to get in. Romeo Gatewood still worked, Romeo was still there, and so I went there after hours one day and Romeo let me in, and I went up there and tried to get in, but they had changed the locks. Romeo got me a key to the newsroom and on pain of being fired himself, I guess, if they had discovered it. He was the building superintendent. So I went up there after about six o'clock the next week, and Romeo took me back there and gave me a set of keys to get me into the library and the newsroom because they had put locks on. And so I unlocked the key to the newsroom—I went in the newsroom. But I got back there to the library, and they had changed the lock on the library. I couldn't get the library open.

So a little bit after that, the *Arkansas Times* asked me to write a big piece on Jim Guy Tucker, a cover story on Jim Guy. Who was Jim Guy Tucker? The guy who was going to be the acting governor. And so I needed to get in the files, and so I again asked permission from Walter Hussman to get—I called Brummett and he said he'd get it for me. And Hussman told him no, that I could not have access to the library to do any research. And so I never got my byline file out of there either.

. . . Somebody went up on Saturday and [*Democrat* editors] were out in the newsroom going through desks and waste cans. And, apparently, Starr said later that he had—in fact, wrote in his column once, shortly before he died—that he had all of this stuff that he had gleaned from the *Gazette* computers and the editors' offices he thought would be interesting to old *Gazette* employees, and he was thinking about writing a series of columns about the stuff that he had found in the editors' offices after the closing. But then he died and didn't get to write it.

Cottingham: Most everybody worked very hard and did not give up and worked as if the *Gazette* would be publishing for the next one hundred years. I do not feel the quality deteriorated. It was a very tense newsroom. In any work environment there are personality conflicts and sometimes those would erupt, exacerbated by the tension in the newsroom. People would yell at each other. There was more of that. . . . [On the last day] the air was heavy; it was hard to breathe. People were using gallows humor and crass and grim jokes. There was some talk about Hussman using security guards to kind of pat us down when we left the *Gazette* to make sure we didn't take anything that was his . . . The *Gazette* was dear to me. It was like a child. It was as hard as the death of a beloved family member for it to close . . . On the final day, somebody had a video camera there. They sold their videotape to, I guess it was Channel 4, the NBC affiliate. This tape, then, became the promo for the station for the next two weeks. They said, "We were there, in the newsroom, when the announcement was made that the *Gazette* would be closed." I was featured on this videotape, sobbing and hugging Jerry Jones, and, for two weeks, I couldn't watch television because there I was, on their promotional commercial, sobbing.

Allbright: I was off in Michigan visiting my daughter and family and came back in the afternoon, got off the plane, and went downtown to pick up mail, to go home, and as I did, people coming out the backdoor with their belongings and possessions. And they were coming out of the building crying.

Smith: I guess I was mainly thinking that, you know, I had had the best job I had ever had, writing editorials at the *Arkansas Gazette,* and I knew that I was not going to get a job again that pleased me as much as that one had, so— and I was over fifty too. In fact, my chances were a lot less than some of the younger people's were of finding employment, finding a good job. But finding a job as a liberal editorial writer on a good newspaper was going to be very unlikely.

Mosby: I sat at home late that Friday afternoon after the *Gazette* had closed, talking to Mary Ann, and she asked a question, "What do you want to do?" I said, "Well, I was supposed to cover the Atkins-Dardanelle game. I don't have anything to write it for, but I'm going to cover it." We drove to Atkins, and I sat in the top of the stands, not in the press box, with Mary Ann. I kept notes on the game, like I had done many times all down through the years, and we went back home. I didn't write anything, but I covered the game.

Shepherd: And the amazing thing to me is I'd never seen anybody take a drink in the newsroom, but when they announced it was closing, whiskey bottles came out of various places. [*Laughter.*] Right on the table, out on the desk, where the dignity of the Old Gray Lady was assaulted a little bit by the fact that it looked like a cocktail lounge in some areas there.

Farris: Someone brought in this case of beer and was handing out beer, and people were lighting up cigarettes and cigars. They were not celebrating, but smoking and drinking as an act of rebellion. One of the Gannettoids said, "You know there's no alcohol allowed," and the guy who brought in the case of beer turned and said, "What are they going to do? Fire me?" [*Laughter.*]

Donald: People were beginning to get fidgety, and a lot of them went out and got beer and some booze and, you know, just said, "Well, we can't put out a paper. We might as well just kind of sit around and enjoy this." . . . Some of them were getting pretty drunk, and they were getting pretty mean. And they got people to stand up and tell what they could recall about their days at the *Gazette*. . . . And then Paul Smith [general manager of the *Democrat*] came in, and somebody was hollering obscenities at him, and I thought that was pretty stupid. . . . As nice a guy as you can meet, and he had all the sympathies for everybody, but he simply explained the very quick situation that the *Gazette* had shut down; the *Democrat* had bought the assets. Said, "That is it. That is all we can tell you." Everybody had to leave, and they were doing—they had to do a lot of stuff to get the people their checks, their pension money, all that sort of thing. Once you were out of the building, you were out of the building. You couldn't get back in. There was a scuffle out in the alley. Some guy from down in advertising . . . I think he was just a clerk, but he was a real hothead. And he walked out in the alley, and some *Democrat* photographer stuck a camera right in his face. And the guy popped him. Popped the photographer. I don't know if anything ever came of it. He wasn't arrested. One of those things. Everybody was mad. But I can remember—I think it was maybe *Democrat* staff members, management members. It wasn't even staff, it was management, or editors, came in and they stood, walked you up to your desk, and you unloaded what was left in your desk that you wanted, in a cardboard box and carried it out, and that was it.

Thompson: How did you feel? Any of you felt that nothing that you could have done personally about it, and so you just accepted it?

Donald: Oh, you could have. You could have kidnapped some certain management people at the *Gazette* earlier, early on, and dropped them in the river. Maybe that would have helped. But, no, there was really nothing you could do. The *Gazette* management wasn't listening to what anybody said. They thought they knew. Well, they also, they had the problem of knowing what the finances were and what the projected financial situation would be, and they had to do something. It just wasn't there. The money just wasn't there.

Mathis: We walked out and the place was occupied with literally armed people. George Fisher, who had won awards and brought great fame and notice and loyalty and love to that paper for years, was not allowed to take his brushes home because, for all they knew, this was company property. It was a Gestapo in there that day. They had closed up all the exits, save one, where you had to march by the little walkie-talkie people. It was humiliating, on top of everything else.

Johnson: There were guards that we had never seen before with pistols on their hips herding us out. They said, "Don't go back to your office. Leave right now. Don't take anything with you. You will receive a notice on when you can come back and pick up your things." It was a real surreal feeling. You have had it happen to you in various times of your life where things are happening, and you think, "Is this really happening?" We all left the building. Some people were laughing, but I was crying. I was interviewed by a reporter from Channel 7 with tears in my eyes. I went home. My wife was at home, and she was crying. It had been on the news by then. It was the equivalent of a close family member passing away. . . . We received notice that there was going to be a candlelight vigil that night in the street in front of the *Gazette*. We went down there, and there were hundreds of people. I remember Sid McMath talking, eulogizing the newspaper. We all went home, and I guess it was within a week we got notice on when to come and get our last paycheck and severance pay.

They sent a notice that we could come down on this day and this time, and someone would escort you back to your office and observe you as you cleaned out your desk. I did not have much left in my office at that time. I got everything that I needed in a small box. There were two *Democrat* employees standing there watching me. I was pretty resentful that they would think I would steal something.

McCord: There was so much tension in the building. If you had struck a match, you would have started a fire. It beat everything I had ever seen . . . It was terrible. It was wrought with people hollering and cursing at each other, you know, saying, "Well, goddamn, look at this," and "Wouldn't you know this is what they would do?" It was just bitterness. We heard about *Gazette* people who had showed up in emergency rooms because of too much drinking and deep depression.

Jordan: Hussman brought in all of those security guards. I resented that. Of course, they confiscated all of the news files and everything, as if we were going to destroy them. Barbara Carter, the personnel manager, she said, "Hey! Wait." And in a box she threw this up in the air towards me. An *Arkansas Gazette* watch. It was inscribed with my name on it. I was going to get it at the banquet in December. And she said, "Hey! Wait. Here's your watch." [*Laughter.*]

Peacock: I was on maternity leave and dashed in for the last day of work when my maternity leave was over. Kate Marymount [city editor] said, "If you ever want to work here again, you better come in." And I had said, "Please, please, please don't let me miss. I want to come back before it's over." Even though it was just such a dreadful terrible time, I wanted to be there even though we all knew it was futile. So I came back the last day and sat down, and the minute I did the computer screens went "schkkk," and that was it. I never got to do one more thing. And took Hannah in, my baby, with me. She stayed with me that last day in her little pram-thing . . . I sat with Kate Marymount, and Jan Cottingham was just weeping, weeping, weeping, and saying, "At least you have your baby." . . . I think, finally, everybody suddenly hated Gannett as much as they hated the *Democrat*. And the *Democrat-Gazette* was so classless in the takeover. They were thrilled. They were dancing in the street. They were taking our name. I think they announced that at the press conference. We did not know that until that day in the newsroom when he said, "We will now be the *Democrat-Gazette*."

Moyer: Looking back, is there anything I could've done differently? Possibly, but considering the force of a huge corporation, the oldest paper west of the Mississippi, where I was in my career, my sophistication level of what I knew, I think I handled it as well as I could. What do I regret? I regret that in the last days I wasn't able to say anything. I had been instructed not to say anything. I wish I would've. At the time, I was thinking about my future career. I had a family. I had two kids and a wife. In retrospect, wish I would've been able to say something to the staff so they'd know how badly I felt. I was devastated by it. It was one of the lowest points I've had in my life. I felt terrible for everybody. I'd grown very fond of so many of these people. I knew their lives were being shattered and that people had kids in college and families to raise, mortgages to pay, and people who had built their whole lives around the *Gazette*. It all came to an end in one afternoon. It took me a while to recover from that. From a personal standpoint, it was a really dark time for me. I had gone in with high hopes, wanting to win the war. It became just the opposite . . . I guess, that final day, I just wanted to say that I was sorry that I didn't figure out a way to make it happen. So much of it had been out of my control. So much of it had been out of the newsroom's control. In fact, we were putting out the best paper I think the *Gazette* had ever been, and it wasn't enough.

Karnatz: I called everyone that I could: Bob Douglas, the [University of Arkansas] journalism crew, my parents. In my case, two of my parents' three children [Sean Harrison is her brother] were losing their jobs in the same day.

Farris: Everything remained untouched months later. There were still coffee mugs sitting on tables and trash bins that had not even been emptied. The newsroom still looked like a newsroom. There were papers on desks. No one had come through and cleaned the place up. It was weird and eerie. You felt like you were being haunted in a way because there were all these remnants of a living, breathing newspaper. . . . There were a dozen of us who worked at the *Gazette,* who just a couple of weeks after the paper folded decided to take our severance checks and all go to Cancún. Deborah Mathis was the person who orchestrated it all. So twelve of us packed our bags and flew to Mexico for a long weekend. And we had a great time. We celebrated, we mourned, and just sort of just took a breather and got away from it all. We swam in the warm seas, hung out in bars, and had a really good time.

Stephens: So the next day they honored our press passes for the Arkansas-Texas football game. So Jim Bailey and Wadie Moore picked me up, and we drove over to the game at War Memorial Stadium. We were just lost. We didn't know how to act; we didn't know anything. And we got off the elevator at the press box, and Orville Henry, who had gone to the *Democrat* earlier, reached out and put his arms around me and hugged my neck, and we all started crying again. Nobody knew even if the sun was going to come up the next day because it was so awful. We watched from the press box. We even went down to the field just to kind of be there. Of course, we didn't have anybody to write for, but we were just kind of there.

Clark: I heard about the sellout when my old art buddies called me in Miami to say that they were having to take their personal effects home with them that night because the next day they weren't going to be allowed back into the building. I wanted to fly home, fly back to Arkansas, be with my pals. It was like a death. So I wanted to be with them. I didn't do it, though. I decided instead to take the money that I would have spent on a plane ticket and send it my friends who were flat out of a job. So I did that.

Cottingham: In ten years, you know, new people come to Arkansas. They never knew the *Gazette* existed. They would never know the legacy and that it would almost be forgotten.

Brantley: I wrote a column saying it looked like the end was near and thanking everybody who had been supportive of us. I didn't know for sure, but I knew that that was the only topic I had left to write about. It was a hard time. I am glad about it, that the gestures in the editorial and in my column and in the paper—the final reporting was even-handed, and the editorial and my column pretty generous, I think, under the circumstances because, by then, we were being treated like criminals by the *Democrat*. They had posted photographers around the building to take our pictures, to make sure we didn't leave with any of Walter Hussman's property. The end of the paper had many low moments. I mean, the grim-faced *Democrat* people coming in with security guards and posting guards at the doors to watch us leave and to check our belongings to make sure we didn't take things. The hardest cut, really, though, was the morning the first *Democrat-Gazette,* in which the headline is something like "It's Over—We Won" effectively, and an exultant, cheering band of *Democrat* employees. They were due their happiness, but there was virtually no mention in the extensive coverage that day of the seven hundred people who had been put out of work. And, if nothing else, it was major industrial closing in Little Rock, Arkansas, the kind of thing that is a boilerplate news story for most newspapers. You say, so-and-so lost their job, what is going to happen to them, the size of the payroll. We were an afterthought to the *Democrat*. They were totally consumed with their victory and their exultation. My son, who was only five years old at the time, but had begun to read, read that streamer headline on page one and said, "Dad, that is so mean." If a five-year-old can understand it, anybody could understand what a mean-spirited newspaper that was that won the war . . .

I had known it was coming, and I did something I am glad I did. I had a drawer in the desk full of old personnel records. Because I had been an editor, I had employee evaluations, nasty notes back and forth among people, payroll records, things that I had accumulated over fifteen years of being a supervisor. Three days before the end, I started cleaning out my desk. I just knew it was over. Two days before the paper closed, I took all of the sensitive documents. They weren't of any value to anybody, but they could have been personally embarrassing to people. I took them home with me and dumped them in a 7–Eleven dumpster so that they wouldn't even be in the *Gazette's* garbage. It turned out to be a good move because we later found out that the building was not emptied, even of trash, until John R. Starr had sent editors over to the building to go through trash cans to make sure nothing important was thrown away. They went through our payroll records, and they shared them with each other. So, to what little degree I was able to protect some of that, people's privacy, I am glad I was able to do that.

Dumas: You [Dhonau] had, I think, that day, written a farewell editorial, a very eloquent piece in my mind, maybe the best piece that you've written. But you had written a farewell editorial on a hunch that we would not know, that we would not be given a chance to run it because we would not be told in advance that tomorrow is the last day of the *Gazette*. But, somehow, that Thursday afternoon, I guess October 17, you decided to run that editorial the next morning. So that editorial appeared the next morning, and on the front page was this lucky picture. Somebody had gone out to Mount Holly Cemetery and hung a wreath on William Woodruff's grave. We had a farewell editorial on the editorial page, and, sure enough, at noon, they shut the computers down and called us all out in the newsroom to announce that the *Gazette* was no more. The paper had been sold and would be closed, and we were all to clean out our desks and be out of the building by five.

12

P.S.

What kind of newspaper was the Arkansas Gazette? *How much did it matter to the state of Arkansas and to the people who lived there?*

Carrick Patterson: I watched on A&E a biography of Jackie Kennedy the other night, and there was a lot of talk about Camelot and that sort of thing. And what that really meant, I think, was how excited those people were to be there, how really vital they felt, how they felt they were doing something important, that they were changing things, that they were doing good, that they were blowing and going, that they were having an influence, and how stimulating it was to be in that intellectual and productive environment. And I think that's what they meant by Camelot, more than the actual accomplishments at the time.

Being at the *Gazette* in the time I was there, before the economic pressures from the newspaper war became so exhausting and all consuming, was a similar environment to that. You were working on something that you thought was really important to do with people that you really respected and that you were learning from. You were working alongside, toward a common goal that everybody pretty much understood and was signed up for. You were having a hell of a good time doing it, and you were feeling good about yourself while you were doing it. Your victories were shared, victories that everyone enjoyed. Your failures were only an incentive to go out and work harder the next day. You were in an environment not only of colleagues but of friends—of almost a vocation, a feeling of a vocation as well as an occupation. And it was an incredible feeling to be part of that. And that's what, I think, everybody who worked there at that time misses the most. It would have been that way without me. I certainly didn't cause it. My dad didn't cause it. My grandfather may have caused it somewhat, but, at the same time, we did help create an atmosphere where it could take place. So I give us credit for that. And, in return, I got to partake of that atmosphere, and it was a wonderful feeling to be part of that group. And I think those who consumed the product felt some of that. And so, to that extent, they're also missing out, now that it's gone.

Smith: I covered a couple of campaigns of David Pryor's, traveling with him and Barbara, just with them all day for weeks at a time. In one of those campaigns, either '72 or '74 I guess it was, we came back into Little Rock late on a Saturday night, flew back into the airport, and he had a car there. A young college guy was driving it, and so the Pryors gave me a ride to the *Gazette,* where my car was parked. So we pull up there, and the lights are shining at the *Gazette.* It is midnight, and I think maybe Pryor said, "Give us a first edition of the paper," or something. Anyway, he, David, turns to this young driver, and he says—I know partly for my benefit but partly because it is true—he said, "You know, Rick, the difference between Arkansas and Mississippi is the *Arkansas Gazette.*"

Hugh Patterson: I remember one time Bill Fulbright saying that he'd always considered himself to be something of a political accident coming from Arkansas and having achieved the position he had, but he said he didn't think it could have ever occurred had it not been for the longtime enlightening influence of the *Arkansas Gazette.*

Powell: I think that the *Gazette's* editorial influence was enormous. Because we were arguing for all of the unpopular, un-Southern things over the years. [State Senator] Ben Allen, for example—of course, he may give more credit than is due—he thinks that we fashioned the course of Arkansas's history. Ben thinks that the *Gazette's* role in those years was the most powerful thing that happened in the state.

Dumas: Did it help avoid the course of Alabama and Mississippi?

Powell: Absolutely. During those twenty-five years that I was on the editorial page, there was only a handful of what I regard as good newspapers in the South. Others were arguing the same old lines that the South had always argued. When you count the good newspapers, there was Little Rock, and for a while there was the Nashville *Tennessean* and the Atlanta *Constitution* before Ralph McGill died. Down in Florida there was the *St. Petersburg Times,* consistently one of the best in the South. In North Carolina, there were the Raleigh *News and Observer* and the *Charlotte Observer,* good newspapers. But most of the big newspapers in the South were pretty bad in the years I was on the *Gazette.* Memphis, Jackson, New Orleans, Birmingham, Mobile, and Richmond—all spoke for the Bourbon South.

They are a little more presentable now, but that's another story. Anyway, the *Gazette*'s influence on Arkansas was profound, critical. In the *Gazette*'s last years, when Walter Hussman was driving us to the wall with cut rates and giveaways subsidized by his media chain, I was talking to Dale Bumpers in his office in Washington one day, and he said that if the *Gazette* fell, Arkansas would get like Mississippi and Alabama. It's already happened, a decade later. The *Democrat-Gazette* has the wildest, most radical Republican commentary in the South, and Arkansas politics is shot to hell.

. . . Where we once had progressive editorials, every day now we have something that resembles the *Manchester Union Leader*. Now the paper really reflects the Old South; only now it's the Republican South rather than the Bourbon Democratic South. The whole attitude of the state is suffering. . . . There's no respite from the cave-dwelling policies which now prevail in that newspaper. They've even tried to scrub up Orval Faubus at Central High. They've tried to present that in Faubus's light rather than in the way it happened. The fall of the *Gazette* is one of the great tragedies in this state's experience.

Brummett: I think the state's political environment is changing. Arkansas had a charming uniqueness, where politicking mattered. The *Gazette* played a role. A tremendously talented generation of moderate Democrats came along. And even before that, McMath and Faubus were progressive early. All of that is changing. . . . The *Gazette* was a big part of it. It was so rich in history. Without the *Gazette* there is a void.

Reed: What kind of newspaper was the *Arkansas Gazette?*

Dumas: Since I spent my life, my career, working for a single newspaper, I probably have a poorer basis for comparison than most newspaper people . . . But I have known hundreds of newspaper people, including many who worked at the *Gazette* and moved on or else worked at other newspapers and ended their career at the *Gazette*. It reinforces my sense that the *Gazette* was a different newspaper, that it was a separate kind of experience. All these interviews with old *Gazette* hands deep into the last century suggest the same thing, that their relationship with the *Arkansas Gazette* was somehow special, even if it was not always happy, that it was unlike the relationship with other newspapers for which they worked or other companies if they followed altogether different pursuits. All journalists, I suppose, think they are on a mission from God, to tell the world the truth, which is probably why the public dislikes us so much. But writing for the *Gazette* transcended even that impulse. I think it was a sense that at the *Gazette* they were part of a stewardship of a peculiar time and place: Arkansas. The *Gazette* had a distinctive role in the state, a special responsibility that no other newspaper filled, certainly not in Arkansas and probably not anywhere else. In no other place, I'm sure, has a newspaper played such a critical part in the entire history of the state. The *Gazette* and Arkansas were yoked irreversibly, from the first days of the territory through the racial crisis, and everyone was aware of it. I came to the *Gazette* in 1960 when its heroic role in the school integration crisis at Little Rock was fresh, especially in my mind. I had always wanted to work for the *Gazette,* but by then it was a rare privilege. It may be that the sense of mission that I and others who had worked there in the last quarter century shared arose simply from that, pride that we were part of a newspaper that stood its ground against bigotry when its own survival was in peril. But I believe it was more than that. It seems to me that it preceded 1957, even in all those years after Ned Heiskell saved the paper, when its editorial pages stood for a principled conservatism that was considerably different from the *Gazette* of the final half century. There had been other instances when the paper had positioned itself between tyranny and the community. There may be a little arrogance in all this, and it may explain after all why the *Gazette* didn't survive. Newspapers are news products, and it is important to learn how to publish a product that pleases the most people, or displeases the fewest. You cater to popular whims and prejudices. Until near the end, that was never on anyone's mind at the *Gazette.*

Donald: The *Gazette* was the paper of record. It was a chronicle. And that was drummed into your skull from the minute you got there, that this is history. Because, you remember, there was a time that the *Gazette*'s feeling was, if it came in by packet boat and was two weeks later, it wasn't news until the *Gazette* printed it.

Trimble: People bitched a lot about the paper among themselves but were furiously loyal to it and defended it against all outsider criticism. . . . It was just so different in that every person had one goal in life, which was to work at the *Gazette.* You didn't see many people who were saying, "Well, I'll work here a few years and then I will go to the St. Louis *Post Dispatch*." Every newspaper person in Arkansas who was any good, their ambition was to work for the *Arkansas Gazette.* And it seemed to me that once they got there, they were content to stay there. . . . I think the *Gazette* was unusual in that we had people who had started out as copy boys and had gone to be telegraph editors, you know. Their careers were spent at the *Gazette.* Other people started out at other papers, smaller papers, but their ambition was to work at the *Gazette.* And its status as an institution was so pervasive that you knew that you were working for something that was bigger than you were. . . . We were very arrogant about the *Gazette,* and we belittled people who weren't good. And sometimes our judgment was correct. Sometimes it may not have been that correct. But if a person who came to work at the *Gazette* was just bad, well, if Shelton couldn't run them off by not giving them assignments, we could be pretty cruel about people who we thought weren't cut out to be *Gazette* people. I think this was a Southern thing. We were very self-effacing at the same time. We were self-effacing and flippant about everything except the work we were doing that was in front of us. We'd work like hell to make it as good as we could. And then we'd throw it in the basket and talk about how terrible it was. It was just not done that you'd toot your own horn. . . . When I left the *Gazette,* after eighteen years, I still considered myself one of the new guys, not that people hadn't accepted me. They had, you know, and I felt really a part of it, but the *Gazette* was such an institution that I had not in my own mind worked myself up to be one of the veterans here. I had been there eighteen years, and I considered myself one of the new guys.

Stern: I thought the *Gazette* was one of the greatest papers. In fact, at the time when the *Denver Post* was regarded as one of the top twenty papers in the country in that period of the 1960s, I always thought the *Gazette* belonged in that top twenty as well, or even the top ten. I considered the *New York Times,* the *Washington Post,* the Louisville *Courier-Journal, St. Louis Post-Dispatch,* the *Arkansas Gazette,* the *Denver Post,* the *Los Angeles Times,* to be really great papers in the 1950s and '60s.

Allen: It set a standard for me that exists to this day. I carried it from the *Gazette* to the *Democrat* to *Newsday* to the *New York Times.* Sometimes I felt like the standards I had were higher than the *New York Times.*

Jordan: I meant that truly when I said that the *Gazette* was the conscience of the state. It gave the direction in which this state should go morally, industrially, and in every way as a community. I mean, thinking of the state as a community. Here's what this community should do.

Griffee: You couldn't afford to hide anything because the *Gazette* wasn't going to hide anything, and you could have egg on your face if you didn't step up to the plate and face things honestly. And, in my way of thinking, that was the *Gazette.* It kept journalism and Arkansas honest, and that was its greatest role, its greatest contribution to this state.

Richard Portis: Bob Douglas was, to me, the *Gazette,* and he set the tone for the morality of the place and the standards of what we could do and wouldn't do. I remember one time—you know, we were a bunch of rowdy smart-aleck, left-wing guys, liberal guys, Bolsheviks—and we were making fun of Lurleen Wallace running for George [for governor of Alabama]. And Douglas says something about, "You guys ought to shut up about that. She's just being loyal to her husband, and that's what she needs to be doing." And we all kind of backed off. Douglas was sort of the moral fiber of that place.

Martha Douglas: You know, with Bob, I always thought the *Gazette* was sort of his mistress, but then I decided that the *Gazette* was his religion, so that made it better.

Lancaster: The *Gazette* was here before Arkansas was, and it had always been the intellectual focus of Arkansas. Everything that Arkansans thought and believed and practiced, both politically and socially, found its way into the *Gazette* in the nineteenth century and on into the twentieth century. It was the conscience of Arkansas. And I think that had to do more with its stature as an opinion organ than as a news gatherer. Its opinions were always interesting to people all over the state because of its statewide concept. It's the same concept that John Barnhill brought to the University of Arkansas football program. That is, everybody in the state would get behind one institution. Athletically, it was the Razorbacks; journalistically, it was the *Gazette*.

McCord: Don't you think that it probably was the *Gazette* that was responsible for Arkansas at one time being the most Democratic state in the Union?

Lancaster: Probably. But *Gazette* editors ran the gamut of political allegiance. I mean, there were Whig editors; there were loco-foco editors; there were Know-Nothing editors. In the first World War there was a senator from Arkansas, Senator William F. Kirby, who was one of the leading opponents of the United States entering World War I. And so for a time there, we had a pacifist *Arkansas Gazette* at a time when that was very, very much looked down on. A precursor of Senator [J. William] Fulbright.

It's true that the Gazette was killed by greed, arrogance, and stupidity. But those qualities were mainly in the upper reaches of the big chain's management. Some of the Gannett people at the Gazette took the paper seriously and grieved its loss. If there were days of ignominy during the last years, there were also days of grace. John Hanchette was Gannett's managing editor of the Gazette for two years, until 1990, before returning to the Gannett News Service. He had won a Pulitzer Prize for reporting during an earlier stint with Gannett.

Hanchette: I drove by [the *Gazette* building]. The parking lot was empty. You know, you remember going in there. You get a real empty feeling. You get a sickening, empty feeling. This was organic. Newspapers are not only familiar, they're organic. They evolve daily. And when it dies, it's not only a death in the family, it's a personal death. . . . There's no real way to mourn, you know. It's not like you can go back and visit a cemetery. People think you're crazy when talk about this sort of thing. It's very strange. And so many of them have gone.

The bosses at Gannett headquarters did not get their way easily. When they pushed for ill-advised changes, the old-timers at the paper pushed back. The national office sent word time after time to whip the Little Rock gang into line. The gang dug in their heels and refused. They undoubtedly knew that the bullies would win, but they never stooped to collaborating with them.

They scattered when it was over. Some found new work in Arkansas, frequently in advertising and public relations. Some moved away and worked for news organizations from coast to coast. A hardy dozen or so gravitated to the Arkansas Times, *a feisty weekly of news and opinion with revenues a fraction of those at the big daily. The* Times *became known in some quarters as the* Arkansas Gazette *in exile. From their perch a few blocks from their former office, the old* Gazette *hands occupied themselves with a steady stream of stories, mainly the state's political ups and downs, that were missed or ignored by the* Democrat-Gazette. *The weekly's newsroom sometimes resembled one of the* Gazette's *after-hours parties, minus the booze. There they worked, huddled together in something more than friendship, a besieged little band, watchful, still hurting, stout of heart.*

They were a little like the North Vietnamese sniper that Michael Herr wrote about in his book Dispatches. *From a tiny hole in the ground outside a U.S. marine encampment at Khe Sanh, the sniper bedeviled the Americans day after day. The marines could see him clearly and fired back every time he raised up to shoot, but they never got him. They used mortars and rifles. They used gunship rockets. They began to call him "Luke the Gook" and developed a perverse affection for him. Finally they called in an aircraft to drop napalm right on the sniper's hole. The air above was bright with fire, and everything for yards around was burnt. For ten minutes there was no sign of life. Then the sniper raised up and fired a single shot. The marines cheered.*

Suggestions for Further Reading

Allsopp, Fred W. *History of the Arkansas Press for a Hundred Years and More.*
Little Rock: Parke-Harper, 1922.

Ashmore, Harry S. *An Epitaph For Dixie.* New York: Norton, 1957.

———. *Civil Rights and Wrongs: A Memoir of Race and Politics, 1944–1994.*
New York: Pantheon Books, 1994.

———. *Hearts and Minds: A Personal Chronicle of Race in America.*
Washington, DC: Seven Locks, 1988.

Dougan, Michael B. *Community Diaries: Arkansas Newspapering,
1819–2002.* Little Rock: August House, 2003.

Faubus, Orval E. *Down From the Hills.* Little Rock: Pioneer Press, 1980.

Meriwether, Robert W., ed. *A Chronicle of Arkansas Newspapers Published
since 1922 and of the Arkansas Press Association, 1930–1972.* Little Rock:
Arkansas Press Association, 1974.

Reed, Roy. *Faubus: The Life and Times of an American Prodigal.* Fayetteville:
University of Arkansas Press, 1997.

Roberts, Gene and Hank Klibanoff. *The Race Beat: The Press, the Civil Rights
Struggle, and the Awakening of a Nation.* New York: Knopf, 2006.

Ross, Margaret. Arkansas Gazette: *The Early Years 1819–1866.* Little Rock:
Arkansas Gazette Foundation, 1969.

Starr, John Robert. *Yellow Dogs and Dark Horses: Thirty Years on the
Campaign Beat.* Little Rock: August House, 1987.

Williams, Nancy A., ed. *Arkansas Biography: A Collection of Notable Lives.*
Fayetteville: University of Arkansas Press, 2000.

Index

Page numbers in italics refer to illustrations.

7, 8, 9, 11–12; on Nell Cotnam,
71–72; on the newsroom atmosphere,
100
Ross, Seaton, 75
Rouby, Jason: background information,
xxiv–xxv; on Harry Ashmore, 174–75;
on school desegregation crisis, 189
Rowland, Spider, 28, 58–59
Rozzell, Forrest, 9
rum balls, 96
Rush, Jerry, 92
Rutherford, Bill, 9, 109, 119

S

salaries, 35, 42, 48–49
Sallee, Bob, 255
Sandy Hook, Connecticut, 61, 62
Santa Barbara, California, 174, 189
savings and loan scandals, 126–27
scandals: business scandals, 125–26;
corruption stories, 127–29; savings and
loan scandals, 126–27; Whitewater
Development Company scandal,
132–33, 134
Schaffer, Archie, 133
school desegregation, 173, 183–93; *see also*
Central High segregation crisis
Schwartzlose, Monroe, 135–36
Scott, Tommy, 89
scuba-diving record, 154–55
Securities and Exchange Commission, 240
security guards, 263–67, 269
segregated obituaries, 194
Seigenthaler, John, 218, 222
sexual harrassment, 37–39
Shadle, Bill, 155
Shaw, Robert, 36, 97, 103
Shelton, Bill, *165*; background
information, xxv, 43–44; as city editor,
43–47, 142; and competition with the
Democrat, 252–53; disaster coverage,
149; and Ernest Valachovic, 98; Faubus
obituary, 162; and John Heiskell, 7;
language and grammar usage, 40, 46;
news coverage, 18, 29, 48; on the news
staff, 47
Shepherd, Aubrey: background
information, xxv; on the Gannett

Company, 200, 206; on John Robert
Starr, 254; on the last days of the
Gazette, 265
Simmons, Bill: background information,
xxv, 36; on copy boys, 102; sports
coverage, 103
Simpson, Dick, 127
slot editors, 111, 122
Smiley, Walter, 262
Smith, Doug: on the *Arkansas Gazette*, 20,
272; background information, xxv; on
Bill Shelton, 45; on copy boys, 102;
Faubus obituary, 163; on the Gannett
Company, 202–3; on Harry Ashmore,
191; on John Heiskell, 191; on the last
days of the *Gazette*, 264; recipes,
117–18; on Winthrop Rockefeller,
138; writing skills, 158
Smith, Gene, *169*
Smith, Griffin, 163–64
Smith, Paul, 226, 265
smoking in the newsroom, 99, 109, 111,
115–16, 117
snakes, 6
Snider, Margie: background information,
xxv; on Bill Clinton, 132; on Ernie
Dumas, 53; on the newsroom
atmosphere, 99
Snook, Rosemary Beryl, 72–73
snowy weather, 103
Social Security Administration, 155–56
society section, 21, 37–38
spandex, cheerleaders and, 204, 208
Speed, Julie Baldridge, xxv, 107
spelling mistakes, 108, 122
Spillman, Brenda, 48
sports coverage: deadlines, 102–3; and
Jerry McConnell, 153–54; and Jim
Bailey, 21, 76; and Joe Mosby, 154–55;
and Orville Henry, 20–21, 76;
Razorback football games, 68, 76,
107–8, 151–53; salary negotiations,
35–36; during segregation crisis,
195
Starr, John Robert: as Associated Press
reporter, 149–50; and Dillard
Department Stores, 242; as editor of
the *Democrat*, 202, 231–32, 245, 247,

ROY REED is the author of *Looking for Hogeye* and *Faubus: The Life and Times of an American Prodigal,* a *New York Times* notable book and winner of a Certificate of Commendation from the American Association of State and Local History. He reported for the *Arkansas Gazette* for eight years before becoming a national and foreign correspondent for the *New York Times* and then a longtime professor of journalism at the University of Arkansas. He lives in Hogeye, Arkansas.